YORKSHIRE

A GAZETTEER OF
ANGLO-SAXON
&
VIKING SITES

YORKSHIRE

A GAZETTEER OF
ANGLO-SAXON
&
VIKING SITES

GUY POINTS

Yorkshire: A Gazetteer of Anglo-Saxon and Viking Sites

RIHTSPELL PUBLISHING
First Published in 2007

ISBN 978-0-9557679-0-6

Front cover – Lilla's Cross, Fylingdales Moor, North Yorkshire.
Back cover – An Anglo-Danish hogback grave cover, All Saints Church, Barmston, East Yorkshire.

Design and Typesetting by:
Heritage Marketing & Publications Ltd
Hill Farm
Castle Acre Road
Great Dunham
King's Lynn
Norfolk
PE32 2LP
Email: publishing@heritagemp.com
www.heritagemp.com

Table of Contents

Part 2

Preface

This book has three objectives. First, it aims to fill a gap by providing a comprehensive gazetteer of places where there is something of interest for those who wish to know more about the Anglo-Saxons and Vikings in Yorkshire. For the purposes of this book "Viking" includes all that may be described as "Anglo-Scandinavian", "Anglo-Danish", and "Anglo-Norse". The dates attributed to the sites and the artefacts included in the text are based on information published both locally and nationally and take account of the author's own experience and knowledge. As a matter of course it is only to be expected that there may be different views from time to time about the accuracy of the dates given.

The second aim is to ease the task of identifying these places by providing precise locations and descriptions of what there is to see. The intention is to enable the reader to know what they are looking for and exactly where to look, and so avoid not knowing whether they have found what they are looking for. To assist in the search, entries are each given a star rating ranging from one star ☆ signifying the material may be difficult to find or to identify with confidence, to up to five stars ☆☆☆☆☆ signifying that the material can easily be found and identified and also provides an excellent example that is full of interest.

The third aim is to provide background material (for use if required) to put the Anglo-Saxons, Vikings and churches into their historical context, plus a glossary of terms, plans and features of Anglo-Saxon churches, and features relating to cross-heads, cross-shafts, grave covers and grave markers.

PART 1 of the book sets out basic information.

PART 2 of the book sets out the places of interest – the "sites". These are divided into five distinct geographical areas: East Yorkshire, South Yorkshire, North Yorkshire, West Yorkshire and York.

List of Photographs

YORK

List of Illustrations

Glossary of Terms

[Terms referred to in the explanations given are also included in the glossary.]

Abacus – The flat slab forming the top of a capital.

Addorsed – Two figures or features placed symmetrically back-to-back.

Affronted – Two figures or features placed symmetrically face-to-face.

Aisle – Part of the church usually running alongside the nave, choir or transepts. It is separated from the nave, choir or transepts by columns or piers.

Alcove – A vaulted recess.

Altar – A table made of wood or stone usually situated at the eastern end of the chancel, or if there is no chancel at the eastern end of the nave. It has been consecrated for the purpose of the celebration of the Eucharist (the sacrament of the Lord's Supper, the Communion).

Ambulatory – An open but often enclosed walkway – mostly at the east end of the chancel surrounding an apse.

Animals Or Beasts – The two terms animals or beasts are often used to describe the same thing. Where animals or beasts were depicted on stonework they were rarely exact representations. Usually animals or beasts were represented by a distinctive stylistic design, often curving and/or with entwined bodies, necks and legs.

Annular – A description for a complete ring; often used when describing a brooch or a representation forming part of a decorative design (see *penannular* below).

Apse – A vaulted semi-circular, sometimes polygonal, eastern end of the nave or chancel.

Arcade – A series of freestanding arches supported by columns or piers between a nave and an aisle. When not freestanding and incorporated into walling they are described as blind arcades.

Arch – Stonework intended to support other arches and the weight of the wall above.

Arms – The four arms of a crosshead, two of which were horizontal, two of which were vertical. The lower vertical arm connected the crosshead to the cross-shaft.

Artefact (Artifact) – An artificial product produced by the application of skill acquired through knowledge and practice.

Ashlar – Stonework prepared and trimmed with a finished surface, "dressed", comprising smooth faced square or rectangular blocks laid with fine joints in regular courses. Ashlar stonework identifies the origin of the fabric as being no earlier than Norman.

Aumbry – A recess or cupboard within a wall specifically to hold sacred vessels.

Baluster – A turned vertical pillar used for supporting a handrail or used for supporting the central pillar in a double window or a belfry window. It can also be used as a decorative feature in coping.

Balustrade – A series of balusters supporting a handrail.

Band – A strip of either flat or thin material used to hold things together; bind around an object. Also commonly used as a strip of stonework to provide a vertical and horizontal border to enclose decoration within a panel, to separate one decorative panel from another, and to separate decoration within an individual panel.

Baptistry – An area for baptism designed to include the font. Usually near the entrance to the church, at the west end of the south aisle or nave, or on the ground floor of the tower. It can also be located at the east end of the south aisle, immediately before the entrance to a south transept or chapel.

Barrel Vaulted – A descriptive term for a building or room with a semi-cylindrical roof.

Barrow – An ancient artificial mound used for burials similar to a howe or a tumulus.

Bas Relief – Shallow moulding or sculpture in wood or stone where a figure, less than half its true proportion, protrudes from the background.

Base – The bottom, the moulded foot of a column or pilaster.

Basilica – A rectangular building with aisles separated by colonnades or arcades from a nave with a clerestory.

Basket Plait Or Basket Ware Design – A design representing the appearance of plaited wickerwork, similar to that found in the construction of a basket.

Battlements – An indented parapet at the top of a wall. The original purpose was as a fortified feature so that archers could shoot through the indentations between the projecting solid sections of masonry.

Bay – A division of an interior space divided by vertical columns or arches or windows.

Belfry – The stage of the tower where the bells are hung, usually the highest stage of the tower.

Bell Cote – An ornamental structure designed to house one or two church bells usually on the roof of a church.

Blocked – The description attached to a doorway, arch or window, where it is no longer open and used for its original purpose and where stonework of some description has been inserted to fill in the former void.

Borre Design – A design representing a ring chain pattern, or a backward looking animal, or an animal(s) gripping the nearest object(s). The design was in use between the mid 9C to the end of the 10C. The design was named after the designs on artefacts found in a rich ship burial found in Borre, Norway.

Boss – A square or round projecting area of stonework often found in the centre of crossheads that can vary in height considerably. Also, it is more commonly used to cover the intersections of the ribs in a vaulted ceiling.

Bracket – A small projecting block of stonework or woodwork used to support the beam of a roof.

Brick – A block of clay that has been kneaded, moulded and hardened to form a definite size and shape (usually rectangular).

Brickwork – A structure formed by using bricks.

Buttress – A section of masonry or brickwork supporting or projecting from a wall. Its purpose is to provide extra strength.

Cable Moulding – Moulding carved in the design of rope.

Cable Work Or Rope Work Design – A design representing the appearance of moulding in the form of a strong, thick cable or rope. It was often found along the vertical edges of cross-shafts.

Canopy – A projection, a hood, over a doorway, niche, statue, altar or pulpit.

Capital – The head or the top part of a column.

Castellated – Decorated with battlements.

Cathedral – The principal church of a diocese, containing the "cathedra" or throne of a bishop – the chair of office.

Cats Cradle Design – A design representing the appearance of an entwined cord producing a symmetrical figure.

Ceiling – An under covering or lining of a roof or floor which conceals timbers, plaster, etc.

Cell – A single chamber or room intended to be inhabited by a single individual.

Celtic Design – Generally characterised by designs where the crosses decorating the stonework have cup-shaped ends of arms with stems joining a central roundel. Inside the crosses the design is intricate and circular without necessarily forming so uniform a style as Anglo-Saxon designs. In reality there is great difficulty in distinguishing Celtic design from Anglo-Saxon since there was undoubtedly considerable cross fertilisation of ideas. What is true is that following the Synod of Whitby the Anglo-Saxon, Anglo-Danish and Anglo-Norse designs became far more diverse than the their Celtic comparators.

Celts – The Celts were the indigenous peoples who retained or acquired land in the western and highland areas of present day Scotland, Cumbria, the Isle of Man, Wales, Cornwall, Ireland and Brittany. They spoke what might be described as an early form of Welsh. They accepted Christianity during the fourth and fifth centuries.

Central Section – The centre of a crosshead on to which the four arms are joined.

Chain Pattern Or Chain Plait Or Chain Work Design – A design representing a connected series of chain-like links passing through each other or joined together.

Chamber – A private room.

Chamfer – A design feature where a square edge or corner of stonework has been cut off to provide a surface with a bevelled (sloped) edge.

Chancel – The east end of the church beyond the nave where usually the altar is located. Originally the chancel was narrow, short and lower in height than the nave. The part of the church intended for use by the clergy and the choir.

Chancel Arch – A large arch forming the division between the eastern end of the nave and the western end of the chancel. The supporting pillars or columns or jambs and the surrounding stonework often provide dating evidence.

Chantry Chapel – A separate chapel within or attached to a church specifically for saying Mass for the soul of an individual.

Chapel – A place of worship dependent on, or subordinate to, a church: a subdivision of a larger church containing an altar.

Choir – The part of the church, cathedral, or monastery, where services are sung by an organised body of singers ("the choir").

Church – A building for public Christian worship. The Christian community.

Clerestory – The upper (top) storey of the nave or chancel walls pierced by windows.

Clergy – An individual who has be ordained so that they can conduct religious services in a Christian church: a collective term for such people.

Coffin – A chest or box in which a human body is enclosed for burial.

Colonnades – A series of columns.

Column – A vertical structure, either round or polygonal in shape. It has a capital, a shaft and a base.

Confronting – A description used to indicate that the decoration on stonework or woodwork includes at least two (the usual number) figures of saints, humans or animals, standing or meeting face to face.

Congregation – A gathering of lay (not the clergy) people into a single body or assembly.

Consecration – The act of making a solemn dedication for a sacred or religious purpose.

Consecration Cross – Painted or carved crosses on the fabric of the church indicating the place(s) where the walls were touched with holy oil during the consecration of the church.

Coping – The course of masonry or brickwork covering the top of a wall.

Corbel – A block of stone or wood protruding from a wall to carry a beam.

Cornice – A projected horizontal moulded feature which sits at the very top of a building or immediately below the ceiling in a room.

Course – A continuous row, range or layer of stones, brick or timber, of the same height throughout, in a wall or face of a building.

Cross – The standard Latin cross comprises a horizontal line placed across a longer vertical line at two-thirds of its height. The representation of a cross signifies a sacred mark or symbol. A generic term used to describe a crosshead with its attached cross-shaft; sometimes with its cross base.

Cross Base – A section of ground or floor-standing stonework specifically designed to support a cross-shaft in a vertical position.

Cross Design – A design depicting the shape of a cross.

Crosshead – A section of stonework or a design with four arms connected to a common centre. Often only one or two or parts of the arms of a stone crosshead survive. Crossheads were supported by a cross-shaft sitting on a cross base.

Cross-Shaft – A four sided vertical section of stonework, comprising two faces and two sides or edges usually for supporting a crosshead. It can vary in height and width and its sides can taper towards the crosshead. It can be decorated with various designs. Sometimes its sits within a specifically designed and purpose built cross base.

Crossing – The central area in a cruciform church forming the junction of the nave, chancel and transepts.

Crucifix – An image depicting Christ on the Cross.

Cruciform – The ground plan of a church shaped in the form of a cross.

Crypt – An underground vaulted chamber usually provided to house relics.

Damaged – Some part of the artefact, section of stonework, survives and it can be identified despite the obvious damage.

Decorated – Where it is possible to identify an artefact or section of stonework that has been decorated with some design.

Design – A combination of details that together go to make up a decorative form of art.

Diocese – The district under the pastoral care of a bishop.

Doorframe – A structure that provides the skeleton for the hanging of a door.

Doorway – An opening or passage which is opened or shut by the presence of a door.

Double Windows/Double Openings – Often used to describe where there are two windows rather than a single window that share the same interior (central) column.

Eaves – The projecting edge of a roof that overhangs the sidewalls of a structure.

Edge(s) – A relatively thin border that terminates a side.

Escomb Quoining – A description applied to quoining where the construction technique in the jambs is similar to that employed in the jambs supporting the chancel arch in the Anglo-Saxon church at Escomb, County Durham. This is where side alternate quoins are laid alternately between a quoin laid so that it has one of its faces standing upright on top of one of the narrow sides of another quoin laid flat below.

Face(s) – The two widest and opposite sides of a crosshead or cross-shaft. Sometimes the wider sides of buildings.

Finial – An architectural decoration on a church, often in the shape of a cross, placed on the apex of a roof or gable, or on each corner of a tower.

Floor – The under surface of the interior of a room on which people stand.

Font – A stone bowl for holding the consecrated water used for baptisms.

Gable – The vertical end of the wall at the end of a ridged roof, from the level of the eaves to the summit, usually triangular in shape.

Gallery – A storey above the aisle opening with arches to the nave.

Gnomon – An axial pillar, rod, or pin, which by its shadow indicates the time of day. Used in the centre of sundials. When missing, the central hole into which it was inserted remains.

Grave Covers Or Grave Slabs Or Grave Markers – Grave covers or grave slabs or grave markers can vary in size, shape and decoration. They can range from a simple stone marker with a cross to a large, shaped stone, decorated with an inscription which may be in letters (Latin or Old English) or runes and decorated with a variety of designs. They may cover the entire surface of a grave or simply mark the site of a grave. Grave Covers or Grave Slabs are usually decorated on the top, although occasionally, they are decorated around the supporting sides.

Grid Iron Design – A design of parallel lines running in horizontal and vertical directions to cross each other.

Groove – A design made by a sunken channel cut into (usually) stone-work or woodwork.

Hammer Head – Hammer shaped item with an unusually expanded head. Some crossheads have hammer heads and these can be identified as where two additional horizontal arms have been integrated into the top vertical arm of the crosshead.

Herring Bone – Where the building material, stone, flints, tiles, bricks, are laid diagonally instead of flat. Sometimes comprising adjoining rows of parallel lines with the effect that any two rows provide a pat-tern in the shape of the letter V or an inverted letter V, or a zigzag pattern where courses are laid in opposite directions.

Hogback Grave Cover Or Hogback Tombstone – A rectangular shaped grave cover in the shape of a low, curved, tegulated roofed longhouse. Some have recumbent bears, or some sort of beast, at the gable ends gnaw-ing at the end of a long, decorated ridge running the length of the top surface. The name hogback is derived from the roof tiles giving the appearance of the bristles on a hog's back.

Hood Or Hood Moulding – A section of moulded stonework projecting over the head of a window, door or lintel.

Howe – An ancient artificial mound used for burials; similar to a tumulus or barrow.

Impost – Horizontal moulding at the springing of an arch sometimes used instead of a capital.

Incised – Lines or a design cut into, or engraved in, an object, usually stonework.

Inscribed – Writing marked on stonework, woodwork, bone, silverwork, gold or metalwork. Commonly found on grave covers or grave slabs or grave markers.

Interlace – A generic term for a design that intricately entangles and weaves together.

Jamb(s) – The straight side of an archway, doorway or window. The stones forming part of the straight side.

Jellinge Design – A design representing long and reptile like S-shaped animals, drawn with double outline and with curling twists in their bodies from their tails to their tongues. The animals are restrained with a number of straps. The design was in use between the end of the 9C to about the year 1000. A design named after the animal that decorates a small silver cup found at the royal burial ground in Jellinge in Jutland in Denmark.

Joists – Horizontal timbers carrying a floor or ceiling.

Key Pattern Design – A design depicting the shape of keys placed together in a regular pattern, similar to *Stepped Work Design* (see below).

Keystone – The central stone in an arch.

Knot Work Or Plait Work Design – A design comprising cords intertwined and knotted together. The cords in plait work design tend to be more straight and angular than knot work design.

Lancet Window – Dates from the "Early English" period. A slender, pointed arched window.

Linear Design – The use of a line or lines, usually to outline the shape of a crosshead or cross-shaft.

Light – A window opening.

Lintel – A horizontal beam bridging a doorway or opening.

Lobby – A covered passage or walkway often used as a waiting room.

Longhouse – A house long in overall physical appearance and often of low height in comparison to its length. Originally, on one side of the entrance there was a living room – sometimes subdivided – and on the other side a byre (a house for cattle).

Long And Short Quoining – This is where quoins are laid alternately between a long, narrow quoin standing vertically (the "long") on top of a flat rectangular quoin laid horizontally (the "short") below.

Masonry – A collective term for stonework built by a skilled craftsman.

Mass – A service to celebrate the Lord's Supper or Sacrament of the Body and Blood of Christ, the Eucharist.

Mass Dial Or Scratch Dial – A device for measuring the passing of the time to indicate the time for the liturgy (service or mass) of the Eucharist (The Sacrament of the Lord's Supper, the Communion). It usually consists of a stone slab incorporated into the fabric of the church, on whose vertical face there is an incised semi-circle with its horizontal line having lines radiating often below but sometimes above. At the central intersection of these lines dividing the day into segments there would be a wooden or metal peg or stele – the "gnomon". The gnomon would cast a shadow and thus denote the time for the service or mass, usually 9 am, noon and Vespers (Evensong). The gnomon is now usually missing but the hole in which it was housed is still identifiable. Often the hole for the missing gnomon assists in identifying the weathered scratches on a vertical slab of stonework as being those from a mass or scratch dial. Mass Dials or Scratch Dials are usually located on the south side of the church often on stonework in the walling near the south side entrance but also on stonework to the east of the entrance on the south wall of the nave/south aisle or chancel. They are also sometimes located on the west side of the church.

Masses – A service specifically intended to intercede on behalf of an individual person's soul.

Megalithic – A description used to identify larger than average sized stones which are not uniform in size or shape used in the construction of walling. Sometimes they are used individually on the corners of a building where the quoining (see *Quoining* below) above is formed of smaller more manageable stones. The very size of these stones makes them so distinctive.

Misericord – A bracket placed under a hinged seat to provide support to the occupant when standing. Under this hinge there can be elaborate carvings depicting various representations.

Monastery – A place of residence and prayer for a community of monks.

Monolith – A single large block of stonework.

Mortar – A mixture of cement or lime, sand and water used to make joints between stones and bricks in buildings.

Moulding – A continuous section of stonework intended as a decorative feature. It usually forms a band of either plain or decorated stonework, sometimes flat, sometimes in relief, or sometimes as roll moulding.

Narthax – A covered porch spanning the whole width of the entrance of a basilica.

Nave – The main body of the church intended for the congregation. It is west of the crossing or chancel and often has north and/or south aisles alongside.

Niche – A vertical arched recess usually intended to house a statue.

Ogee – A double curved line made up of a convex and a concave part.

Ornamented – Something that has been embellished with decoration.

Oratory – A small room or chapel intended for private prayer.

Panel – A square or oblong or circular compartment sunk or raised from the surface of stonework, woodwork, bone, silverwork, gold or metal-work with a defined border or frame. Within the panel it can contain decoration that may include lettering or runes, figurative or scenic images, religious or mythological scenes, or purely abstract designs.

Parapet – A low wall to provide protection where there is an abrupt drop. Usually a wall extending above a roof at the eaves or gable end.

Parclose Screen – A screen which separates a chapel from the rest of the church.

Parvise Chamber – A room over the porch.

Passage – A corridor linking one place to another allowing the movement of people.

Pellet(s) – A moulding comprising a flat band on which there is a row of small spherical shapes in relief.

Penannular – A description for an incomplete ring; often used when describing a brooch or a representation forming part of a decorative design (see *annular* above).

Pew – A specified place where a seat is usually provided. Often there are separate pews for worshippers, the choir and officiating priests.

Pier – A large section of stonework that supports an arch.

Pilaster – A vertical strip of stonework protruding from a wall.

Pillar – A vertical section of usually circular or polygonal stonework whose height is much greater than its diameter.

Piscina – A basin, with a drainage hole, incorporated into the fabric of a wall used for washing Communion or Mass vessels.

Pitch – The shape or angle of a roof.

Plait Work Or Knot Work Design – A design comprising cords intertwined and knotted together.

Plant Scroll Design – A design resembling a plant with a branch or stem supporting leaves.

Plaster – A composition of lime, sand and usually hair, used for covering walls and ceilings.

Plinth – Projecting stonework beneath a wall or column whose upper edge is usually chamfered.

Pointing – The mortar jointing between blocks of stonework or bricks.

Porch – The structure surrounding and enclosing an entrance. Used for both secular and religious purposes. Sometimes there is an upper chamber that was often used to accommodate a priest.

Portico/Porticus – An ambulatory comprising a roof supported by regularly spaced columns. Often attached as a porch to a church.

Portrait – A representation of a figure, including Christ, angels, saints, humans and gods, animals or some hybrid, as seen from the front with their eyes looking directly at the viewer.

Priest – A minister of religious worship, a clergyman, an ecclesiastic not a bishop or archbishop.

Priests – When priests were depicted on stonework they are shown with either a Celtic or Roman tonsure (see Tonsure below) and usually hold either a book, often The Bible or sometimes a cross. Additionally those following the Celtic form of Christianity were often carved with their feet pointing the same way sideways.

Profile – A representation of a figure, including Christ, angels, saints, humans and gods, animals or some hybrid, as seen from the side.

Pulpit – A raised and sometimes enclosed structure used for the preaching of sermons.

Quoin(s) – A dressed section of stonework that supports the corners of the church or building. One side of a quoin forms the last stone in one wall and another side of the same quoin forms the last stone in the wall adjoining. Usually quoins are distinctly larger than other sections of stonework in the rest of the walling. They are not usually uniform in shape and size. Most sides of the quoins are hidden by the interior fabric of the walling. Quoins are also used to define the construction of the stonework forming the jambs to internal and external doorways, arches, windows and belfry openings, whether open or blocked. See also *Long and Short Quoins* (above) and *Side Alternate Quoins* (below).

Quoining – A serious of quoins placed one on top of another (see *Quoins* above).

Recess – A niche or alcove.

Relief – A design protruding from the surface of the stonework or woodwork.

Removal Of Plasterwork – The effect when plaster is removed from walling. The walling is left scarred with the marks of chiselling.

Rendered – A process resulting in the shape of a section of stonework being altered and smoothed to fit in a particular place, for example, the side of a cross-shaft being rendered so that it can fit into a particular section of walling. This often results in any decoration being damaged or completely removed.

Rendering – Where a coat of plasterwork or whitewash has been applied to stone surfaces, usually for protective purposes. Often covering a wall to provide a uniform surface.

Reredos – Usually a painted or carved screen behind and above an altar.

Respond – A half-column supporting a single arch or pier at the end of an arcade.

Ring Head Crosshead – A crosshead where each of the angles between the four arms is linked by an additional curved "ring" of stonework – the shape of the ring can vary from a quarter to a full circle.

Ring Work Or Ring Chain – A design comprising circles, also concentric circles connected by thin entwined threads, cords or strands.

Ringerike Design – A design that is distinguished by elongated plant-like tendrils often sprouting from the core of the decoration whether abstract or animal. The design was in use in the 11C. A design named after a group of ornamental slabs found in the Ringerike district in Norway.

Roll Moulding – A decorative cylindrical feature of stonework usually in a band.

Rood Or Holy Rood – A representation of a cross or crucifix usually on a beam or painted above the chancel arch. Sometimes used to decorate crossheads or cross-shafts.

Rood Loft – A gallery built above the rood screen. Sometimes used by singers during a service, also used for maintenance purposes.

Rood Screen – The screen separating the nave from the chancel. Originally a crucifix flanked by the Virgin Mary and St John the Evangelist would surmount it. Originally it would have had an elaborate design.

Roof – The upper covering of a building. Terminology connected with a roof:

  Beam – A major horizontal timber consisting of a large piece of square timber long in proportion to its width and breadth.

  Braces – These are supporting timbers to provide strength to the frame.

  Collar – A horizontal timber joining a pair of rafters together.

  Rafters – A pair of timbers resting on the top of the wall and sloping to meet at the ridge.

  Ridge – The top external edge of the roof.

  Roofline – Marks in the stonework indicating the former ridge of a roof.

  Strut – A short supporting timber usually vertical.

  Truss – A transverse framework of timbers placed at each bay in the roof that carry the longitudinal roof timbers supporting the rafters.

  Tie Beam – A horizontal transverse beam connecting the foot of the rafters, usually at wall level.

  Collar Beam – A tie beam found higher up the slope of the roof.

  Hammer Beam – A horizontal transverse beam usually projecting from the top of the wall level and acting as ends to a tie beam but with the middle section removed. The beams may be single or double and are supported on braces and struts.

Crown Post – A vertical piece of timber standing centrally on a tie beam and supporting a collar beam.

Rope Work Design – See *Cable Work Design* above.

Rosette – A decorative ornamental design resembling a rose with a distinctive centre with flower-like petals radiating from it.

Rubble – Rough and ready building material not shaped and not laid in regular courses.

Rude – A description used when the stonework or design is simple and usually demonstrably undertaken by a craftsman with little skill or understanding of what is required. Poor quality workmanship, not necessarily early in date.

Runes Or Runic Or Futhorc Alphabet – Originally designed for carving on wood or stone. The characters take the form of straight strokes with angular forms. Futhorc denotes the first six letters of the alphabet f, u, "th" being a thorn, i.e. "Ð" or "ð", and hence one letter, o, r, and c. The Anglo-Saxon runic alphabet contained thirty one characters. These are:

f   u   Þ(th)   o   r   c   g   w   h   n   i   j   z(ih/ix)   p   x   s

t   b   e   m   l   n(ng)   d   œ(oe)   a   æ(ae)   y   ēā   ḡ   k   k̄

NB: Letters in brackets indicate sound value.

Ryedale Dragon Design – A design usually comprising a single, bound beast or dragon shown in S-shape with its jaws open. The design is similar to the *Jellinge Design* (see above). The design features on a number of examples of cross-shafts and grave covers in the Ryedale area in North Yorkshire – hence the name.

Sacristy – Now more commonly known as the vestry. Used for storing sacred vessels and vestments.

Sanctuary – The area immediately around the main altar of a church.

Sarcophagus – An elaborately carved stone coffin.

Sceat (Singular) And Sceattas (Plural) – These were small, thick silver pennies similar in size, weight and appearance to Thrymsas. They were in general circulation between 680 and 760. Wider silver pennies first introduced during the reign of King Offa of Mercia (757-796) gradually replaced them.

Scramasax – A larger version of the seax specifically used as a weapon rather than a household or hunting item. A short, single edged sword.

Screen – An internal partition, with doors when required, dividing a room or building. Sometimes an external wall in front of a building.

Scroll Design – A design resembling a roll of paper, a convoluted or spiral ornament, or a circuitous design similar to the trunks or branches of a plant or tree. (See also, above *Plant Scroll Design*, and below *Vine Scroll Design* and *Tree Scroll Design*.)

Seax – A knife or large dagger, sometimes a short single edged sword used for domestic or hunting purposes. This weapon gave its name to the people known as the "Seaxe" – the Saxons.

Sedilia – A seat for officiating priests usually on the south side of the chancel.

Shaft – A vertical round or polygonal section of stonework.

Side(s) – A generic description for all the faces, edges and any other description used for the sides of a section of stonework or a building.

Side Alternate Quoining – This is where the quoins are laid alternately between a quoin laid so that it has one of its faces lengthways on top of one of the short sides of another quoin below.

Side Wall – A wall forming a supportive part of a structure.

Sill – The horizontal section of stonework or woodwork at the bottom of a window or doorframe.

Slab – A flat and broad section of stonework.

Soffit – The underside of an arch.

Spandrel – The triangular space between adjacent arches.

Splay(ed) – An angled jamb of a window used to increase the amount of light coming into a building. Usually found on the internal face of a window but sometimes also found on the external face as well.

Spring(ing) – The point where an arch rises from its supports.

Squint (Hagioscope) – A hole in a wall to allow sight of an altar from a position in the church otherwise blocked by stonework.

Stage – A storey or floor of a building.

Statue – A sculptured representation of a deity, human or animal or beast.

Stele – An upright, often cylindrical, axial section of stonework decorated with sculptured designs or inscriptions.

Stepped Work Design – A design depicting a series of steps placed together in a regular pattern similar to *Key Pattern Design* (see above).

Stonework – Masonry comprising stones sometimes without mortar.

Storey – A stage of a building at one level. A building has stories one above another.

Stoup – A recess or niche to hold holy water.

"St Cuthbert Style" Cross Design – A design similar to that of the pectoral cross buried with St Cuthbert in Durham Cathedral in 687 AD. The arms of the cross are concave and the ends of the arms of the cross are convex.

Strands/Stranded – The threads or cords in an interlace design.

Strap Work Design – A plain design resembling a flat band or strap.

String Course – A distinctive line of horizontal stonework that protrudes around the external fabric of a wall. It often separates the various stages of a tower.

Strip Work – A long narrow section of stonework often used to outline a particular architectural feature, for example, a doorway.

Structure – The way in which a building has been put together.

Stycas – A copper coin or debased sceat that contained no silver, issued in Northumbria. It was in circulation towards the end of the 8C up until the mid 9C.

Sun Dial – A device for measuring the passing of the time of the day. It usually consists of a stone slab incorporated into the fabric of the church, on whose vertical face there is an incised semi-circle with its horizontal line having lines radiating often below but sometimes above. At the central intersection of these lines dividing the day into segments there would be a wooden or metal peg or stele – the "gnomon". The gnomon would cast a shadow and thus denote the day time: the absent half circle denoting night time. The gnomon is now usually missing but the hole in which it was housed is still identifiable. Often the hole for the missing gnomon assists in identifying the weathered scratches on a vertical slab of stonework as being those from a sun dial. Most Anglo-Saxon sundials were divided into four (day) segments (eight in total for day and night) but there were exceptions where sundials were divided into twelve (day) segments (twenty-four in total for day and night). Dividing day and night into eight segments was a Germanic tradition rather than the Roman tradition of a twenty-four hour day and night.

Sunk(en) – Where the surface of a specific area of a section of stonework or woodwork has been lowered so that it is below the general surface.

Tegulated – A design comprising, or arranged like, a series of overlapping tiles. Such a design originated with roofing tiles and armour.

Terracotta – Moulded and fired unglazed clay.

The Four Evangelists Design – A decorative design depicting the Four Evangelists: Matthew represented by a winged man; Mark represented by a winged lion; Luke represented by a winged ox; and John represented by an eagle.

Through Stone – A stone that extends through the entire thickness of a wall.

Thrymsas – A small, thick gold coin minted from around the 630s, they were also known as gold shillings. They were superseded by thin silver pennies known as sceattas which were made from pure silver and were the same size and weight and general appearance as Thrymsas.

Tiles – A thin flat slab of burnt clay covering the roof of a building (unglazed) and, less common, the floor of a building (sometimes glazed).

Tomb-Chest – A large stone coffin (like the size of a chest piece of furniture) often decorated.

Tonsure – There are two types of tonsure: The Celtic Tonsure is where the hair is shaved at the front of the head, from ear to ear. Roman Tonsure is where the hair is shaved in the middle of the head so that the surrounding hair might be a symbol of the Crown of Thorns.

Tooled – A worked or shaped piece of stonework, woodwork leatherwork or metalwork.

Torus – A roll moulding design used on a column base.

Tower – A structure taller in height than its width, mostly square in plan but occasionally it may be polygonal or circular. The tower is usually attached to the west end of the church, occasionally detached. In a cruciform church the tower is more centrally placed, between the east end of the nave and the west end of the chancel. The tower sometimes provided accommodation for a priest, a refuge for people in times of attack and safety from floods. It also housed the church bells and was sometimes used as a schoolhouse.

Tracery – Intricate ornamental stonework separating the lights (encased windows) in the upper part of Gothic (late 12C to mid 16C) windows. The stonework to support glass within a large window aperture.

Transept – The transverse sections (arms) of a cruciform church.

Transom – The horizontal bar across the openings of a window.

Tree-Scroll Design – A design resembling a tree with a main stem or trunk supporting branches.

Triforium – An arcaded wall passage below the clerestory.

Tumulus – An ancient artificial mound used for burials; similar to a barrow or a howe.

Typaneum – The space enclosed between a horizontal lintel and the enclosing arch above it. The space is often filled with ornament or sculpture. Typaneums are most often found above doorways but also above windows, particularly double belfry windows.

Urnes Design – A design that is distinguished by elongated stylised animals and snake-like creatures ensnared with strands and ribbons. The design was in use during the 11C and 12C and it is sometimes referred to as "the last art form of the Vikings". The design is named after the wood carvings on Urnes Church in Norway.

Vault – An arched stone ceiling.

Vestibule – The entrance lobby.

Vestry – A room primarily now used as a robing room by the clergy and choir. Formerly, it also stored the church plate and church records.

Vine Scroll Design – A design resembling a trailing or climbing plant like a vine sometimes with distinctive grapes.

Voussoir – Each of the wedge-shaped, tapered, stones forming an arch.

Wall – An enclosing structure of stones or bricks or timber laid in courses. For defensive structures walls may also be made of earth.

Weathered Or Weathering – An artefact, or section of stonework, seasoned by the weather rather than deliberately damaged.

Wheel Head Crosshead – A crosshead whose four arms are linked to each other near their circumference by a curved section of stonework to give the overall appearance of a wheel – the arms forming the spokes of the wheel.

Wheel Head Design – A design or section of stonework with a circular frame with spokes radiating from a central point.

Whitewash – A liquid composition of lime and water to provide a lighter colouration to building surfaces.

Window – An opening to let light into a building.

Worn – An artefact or section of stonework, showing the results of wear through use.

Zoomorphic Design – A design representing or imitating animals.

Layout of Gazetteer

The sites are divided into five distinct geographical areas:

1. East Yorkshire.
2. North Yorkshire.
3. South Yorkshire.
4. West Yorkshire.
5. York.

At the beginning of each geographical entry the number of sites is identified and there then follows a list of all the sites in each star-rated category. The significance of the star rating is explained. [Note: After the star ratings in North Yorkshire two, South Yorkshire one, and West Yorkshire one, entries identify sections of stonework that are in private ownership where access is not possible – their locations are not provided.]

For each of the five distinct geographical areas, each site is then listed:

1. In alphabetical order based on the name of the hamlet, village, town or city. [Note: the entries are not in star-rating order.]

2. By a title identifying the nature or the association of the site. For example: St James's Church, Lilla Cross, Weston Park Museum, Battle.

3. Where appropriate, where there is more than one entry for a particular hamlet, village, town or city, each title identifying the nature or association of the site is listed and numbered in alphabetical order. For example:

WHITBY

(1) *Abbey (EH) etc*
(2) *Cholmley House Visitor Centre (EH) etc*
(3) *St Mary's Church and Caedmon's Cross etc*
(4) *Whitby Museum and Pannet Art Gallery etc*

Where appropriate, the letters "EH" or "NT" appear denoting the site as in the custodianship of English Heritage or the National Trust. For example, Whitby Abbey (EH), Conisbrough Castle (EH), East Riddlesden Hall (NT).

4. Beneath the title identifying the nature or association of the site there is the National Grid Reference identifying the precise location of the site. For example: TA 204688, SE 705900, SK 267925.

5. Next to the National Grid Reference there is the "star" rating. The key to the star-rating is:

    RATING ☆ This signifies that material may be difficult to find or identify with confidence.

    RATING ☆☆ This signifies that material can be found and identified but it is not particularly well looked after or a "good example".

    RATING ☆☆☆ This signifies that material can easily be found and identified.

    RATING ☆☆☆☆ This signifies that material can easily be found and identified, and provides good examples.

    RATING ☆☆☆☆☆ This signifies that material can easily be found and identified, providing excellent examples that are full of interest.

6. Next to the star rating the words "Access is possible" often appear. This indicates that visits have to be arranged in the company of a "key holder". Where these words do not appear this indicates that the sites, including churches are usually open during reasonable daylight hours and access does not require any special prior arrangements.

7. There then follows the full entry. Each entry follows the following format:

    *   A description of how to get to, or how to identify the site. Where road names are identified in the text this signifies that there are street sign(s) currently in the vicinity. Where no street signs can currently be identified, the text includes the words "(there are no street signs)" and consequently no road names are given.

    *   A brief mention of any pertinent historical facts relating to the particular site. For example: "The church retains much late 7C/ early 8C material with 12C, 13C and 15C alterations." "The assassination attempt on King Edwin..." "The Museum displays Sheffield metal ware, cutlery..."

    *   Where necessary, especially in churches, further information is given to identify where particular Anglo-Saxon, Anglo-Danish, Anglo-Norse items or material are located.

For Church sites the entries follow the following sequence:

A. Items or material located internally are given first, followed by any external items or material. Separate items in the churchyard are the last to be identified.

B. Where there is a considerable number of specific items/stonework these are numbered sequentially.

C. The item is:

(i)   Identified.

(ii) Located precisely. Where necessary distances from walls, ends of window ledges etc, are given in both Imperial [Ins = inches, Yds = yards] and metric measurement, rounded down to the nearest centimetre [Cms = centimetres, M = metres].

(iii) Measured approximately in both Imperial [Ins = inches, Yds = yards] and metric measurement, rounded down to the nearest centimetre [Cms = centimetres, M = metres].

Measurements are given in height, abbreviated H; width, abbreviated W; and depth, abbreviated D. In the case of coffins, hogback grave covers and baluster shafts, length, abbreviated L – in most, but not all, cases length replaces depth.

Where material has been incorporated into the fabric of a wall it is usually only be possible to give the measurements of height = H, and width = W.

Where it is clear that the item has not been placed in its proper alignment the height, width and depth descriptors are given as it currently appears with, in brackets, their true descriptors. For example: "The section of stonework measures 14 Ins/35 Cms H (W) by 7 Ins/17 Cms W (H)".

(iv) The detail of the measurements given relating to cross-shafts may vary from one example to another because of the nature of their construction. Thus the shape of the cross-shaft may be:

- Four sides (i.e. two faces and two other sides) with equal dimensions.

- Two faces having the same dimensions and the two other sides each having the same dimensions but differing from the faces.

- Four sides (both faces and two other sides) each having tapering dimensions from bottom to top with equal dimensions.

- The two faces having the same dimensions tapering from bottom to top and two other sides each having the same tapering dimensions from bottom to top, but differing dimensions from the faces.

(v) Where possible, the nature of any decoration on the item is identified.

ACCESS TO CHURCHES

Printed details about access to churches in touring guides and local guidebooks are not always reliable. The best way to obtain contact details for a particular church, prior to a visit, is to go to the Church of England web site at *http://www.cofe.anglican.org.* This is subject to change and improvement. On entry to the site click on the "Find us" (Find Churches, parish websites, email & phone numbers.). This leads on to the "Where to find us" page which provides the option to search either by "information sheets" or by "parish websites" (becoming "Parish church web sites" when clicked for search). Both these provide options to search parishes by phrase, first letter of parish or by diocese – the information sheets entry also provides a search by postcode option). Some, but not all, churches will have their own web site but the details provided may not always contain the information required.

If web site enquiries prove unsuccessful then the most reliable source is the current "Crockford's Clerical Directory" published by Church House Publishing. This Directory includes details of Church of England clergy and identifies the church(es) for which they are responsible. Copies of this Directory can be obtained from Church House, Great Smith Street, London SW1P 3NZ if enquiries of booksellers and public libraries are unsuccessful.

When writing to the incumbent (e.g. vicar, curate-in-charge etc), explain the reason for your interest, and enquire whether it is possible to visit the church, their co-operation is usually forthcoming. As vicars/curates do not necessarily live near every church for which they are responsible, they may put you in touch with a churchwarden or another local resident.

Sometimes at the time of a visit details of the key holder can be obtained by looking at the notices on the internal walls of the porch or on the door into the church itself. The notices can range in size and quality from printed notices behind glass-fronted notice boards to scraps of paper pinned to the door with the details handwritten. (The porch entrances to churches are usually on the south side, occasionally on the west and rarely on the north.) Opening times of the church and the names and addresses of key holders are sometimes included on church notice boards located by the entrance gate(s) to the churchyard, or the driveway/pathway leading to the church – these notice boards primarily give the details of the church services. Where there are no such notices, local post offices and the local tourist information office may be able to assist.

MUSEUMS

As with all museums, the displays and the exhibits they contain may be changed, re-sited, removed from display and/or put in store, or loaned to other museums or suitable repositories. Before visiting a museum it is worth checking in advance whether the displays listed in the Gazetteer are still in place in the same location(s) set out in the text. Individual exhibits may have been rearranged in terms of their display, the order in which they are displayed and their relationship to other exhibits; some exhibits may have been removed from display. The text in the Gazetteer reflects the descriptions and/or notices accompanying exhibits at the time of visiting. These too may have been revised, amended, added to or removed.

ABBREVIATIONS COMMONLY USED THROUGHOUT THE TEXT

A-D	=	Anglo-Danish
A-N	=	Anglo-Norse
A-S	=	Anglo-Saxon(s)
C	=	Century
Cms	=	Centimetres
D	=	Deep/Depth
EH	=	English Heritage
H	=	High/Height
Ins	=	Inches
L	=	Long/Length
M	=	Metres
NT	=	National Trust
W	=	Wide/Width
Yds	=	Yards

Part 1

Background

WHO WERE THE ANGLO-SAXONS?

The Anglo-Saxon period is defined as the years from 400 up to 1100 AD. The predecessors to the Anglo-Saxons in Britain were the Romans with the native British; how much these peoples could be accurately described as "Romano-British" and how much the native British retained their separate identity is a matter of conjecture. However, when the Romans left Britain in 410AD the remaining Romano-British population is thought to have been mostly Christian.

Around 428 AD Vortigern, a British ruler, invited the Angles and the Saxons to the country to help fight the Picts who at that time dominated modern day Scotland. Traditionally these Angles and Saxons were led by Hengist and Horsa. In return for their services Vortigern offered them land. On seeing how rich and sparsely populated the country was, the Angles and the Saxons rebelled around 441 AD and took land on their own behalf. Growing populations in the Anglo-Saxon homelands, the need for farmers to seek better land for their crops, and for some, the fear of their land being flooded by the rising North Sea, prompted migration of the Anglo-Saxons to Britain.

Initially the Anglo-Saxons crossed the North Sea in relatively small groups in the late fourth and early fifth centuries, but subsequently their numbers increased so that during the later fifth and sixth centuries they began to dominate the population. As well as warriors the settlers were predominantly arable farmers wanting better and more land for their crops and families. As the number of Anglo-Saxon settlers increased, the British language of the native Romano-British population was replaced by English, reflecting the domination of the newcomers. In lowland Britain this was exemplified by the use of English to describe names for topographical features, settlements and groups of settlers. In response, the Romano-British population moved westwards into Cornwall, Wales and Brittany either as a result of warfare or their own volition.

The **Angles** came from the Danish peninsula, some of the islands in the Danish archipelago and southern Norway. They settled north of the River Thames and established the kingdoms of Bernicia (roughly modern day Northumberland, Durham, parts of Cumbria and parts of southern Scotland), and Deira (roughly modern day Yorkshire). After 600AD Bernicia and Deira were united to become the kingdom of the "people north of the River Humber", "Northanhymbre" – Northumbria. The kingdom of Northumbria extended from the Rivers Humber and Mersey in the south up through all the land south of the Firth of Forth in modern day Scotland, including Edinburgh. ("Edwin's burgh", named after King Edwin of Northumbria who reigned 616-633. He was baptised in 627 at York.)

The Angles also established the kingdoms of Lindsey (roughly modern day Lincolnshire), Mercia (roughly modern day Cheshire, Derbyshire, Nottinghamshire, Leicestershire, Staffordshire, Shropshire, Herefordshire, Worcestershire, Warwickshire, Northamptonshire, Bedfordshire, Hertfordshire, Greater London, Middlesex, Buckinghamshire, Oxfordshire and Gloucestershire), and East Anglia (roughly modern day Norfolk, Suffolk and Cambridgeshire).

The **Saxons** came from North Germany; they lived to the southwest of the Angles on the North Sea coastal plain around and up to the River Wesser. They settled mostly to the south the River Thames and established the kingdoms of Wessex (roughly modern day Devonshire, Somersetshire, Dorsetshire, Wiltshire, Berkshire and Hampshire), Essex (roughly modern day Essex but with parts of Greater London, Hertfordshire and possibly parts of Surrey), and Sussex (roughly modern day Sussex but extending into parts of Hampshire and Surrey).

The **Jutes** came from Jutland in Denmark. The Jutes settled in Kent, the Isle of Wight and the coastal lands in Hampshire opposite the Isle of Wight.

The **Freisians** were from the north of Holland; their numbers were increased by Angles and Saxons who used Frisia as a staging point in their migration. The Frisians settled mostly in Kent. Franks from the German Rhineland also settled in Kent.

WHO WERE THE VIKINGS?

The Viking period is defined as the years from 793 to 1100 AD. The Vikings were people from modern day Denmark, Norway and Sweden. The "Age of the Vikings" was prompted by:

- Economic factors. The populations were expanding; there was not enough land and wealth for everyone in the homelands.

- The climate. The northern hemisphere was experiencing a periodic improvement in climate making formerly inhospitable land desirable. In contrast, some areas experienced a rise in water levels making the land less hospitable.

- Political factors. Warfare, consolidation and enlargement of kingdoms resulted in numbers of people becoming displaced.

- Technological factors. The improvement of their ships in terms of construction, speed and manoeuvrability, and their ability to navigate.

Among the first recorded attack of the Vikings on England is the one on Lindisfarne off the Northumberland coast in 793. Initially, these raids by both Danish and Norwegian Vikings comprised a series of small-scale raids on undefended coastal sites by a few ships intent on acquiring portable wealth for either trade or for use at home. As the success of these early raids became known, larger groups of between thirty and forty ships became involved. These groups targeted rich trading centres and developed a systematic pattern of raiding. These larger groups had the advantage over those who opposed them in that they could land and attack wherever they liked; unlike their opponents they did not have to stretch their resources to defend everywhere from surprise attack. Raids by these larger groups then developed into attempts at conquest of the country by armies involving hundreds of ships.

Viking conquest of England began in 865AD with "The Great Army" led by two sons of Ragnar Lothbrok, Ivar "the Boneless" and Halfdan. They landed in East Anglia and in the succeeding years the army moved back and forth between York, Mercia, East Anglia (where they killed King (Saint) Edmund the Martyr of East Anglia in 869), Wessex, London and Northumbria. In 874 the Great Army divided into two. One part, under the leadership of Halfdan went to the area around the mouth of the River Tyne in Northumbria. This resulted in 876 with the settlement of many of his soldiers in lands in modern day Yorkshire. The second part of the Great Army under the leadership of Guthrum, Oscytel and Anund moved to the Cambridge area. In 876, this part of the army attacked Wessex, moving between Wessex and Mercia in succeeding years. King Alfred's Treaty of Wedmore with Guthrum in 886 divided much of England between Saxon Wessex and Anglian south and west Mercia. The Viking "Danelaw" covered much of England north and east of a line from London to the Mersey. Part of northern Northumbria, with its capital at Bamburgh, Northumberland, remained English (Anglian) rather than Viking. Over the next sixty years the English gradually re-imposed their authority of the areas settled by the Great Army and their descendants.

During 900-925 AD Norwegian settlements extending from west of the Pennines to York were augmented by displaced Vikings from Ireland.

In 1014 the Vikings conquered all of England under Sweyn Forkbeard, King of Denmark and Norway. Shortly after his success Sweyn died and was succeeded by Canute who initially battled with King Edmund II "Ironside" for control of the country. With Edmund's death in 1016, Canute reigned as the unopposed King of England. Canute reigned until 1035. He was succeeded as King of England by Harold I (1035-1040). Harold I was in turn succeeded by Hardecanute (1040-1042). On Hardecanute's death in 1042 Viking rule of England ceased. Hardecanute was succeeded by Edward the Confessor (1042-1066).

The next Viking attempt at conquest of England occurred in 1066. A Norwegian led army under Harold III "Hardrada" of Norway landed in Yorkshire. After initial success at the battle of Fulford Harold Hardrada and his army were comprehensively defeated by King Harold II of England at the battle of Stamford Bridge.

In 1069 King Sweyn Estrithson of Denmark sent a composite fleet of Danes and Norwegians to join the English in their attempts to overthrow William I. After testing defences in Dover, Sandwich, Ipswich and Norwich the fleet went to safe anchorages in the River Humber. In 1070 King Sweyn himself led another Viking fleet to join the fleet he had sent in 1069. These Vikings were involved in the events orchestrated by Hereward leader of the English in the Isle of Ely. In the summer of 1070 Sweyn and William made a peace treaty involving William paying money to Sweyn to leave the country. There were no further attempts by the Vikings to effect a conquest of England.

THE CHURCH – THE CELTIC AND ROMAN CHURCH, AND THE SYNOD OF WHITBY

In 664 King Oswy, King of Northumbria, called a synod at Whitby to resolve the differences between the adherents of the Celtic and Roman forms of Christianity.

The churches following the **Celtic or Irish traditions** of Christianity were distinguished by their self-contained monastic communities often in remote places. Bishops were under the jurisdiction of abbots or were themselves both bishop and abbot. The communities practised ascetic discipline, living lives as simply as possible in poverty. Their monasteries were always built in wood, not stone, within characteristically shaped oval enclosures.

The churches following the **Roman traditions** of Christianity were organised on a centralised, hierarchical structure with monasteries and bishops, a universal church opposed to insularity and parochialism. Despite it's Rome based centre and Latin based culture, the clergy developed the use of the vernacular speech because of the need to communicate with a largely illiterate flock. The church was administered by bishops who with their clergy lived a communal life. Where possible churches were built in stone and decorated. Whilst admiring many aspects of Celtic Christianity, those following the Roman traditions of Christianity were critical of the way in which followers of the Celtic tradition calculated the timing of Easter and that they had not converted their pagan neighbours, the Angles, Saxons and Jutes earlier.

Following the appointment of Colman as bishop of Northumbria in 660 AD the dispute between those following the "Roman" and "Irish" (Celtic) traditions of Christianity culminated in King Oswiu (Oswy), King of Northumbria, calling a synod in 664 at the monastery of Abbess Hild (Saint Hilda), at Streanaeshalch (Whitby). The principal advocate of the "Roman" party was Wilfred (later bishop and Saint) and the principal advocate of the "Irish" party was Colman. The dispute centred on the method of calculating the timing of Easter. Colman based his arguments on the authority of Saint John the Apostle, the authority of Anatolius a disciple of John the Apostle, the teachings of the church in Iona and the tradition of Saint Columba. Wilfred based his arguments on the authority of Saint Peter the keeper of the "Keys of Heaven" whose authority had been inherited by his church in Rome, the folly of only the two "outer" islands of Christianity using a different method of calculating Easter, and the advantages of conformity across the Christian world. The Synod determined that the "Roman" rather than the "Celtic" form of Christianity would be adhered to in England. Most accepted the decision but Colman, many of his Irish clergy, and some English monks, left for Iona.

THE CHURCH – EXEMPLAR CHURCH PLAN

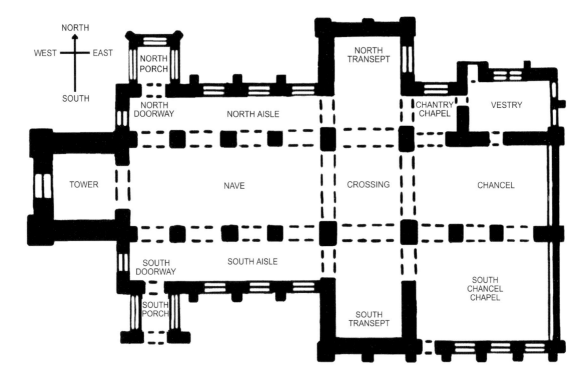

This is an example of a church plan showing the most commonly identified parts of the church. An exception is made of the baptistry which has no set location. Often the baptistry is located on the ground floor of the tower or at the west end of the south aisle where there is sufficient space between the south doorway and the west wall of the south aisle. In addition it might also be located at the east end of the south aisle, immediately before the entrance to a south transept or chapel or in the south transept.

CHURCH BUILDING STYLES AND ARCHITECTURE

Churches are undoubtedly the main providers of extant Anglo-Saxon, Anglo-Danish and Anglo-Norse evidence. However, much of what can be seen today was incorporated into later work when substantial additions, rebuildings and restorations took place.

As a general guide, characteristics of church building styles and architecture can be described as:

1.   **The Celtic monastic tradition**. This is the characteristic of the "conversion" period in the seventh century. Although no structures

survive from this period, later buildings - and particularly the churchyards - adhere to the Celtic tradition of monastic layout. These comprised an oval monastic enclosure in which there were groups of circular huts for the monks who lived in hermit-like cells. The church was the only substantial structure. All the buildings were made of wood, wattle and daub and thatch. The priests adopted an itinerant lifestyle to spread Christianity and often built a wooden cross at sites where they preached. Examples of existing churchyards which follow the layout of a Celtic monastery are to be found at All Saints Church Bramham and St John's Church Stanwick.

2.   **The Anglo-Saxon period**. Despite the outcome of the Synod of Whitby in 664 where it was agreed that the "Roman" rather than the "Celtic" form of Christianity would be followed, the Celtic monastic tradition continued in some respects in terms of simple, rather than decorative, church architecture, and the use of preaching crosses by itinerant priests. The Anglo Saxons used "Minster" churches as the centre from which priests went out into the countryside to preach, thus creating a community of clergy who undertook pastoral functions over a wide area. Between 1000AD and 1150AD the territory covered by individual Minster Churches was fragmented into smaller ones which became the parishes surviving today in rural areas. These Minster churches would be something similar to what the Church of England describes today as "team ministries". Examples of Minster churches are to be found at the Minster Church of All Saints Dewsbury, and the Minster Church of Holy Trinity Stonegrave. From the eighth century churches began to be built and rebuilt in stone, for example, St Peter's Hackness; All Saints Ledsham.

3.   **The combined Anglo-Saxon/Anglo-Danish/Anglo-Norse period**. With the coming of the Danes in the ninth century and the Norse in the tenth century many churches were destroyed. However, as times became more settled and the Danes and Norse were converted to Christianity, churches were rebuilt and in particular decorated crosses, combining both cross-shaft and crosshead were raised. These crosses were used both for preaching purposes and as memorials to specific individuals. During this period "hogback" grave covers were also introduced.

4.   **Norman or Romanesque** 1066-1170. The tops of the arches and windows were semi-circular in shape. Typically, the building style emulated the Roman style that was simply known as "Romanesque" in Europe.

5.   **Transitional** 1170-1200. The period when the style of architecture changed from Norman/Romanesque to Early English.

6.   **Gothic style**. This is divided into three distinct phases.

(i)   Late 12th century to late 13th century Early English. Typified by tall, narrow pointed arches and lancet windows.

(ii)   Late 13th century to mid 14th century Decorated. Typified by architecture involving more decoration particularly in the use of more complex windows with several lights with tracery surmounted by pierced decorated stonework.

(iii)   Mid 14th century to mid 16th century Perpendicular. Typified by taller and wider windows, with more complex tracery and with ornamental stonework becoming more common. Towers were built to house bells and the ornamentation of the towers became common.

7.   **Elizabethan, Stuart, Jacobean** 1558 to 1714. Few churches were built during this period. However, many monuments and brasses do survive from this period. Elizabeth 1, who reigned 1558-1603, decreed that the congregation should no longer have to stand in church but be provided with seating.

8.   **Georgian** 1715 to 1837. Churches were built in the "classical" style based on Ancient Greek and Roman styles of architecture.

9.   **Victorian** 1837 to 1901. Many churches were restored or rebuilt during this period, often in a style imitating work of an earlier period particularly mock medieval Gothic.

ANGLO-SAXON CHURCHES

Most rewarding are visits to churches with known Anglo-Saxon or Anglo-Danish or Anglo-Norse material, or current structures known to be on the site of an Anglo-Saxon or Anglo-Danish or Anglo-Norse church, for instance, because of an entry in the "Domesday Book". In addition visitors should remember that Anglo-Saxon and Anglo-Danish or Anglo-Norse (Viking) workmanship did not simply cease after 1066, it continued and is sometimes referred to as "Saxo-Norman". When investigating sites of Anglo-Saxon or Anglo-Danish or Anglo-Norse interest, do not be put off by the age of the present structure; often during nineteenth century restorations, Anglo-Saxon and Anglo-Danish and Anglo-Norse material was re-discovered and incorporated into new, or restored, internal or external fabric in the church or displayed, usually internally, rarely externally.

Unfortunately, church guidebooks and leaflets provide no comprehensive catalogue of extant material. Often there is no guidebook or leaflet at all. However, guidebooks and leaflets should always be consulted since they may provide useful additional information not evident from simply looking around the church. Don't be put off by the failure of authors to distinguish between Anglo-Saxon and Anglo-Danish and Viking and Norse and Norman and by phrases such as "Pre-Conquest", "Early Norman" or "Early Medieval".

PLANS OF ANGLO-SAXON CURCHES

1. Simple Design

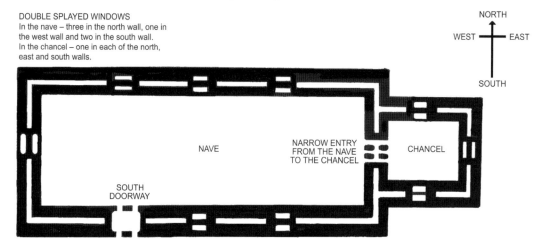

DOUBLE SPLAYED WINDOWS
In the nave – three in the north wall, one in the west wall and two in the south wall.
In the chancel – one in each of the north, east and south walls.

NORTH
WEST —— EAST
SOUTH

NAVE

NARROW ENTRY FROM THE NAVE TO THE CHANCEL

CHANCEL

SOUTH DOORWAY

2. Roman Basilica Design

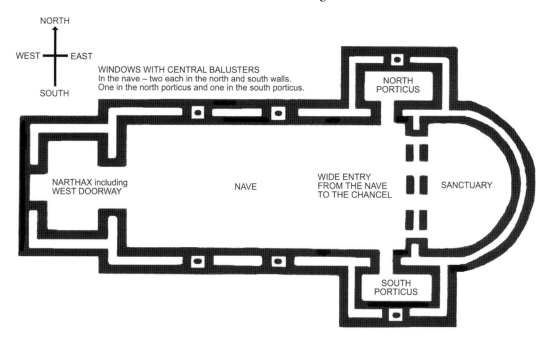

NORTH
WEST —— EAST
SOUTH

WINDOWS WITH CENTRAL BALUSTERS
In the nave – two each in the north and south walls.
One in the north porticus and one in the south porticus.

NORTH PORTICUS

NARTHAX including WEST DOORWAY

NAVE

WIDE ENTRY FROM THE NAVE TO THE CHANCEL

SANCTUARY

SOUTH PORTICUS

DEVELOPMENTS IN THE STRUCTURE OF ANGLO-SAXON CHURCHES

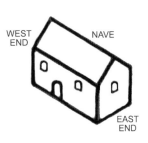

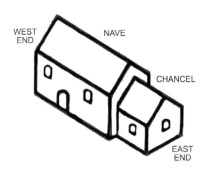

The first two examples show initially a simple, small, narrow, rectangular church that subsequently has had a shallow apse or chancel added to the eastern end of the nave.

The third example shows a simple, narrow, rectangular church, larger than the two previous examples. It comprises a three stage western tower attached to a wider rectangular nave. Added to the eastern end of the nave there is a smaller, shallower eastern apse or chancel.

The fourth example shows a cruciform (cross) shaped church. The large western nave is attached at its eastern end to a three stage tower of similar width. Attached to both the north and south sides of the tower, there is a north and south porticus, both smaller than the tower in width and height. Attached to the east end of the tower is a chancel, narrower in width than the tower and shallower in length than the nave.

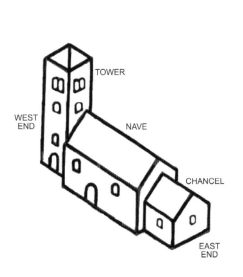

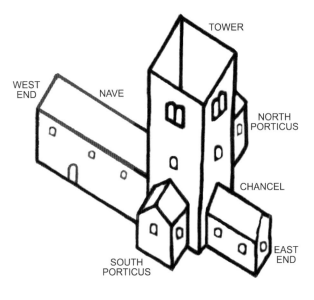

CONSTRUCTION OF THE CHURCH

Typical Anglo-Saxon churches were rectangular in plan and were very high in relation to their length and width. Some churches had a western porch or tower and some an eastern apse or chancel. Doorways, arches and windows were generally narrow in comparison with their height.

Originally Anglo-Saxon churches would have been constructed in wood. However, apart from Greensted Church in Essex, none now survive. Fortunately many Anglo-Saxon churches were rebuilt in stone or built in stone to begin with and it is these churches that survive in some degree. Stonework in typical Anglo-Saxon churches is characterised by:

- The use of irregularly-shaped, roughly faced plain stones (rubble) built in irregularly shaped courses often including large megalithic stones. Rarely did the Anglo-Saxons use the uniform-shaped stones built in regular courses or use ashlar stonework favoured by the later Norman builders.

- The re-use of existing tooled stonework from nearby Roman remains where available.

- The use of herring-bone masonry with lines of tooled stonework set at right angles to each other. These are a late Anglo-Saxon development and now such masonry is not considered so indicative of Anglo-Saxon origin.

In England both the Danes and the Norse built churches in the Anglo-Saxon style.

FEATURES OF CONSTRUCTION

Walls

- The thickness of the walls of a church can be indicative of Anglo-Saxon origin. Apart from walls in the towers, most Anglo-Saxon walls were less than 36 inches/91 centimetres thick, although there are the occasional exceptions where the walls were thicker. The high quality of the mortar used by the Angle-Saxons in the construction of their walls is demonstrated by the original thin walls later being used to carry the weight of arches for which they were not originally intended.

- Both string courses and pilaster strips dividing up walls are simple in design, usually square in shape and thin, and usually protrude from the wall.

An example of "Regular" Anglo- Saxon walling found in churches:

The pieces of stone work are laid in regular courses but the stones themselves vary in shape and size. The left hand end wall has "standard side alternate" quoining (see below).

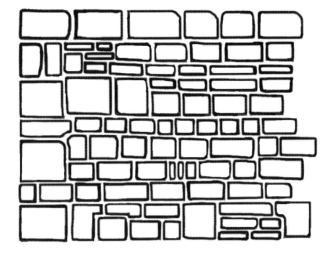

An example of "Irregular" Anglo- Saxon walling found in churches:

The pieces of stone work are irregularly shaped and sized and they are laid randomly. The left hand end wall has "standard side alternate" quoining (see below).

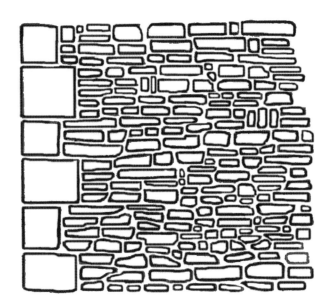

QUOINS

Quoins comprise a dressed section of stonework that supports the corners of the church or building. One side of a quoin forms the last stone in one wall and another side of the same quoin forms the last stone in the other wall adjoining. Anglo-Saxon quoins are usually distinctly larger than other sections of stonework in the rest of the walling. They are not usually uniform in shape and size. Quoins are also used to define the construction of the stonework forming the jambs to internal and external doorways, arches, windows and belfry openings, whether open or blocked.

1. "Side Alternate Work".

(a)   Standard Side Alternate Work

This example of quoining is known as "Standard Side Alternate Work". The quoins are laid with their long sides parallel to the top and bottom of the walling, with one of their faces and one of their short sides exposed - the other face and sides are hidden by the interior fabric of the walling. The courses of the quoins alternate a face lengthways above a short side of the quoin below. This is the most common form of quoining that can easily be identified. *Hatched lines indicate the full shape of the quoins incorporated and hidden by the fabric of the walls.*

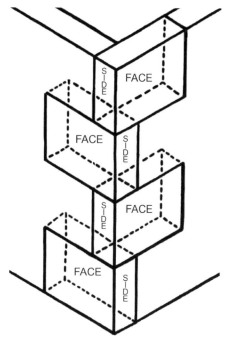

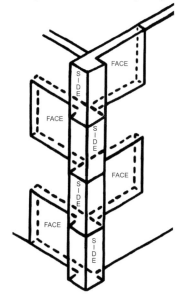

(b)   Cut Back Side Alternate Work

This example of quoining is known as "Cut Back Side Alternate Work". This is where the corner of the quoin protrudes from each of the two walls for which it forms the junction. The stones forming the quoins are deliberately cut back to give this appearance. *Hatched lines indicate the full shape of the quoins incorporated and hidden by the fabric of the walls.*

(c)   Face Alternate Work

This example of quoining is known as "Face Alternate Work". This is where the quoins are laid as though they were bricks or small blocks. (NB. Brickwork is not a feature of A-S churches apart from those churches where Roman bricks have been reused.) The quoins are laid with their faces parallel to the top or bottom of the walling, with one of their long sides and one of their short sides exposed - the faces and the other sides are hidden by the interior fabric of the walling. The courses of the quoins alternate a long side above a short side of the quion below. It is a less common variant of the "side alternate" quoining. *Hatched lines indicate the full shape of the quoins incorporated and hidden by the fabric of the walls. NB: to avoid confusion hatching and identification of the sides has been restricted to one example on each wall.*

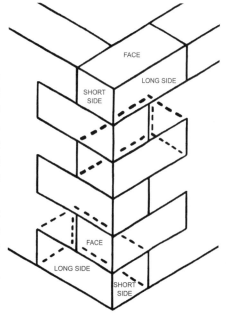

(d)   "**Megalithic Work**". This is where large quoins of irregular shape and size are usually laid in standard side alternate pattern (see the example of a Tower Arch on Page 38). The quoins are laid with their long sides parallel to the top or bottom of the walling, with one of their faces and one of their short sides exposed - the other face and sides are hidden by the interior fabric of the walling. The courses of the quoins alternate a face lengthways above a short side of the quoin below. The quoins are very distinctive and are easily recognisable as "megalithic".

2. "**Long and Short Work**".

(a)   Standard Long and Short Work

This example of quoining is known as "Standard Long and Short Work". The courses of the quoins alternate between a square-shaped quoin lying flat horizontally on one of its hidden faces with two of its sides exposed and forming the "short side" (its hidden faces are parallel to the top or bottom of the walling), and a narrow, rectangular-shaped quoin standing vertically on one of its hidden smallest sides with one of its faces and one of its other sides exposed and forming the "long side". The other sides and faces of the stonework are hidden by the interior fabric of the walling. Sometimes this quoining is described as "Escomb" named after the construction technique used in the jambs supporting the chancel arch in the Anglo-Saxon Church at Escomb, County Durham. The face of one quoin stands upright on top of one of the narrow sides of another quoin laid flat below. *Hatched lines indicate the full shape of the quoins incorporated and hidden by the fabric of the walls.*

(b)   Cut Back Long and Short Work

This example of quoining is known as "Cut Back Long and Short Work". This is where the corner of the quoin protrudes from each of the two walls for which it forms the junction. The stones forming the quoins are deliberately cut back to give this appearance. *Hatched lines indicate the full shape of the quoins incorporated and hidden by the fabric of the walls.*

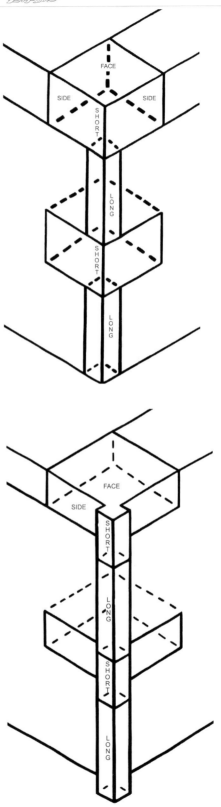

ARCHES

Typical characteristics of Anglo-Saxon arches:

- They have no central "key" stone.

- They were cut straight through the wall, either lined with through stones or built wholly of rubble just like the walls into which they have been cut.

- They were often supported by stonework similar in design to quoining.

- They were built using plain square sections of stonework or they were built wholly of rubble.

- They were not recessed or built of ashlar cut to convenient sizes; the voussoirs are irregular in shape.

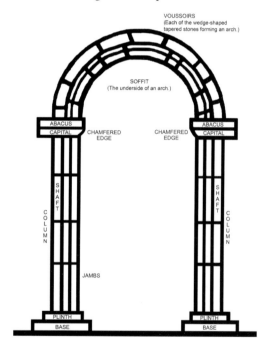

(a)   **A Chancel Arch**

This is an example of a chancel arch. It comprises:

- Two sets of individually shaped through stones placed one on top of each other each forming an arch. Neither of these two arches has a central key stone. The inner arch is the same depth as the outer arch but it has been shaped with a recess along part of its width. The design of this recess has been continued down both of the inner shafts supporting the capitals that in turn support the arch itself. The designs used on these arches can vary greatly: from no design at all, to abstract designs, to designs depicting animals and people forming a scene.

- Supporting through stones laid flat and forming the capitals on each side of the arch. The abacus forms the top slab of each of the capitals on both sides of the arch. The lower slab of each of the capitals on both sides of the arch has a chamfered edge. Like the arch itself, the designs on these capitals can vary greatly. Sometimes it is only the capitals, rather than the arches, that have any form of detailed design.

- Two columns either side of arch supporting the capitals and the arch itself. These columns each contain two shafts, the inner shaft on each side recessed along part of its width. Unlike the capitals and the arch itself the two columns are not through stones. The columns are cut into the stonework forming the depth of the walling supporting the arch. (This stonework may comprise one or more sections of stonework.) The columns each stand on plinths which themselves stand on a raised base standing on the floor.

- The vertical stonework forming the straight edges of the inner walls facing opposite each other are the jambs.

(b) Internal Tower Arch or Internal Doorway

This is an example of an internal tower arch or internal doorway. It comprises:

- An arch cut out from a large solid section of stonework forming a through stone. There is no design on the stonework.

- Supporting through stones laid flat on each side of the base of the arch and on top of the quoining below. Again there is no design on the stonework.

- Megalithic quoins laid in standard side alternate fashion (see page 35). The lowest quoins stand directly on the floor. There is no decoration on the quoining.

- The vertical stonework (the megalithic quoining) forming the straight edges of the inner walls facing opposite each other are the jambs.

DOORWAYS

Typical characteristics of Anglo-Saxon doorways:

- They were usually tall and narrow. Internal doorways in particular were tall and narrow for their height.

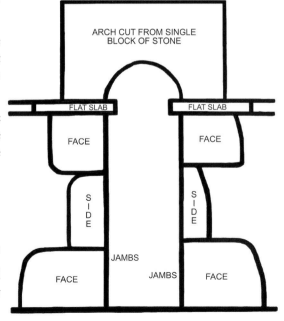

- They were cut straight through the wall, either lined with through stones or built wholly of rubble just like the walls into which they have been cut.

- Most doorways were round headed and some may have had round heads externally and flat heads internally or vice versa.

- Some doorways were covered by flat lintels and some by pairs of stones.

- The arches of the doorways were often supported with through stones that were laid in quoining fashion, as in "Standard Side Alternate Work", or "Face Alternate Work", or "Long and Short Work" (see pages 34 to 36).

- Decoration on external doorways was not common but where it existed it was usually abstract in design.

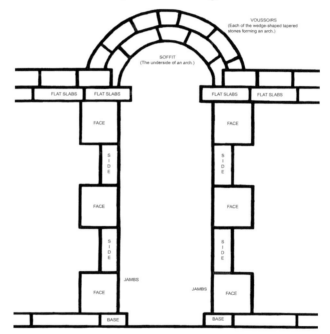

This is an example of an external doorway. It comprises:

- Two sets of individually shaped through stones placed one on top of each other each forming an arch. Neither of these two arches has a central key stone.

- Supporting the stones forming the outer arch on each side of the base of the arch, and on top of the flat through stones below, there are single stones with their faces parallel to the top and bottom of the doorway.

- Through stones laid flat on each side of the base of the arch supporting both sets of stones forming the arches and the additional stones supporting only the outer arch. These stones are laid on top of the quoining below.

- Quoins laid in standard side alternate fashion (see pages 34 – 35). The lowest quoins stand on stones forming an additional base for the floor of the structure.

- The vertical stonework forming the straight edges of the inner walls facing opposite each other are the jambs.

WINDOWS

Typical characteristics of Anglo-Saxon windows:

- They were usually narrow and small.

- Some windows were "single-splayed". This means that the narrowest aperture of the window was at, or close, to the outer (external) face of the wall of the church and the opening widens towards the interior of the church.

- Some windows were "double-splayed". This means that the narrowest aperture of the window was close to the centre of the wall of the church and the opening widens both outward towards the outer (external) face of the wall of the church and inward towards the inner (internal) face of the wall of the church.

- The tops of both single and double headed Anglo-Saxon windows were often cut from a single piece of stone.

- Windows were cut straight through the wall, either lined with through stones or built wholly of rubble just like the walls into which they had been cut.

- The arches of the windows were often supported with through stones that were laid in quoining fashion, as in "Standard Side Alternate Work", or "Face Alternate Work", or "Long and Short Work" (see pages 34 – 36).

- Blocked windows. Many surviving Anglo-Saxon windows and parts of Anglo-Saxon windows have subsequently been blocked in by the later addition of stonework often when more modern, usually larger, windows were inserted into the walls. Often, only part of the Anglo-Saxon window survives, for example, the single stone containing the rounded top, or part of the supporting arch or quoining for one of the sides of the window, or where half of the Anglo-Saxon window survives where the missing half has been replaced by part of the support or arch for a more recently inserted window. Sometimes these blocked windows can be identified both internally and externally in the church and sometimes they can only be identified internally or externally.

Note: Windows may have had wooden shutters wedged into a rebate cut into the external stonework of the window surround. Such shutters would be closed in bad weather. In the belfry stage of a tower the openings (windows) would not have shutters; they would be left open at all times.

The following two illustrations provide two typical examples of Anglo-Saxon windows commonly found where fabric survives from an Anglo-Saxon church. On the left below the window head has been made out of a single, large, oblong block of stone with the top of the round headed window cut out. The window head is supported by stonework laid as in standard side alternate quoining. The window is incorporated into "regular" Anglo-Saxon walling (see above).

On the right below the window head has been made out of a single, large, rounded block of stone with the top of the round headed window cut out. The window head is supported by stonework laid as in standard long and short quoining. The window is incorporated into "irregular" Anglo-Saxon walling (see above).

BELFRY OPENINGS

The purpose of belfry openings was to let out the sound of the church bells. To gain the widest coverage of sound the belfry openings were nearly always situated in the top stage of the church tower. Subsequently, a later, (not Anglo-Saxon) stage may have been added to the top of the tower. Thus the church may appear to have two belfry stages. Typical characteristics of Anglo-Saxon belfry openings:

- They were commonly "double opening" (i.e. with two windows sharing the same interior (central) column) rather than single opening (i.e. with one window).

- Anglo-Saxon belfry openings were not recessed like Norman belfry openings.

- The two windows forming the belfry openings were usually less narrow and tall than standard Anglo-Saxon windows used elsewhere in the church.

- Belfry openings were cut straight through the wall, either lined with through stones or built wholly of rubble just like the walls into which they were cut.

- Belfry openings were not splayed (see above) like some Anglo-Saxon windows.

- The window heads of the two windows in a belfry opening may have been formed out of two separate, solid blocks of stonework with the semi-circular tops of the widows carved out, or they may have been formed from individual wedge-shaped tapered stones (as in voussoirs). Alternatively, the window head may have comprised stones forming a triangular shape.

- The arches of the belfry openings were often supported with through stones that were laid in quoining fashion. Whilst some of the quoining can be as in "Standard Side Alternate Work", or "Face Alternate Work", or "Long and Short Work" (see pages 34 – 36), some may also be more random in design following no particular template.

- The windows in the belfry openings were left open and not glazed

This is example of an Anglo-Saxon belfry opening commonly found in the top stage of the tower of an Anglo-Saxon church. It comprises:

- Individually wedge-shaped tapered through stones (voussoirs) forming two interlocked curved window heads.

- Supporting through stones laid flat in the width of the window to support the ends of the window heads incorporated into the fabric of the wall of the tower. These flat stones themselves are supported by vertically placed through stones of varying width standing one on top of another. These vertically placed through stones stand on top of through stones laid flat in the width of the opening.

- The shared vertical stonework separating the two windows forming the opening has a through stone laid flat to support the stonework interlocking the two window heads together. Beneath this through stone there is rounded baluster. Beneath the baluster is a through stone laid flat.

• The whole bottom of the belfry opening simply uses a course of Anglo-Saxon fabric laid in a "regular" fashion.

CROSSHEADS, CROSS-SHAFTS, CROSS BASES AND GRAVE COVERS OR GRAVE SLABS AND GRAVE MARKERS

Vertically standing crosses, comprising a crosshead supported by an attached cross-shaft (sometimes inserted into a ground or floor standing cross base) were raised for various purposes:

- Denoting the site where a priest would conduct a Christian service before a church was built.
- Memorials to the dead.
- Votive offerings for the living.
- Places of prayer.
- Boundary and grave markers.
- Commemorating significant sites in the life of a saint or to mark the route of their funeral.

Fragments from Anglo-Saxon, Anglo-Danish and Anglo-Norse crosses (including crossheads, cross-shafts and cross bases), grave covers or grave slabs, and grave markers are sometimes incorporated into the later fabric of the church, both internally and externally.

There is no particular part of the church where such fragments are concentrated, and they can be situated anywhere from ground level to nearly the top of the tower, nave, aisle or chancel. Sometimes they can be detected only with the aid of binoculars. Often fragments are found internally sitting loosely or in groups on the floor of the tower, or on the floor of the north or south aisle, or on window ledges, ledges inside the porch, or sitting in niches, or hidden behind curtains screening blocked doorways. Sometimes, much weathered fragments of crosses (including crossheads, cross-shafts and cross bases), grave covers or grave slabs, and grave markers, can be identified standing outside in the churchyard.

Whilst occasionally crossheads can be found almost intact, it is much more common to find that only an arm, or part of an arm, has survived. The cross-shafts have invariably been broken into sections, and occasionally, some of these sections have been reunited. It is unusual when cross-shafts survive intact and even rarer if they survive with their crosshead. Cross bases, grave covers or grave slabs, or grave markers are similarly susceptible to damage. It was common for crosses (including crossheads, cross-shafts and cross bases), grave covers or grave slabs, and grave markers to be decorated with various designs – see the entries in the following pages. How well the decorations on the remaining sections or fragments of stonework have survived, is often dependent on how long the stonework has been exposed to the elements and whether they now are housed inside the church.

The designs used on crossheads, cross-shafts and grave covers can roughly be dated on the following lines:

1.   Late eighth century to early ninth century. These designs are characterised by complex and intricate designs that are symmetrical, well-proportioned and balanced. They often involve flowing lines of interlace, which twist and wrap around each other. Animals and figures are well drawn.

2.   Mid ninth century to early tenth century. These designs tend to use less difficult patterns and animals and figures are less well drawn. A general lowering of quality often ascribed to the disruptive impact of the Vikings.

3.   Late tenth century to early eleventh century. The designs demonstrate something of a renaissance, approaching, but not reaching, the standard of the late eighth century to early ninth century.

4.   Late eleventh century to early twelfth century. The designs show a general degradation, a debasement of designs and of the clarity of animals and figures. The reason is ascribed to the disruptive impact of the Normans.

Designs can involve Christian and mythological subjects sometimes depicting a biblical or mythological story. They include the depiction of Christ Crucified, the Evangelists, Saints, priests and biblical stories. They can also include Odin, Sigurd, Fafnir and Weland forming part of a well known myth. Designs can include runic inscriptions and words. Designs do not represent an accurate, lifelike representation of the individual(s) or animal(s) depicted. However, abstract designs are the most common with some form of interlace pattern forming the core.

Designs on the same section of stonework do not necessarily involve one subject or type of decoration. Individual people can be interposed between abstract designs, groups of people, and words and runes. Just because there is one design on a particular side of a section of stonework it does not follow automatically that the three other sides have the same design.

ILLUSTRATIVE EXAMPLES OF STONEWORK

1. A Complete Crosshead, Cross-shaft and Cross Base

This is a composite example of a complete crosshead, its complete supporting cross-shaft and its complete cross base. Such an example is likely to have been found where a priest would conduct a service before a church was built.

The example shown has a common crosshead at its top. The crosshead comprises four arms in a standard cross shape. On both the front and rear faces of the crosshead there is a central incised circle or a protruding boss. Both faces of the crosshead are decorated with single stranded interlace design.

The cross-shaft supporting the crosshead has four panels, each decorated with a different design. The top panel shows an evangelical figure, probably a saint since there is a stylised halo surrounding his head, and he is also holding a book. Beneath this saint the panel below shows an example of "vine scroll" design. It consists of a trailing vine laden with grapes. In the panel beneath this vine scroll design there is a warrior with a pointed helmet, a spear, a sword, a scramasax (a short single edged sword) at his waist, an axe and a shield (not to scale). Beneath the warrior the panel below shows an example of a "common interlace" design. It consists of threads entangled and woven together to give the appearance of constantly alternating threads.

The reverse face of this example of cross-shaft would have a similar number of panels that may or may not contain different designs. The other two sides of this cross-shaft could also contain panels with a similar number of different designs although it is more likely that these would be decorated with one continuous abstract design.

The cross-shaft of the illustrated example would have fitted into a cross base similar to that shown. The cross base is decorated with scroll design often described as "tree scroll" design. The design resembles a tree with a main stem or trunk supporting branches.

The crosshead, sections of the cross-shaft and the cross base would have been fixed together by mortice and tenon joints cut into the sections of stonework so that they were secure standing one on top of another. The complete cross might stand up to say 8 Yds/7 M high with the crosshead providing a span of 60 Ins/152 Cms.

2. A memorial cross

This is a composite example of a complete crosshead and its complete supporting cross-shaft standing on a plain stepped plinth. Such an example would most likely have been a memorial to some locally important person or a boundary or commemorative marker.

The example shown has a wheel head crosshead at its top. A wheel head crosshead comprises four arms in a standard cross shape connected with each other near their circumference by sections of stonework forming a wheel shape. On both the front and rear faces of the crosshead there is a central incised circle or a protruding boss. Both faces of the crosshead are decorated with single stranded interlace design.

The cross-shaft supporting the crosshead has one panel on each of its four sides all decorated with ring chain design.

The edges of this illustrative example have rope work moulding design down each vertical edge.

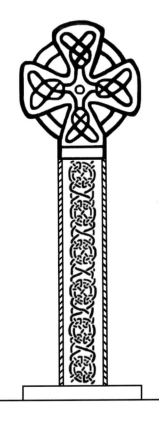

The cross-shaft of the illustrated example would have fitted into the stepped plinth shown. The stepped plinth has no decoration on any of its sides.

The crosshead, sections of the cross-shaft and the stepped plinth would have been fixed together by mortice and tenon joints cut into the sections of stonework so that they were secure standing one on top of another. The complete cross might stand up to say 60 Ins/152 Cms high with the crosshead providing a span of 15 Ins/38 Cms.

CROSSHEADS

Crossheads can vary in shape and size; they do not follow standard dimensions and can also vary greatly in height and width. The decoration on the two faces is usually consistent, but not always, and where there is decoration on the ends of the arms this is also usually consistent on each of the ends of the arms.

The arms of such a crosshead can vary in shape from being square-edged, 90 degree arms, to curved edges where the sides of the arms virtually touch each other. Where this happens, the appearance is given of four fully opened fans giving the impression of a circular crosshead with closed small circular openings in between the arms. The ends of the arms of the crosshead can also vary in shape from square-edged with 90-degree angles to round like the sides of an opened fan.

The design of the decoration of the crosshead can vary greatly dependent on the wishes of the patron and the skills of the craftsman: interlace design is the most common. On occasions the front and the rear faces of the crosshead may be decorated with representations of Christ Crucified, or human or animal figures. Very rarely the faces may be incised with writing or runic inscriptions.

1. Standard

This is a typical example of a standard crosshead with a common design and decoration. The example comprises four arms in a standard cross shape. On both the front and rear faces of the crosshead there is a central incised circle or a protruding boss. Both faces of the crosshead are decorated with single stranded interlace design.

2. Wheel head

This is a typical example of a wheel head crosshead with a common design and decoration. The example comprises a standard cross shape whose four arms are linked to each other near their circumference by a curved section of stonework to give the overall appearance of a wheel – the arms forming the spokes of the wheel. On both the front and rear faces of the crosshead there is a central incised circle or a protruding boss. Both faces of the crosshead are decorated with single stranded interlace design.

The stonework forming parts of the wheel linking the arms of the crosshead can vary in diameter (height). Sometimes the distance between the top edges of the stonework forming the wheel and the top edges of the arms of the crosshead, and the bottom edges of the wheels and the centre of the crosshead, are so small that they give the appearance of a virtually solid circular crosshead.

The "eyes" in the four quartered angles of the arms of the crosshead can also vary in shape forming a complete circle rather than just a section from a circle within the stonework forming the wheel.

3. Ring head

This is a typical example of a ring head crosshead with a common design and decoration. The example comprises four arms in a standard cross shape where each of the angles between the arms is linked by an additional curved "ring" of stonework. On both the front and rear faces of the crosshead there is a central incised circle or a protruding boss. Both faces of the crosshead are decorated with single stranded interlace design.

The circular shape of the additional protruding stonework minimally affects the design of the decoration of the faces of the crosshead and, at its maximum, affects the shape of the crosshead so that the arms are sinuous in outline. The protruding stonework forming the rings linking the arms of the crosshead can vary in diameter (height) from being just about identifiable to forming a complete additional circle of stonework in the angle between the arms of the crosshead. The impact on design of these rings can be markedly reduced where the arms of the crosshead are fan shaped.

4. Hammer head

This is a typical example of a "hammer head" crosshead with a common design and decoration. The example comprises four arms in a standard cross shape attached to which there are two additional horizontal arms. These two additional horizontal arms are integrated into the top vertical arm of the crosshead. This gives the overall appearance of what is described as a hammer head. On both the front and rear faces of the crosshead there is an incised circle or a protruding boss in the centre of the two top horizontal arms and the centre of the lower four arms of the crosshead. Both faces of the crosshead are decorated with single stranded interlace design.

The top two horizontal arms of the crosshead can differ in height and width from the other arms, they can have similar, or much larger or much smaller, dimensions to the other arms, with variations in between. The overall appearance can be that the crosshead is top heavy. Very rarely, the arms may be connected by additional stonework forming wheels and similar to a wheel head cross – see 2 above.

These hammer head crossheads are of later, generally 11C date, displaying poorer quality workmanship and design.

CROSS-SHAFTS

Cross-shafts can vary in shape from having the two wider faces and the two narrower sides parallel from top to bottom to tapering from a wider bottom, to a narrower top. Cross-shafts can also be circular with a regular circumference from top to bottom as well as tapering from a wider bottom to a narrower top. They do not follow standard dimensions and can vary greatly in height and width. Similarly, decoration on the cross-shaft can vary from being consistent to different on each of the four sides, or different around the circumference. Sometimes on the cross-shaft, panels separate the designs on the same side or on the circumference. These panels can depict a different design or scene, and they are often used to depict a biblical or mythological story.

1. Interlace Design

This is a typical example of a section of stonework from a cross-shaft decorated with a variation of the most common form of interlace design often described simply as "interlace" design. It consists of threads intricately entangled and woven together to give the appearance of constantly alternating threads. Although this example has regular sized and spaced threads of interlace many examples are more erratic in design with the interlace varying in terms of number of threads, some times referred to as "strands" and the thickness and degrees of intertwining. The edges of this illustrative example are a pair of parallel lines down each vertical edge.

2. Knotwork or Plait Work Design

This is a typical example of a section of stonework from a cross-shaft decorated with a variation of the interlace design often described as "knot work" or "plait work" design. It consists of thick cords intertwined and knotted together. The cords in plait work design tend to be more straight and angular than knot work design. Although this example has regular spaced circular concentrations of knot work or plait work, many examples are more erratic in design with cords of varying thickness and degrees of intertwining. The edges of this illustrative example are a pair of parallel lines down each vertical edge.

3. Ring Work or Ring Chain Design

This is a typical example of a section of stonework from a cross-shaft decorated with a variation of the interlace design often described as "ring work" or "ring chain" design. It consists of intertwined concentric circles connected by thin intertwined cords or strands. Although this example has regular spaced circular concentric circles, many examples are more erratic in design with single circles of varying shape connected by varying degrees of intertwining cords or strands. The edges of this illustrative example show rope work moulding down each vertical edge.

4. Scroll or Plant Scroll or Vine Scroll or Tree Scroll Design

This is a typical example of a section of stonework from a cross-shaft decorated with a variation of the scroll design often described as "plant scroll", "vine scroll" or "tree scroll" design. It consists of a climbing or trailing vine laden with grapes (sometimes without grapes). Although this example has regular spaced circular concentrations of vine scroll many examples are more erratic in design with vines less regular and ornate in shape. The edges of this illustrative example have rope work moulding design down vertical edges.

Scroll design in its most basic form resembles a roll of paper or a convoluted or spiral ornament. Scroll design can comprise a plant with a branch or stem supporting leaves. Sometimes plant, vine or tree scroll design can contain stylised animals, birds and human figures.

5. Key Pattern or Stepped Work Design

This is a typical example of a section of stonework from a cross-shaft decorated with a design that is described as "key pattern" design and is sometimes referred to as "stepped work design". It consists of a series of shapes that can be envisaged as depicting the shape of keys placed together in a regular pattern; arguably more recognisable as a series of steps - as though the steps of a plinth. Although this example has regular spaced keys or steps, many examples are more erratic in design with a fewer number of keys or steps less regular in shape and size. The edges of this illustrative example have a simple diagonal line design down vertical edges.

6. Depiction of a Saint

This is a typical example of a section of stonework from a cross-shaft decorated with a panel containing the depiction of a saint. The figure is stylised and not a lifelike representation. The critical feature determining whether the figure is a saint is the addition of a halo surrounding the head. The halo can vary in size and shape, and as in the figure shown, the halo can given the appearance of a hood or cape. Saints are often shown holding books as in this example.

In addition to the depiction of Christ, with a halo, other religious figures depicted might include the "Four Evangelists" - Matthew represented by a winged man, Mark by a winged lion, Luke by a winged ox and John by an eagle. Ordinary priests may also be depicted. The edges of this illustrative example are a pair of parallel lines down vertical edges.

7. Depiction of a Warrior

This is a typical example of a section of stonework from a cross-shaft decorated with a panel containing the depiction of a warrior. The figure is stylised and not a life like representation.

The warrior depicted in this example wears a pointed helmet, has a spear by his right hand side, has a scramasax (a short single edged sword) about his waist, has an axe by his left leg, has a sword (not to scale) by the left side of his head and left arm, and he has a shield (not to scale) by the top of the left side of his head. The edges of this illustrative example are a pair of parallel lines down vertical edges.

8. Jellinge Design

This is a typical example of a section of stonework from a cross-shaft decorated with a panel containing what is known as "Jellinge" design. The design is typically distinguished by long and reptilian S-shaped animals drawn with double outline with curling twists in their bodies from their tails to their tongues. The animals are restrained with a number of straps. The edges of this illustrative example are a pair of parallel lines down vertical edges.

The design was in use between the end of the 9C to about the year 1000. The design is named after the animal that decorates a small silver cup found at the royal burial ground in Jellinge in Jutland in Denmark.

9. Ringerike Design

This is a typical example of a section of stonework from a cross-shaft decorated with panels containing what is known as "Ringerike" design. The design is typically distinguished by elongated plant-like tendrils often sprouting from the core of the decoration whether abstract or animal. The edges of this illustrative example are a pair of parallel lines down vertical edges.

The design was in use in the 11C. The design is named after a group of ornamental slabs found in the Ringerike district in Norway.

10. *Borre Design*

This is a typical example of a section of stonework from a cross-shaft decorated with a panel containing what is known as "Borre" design. The design is typically distinguished by a ring chain pattern, as shown here, or a backward looking animal, or animal(s) gripping the nearest object(s). The edges of this illustrative example are a single line down the vertical edges.

The design was in use between the mid 9C to the end of the 10C. The design is named after the design on artefacts found in a rich ship burial found in Borre in Norway.

CROSS BASES

A Cross Base

This is a typical example of a cross base, square in design and decorated with a scroll design often described as "tree scroll" design. It consists of a tree with a main stem or trunk supporting branches. The edges of this illustrated example are undecorated and the base stands squarely on the ground.

The cross base is specifically designed to support a cross-shaft with its crosshead in a vertical position. The cross base can vary in shape from being square to trapezium. It can also be low and flat and contain sockets for two cross-shafts and their crossheads.

Some cross bases may have been undecorated but certainly many now appear so because of the effects of weathering.

The base of cross bases may stand directly onto the ground but they may themselves be supported by plinths, some of which may be stepped.

GRAVE COVERS OR GRAVE SLABS OR GRAVE MARKERS

Grave covers or grave slabs or grave markers can vary in size, shape and decoration. They can range from a simple stone marker with a cross to a large shaped stone, decorated with an inscription which may be in letters (Latin or Old English) or runes and decorated with a variety of designs. They may cover the entire surface of a grave or simply mark the site of a grave. Grave covers or grave slabs are usually decorated on the top, although occasionally they are also decorated around the supporting sides.

1. Ryedale Dragon Design

This is a typical example of a grave cover or grave slab. This particular example is decorated with the "Ryedale Dragon" design. It consists of a

single bound beast or dragon shown in S-shape with its jaws open. The whole design fills one face of the grave cover and the edges have two parallel lines following the curve of their shape. (The design is similar to the Jellinge design – see above). The design features on a number of examples of cross-shafts and grave covers in the Ryedale area of North Yorkshire – hence the name.

2. "Hogback Grave Cover or Hogback Tombstone"

This is a grave cover, an example of what is often described as a "hogback tombstone". A hogback grave cover has a recumbent often muzzled beast

at each end with its snout gnawing at the end of a long decorated ridge running the length of the top surface with its upper paw clasping the section of stonework. It is decorated with a curved, tegulated roof and between the two lower paws of the beasts the stonework is decorated with single stranded interlace design enclosed within a triangular pattern.

This hogback grave cover would have stood vertically rather than laid flat across a grave. It would be three dimensional. With the beasts forming the shape of both faces and the two ends of the grave cover, both faces would have been decorated with similar designs. If the two ends (the backs of the beasts) had been decorated they would probably have been decorated with some form of interlace design.

3. Grave Marker – Simple Design

This is an example of a grave marker with a simple design. It may have originally stood vertically or it may have lain horizontally to mark a grave. Just the front or top facing face is decorated. The cross decoration is centrally placed and the arms of the cross extend across the entire face of the grave marker.

Grave markers are physically much smaller than grave covers or grave slabs. Grave markers can vary in size, shape and decoration. The shape of the grave marker may be round or square. The border surrounding the cross design is optional. The design of the cross may extend over the entire face of the grave marker or it may just be simple and small.

Dependent on the size of the grave marker the arms of the cross depicted can be longer vertically than horizontally: the arms of the cross can also be of equal length. The arms of the cross can also vary in size and shape. The designs on the grave marker can include animal and abstract designs between the arms of the cross.

Occasionally the design also includes lettering within the lines of the cross, sometimes between and around the ends of the arms, and sometimes beneath the cross. Lettering identifying who is commemorated is usually positioned around the cross in a horizontal fashion but it may also be positioned vertically.

4. Grave Marker – Intricate Design

This is an example of a grave marker with an intricate design. Originally it may have stood vertically or it may have lain horizontally to mark a grave. Just the front or top face is decorated. The cross decoration is centrally placed with a central boss and with the arms decorated with a single stranded interlace design. The whole cross is surrounded with an interlace design contrasting with that used inside the central cross design.

LOCATION & IDENTIFICATION OF MATERIAL IN CHURCHES

Anglo-Saxon, Anglo-Danish and Anglo-Norse material can usually most easily be identified in situ in:

- The lower stages of the tower (both internally and externally).

- The four corners of the nave (both internally and externally).

- In the area between and above the "new" arches in the nave walls opening into the north and south aisles (internally).

- On either side of the chancel arch (internally).

- Plain, circular or "tub" shaped, font bowls. Most are displayed inside the church, and some may not be the font currently used. Other fonts can be found outside the church abandoned in the churchyard often in the vicinity of the south porch.

Sun dials were also a feature of Anglo-Saxon, Anglo-Danish and Anglo-Norse churches. They are sometimes located externally over the apex of the more recently added south porch, or about the same height inserted somewhere along the external south wall of the nave. Sometimes sun dials are removed from their original position and incorporated into new building, such as the south face of the south porch. Sun dials can also be found internally, on the old outer face of the south wall of the nave, subsequently enclosed by a later south aisle. Sun dials are usually found near to the south door of the church, the lay folk's door, where church ceremonies were conducted utilising the instructive information contained on or by (where there was an accompanying inscription) the sun dial. They are sometimes located on the west side of the church.

Occasionally, the outline plan of an Anglo-Saxon or Anglo-Danish or Anglo-Norse church is indicated by either stone or brickwork where the present structure of the church overlays, or is adjacent to, or near to the site. An outline plan of an Anglo-Saxon or Anglo-Danish or Anglo-Norse church, also sometimes occurs when church has been demolished and has not been replaced.

ILLUSTRATED EXAMPLES (NONE OF THESE ARE BASED ON SURVIVING CHURCHES.)

The examples shown below are intended to show where Anglo-Saxon or Anglo-Danish or Anglo-Norse material may survive in the external fabric of the present structure of the church.

Whilst sections from crossheads, or complete crossheads, are by their very shape relatively easy to locate and identify with confidence, the same cannot be said of sections of stonework from cross-shafts. Sections of stonework from cross-shafts in particular may have a design, which due to weathering, appears as an indistinct mass. Sometimes the design may be so indistinct as to lead to doubt whether the precise location of the section of cross-shaft has been correctly identified. (It is often the design on a section of stonework that can help confirm that it is from a cross-shaft.)

Key to the lettered numbering used in the three illustrated examples

The prefix "C", "N", "T" or "CH" to the numbers indicates whether the item is related to the Chancel, Nave, Tower or Churchyard. The key to the items identified is:

CHANCEL

C1   Quoins: Standard Long and Short Work.

C2   Walling: An example of regular walling. Anglo-Saxon, Anglo-Danish and Anglo-Norse walling often survives in patches; it has not been affected by later extensions, restorations etc.

C3   Window: Window head has been made out of a single block of stone supported by stonework laid as in standard side alternate quoining.

C4   Doorway: The arch is formed of individually shaped through stones, with no central key stone, and is supported by quoins laid in standard side alternate fashion. The doorway is now blocked.

C5   Complete and Parts of Crossheads: These include crossheads and wheel head crossheads all with common designs and decorations. Some examples have typically their lower vertical arms removed with their two horizontal arms squared off at the bottom to fit in a course of stonework. Some examples comprise only a single arm.

C6   Section from a Cross-shaft: Decorated with a common interlace design.

NAVE INCLUDING SOUTH PORCH

N1   Quoins: Standard Side Alternate Work.

N2   Walling: An example of regular walling. Anglo-Saxon, Anglo-Danish and Anglo-Norse walling often survives in patches; it has not been affected by later extensions, restorations etc.

N3   Windows: Window head has been made out of a single block of stone supported by stonework laid as in standard side alternate quoining.

N4   Parts of Windows: One window head has been retained when the south porch was built. (The rest of the window has been removed.) Another part of a window comprising, the east end of the window head, and the east supporting quoining, has survived when a new, larger tracery window was inserted into the walling around 1300. (The western part of the window has been removed.)

N5   Doorway: The arch is formed of individually shaped through stones, with no central key stone, and is supported by quoins laid in standard side alternate fashion. The doorway is now blocked.

N6   Complete and Parts of Crossheads: These include crossheads and wheel head crossheads all with common designs and decorations. Some examples have typically their lower vertical arms removed with their two horizontal arms squared off at the bottom to fit in a course of stonework. Some examples comprise only a single arm.

N7   Sections of stonework from Cross-shafts. As a useful piece of solid stonework, sections of stonework from cross-shafts were often re-used to help in a later restoration of the church fabric. Decoration on such re-used sections of stonework from cross-shafts is often indistinct. Usually, the decoration is some form of common interlace design or a knot work design.

N8   Sun Dial. The stone slab containing this particular example has been removed from its original position and incorporated into the fabric of the south wall of the south porch.

TOWER

T1   Quoins: Standard Long and Short Work (Examples 1 and 2); Standard Side Alternate Work (Example 3).

T2   Walling: An example of irregular walling. Anglo-Saxon, Anglo-Danish and Anglo-Norse walling often survives in patches; it has not been affected by later extensions, restorations etc.

T3   String Courses: These separate the first and second stages of the tower.

T4   Belfry Opening with a central baluster separating the two openings.

T5   Window: Window head has been made out of a single block of stone supported by stonework laid as in standard side alternate quoining.

T6   Re-used Window head. In Example 2, the single block of stone forming a window head has been placed on one of its ends to stand vertically, and then re-used to form a quoin. In Example 3, the single block of stone forming a window head has been inverted and used to patch up the walling.

T7   Doorway: The arch is formed of individually shaped through stones, with no central key stone, and is supported by quoins laid in standard side alternate fashion. The doorway is now blocked.

T8   Complete and Parts of Crossheads: These include crossheads and wheel head crossheads all with common designs and decorations. Some examples have typically their lower vertical arms removed with their two horizontal arms squared off at the bottom to fit in a course of stonework. Some examples comprise only a single arm.

T9   Sections of stonework from Cross-shafts. As a useful piece of solid stonework, sections of stonework from cross-shafts were often re-used to help in a later restoration of the church fabric. Decoration on such re-used sections of stonework from cross-shafts is often indistinct. Usually, the decoration is some form of common interlace design or a common knot work design.

CHURCHYARD

CH1 Part of a section of stonework from a cross-shaft standing on a stepped plinth. Part of a crosshead has been placed upon this section of stonework from a cross-shaft. Often, as in this example, there is no original connection between the section of stonework from the cross-shaft, and the part of the crosshead. The two have simply been placed together for aesthetic reasons.

CH2 Part of a section of stonework from a cross-shaft standing directly on the ground. It is doubtful it is in its original position. It was probably placed in its current position after its discovery, perhaps, during a 19C church restoration. (Much Anglo-Saxon or Anglo-Danish or Anglo-Norse material was rediscovered during the extensive church restorations undertaken in the 19C.)

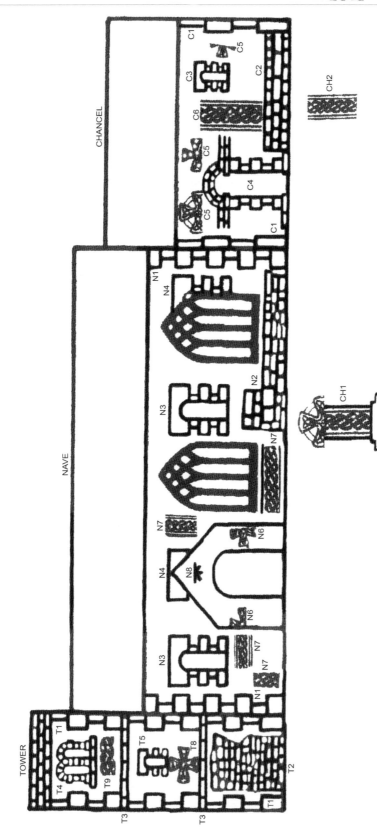

Example 1. The south face of the tower, nave (including south porch) and/or the later attached south aisle, and the chancel

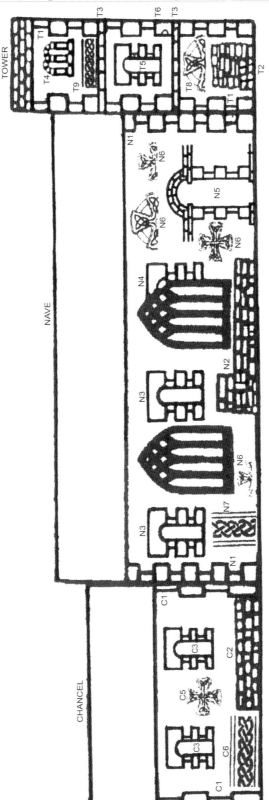

Example 2. The north face of the tower, nave and/or the later attached north aisle, and the chancel

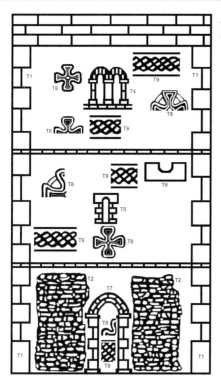

Example 3. The west face of the tower

SUGGESTED FURTHER READING

Anglo-Saxon England by Sir Frank Stenton. Published by Oxford University Press. First published in 1943

The Anglo-Saxons edited by James Campbell. Published by Phaidon Press Limited. First published in 1982

A guide to Dark Age Remains in Britain by Lloyd and Jennifer Laing. Published by Constable and Company Limited. First published in 1979

Anglo-Saxon Architecture by H M Taylor and Joan Taylor. (Three Volumes.) Published by Cambridge University Press. First Published in 1965

Northumbrian Crosses of the Pre-Norman Age by W G Collingwood. First Published in 1927, reprinted in 1989 by Llanerch Enterprises

The Corpus of Anglo-Saxon Stone Sculpture – Grammar of Anglo-Saxon Ornament: A General Introduction to the Corpus of Anglo-Saxon Stone Sculpture by Rosemary Cramp. Published by Oxford University Press. First Published in 1991

Corpus of Anglo-Saxon Sculpture, Volume III: York and Eastern Yorkshire by James Lang. Published by Oxford University Press. First Published in 1991

Corpus of Anglo-Saxon Stone Sculpture, Volume VI: Northern Yorkshire by James Lang. Published by Oxford University Press. First Published in 2002

Part 2

East Yorkshire

In East Yorkshire 34 sites of Anglo-Saxon & Viking interest have been identified and entered in the text.

15 sites have been entered and rated with one star ☆

This signifies that material may be difficult to find or identify with confidence. These entries are:

Bridlington – Priory
Boynton – St Andrew's Church
Easington – All Saints Church
Flamborough – Dane's Dyke
Goodmanham – All Hallows Church
Harpham – St John of Beverley Church
Harpham – St John's Well
Holme-On-Spalding Moor – All Saints Church
Howden – Minster
Leconfield – St Catherine's Church
Lisset – St James Church
Pocklington – All Saints Church
Shiptonthorpe – All Saints Church
Stamford Bridge – Site of Old Bridge
Stamford Bridge – Battleflats

11 sites have been entered and rated with two stars ☆☆

This signifies that material can be found and identified but it is not particularly well looked after or a "good example". These entries are:

Beverley – 3 Sanctuary Crosses – Hessle, Killingwoldgraves and
    Walkington
Great Driffield – All Saints Church
Kirby Underdale – All Saints Church
Leven – Holy Trinity Church
Little Driffield – St Mary's Church
Londesbrough – All Saints Church
Lowthorpe – St Martin's Church

North Frodingham – St Elgin's Church
Stamford Bridge – Monument

4 Sites Have Been Entered And Rated With Three Stars ☆☆☆

This signifies that material can easily be found and identified. These entries are:

Barmston – All Saints Church
Catwick – St Michael's Church
Sewerby – Sewerby Hall, Museum of East Yorkshire
Sutton-Upon-Derwent – St Michael's Church

3 sites have been entered and rated with four stars ☆☆☆☆

This signifies that material can easily be found and identified, and provides good examples. These entries are:

Aldbrough – St Bartholomew's Church
Beverley – Minster
Hull – Hull and East Riding Museum

1 site has been entered and rated with five stars ☆☆☆☆☆

This signifies that material can easily be found and identified, providing an excellent example and is full of interest. This entry is:

Nunburnholme – St James Church

ALDBROUGH
St Bartholomew's Church

TA 244387   Rating: ☆☆☆☆   Access is possible.

In the north-eastern part of Aldbrough, the church is located on the north side of "Church Street" (there is a street sign). Note: Church Street is a continuation of "North Street" (there are street signs).

The present structure dates mainly from 1353-77 and the restoration in 1870.

Internally, there is an A-S sundial located separating two arches in the middle of the walling comprising the south wall of the nave, 132 Ins/335 Cms up from the floor. The sundial has been incorporated into stonework picked out and protruding from the rest of the whitewashed south wall and is viewed from the south aisle. The sundial is circular and is 16 Ins/40 Cms in diameter. It is divided into eight equal segments with the hole in the middle for the missing gnomon clearly identifiable. Around the circumference there are written in Old English words that have been translated as "Ulf had this church built for himself and for Gunwara's soul".

ALDBROUGH: St Bartholomew's Church. Anglo-Saxon sun dial with inscription in Old English.

Internally, there is a section of stonework in a triangular shape reminiscent of the top of a pointed A-S window head or part of the moulding above a doorway. It is located 2 Ins/5 Cms beneath the sundial and has also been incorporated into the same picked out stonework in the south wall of the nave. This section of stonework measures 12 Ins/30 Cms H by 10 Ins/25 Cms W.

Internally, two small narrow windows that may have A-S window heads have been exposed following the removal of the surrounding whitewash. These can be identified incorporated into the south wall of the "Melsa chapel" (the east end of the north aisle) forming the north wall of the chancel. These are located:

1.   12 Ins/30 Cms above and 12 Ins/30 Cms to the west of the centre of the arch above the tomb of a female incorporated into the

south wall of the chapel and the north wall of the chancel. In total the stonework comprising the window, including the widow head, measures 20 Ins/50 Cms H by 14 Ins/35 Cms W. The window head measures 12 Ins/30 Cms H by 14 Ins/35 Cms W. The exposed stone vertical supports are not A-S. The window head is incised with circle designs.

2.   60 Ins/152 Cms west of the east wall of the chapel and 79 Ins/200 Cms up from the floor. In total the stonework comprising the window, including the widow head, measures 45 Ins/114 Cms H by 24 Ins/60 Cms W. The window head measures 13 Ins/33 Cms H by 24 Ins/60 Cms W. The exposed stone vertical supports are not A-S. The window head is incised with circle designs.

Externally, an A-S window head can be identified incorporated into the fabric of the south wall of the chancel, abutting the centre of the top of the stonework framing of the only window in the south wall of the chancel. It consists of a curved (top) section of a window aperture set in a larger single section of stonework. The section of stonework measures 15½ Ins/39 Cms H by 22 Ins/55 Cms W. It is decorated with Ringerike design including two animals with necks adjacent but their heads facing the opposite way, their bodies and tails all surrounded by vegetation. The semi circle in the centre of the bottom edge of this section of stonework, confirms that it was the solid window head from an A-S window.

BARMSTON
All Saints Church
TA 156588   Rating: ☆☆☆

200 Yds/182 M east of the A165, the entrance to the drive leading up to the church is located on the south side of "Sands Lane" (there is a street sign). The church is easily identified from the road. Proceed up the drive to reach the churchyard entrance after about 70 Yds/64 M. (18 Yds/16 M along this drive there is a large, wooden, freestanding church notice board.)

The present church on the site dates from the 12C.

Internally there is a section of stonework from an A-D hogback grave cover. It is located sitting on the floor in the south west corner of the south porch, between 2 Ins/5 Cms and 3½ Ins/8 Cms east of the west wall. The section of stonework measures 18 Ins/45 Cms H, by 12 Ins/30 Cms W, by 24 Ins/60 Cms L. It is clearly decorated with the distinctive face of a bear like animal and knot work design on the roof. There is no other decoration that can now be identified due to weathering and damage. It dates from the early 11C. The hogback grave cover was brought to Barmston by William Dade who was rector in the 18C.

BARMSTON: All Saints Church. An Anglo-Danish hogback grave cover. It is decorated on the "roof" with knot work design and at one end it has the distinctive face of a bear-like animal.

BEVERLEY
(1) Minster
TA 037393   Rating: ✮✮✮✮

The distinctive Minster is situated in the southern part of Beverley. The south side of the Minster is adjacent to the north side of the B1230.

At the junction of the roads "Minster Moorgate", "Highgate" and "Minster Yard North" (there are street signs), the entrance to the Minster is situated adjacent to the south side of Minster Yard North. Entry to the Minister is gained through the north entrance.

St John of Beverley (640-721) founded the original church on this site. In 934, on hearing of St John's sanctity, King Athelstan (924-939) came to Beverley and took with him the Banner of St John. He left a dagger on the high altar as surety to a pledge that if victorious in his forthcoming campaign against the Scots, he would return the banner and endow the church. King Athelstan won his battles against King Constantine of Scotland and to mark his success, the town of "St Johnstone" is said to have been so-named in honour of St John.

BEVERLEY: Beverley Minster. The Frith Stool – Bishop's Throne – Sanctuary Chair. Photograph reproduced with the permission of the Vicar and Church Wardens of Beverley Minster.

King Athelstan again took the Banner of St John with him when he achieved his victory over the Norse and all the Celts at the Battle of Brunanburgh in 937. In 938, in honour of the earlier pledge he made, King Athelstan re-founded the church as a college for secular canons and granted the right of sanctuary. In 1726 when St John's relics were rediscovered a small, corroded dagger was also found (possibly Athelstan's surety to his pledge in 934).

The present structure is the fourth church on this site. It dates mainly from three significant building stages, circa 1220, circa 1320 and circa 1420.

Internally, there is a late 7C A-S frid (frith) stool (a stone chair). It is situated in the chancel 7 Ins/17 Cms north of the steps in front of and by the sides of the high altar and between 3½ Ins/8 Cms and 9 Ins/22Cms to the west of (in front of) the reredos. The frid stool measures 33 ¼ Ins/84 Cms H, between 34¼ Ins/86 Cms to 32½ Ins/82 Cms W, by 22 Ins/55 Cms D. The seat part of the frid stool has a 14½ Ins/36 Cms radius D and a 23¼

Ins/59 Cms diameter W. There is some damage on the frid stool and there is no decoration on any of the sides. However, there is an inscription on the back of the seat which reads: "HAEC SEDES LAPIDEA FREEDSTOLL DICITVR I.E. PACIS CATHEDRA AD QVAM REVS FVGIENDO PERVENIENS OMINODAM HABET SECVRITATEN" translated: "The chair of peace was a full refuge and safety from the immediate infliction of punishment for any crime whatsoever." It is impossible to identify this writing given the present location of the frid stool. The frid stool is the Episcopal throne of a bishop. The fact that there is such a throne in Beverley confirms that the church was governed by a bishop and suggests a suffragen (supporting) cathedral. It is thought that Beverley, along with Ripon and Whitby, were suffragen cathedrals of York. Originally used as the Episcopal seat of St John it became a sanctuary chair when the right of sanctuary was granted in 938.

Internally, there is a diamond-shaped tomb slab denoting the resting place of St John of Beverley. It is situated surrounded by a low wooden frame in the centre of the floor near the east end of the nave and less than 10 Yds/9 M west of the crossing. The tomb slab is incised with the words: "Here lies the body of Saint John of Beverley; Founder of this church; Bishop of Hexham, A.D. 687-705; Bishop of York, A.D. 705-718. He was born at Harpham, and died at Beverley, A.D. 721." (Note: the punctuation is now mostly missing.)

BEVERLEY
(2) Sanctuary Crosses

The Minster provided the right of sanctuary to fugitives under the law. Six successive boundaries were marked by stone crosses within a radius of about 3 miles of the Minster (a "leuga" from the church). Penalties for apprehending a fugitive within this radius increased the closer one came to the high altar and frid stool in the Minster. The right of sanctuary was granted by King Athelstan in 938 and was abolished in 1624.

Three of the outer boundaries survive each about 2 miles from the Minster. The "crosses" are more accurately weathered sections of stonework from different cross-shafts. There are no identifying notices either attached to the crosses themselves or nearby.

"Hesssle" Cross
TA 025363   Rating: ✫✫

The cross is situated standing in the grass verge 55 Ins/139 Cms from the east side of the A164. It is enclosed by a wooden fence standing 38½ Ins/97 Cms H. The enclosure is diagonally opposite (to the north-east) a large roadside directional sign denoting "Beverley A164" and "York

A1079, Driffield (A164)". It is 530 Yds/301 M south of the junction of the A164 and the A1079.

The cross stands on a plinth measuring between 14 Ins/35 Cms and 19 Ins/48 Cms H, by 41 Ins/104 Cms W, by 41 Ins/104 Cms D. The section of stonework from a cross-shaft measures 27 Ins/68 Cms H, by 16 Ins/40 Cms W, by 14 Ins/35 Cms D. The initial appearance of the cross-shaft is round but on inspection it has angled corners. There is no decoration on any of the sides.

"Killingwoldgraves" Cross
TA 006397   Rating: ☆☆☆

The largest of the surviving crosses, the Killingwoldgraves cross is situated in a field adjacent to the south side of the A1035, 280 Yds/254 M east of the junction of the A1035 and the A1079. The cross is 22 Yds/20 M south of the south side of the A1035 and is enclosed by a wooden fence standing between 41 Ins/104 Cms and 61½ Ins/156 Cms H.

The cross stands on a plinth measuring between 13½ Ins/34 Cms and 17 Ins/43 Cms H, by 35½ Ins/104 Cms square. The section of stonework from a cross-shaft measures 60¼ Ins/153 Cms H, tapering 14½ Ins/36 Cms to 13 Ins/33 Cms W, tapering 13¾ Ins/34 Cms to 11½ Ins/29 Cms D. For most of the entire height of each side of the section of stonework there are two vertical grooves running between 6 Ins/15 Cms and 7½ Ins/19 Cms apart. There is no other decoration on any of the sides.

BEVERLEY: Killingwoldgraves. Sanctuary Cross. A section of stonework from a cross-shaft standing on a plinth.

"Walkington" Cross
TA 004374   Rating: ☆☆☆

The cross is situated adjacent to the south side of the pavement on the south side of the B1230, "East End" (there are street signs). It is surrounded by a three sided 37¾ Ins/95 Cms H wrought iron fence. It is 61 Yds/55 M west of the nearby crossroads where there are signs including "Walkington, North Cave B1230" and "Hessle A164".

The cross stands on a plinth that measures 6½ Ins/16 Cms H, by 25 Ins/63 Cms W, by 27 Ins/68 Cms D. The section of stonework from a cross-shaft measures between 18½ Ins/46 Cms and 21½ Ins/54 Cms H, by 10 Ins/25 Cms W, by 13 Ins/33 Cms D. The initial appearance of the cross-shaft is round but on inspection it has angled corners. There is no decoration on any of the sides.

BOYNTON

St Andrew's Church

TA 136679   Rating: ☆

The church is easily identified at the southern end of Boynton 260 Yds/237 M south of the B1253. It is on the east side of the road running through the village (there are no street signs).

Probably on the site of an A-S church, the present structure dates from the rebuilding of 1767-76 apart from the tower which dates from the early 15C.

Externally, there is a section of stonework that depicts a "Celtic" cross. It has been incorporated into the south west face of the south west facing buttress for the tower. It is easily located 40 Ins/101 Cms up from the ground. The design comprises a crosshead and cross-shaft and measures in total 13½ Ins/34 Cms H by 6½ Ins/16 Cms (crosshead) and 3½ Ins/8 Cms (cross-shaft) W. The crosshead has a diamond shaped cross in the centre surrounded by two concentric circles. There is no other decoration on either the crosshead or the cross-shaft due to weathering. It is difficult to date but it probably dates from the early 12C despite its earlier style.

Externally, there is a scratch dial incised on the south face of the quoining in the south west corner of the nave. The quoining on which the scratch dial has been incised is 43½ Ins/110 Cms up from the ground. The scratch dial is clearly defined with a circle with a diameter of 7½ Ins/19 Cms. Within the circle there are radiating lines dividing it into 24 segments. The distinctive hole in the centre of the circle for the missing gnomon is easily identifiable. There is no writing or design on the scratch dial. It too is difficult to date but it probably dates from the early 12C.

BRIDLINGTON

Priory

TA 176679   Rating: ☆

The Priory is located in the northern part of Bridlington in the "Old Town". Both the Priory and the "Bayle" Museum are signposted in the town. (The Bayle Museum is located in the Priory Gatehouse. It does not contain any items of A-S or A-D interest.)

The large Priory Church is easy to identify on the south side of "Sewerby Road" (there are street signs). The western entrance to the Priory is on the east side of a green on the east side of "Kirkgate" (there is a street sign) that leads into Sewerby Road.

The Augustinian Priory founded circa 1113 replaced an A-S church that was situated near the north-west tower of the present church. Construction of the present building began around 1150 following the desecration and fortification of the priory by the Earl of York and his troops in 1143/44. Much of the present structure dates from the early 13C. In 1539 many of the monastic buildings were pulled down, as was part of the church. Traces of some of the monastic buildings can be seen on the south side of the priory church.

Internally, foundations, comprising a course of moulded stones from the A-S church, can still apparently be seen. These are located under the foundations of the north side of the nave, on either side of the north porch (they are hidden from view at present).

Externally, a line of modern brickwork follows the line of the northern wall of the church forming a curve to skirt around the north porch. This brickwork is some 48 Ins/122 Cms from the exterior northern walling of the church and stands 24 Ins/60 Cms H. At intermittent intervals abutting this brickwork, there are some single sections of stonework, about 24 Ins/60 Cms H by 12 Ins/30 Cms W. Some of these have clearly been incorporated into concrete with the clear intention to give a uniform appearance. Some are decorated but unfortunately it is not clear what they are, or where they come from, or, what age they are, but clearly someone has considered they are worthy of preservation.

CATWICK
St Michael's Church
TA 131454   Rating: ☆☆☆   Access is possible.

At the eastern end of Catwick turn off the B1244, "Main Street" (there are street signs), and head in a southerly direction along "Rise Lane" (there is a street sign). After 200 Yds/182 M turn off Rise Lane and head in a westerly direction along "Church Lane" (there is a street sign). 200 Yds/182 M along Church Lane, the church, which is easily identified, can be reached by taking the gravel footpath that heads off the road in a northerly direction and runs along the western end of the churchyard. (Where the footpath reaches the road there is a free-standing wooden directional signpost "Public Footpath".) The churchyard entrance adjoining the footpath is 22 Yds/20 M from the road.

The A-S church on this site was replaced by the present structure in 1272. Much of the church was restored and rebuilt in 1862-63.

Internally, there is a section of stonework from the original A-S church on this site. It is located incorporated into the north wall of the chancel, and is situated 144 Ins/365 Cms up from the floor, and 36 Ins/91 Cms west of the altar rail. It measures 18 Ins/45 Cms H by 12 Ins/30 Cms W. It depicts St Michael from head to feet.

EASINGTON
All Saints Church
TA 398191   Rating: ☆

The church is prominently situated adjacent to the south side of the B1445, "North Church Side" (there is a street sign), which runs through the centre of Easington.

The present structure dates from the late 12C, 13C and 14C.

Internally, the stonework comprising the four corners of the nave is apparently A-S. The quoining in the southwest and northwest corners of the nave, which have not been whitewashed, and protrude from the later walling, are clearly identifiable as A-S workmanship. The southeast quoining in the nave is not exposed, but there is a section of protruding walling which evidently is also A-S. In the northeast corner of the nave there is no discernible trace of A-S stonework.

Internally, in the north aisle, the lintels above the two easternmost windows are said to be A-S, but these are the more common medieval grave covers incised with a sword design.

Internally, on the southern face of the easternmost pillar on the south side of the nave, some 36 Ins/91 Cms up from the ground, an outline of a Viking longship has been cut into the stonework. There is no indication of when this longship was drawn.

FLAMBOROUGH
Dane's Dyke
Running from TA 215692 to TA 213732   Rating: ☆

This "Dyke" is a large earthwork with a bank nearly 20 feet/6 M H and a west facing ditch nearly 60 feet/18 M W. The Dyke runs for about 2½ miles in length and cuts off the peninsula of Flamborough.

Rather than an Iron Age or Roman construction, it is now thought the Dyke was built by an Anglo-Saxon or Viking war band attracted to the defensive capabilities of the Flamborough headland.

Although the Dyke is now often hidden amongst trees and vegetation, it can easily be identified running north and south from the B1229 at TA 213712 and running south from the B1255 at TA 213701.

At TA 213701, opposite the junction of the B1255 and a drive cum minor road leading off southwards, there are "Danes Dyke" directional signs identifying the entrance to the drive leading to a Nature Trail. 10

Yds/9 M along this drive there are more signs (relating to car parking – but not to the Dyke).

At the Nature Trail exit, at the junction with the B1255 at TA 219701 (farther east of the entrance), there are freestanding wooden signs relating to Danes Dyke, the location of the entrance to the Nature Trail and parking. (Only at this site there are clear signposts identifying the Dyke.)

GOODMANHAM
All Hallows Church
SE 889432   Rating: ✰

The church, on the slope of a hill, is clearly visible adjacent to the north side of the minor road running south-west/north-east through Goodmanham.

When writing in 731 Bede referred to Goodmanham as the site of a pagan temple that acted as a centre of worship to Woden in northern England. It was here in 625 that the high priest Coifi desecrated the pagan temple after hearing the preaching of Christianity by St Paulinus at the Great Council held by King Edwin of Northumbria at nearby Londesborough (no trace survives of the hall where this took place).

The present structure apparently dates from 1130 with additions in the 13C and 14C.

Internally, there are various sections of stonework incorporated into the fabric that suggest an earlier construction date than 1130. Examples of such stonework include the chancel arch and the surrounding stonework, walling in the south wall of the nave, a small window in the southwest corner of the nave, and a blocked doorway (?) at ground level in the north wall of the tower.

Internally, there is a plain and worn hexagonal-shaped A-S font. It is situated in the northwest corner of the nave, standing on the floor on a shallow plinth. The font may date from the 9C.

Externally, in the churchyard, there is a wooden cross standing about 120 Ins/304 Cms H, cemented at its base, some 50 Yds/45 M west of the church. (Is this the site of the pagan temple?)

GREAT DRIFFIELD
All Saints Church
TA 022580   Rating ✰✰

In the centre of Great Driffield, the easily identifiable church is set back from the west side of "Middle Street North" (there is a street sign).

On the site of an A-S church, some 12C, 14C and 15C material survives despite restoration in 1880.

Internally, there are two sections of 11C A-S stonework incorporated into the fabric of the walling contained in the tower-ringing chamber of the church which is located on the floor above the organ. These are:

1.   A section of stonework incorporated into the walling of the north wall of the tower-ringing chamber. It is incorporated into the northwest corner of the ringing chamber, 3 Ins/7 Cms up from the floor and measures 9 Ins/22 Cms H by 41 Ins/104 Cms W. It is decorated with distinctive rounded "torus" moulding along its entire width.

2.   A section of stonework incorporated into the walling of the south wall of the tower-ringing chamber. It is incorporated into the southwest corner of the ringing chamber, 60 Ins/152 Cms up from the floor enclosed within a cupboard that can be opened to view. This section of stonework measures 9 Ins/22 Cms H by 29 Ins/73 Cms W and is decorated with distinctive rounded "torus" moulding along its entire width.

Although the church is open, to gain access to the tower special arrangements have to be made with the vicar at The Vicarage, Downe Street, Driffield, East Yorkshire, YO25 6DX.

HARPHAM
(1) St John of Beverley Church
TA 092616   Rating: ☆

At the minor crossroads in the centre of Harpham, turn off Main Street (there is a street sign) and proceed in a south easterly direction along Crossgates (there is a street sign), a "no through road" (there is a sign), following the directional sign "To the Church". After about 160 Yds/146 M, opposite the street sign "Daggett Lane", turn off Crossgates and head in a westerly direction along a drive to reach the easily identified church.

The church is basically Norman but was extensively restored in the 14C.

Internally, there is a small splayed window that may be A-S in origin incorporated into the south wall of the nave. It is the most westerly of the three windows in the south wall of the nave. The stonework surrounding the outer splay of the window is complete apart from the eastern vertical support which presumably was removed when the adjacent "new" window to the east was built.

Internally, there are two coffins that could be A-S in origin. They are located adjacent to the north wall of the north chapel. They are supported by stone plinths raising them between 12 Ins/30 Cms and 13 Ins/33 Cms off the floor. The more easterly of these coffins measures 78 Ins/198 Cms L, tapering 26 Ins/66 Cms to 18 Ins/45 Cms W, by 15½ Ins/39 Cms D. There is a socket for the head. The most westerly of these coffins measures 84 Ins/213 Cms L, tapering 26½ Ins/67 Cms to 18½ Ins/46 Cms W, by 17½ Ins/44 Cms D. There is a socket for the head.

HARPHAM
(2) St John's Well
TA 095617   Rating: ✫

From the crossroads in the centre of Harpham, proceed in an easterly direction along "East End" (there is a street sign), a "no through road" (there is a sign), as directed by the "St. Johns Well" sign. The well is easily located at the east end of Harpham past the last farm on the north side of the road about 350 Yds/320 M from the crossroads.

Amidst the grass verge on south side of the road there is a 60¼ Ins/153 Cms H iron railing surround standing on a 12½ Ins/31 Cms H concrete plinth. This iron railing surrounds the concrete construction, 45 Ins/114 Cms H with a 24 Ins/60 Cms diameter, housing the well head itself.

On the north side of this concrete housing there is an opening for access to the waters of the well itself. A stone plaque, placed at a 45 degree angle between the concrete plinth and concrete well housing, on the north side of the construction, commemorates "St John's Well, Birthplace, Harpham, 640 AD." There is no decoration on the concrete housing. Apparently the waters in this well never fail to spring even in the driest of summers.

HOLME-ON-SPALDING-MOOR
All Saints Church
SE 821389   Rating: ✫

In an isolated position, separate from the north-east side of Holme-on-Spalding-Moor, the church is prominently situated on top of a hill about 1050 Yds/960 M from the junction of the A163 and the A614.

Turn off the A163 and proceed in a southerly direction along an un-named and un-signed, narrow lane (near to the junction there is a road sign indicating a junction of a major and a minor road). This lane winds its way uphill and reaches the church after about 350 Yds/320 M.

On the site of an A-S church, the present structure contains some Norman material but it mostly dates from the 13C. The church was restored in 1906-11.

Apparently, at some height on the inside of the belfry wall of the tower, there is what is described as a crude A-S carved stone depicting a figure with a lamb. The carving cannot be viewed and access to the church is restricted.

HOWDEN
Minster
SE 748283   Rating: ☆

The large, partly ruined, Collegiate Minster church is easily located in the centre of Howden. 40 Yds/36 M south-west of the junction of the A63 and the B1228, the west end of the Minster church is located some 15 Yds/13 M east of the junction of "Bridgegate" (there is a street sign) and "St John's Street/St Johns St" (there are two street signs opposite each other). Opposite the Bridgegate/St Johns Street junction there is a very small square on the south side of which there is a street sign "Corn Market Hill". [Bridgegate is part of the B1228. "Pinfold Street/Pinfold St." (there are street signs) is a continuation of Bridgegate as it proceeds in a southwest direction, and it is also part of the B1228.] The Minster is bounded on the north by the pedestrian passage "Churchside leading to Market Place" (there is a street sign).

Although the Minster is on the site of an A-S church, the earliest surviving fabric consists of a few carved fragments and re-used masonry from the Norman church. Most of the surviving Minster dates from the mid 13C to the 14C.

Internally, the window in the north transept includes a depiction of Roger de Hoveden, Rector of Howden from 1174 to 1197. In his History of England Roger incorporated chunks of a now lost Viking saga.

HULL
Hull And East Riding Museum
TA 102286   Rating: ☆☆☆☆

The Museum is located in the "Museums Quarter" in the centre of Hull on the east side of "High Street" (there are no street signs but there are signs to the Museums Quarter). The Museum is housed in Number 36 High Street. The appropriate building has the number "36" painted on the south face of the north wall by the imposing large iron gates in front of the original entrance. A plaque on the wall by this former entrance informs "Hull and East Riding Museum main entrance on Chapel Lane Staith". To the north of this former entrance, attached to the west facing walling, there is a blue plaque: "On the site of the Old Custom House, this building opened as a Corn Exchange in 1856, architects Bellamy & Hardy of Lincoln. It reopened as the Museum of Commerce and Transport in 1925."

Proceed in a northerly direction along the High Street until, on the east side of the road, there is a brick wall with the words "The Museum Quarter" protruding from it, the adjacent roadway is "Chapel Lane Staith" (there is a street sign). Turn off the High Street and proceed in an easterly direction along Chapel Lane Staith, pass through the large iron gate with large letters "MQ" on a central roundel. The modern, purpose built, entrance to the Museum is on the south side of Chapel Lane Staith, 25 Yds/22 M from the High Street. It has the words "Museum Entrance" in large letters on its glass front.

As with all museums, the displays and the exhibits they contain may be changed, re-sited, removed from display and/or put in store, or loaned to other museums or suitable repositories. Before visiting the museum it is worth checking in advance whether the displays listed in the text below are still in place in the same location(s) set out in the text. Individual exhibits may have been rearranged in terms of their display, the order in which they are displayed and their relationship to other exhibits, some exhibits may have been removed from display. The text in the entry reflects the descriptions and/or accompanying notices to the exhibits at the time of visiting. These too may have been revised, amended, added to or removed.

The Museum houses both natural history and archaeology displays. The archaeology displays include the 2,300 year old "Hasholme Boat", a reconstruction of an Iron Age village, a reconstruction of a Roman Town and a Roman bath house as well as Roman mosaics and a display relating to the "Saxon" settlers.

In the Museum the "Anglo-Saxon and Medieval Galleries" are located on the first floor, adjacent to the top of the stairs. NOTE: The numbers indicated below are the same numbers identifying artefacts in their respective displays. Likewise the descriptions detailed below are those descriptions that accompany the displays themselves.

(A) The first display gallery depicts the prow of an A-S ship with people landing, with a notice explaining "Coming and going. The end of Roman rule left a power vacuum in Britain". The displays contain:

Finds from the cremation cemetery at Sancton, East Yorkshire:

1 – 13.	Cremation urns, many decorated with stamped designs.
14.	Part of the cremated human remains from an urn.
15.	Decorated copper alloy fragment of square-headed brooch. 6th century AD.
16.	Square-headed or cruciform brooch fragment. 6th century AD.

17.   Bow brooch fragments. 5th century AD.
18 – 19.   Iron knives. 19 has traces of a ? horn handle.

Grave Goods – Crafts & Hobbies:

20.   Whetstone
21.   Glass beads fused by heat.
22-24.   Bone, chalk and fire clay spindle whorls.
25.   Vessel glass fragments, melted.
26.   Game counters, part of a set.

Grave Goods – Personal Care:

27.   Knife or shears blade.
28 – 30.   Copper alloy tweezers.
31.   Copper alloy shears, a symbolic item.
32 – 33.   Miniature copper alloy knife and tweezers, forming a set.
34 – 35.   Miniature tweezers, shears and knife.
36-38.   Set of miniature tweezers, shears and knife.
39.   Miniature shears.
40.   Miniature iron knife, with traces of ? horn handle.
41.   Decorated antler object, perhaps a handle.
42.   Double-sided antler comb, put unburnt into an urn. 6th
           to 7th century AD.
43.   Miniature comb, put unburnt into an urn. 5th to 6th
           century AD.
44 – 45.   Fragments from decorated single-sided antler combs. 5th
           to 6th century AD.
46.   Forty fragments of burnt ivory, perhaps casket fittings.
47.   Vessel glass distorted and fused by heat.

Finds from inhumation (not cremated) burials of women: all dated to
the 6th century AD:

Dress Accessories 500-600 AD:

1 – 2.   Pair of silver wire ear-rings with blue and red glass beads.
           Cheesecake Hill, Driffield.
3 – 4.   Pair of copper alloy annular brooches. Kelleythorpe,
           Driffield.
5.   Cruciform brooch. Londesborough.
6.   Ring-headed pin. Cheesecake Hill, Driffield.
7 – 8.   Set of paired sleeve clasps or "cuff links". Londesborough.
9.   Strap-end (two halves). Staxton.
10.   Buckle, copper alloy with high tin content. Kelleythorpe,
           Driffield.
11.   Meerschaum bead or toggle. Staxton.
12.   Iron knife. Staxton.
13.   Pair of copper alloy girdle hangers. Londesborough.

Anglian brooches and pendants:

14.	Headplate of gilded copper alloy radiate brooch, of Jutish type. Staxton.
15.	Radiate brooch. Kent (where this style was more commonly worn).
16-17.	Silver bracteates or pendants. Hornsea, and Kelleythorpe, Driffield.
18-19.	Copper alloy square-headed brooches. Hornsea, and Kelleythorpe, Driffield.
20.	Cruciform brooch. Staxton.
21.	Small long brooches (worn as a pair like annular brooches). Staxton.
22 – 23.	Penannular brooches (perhaps a Celtic style). Kelleythorpe, Driffield.
24.	Crook-headed pin. Kelleythorpe, Driffield.

Objects hung from belt or girdle:

25.	Buckle and plate, with textile traces preserved.
26.	Buckle. Hornsea.
27.	Pair of girdle hangers. Staxton
28.	Antler ring (for suspending other objects). Londesborough.
29.	Half of an elephant ivory bag-ring or frame. Staxton.
30 – 31.	Amulets or lucky charms: a cowrie shell (for fertility), and a tooth. Staxton.

Noblewoman 600-700 AD:

These objects all come from the same grave at Green Lane Crossing, Garton, together with No.13 in the case to your right.

1.	Copper alloy veil or hair pin.
2 – 3.	Pair of silver slip-knot ear-rings.
4.	Necklace of amethyst (from the eastern Mediterranean) and glass beads.
5.	Silver narrow-banded annular brooch.
6.	Copper alloy annular brooch.
7.	Gold and garnet pendant.
8.	Copper alloy buckle.
9 – 10.	Spindle whorls, perhaps tucked into a belt, one might be a toggle to fasten it.
11 – 13.	Blue glass fragment, and two glass studs, perhaps held in a bag.
14.	Iron spoon or spatula, presented here as another part of the bag-group.
15.	Copper alloy workbox hung on an iron chain.

Anglian Cross fragments 700-800 AD:

16 – 18.   Fragments from three stone crosses. Wharram Percy. No.17 dated 800 A.D. Backdrop shows a 7th century gold and garnet cross from Burton Pidsea.

Coffin fittings:

19.   Iron coffin fitting. Green Lane Crossing, Garton. Late 7th to 8th century AD.

20.   Coffin fitting. Fimber church. 8th century or later.

21 – 27.   Coffin fittings. Green Lane Crossing, Garton. Late 7th to 8th century.

Anglian Freemen 500-700AD:

1.   Iron spearhead. Staxton. 6th century.

2.   Sword. Acklam Wold. 7th century,

3.   Shield boss and fittings. Kelleythorpe, Driffield. 6th century.

4.   Buckle (to fasten strap for sword) Boynton/East Yorkshire ? 6th century.

5.   Copper alloy strap-end. Boynton/East Yorkshire ? 6th century.

6.   Iron buckle. Boynton/East Yorkshire ? 6th century.

Symbols of Status:

7.   Glass and gold pendant. Green Lane Crossing, Garton. 7th century.

8.   Marbled blue glass pendant. Everthorpe. 7th century.

9.   Gold bead. Castledyke, Barton on Humber (North Lincolnshire). 7th century.

10.   Annular brooch (narrow headed) Eastburn. 7th century.

11.   Annular brooch. Garton Slack. 7th century.

12.   Coptic bowl (imported via the Mediterranean). Shiptonthorpe. ?7th century.

From the Feast:

13.   Iron bucket hoops. Green Lane Crossing, Garton (found in the noblewoman's grave shown by the upright figure to the left of this case). 7th century.

14.   Copper alloy bindings for a bucket (wood is modern). Staxton. 6th century.

15 – 16.   Enamelled escutcheons (decorative mounts) from a hanging bowl. Market Rasen, Lincolnshire. 7th century.

17.   Copper alloy escutcheon from hanging bowl. 7th century. Cottam "B".

18.   Openwork buckle of Frankish style. Driffield. Late 6th to 7th century.

19 – 20.   Handle from Frankish bowl, and fragment from a stand to support it. Castledyke, Barton on Humber, North Lincolnshire. 7th century.

Anglian & Viking Metalwork, 750-1000:

Metal-detected finds from the Haldenby collection help us compare different sites.

Dress Accessories from Cottam "A":

1 – 5.   Copper alloy strap-ends 8th to 9th century AD.

6.   Gilded chip-carved fragment of a linked pin (one of a pair). 8th century AD.

7.   Silver globular pin-head. 8th to 9th century AD.

8 – 9.   Copper alloy facetted-headed pins. 8th to 9th century AD.

10 – 11.   Rings. 10 is possibly an ear ring. 8th to 9th century AD.

Dress Accessories from Cottam "B":

12 – 28.   Copper alloy strap-ends. 8th to 9th century.

29 – 32.   Gilded chip-carved linked pins. 8th century AD.

33 – 50.   Iron or copper alloy globular and facetted-headed pins. 8th to 9th century AD.

51 – 57.   Flat-headed pin fragments. 8th to 9th century AD except No. 56, which may alternatively be from an Iron Age wheel-headed pin.

58.   Gilded chip-carved copper alloy ? book mount. 8th century AD.

59 – 65.   Brooch fragment, hooked tag, buckle plates, rings and buckle. 8th to 9th century AD.

66 – 67.   Copper alloy ? stylus and balance arm (see next case). 8th to 9th century AD.

Finds from South Newbald:

68 – 75.   Copper alloy strap-ends. 8th to 9th century AD.

76 – 79.   Chip-carved and gilded pin-heads and fragments. 8th century AD.

80 – 96.   Copper alloy globular and facetted pins and pin-heads. 8th to 9th century AD.

97 – 98.   Silver pin-heads. No. 97 is facetted; No. 98 is a fanged cat's head. 8th century AD.

99 – 102.   Copper alloy flat-headed pin fragments. 8th to 9th century AD.

103 – 4.   Gilded chip-carved copper alloy fragments. 8th century AD.

105 – 7.   Hooked tags. 8th to 9th century AD.

108 – 9.   Copper alloy mounts or terminals. 8th to 9th century AD.

110 – 11.   Decorated mounts or terminals. 8th to 9th century AD.

Other sites in East Yorkshire:

112 – 16. Copper alloy strap-ends and pins. Wharram Percy. All 8th to 9th century AD, except ring-headed pin shaft No. 113, which may alternatively be Bronze Age.

117 – 18. ?Ring bezel or seal and strap-end. Hayton. 8th to 9th century AD.

119.   Buckle. Drewton. 8th to 9th century AD.

120.   Flat-headed pin. North Cave. 8th to 9th century AD.

121.   Silver boss. North Ferriby. 8th century AD.

122.   Silver strap-end. Pocklington. 8th century AD.

123.   Copper alloy strap-end. Millington. 8th to 9th century AD.

124 – 5. Globular-headed pin and gilded buckle tongue. Welton. No. 124 8th to 9th century AD; No.125 7th century AD.

Viking Age finds from East Yorkshire:

126.   Ornamental strap-end. Elloughton. 10th to 11th century.

127 – 9. Strap-ends. South Newbald, North Newbald, Cowlam. 10th to 11th century.

130 – 1. Decorated strap-ends. Cowlam and Cottam "B". 10th to 11th century.

132 – 5. Brooches, silvered or gilt. No.132 Beverley; Nos. 133-4 (with Jellinge style ornament) Cottam; No. 135 Wetwang Blealands Nook. 10th to 11th century.

136 – 8. Buckles. Cottam "A". Welton, Cowlam. 10th to 11th century.

139 – 40. Copper alloy harness bells. Cowlam, Welton. 10th to 11th century.

(B) The adjacent display gallery depicts a Viking boat. The displays contain:

Farming Life 850-1150:

1.   Iron bell and clapper. Church bells came to mark the passage of the day – still a much-loved sound of rural life. Unprovenanced. 9th to 10th century AD.

2.   Spade, made of radially split oak; an iron blade would be added. Barrow on Humber, North Lincolnshire. Medieval.

3 – 4.   Mattock or mallet heads. No. 3 is oak, No. 4 is prunus sp (wood of plum, cherry or blackthorn). Eastgate, Beverley. 11th to 12th century.

5.   Mattock head, oak. Lurk Lane, Beverley. 10th to 11th century.

6 – 9.   Whetstones for sharpening the blades of iron tools. Nos. 6, 8 and 9 from Lurk Lane, Beverley, 9th to 11th century.

No.7 has grooves for sharpening finer points. Dominican Priory, Beverley, 10th-13th century.

Bone and Antler Working 650-1150:

1.   Double-sided comb and comb-case. Kelleythorpe, Driffield. 6th to 7th century AD.
2.   Double-sided comb. Green Lane Crossing, Garton. Late 7th century AD.
3.   Straight-sided comb. Elmswell. 7th to 8th century AD.
4.   Single-sided comb. Lurk Lane, Beverley. Mid 9th century AD.
5.   Handled comb. Paddock Hill, Thwing. 8th to 10th century AD.
6.   Single-sided comb. Paddock Hill, Thwing. 8th to 10th century AD.
7.   Single-sided comb and comb-case. Eastgate, Beverley. 12th century.
8 – 9.   Pins made from pig fibulas. Lurk Lane, Beverley. 9th century AD.
10.   Polished bone pin. Lurk Lane, Beverley. 9th century AD.
11.   Antler spoon. Lurk Lane, Beverley. 9th to 11th century AD.
12.   Red deer antler. Side-plates for combs were made from tines, while tooth-plates were sawn as slices from the beam. North Ferriby. Date unknown.
13.   Antler tine with hatched cuts. Lurk Lane, Beverley. 9th to 11th century AD.
14 – 17.   Waste from another working. Nos. 14-15 from Eastgate, Beverley; No. 16 from Lurk Lane, Beverley; No. 17 from Blackfriargate, Hull. 9th to 13th centuries.

Anglian & Viking Coins, 700-950 AD:

1.   Copper-alloy scales and set of Roman and early Saxon objects re-used as weights. Castledyke. From a grave of the 7th century AD.
2.   Silver sceats (pronounced "shats"). Although most of these are Northumbrian, one piece was struck in Southern England and another on the Continent. Cottam. Early 8th to mid 9th century AD.
3.   Two silver Northumbrian sceats and a copper-alloy styca. Cottam. Late 8th to mid 9th century AD.
4.   Southern English and Northumbrian sceats. Welton. Early to mid 8th century AD.
5.   Southern English and Continental sceats. North Ferriby. Late 7th to mid 8th century AD.
6.   Northumbrian silver sceats and copper-alloy stycas. South Newbald. Mid 8th to mid 9th century AD.

7.   Silver sceats and copper stycas. Although most of the coins were produced in the Kingdom of Northumbria, the two earliest pieces were struck in Southern England and on the Continent. Thwing. Late 7th to mid 9th century AD.

8.   Northumbrian silver sceats. Lurk Lane, Beverley. 8th century AD.

9.   Part of a hoard of Northumbrian copper-alloy stycas. Lurk Lane, Beverley. Buried about 850 AD.

10.   Part of a Roman tile, re-used as a mould for casting metal ingots. Lurk Lane, Beverley. Probably 10th to early 11th century AD.

11.   Copper-alloy weight. Newbald. Early 10th century AD.

12.   Silver penny, struck by the Viking rulers of York. Unprovenanced. Early 10th century AD.

13.   Silver penny, struck by the Viking rulers of York. Lurk Lane, Beverley. Early 10th century AD.

(C) The next display gallery contains displays entitled "William moves North". The displays contain:

Warrior Class 950-1100:

1.   Sword. Skerne, near Driffield. 10th century AD.

2 – 3.   Axeheads. Malton and Leven. Medieval.

4 – 6.   Spearheads. River Hull, Wilfholme. 10th to 11th century AD. No. 5 is an unprovenanced ferrule or butt-spike from a spear.

7 – 8.   Spearhead. Unprovenanced. Medieval.

9.   Spearhead. Skerne. 10th century AD.

10.   Spearhead. North Grimston. ? 8th to 9th century AD ?

Mounted Elite 850-1400:

11.   Iron prick spur fragment, with surface tinning. Lurk Lane, Beverley. 8th to 9th century AD.

12.   Prick spur fragment with brass binding. Dominican Priory, Beverley. 9th to 11th century AD.

13 – 14. Prick spurs. Dominican Priory, Beverley. 12th century.

15.   Rowel spur. Ebberston. 14th century.

16.   Copper alloy spur. Riplingham. 13th to 14th century.

17 – 18. Rowel spurs, No. 18 with leather strap. Wawne. 15th to 16th century.

19.   Copper alloy stirrup mount. Elloughton. 10th to 11th century.

20.   Strap distributors from horse harness tinned. Lurk Lane, Beverley. 10th to 11th century.

21.   Harness ring. Crayke. 10th to 11th century.
22.   Jointed horse bit. Crayke. 10th to 11th century.
23.   Bridle bit cheek-piece. Eastgate, Beverley. 10th to 11th century.
24.   Loose side link. Lurk Lane, Beverley. ? 9th to 11th century?
25-27. Harness fittings. No. 25 North Ferriby, Medieval; No. 26 Unprovenanced, and No. 27 Lurk Lane, Beverley, both 13th to 14th century.

KIRBY UNDERDALE
All Saints Church

SE 808586   Rating: ★★

The church is situated on the eastern edge of Kirby Underdale. The churchyard is adjacent to the north side of the road that approaches the village from a south-easterly direction.

Although restored in 1871, the church retains 11C, 12C, 13C and 14C material.

Internally, the stonework in the nave walls contain A-S material including evidence of herring-bone masonry around and above the more recently inserted arches into the north and south walls of the nave.

Internally, the rounded stonework heads of the arch above A-S windows can easily be identified incorporated into the fabric of both the

KIRKBY UNDERDALE: All Saints Church. Anglo-Saxon window heads and fabric retained in nave walls.

north and south walls of the nave. The westerly end of the part of the arches that survive is situated – on (in the north wall), – or just above (the south wall) – the point of the arches inserted into the walls of the nave. The examples incorporated into the fabric of the south wall of the nave are less complete. The example nearest the east end of the north wall of the nave can also be viewed from inside the north aisle.

Internally, there is A-S herring bone masonry in the south wall of the tower 72 Ins/182 Cms up from the floor.

Externally, there is a coffin that may be A-S. It is located 104 Ins/264 Cms west from the west wall of the south porch and between 6 Ins/15 Cms and 12½ Ins/31 Cms south of the south wall of the south aisle. The coffin sits on a number of unrelated sections of stonework whose origin and purpose is unclear. The coffin measures 81½ Ins/207 Cms L, tapering 27 Ins/68 Cms to 19 Ins/48 Cms W, tapering 17½ Ins/44 Cms to 13½ Ins/34 Cms D. There is no socket for the head of the body for this coffin and there is no decoration on any of the sides.

Externally, there is a substantial section of stonework from the base of a boundary cross of uncertain age. It contains a socket for the base of a cross-shaft. The east side of the cross base is missing. It is located 10 Yds/9 M south of the south porch, and 132 Ins/335 Cms west of the footpath leading northwards to the entrance to the south porch. The base of the boundary cross measures 17½ Ins/44 Cms H, by 36 Ins/91 Cms W, by 24 Ins/60 Cms D.

LECONFIELD
St Catherine's Church
TA 015438   Rating: ☆   Access is possible.

In the northern part of Leconfield, turn east off the A164 as indicated by the separate directional signs "Arram" and "St Catherine's Church". Proceed as directed in an easterly direction along "Arram Road" (there is a street sign). The church is easily located on the north side of Arram Road, about 440 Yds/402 M from its junction with the A164.

The present structure dates from the 13C; it was restored during the 19C.

Externally, part of the top of an A-S window head, and part of its vertical supports on either side, have been incorporated into the fabric of the church. It is located in the centre of the west wall of the south aisle, 85 Ins/215 Cms up from the ground. The surviving A-S stonework of this blocked-up window measures 26 Ins/66 Cms H by 28 Ins/71 Cms W. Although most of the walling in this part of the church is brickwork, the remains of the window are partially surrounded by stonework, which, along with the window, formed part of an earlier church on this site.

[Note: the surviving A-S material from the window head can only be viewed externally; there is no surviving evidence internally.]

LEVEN
Holy Trinity Church

TA 107452   Rating:☆☆   Access is possible.

In the centre of Leven, the church is easy to identify set back from the west side of the road running north/south through the village.

The church was built during 1843-45.

Internally, there is a section of stonework from an A-S cross-shaft. It is located in the south-east corner of the nave standing on the floor beneath the south-west side of the pulpit. It is between 2 Ins/5 Cms and 3¼ Ins/8 Cms north-west of the pillar in the south-east corner of the nave. The section of stonework measures 24 Ins/60 Cms H, tapering 11½ Ins/29 Cms to 7½ Ins/19 Cms W, by 8 Ins/20 Cms D. It is decorated on all four sides with knot work design (the southeast side is rather weathered but some knot work decoration does survive). It dates from the 9C.

Internally, there is a section of stonework from part of an A-S cross-base. It is located sitting on the floor in the south-east corner of the south transept, 10½ Ins/26 Cms north of the south wall and 10 Ins/25 Cms west of the east wall of the south transept. It measures between 16 Ins/40 Cms and 17 Ins/43 Cms H(D), by 12 Ins/30 Cms W, tapering 11½ Ins/29 Cms to 10½ Ins/26 Cms D (H). It has no decoration on any of the sides. This section of stonework has clearly been re-shaped and re-used as building material. It dates from the 9C. The cross-base probably supported the cross-shaft from which the section of cross-shaft in the church formed part.

LISSETT
St James Church

TA 144581   Rating: ☆   Access is possible.

In the southern part of Lissett, the church is located on the west side of "Main Street" (there are street signs) about 150 Yds/137 M north of its junction with the A165.

Apart from a 12C doorway, the present structure dates from 1876.

Externally, there is a section of stonework that apparently comes from an A-D hogback grave cover. It has been incorporated into the fabric of the church just above the apex to the arch over the entrance to the south door in the south porch. It measures 8 Ins/20 Cms H by about 6 Ins/15 Cms W. It clearly has a carving on it, but what it is precisely is difficult to determine because of whitewashing.

LITTLE DRIFFIELD
St Mary's Church

TA 010578   Rating: ☆☆   Access is possible.

In the southern part of Little Driffield, the church is located close to the east side of "Church Lane" which approaches the village from the south (there are street signs at its junction with the road running west/east through Little Driffield, "York Road" (there are street signs)).

The present fabric dates mainly from the restoration in 1889 but 12C and 14C fabric does survive.

Internally, there is a tablet that records: "Within this Chancel lies interred the Body of Alfred, King of Northumberland, who departed this Life January 19th. A.D. 705 in the 20th. Year of his Reign.". (It should be Aldfrith or Alfrid who reigned 685-704 as King of Northumbria.) It has been incorporated into the north wall of the chancel, 140 Ins/355 Cms up from the floor.

Internally, the tower arch is A-S in origin and the surrounding stonework incorporates material of a similar date.

Internally, there is a section of stonework from part of an arm of a 10C A-S wheel head cross. It is located sitting on the window ledge under the tower at the west end of the church amongst miscellaneous sections of stonework of various shapes, sizes and ages. The section of A-S stonework is situated in the front (easternmost) row of stonework, 3 Ins/7 Cms north of the southern end of the window ledge. It measures between 3 Ins/7 Cms and 5 Ins/12 Cms H (W) by 7½ Ins/19 Cms W (H), by 8¼ Ins/20 Cms D. It is decorated with knot work design on both the west and east faces and the end of the arm: there is no decoration on any of the other sides.

LONDESBROUGH
All Saints Church

SE 868454   Rating: ☆☆*   Access is possible, but as the A-S material can be identified in the porch access to the church is not essential.

The church is on the south side of the most southerly road running in a south-west/north-east direction in Londesbrough.

The present structure dates from the early 13C.

Externally, an A-D "St Cuthbert style" crosshead has been incorporated into the fabric of the church. It is situated above the arch over the south doorway into the church, under the apex of the roof of the surrounding porch. The crosshead is easy to identify despite being obscured by the wooden roof supports for the porch. It measures 24 Ins/60 Cms H by 21 Ins/53 Cms W. It is decorated with interlace design and the central boss can be identified. It dates from the 11C.

LOWTHORPE
St Martin's Church
TA 079608   **Rating:** ☆☆

The church is located at the northern end of Lowthorpe, well set back from the north side of the road that runs south-east/north-west through the village. By the side of the road there are gates to a hidden drive that leads to the churchyard. Just south of these gates, in the grass verge, there is a freestanding wooden church notice board. On the taller of the two uprights supporting this notice board there is a directional sign "Church and monastery ruin". Pass through the gates and proceed along the drive for about 106 Yds/96 M to reach the gate to the churchyard.

On the site of an A-S church, most of the present structure dates from the 13C and the extensive rebuilding in 1333. There were additions in the 15C. During 1776-77 a brick wall was built behind the chancel arch thus reducing the "used" part of the church to its present size. The chancel of the former collegiate church was abandoned and left in ruins.

Internally, there is a virtually complete A-S crosshead with part of its attached cross-shaft. It is located affixed by two iron bars to the west wall of the nave, 25 Ins/63 Cms north of the south wall of the nave. Beneath the crosshead there is the 14C memorial comprising the life-size double effigy of a man (possibly Sir Thomas Heslerton) and a woman. In total the crosshead and cross-shaft measure 26½ Ins/67 Cms H. The crosshead measures 16½ Ins/41 Cms H, by 17 Ins/43 Cms W, by 6 Ins/15 Cms D. The section of cross-shaft measures 10 Ins/25 Cms H, by 12½ Ins/31 Cms W, by 6½ Ins/16 Cms D. The east sides of both the crosshead and section of cross-shaft are clearly decorated with interlace design. The edges of the arms of the crosshead, and the north and south sides of the section of cross-shaft have a slight indication of some decoration, the design of which cannot now be identified with confidence. There is no decoration on the west sides of both the crosshead and section of cross-shaft due to damage. The crosshead and section of cross-shaft date from the 10C.

NORTH FRODINGHAM
St Elgin's Church
TA 090534   Rating: ★★   Access is possible.

The church is located at "Church End", 400 Yds/365 M west of North Frodingham. Church End is separate from the village itself. The church is situated adjacent to the north side of the B1249.

Most of the present structure dates from 1878 and 1892.

Internally, there is an almost complete (apart from the top arm) 10C A-D wheel head cross and part of its attached cross-shaft. It is located on the raised floor by the east face of the first freestanding pillar on the north side of the nave. The cross stands on top of a large section of unrelated stonework. This unrelated section of stonework stands 17 Ins/43 Cms H and is decorated with a face with arms raised in support. (There are also two small fragments of unrelated stonework sitting on this section of stonework.) The crosshead and part of its cross-shaft measures 15 Ins/38 Cms H, by 20 Ins/50 Cms W, by 6 Ins/15 Cms D. The wheel head cross is decorated on its east face with interlace design, including apparently birds and beasts, but these are difficult to identify. No other decoration is apparent on any of the other sides or on any of the sides of the attached section of cross-shaft.

NUNBURNHOLME
St James Church
SE 847478   Rating: ★★★★★   Access is possible.

At the southern end of Nunburnholme, the church is close to the east side of "Church Lane" (there is a street sign, but not near the church) that runs south-west/north-east through the village.

Probably on the site of an A-S church, the present structure dates mainly from the 12C, 13C and 14C. The church was restored in 1872-73 and the tower dates from 1902.

Internally, there is a section of stonework from an A-S cross-shaft (cement has been used to join two sections of stonework together as one). It is located standing on a 21½ Ins/54 Cms H stepped plinth 59 Ins/149 Cms east of the west wall of the tower. The section of stonework measures 60 Ins/152 Cms H, tapering 14½ Ins/36 Cms to 10½ Ins/26 Cms W, tapering 12 Ins/30 Cms to 10 Ins/25 Cms D. The decoration is as follows:

1.   East Side: Top Section – two spiral ornaments and a pair of arms with hands grasping the top of a semi-circular arch underneath

NUNBURNHOLME: St James Church. Anglo-Saxon cross-shaft depicting a seated helmeted warrior with a sword in his left hand.

which there is a helmeted warrior seated on a stool with a sword in his left hand. Bottom Section – a large seated figure with two smaller figures below with the large hands of the larger figure touching the heads of the two smaller figures. This depicts either a Crucifixion scene or Odin with his two ravens!

2. South Side: Top Section – two spiral ornaments and a pair of arms with hands grasping the top of a semi-circular arch underneath which there is a small beast with its jaws open. Underneath this beast there is an arch above a draped figure of a saint with a book. Bottom Section – two beasts one above the other with interlace design.

3. West Side: Top Section – a pair of birds facing each other underneath which there is a depiction of the Virgin and Child, the Child is holding a book. Bottom Section – a headless seated figure holding a book underneath which there is a centaur (animal) with a small round object, possibly a head, slung over its right shoulder.

4. North Side: Top Section – two spiral ornaments and a pair of arms with hands grasping the top of a semi-circular arch underneath which there is a large figure. The figure with its distinctive head-dress and the book satchel is typical of depictions of priests following the Celtic form of Christianity. Bottom Section – a large draped figure holding a cup, probably a priest giving the Mass, with two smaller figures (one has the head of a beast) sitting below his feet. These smaller figures may depict Sigurd and the animal headed Regin eating rings taken from the dead dragon Fafnir.

This section of stonework from a cross-shaft is now dated as mid 9C. Its decoration involved the work of more than one sculptor. It is now argued that the cross-shaft has been wrongly reconstructed, the top section of the south side should have the bottom section of the north side beneath it. The reasoning is that these sections both have a raised band with round pellets forming a side border and in the top section there is a similar raised band with round pellets forming an arch. It is suspected that the missing middle section of this cross-shaft and the crosshead are still incorporated into the walls or the foundations of the nave of the church.

Internally, the arch for the blocked north doorway may be A-S or Saxo-Norman. It is located opposite the south door into the church, 61

Ins/154 Cms east of the west wall of the nave and 61 Ins/154 Cms up from the floor. The wooden panelling supporting the ends of the church pews hide the lower surviving stonework. The arch measures 40 Ins/101 Cms H, by 69 Ins/175 Cms W, by 13 Ins/33 Cms D. Externally, the arch and the supporting vertical stonework of this doorway can be identified. (Note: the vertical stonework displays little clear evidence of long and short quoining.)

POCKLINGTON
All Saints Church

SE 802490   Rating: ☆

In the centre of Pocklington, the churchyard is some 15 Yds/13 M north of "Market Place" (there is a street sign). It is situated on the east side of the road known as "Pavement" (there is a street sign).

The present structure was mostly built during the period 1200 to 1450. It was last renovated in 1890. Apparently under the present structure foundations of an A-S church survive, but where they are precisely has not been identified.

Internally, the present font includes a shallow, undecorated bowl that dates from the 11C. It is located in the centre of the baptistry underneath the tower.

Internally, also in the baptistry, there is the "Sotheby Cross" standing on a stepped plinth in all about 120 Ins/304 Cms H. It is located less than 180 Ins/457 Cms to the north of the font. The "cross" is really a cross-shaft. The cross dates from the 14C and commemorates the fact that St Paulinus preached here in 627.

SEWERBY
Sewerby Hall – Museum of East Yorkshire

TA 203690   Rating: ☆☆☆

In the centre of Sewerby, less than 60 Yds/54 M north of the junction of "Main Street" and "Church Lane" (there are street signs – the Church Lane signs are not at this end of the road), there is a gateway on the east side of Church Lane. On either side of this gateway, immediately behind the adjacent walling, there are large freestanding signs "Welcome to Sewerby Hall and Gardens". Pass through this gateway and into the car park. The Hall can be reached from various footpaths leading from the car park.

The easily identifiable ornate gateway to the gardens of the Hall, through which pedestrians can pass, is at the junction of Church Lane and

"Seagate" (there are street signs). This junction is opposite the junction of Church Lane and Main Street. There are no distinguishing signs on this gateway, or its attached buildings.

The Hall is about 200 Yds/255 M northeast of Church Lane and can be reached by a choice of obvious pathways through the gardens (there are a number of directional signs on the way).

As with all museums, the displays and the exhibits they contain may be changed, re-sited, removed from display and/or put in store, or loaned to other museums or suitable repositories. Before visiting the museum it is worth checking in advance whether the displays listed in the text below are still in place in the same location(s) set out in the text. Individual exhibits may have been rearranged in terms of their display, the order in which they are displayed and their relationship to other exhibits, some exhibits may have been removed from display. The text in the entry reflects the descriptions and/or accompanying notices to the exhibits at the time of visiting. These too may have been revised, amended, added to or removed.

The Hall was built between 1714 and 1720 and has 19C additions.

The Hall houses the Museum of East Yorkshire that has displays relating to local history. The items of Anglo-Saxon and Viking interest are all housed in the "Archaeology Gallery" on the ground floor. (The Archaeology Gallery is the second gallery from the west side of the shop on the ground floor to the left of the entrance to the Hall.) The Gallery contains the following displays and illustrated information notices of Anglo-Saxon and Viking interest.

1.   An A-S cemetery was found at Home Farm on the edge of Sewerby Gardens. The cemetery contained the graves of 59 people who came from farming families and who were buried between 400 and 700 AD.

The Gallery displays a reconstruction of "Grave 49". This grave contained the body of a wealthy A-S woman who died between age 17 and 25. The reconstruction includes the following original items found in the grave:

a. A bronze cruciform brooch dating from the early 6C.
b. A bronze cruciform brooch dating from the late 6C.
c. A bronze square-headed brooch dating from the late 6C.
d. A bronze annular brooch with an iron pin dating from sometime in the 6C.
e. A bronze annular brooch dating from sometime in the 6C.

On top of Grave 49 there was another burial of a female who was aged between 35 and 45. She was buried in an unusual position and because of this fact it is supposed she may either have been the wealthy woman's slave, or, perhaps, the "suspect" responsible for the wealthy woman's death.

2.   There is a notice about the "Danes Dyke" earthwork. This earthwork is 2½ miles long with an earth bank 18 feet (5.4 M) H in places and a ditch over 60 feet (18 M) W. The Dyke is thought to have originated in the Bronze Age. However it was strengthened and used as a temporary camp for the army of King "Eda" in the 7C. (It may have been used as an army camp but King "Eda" is probably meant to mean King "Ida" of Northumbria who lived during the 6C and so there must be some doubt about the accuracy of this information.) (See the entry for Flamborough, East Yorkshire.)

3.   There is a notice about "The Viking Legacy" identifying places in the locality with names of Viking origin.

4.   In a separate freestanding display stand with a descriptive information notice there are:

a.   A gold and garnet pendant dating from the 7C.

b.   A gilt bronze sword pommel dating from between 600 and 650 AD. It is decorated with interlace design and it has cloisonné cells for garnets and beaded wire decoration.

c.   An "S" shaped copper and alloy garnet brooch dating from sometime in the 6C/7C. It has traces of gold and silver in its decoration.

d.   A notice about A-S decorative metalwork.

SHIPTONTHORPE
All Saints Church

SE 852431   Rating:☆   Access is possible.

In the southern part of Shiptonthorpe, the church is easily located on the north side of the A1079 (T), "Town Street" (there is a street sign).

Externally, there is a section of stonework that may be A-S in origin. It is located incorporated into the south facing fabric of the south porch, immediately above the centre of the arch framing the porch entrance. It measures 15½ Ins/39 Cms H by 11 Ins/27 Cms W. It is decorated with the distinctive figure of a bishop who has his right hand raised in a blessing and in his left hand he holds a bishop's crosier. The head, body, legs and feet of the figure are stylistically A-S, the only doubt is the bishop's crosier. The representation of a crosier does not appear on any similar decorative stonework of the A-S period, perhaps it is of a later date but carved by those trained in the A-S style.

STAMFORD BRIDGE

In Stamford Bridge, on the south side of the modern bridge carrying the A166 over the River Derwent, take the minor road "Viking Road" (there are street signs) that heads in a southerly direction. Adjacent to the west side of Viking Road identify the small brick built building housing an electricity sub station. It is easily identified adjacent to the south side of the drive leading to the car park and picnic area (by the south bank of the River Derwent and immediately to the west of the modern bridge). Attached to the walling on the north side of this building there is a map and description of the battle that took place in the vicinity on the 25 September 1066.

STAMFORD BRIDGE
(1) Battle Monument
SE 713556   Rating: ☆☆

On the north side of the A166 in the centre of Stamford Bridge, and on the south bank of the River Derwent, locate a brick-built enclosure. It is situated on a small grassy mound by the south side of a drive leading to the "Corn Mill" (now riverside apartments and houses).

Inside the enclosure there is a solid rough stone pillar whose top is shaped something similar to a pyramid. The pillar measures 54 Ins/137 Cms H, between 19½ Ins/49 Cms and 12 Ins/30 Cms W, between 17 Ins/43 Cms and 11¼ D. It sits on a large, flat stone plinth that measures between 13½ Ins/34 Cms and 16½ Ins/41 Cms H, between 45 Ins/114 Cms and 43 Ins/109 Cms W, by 37 Ins/93 Cms D. Attached to the plinth there are two undated plaques commemorating the battle, one in English on the west side and one in Norwegian on the south side. Neither the stone pillar nor the stone plinth has any decoration on any of their sides.

Incorporated into the rear wall of the brick-built enclosure is the modern notice "1066 The Battle of Stamford Bridge King Harold of England defeated his brother Tostig and King Hardraada of Norway here on 25 September 1066".

STAMFORD BRIDGE
(2) Site of Old Bridge
SE 714557   Rating: ☆

In the centre of Stamford Bridge locate the modern weir about 180 Yds/164 M to the east of the modern bridge carrying the A166 over the

River Derwent – in the vicinity this part of the River Derwent is known as "The Shallows".

The old bridge on this site that featured in the initial stages of the battle of Stamford Bridge in 1066 was probably located just to the east of the weir, and to the north east of the monument identified in "1" above. At the time of the battle there was a stone ford and a bridge at the point where a Roman road had crossed the river. The river was much shallower, possibly just ankle deep, before the introduction of the weir. There is a public footpath running alongside the south bank of the River Derwent that passes the site of the old bridge and runs behind the boundaries (both walls and fences) of the gardens to the adjacent houses.

STAMFORD BRIDGE
(3) Battleflats
SE 714557/SE 721553   Rating: ☆

To reach the main area of the battle (known as "Battleflats") in Stamford Bridge, turn off the A166 and head in a south east direction along a minor road as indicated by the two signposts "High Catton 1½ and Low Catton 1½" and "Fangfoss". Less than 200 Yds/182 M along this road, at the junction where the Church of St John the Baptist is situated, take the minor road signposted "Full Sutton, Fangfoss" that heads in an easterly and then a south-easterly direction.

Under 200 Yds/182 M along this road, on the northeast side, there is a modern housing estate; the road leading off is called "Battleflats Way". The original Battleflats was a larger area than the confines of this road suggest! The area over which the main battle was fought was in the fields to the south-east of this modern housing estate.

On the 25th September 1066 King Harold II decisively defeated King Harald Hardrada of Norway and Earl Tostig at this battle site.

SUTTON-UPON-DERWENT
St Michael's Church
SE 705474   Rating: ☆☆☆   Access is possible.

At the north end of Sutton-upon-Derwent the church is easily located adjacent to the west side of the B1228, 350 Yds/320 M south of where the B1228 crosses the River Derwent.

On the site of an A-S church, the present structure dates mostly from the early 12C. Additions were made in the 13C, 14C and 15C. The church was restored in 1841.

Internally, there is a substantial section of stonework from an 11C A-D cross-shaft. It is located standing in the western end of the nave 55

Ins/139 Cms east of the tower. The section of stonework stands on a 5 Ins/12 Cms H floor-standing plinth which is attached to the western end of the base of the plinth surrounding the font. A concrete support for the section of stonework has been provided at the north and east sides and the eastern part of the south side to enable it to stand in an upright position. The section of stonework stands between 22½ Ins/57 Cms and 18 Ins/45 Cms H, by 16 Ins/40 Cms W, tapering 13½ Ins/34 Cms to 12½ Ins/31 Cms D. It is decorated with Jellinge design on all four sides with cable pattern along all four vertical edges. The decoration includes on the south side a bird; on the north side a beast and on the west side a man (the Jellinge decoration on east side does not include any humans, beasts or birds).

Externally, there is a much-weathered section of stonework that may be from an A-S cross-shaft. It is located 162 Ins/411 Cms east of the east wall of the south porch and 56 Ins/142 Cms south of the south wall of the south aisle. The section of cross-shaft measures 23 Ins/58 Cms H, by 12 Ins/30 Cms W, by 5½ Ins/13 Cms D. It is very weathered and there is no apparent decoration. However, on the east face there does appear to be some indistinct decoration and lettering (it appears to have been used as a memorial headstone).

North Yorkshire

In North Yorkshire 159 sites of Anglo-Saxon & Viking interest have been identified and entered in the text.

49 sites have been rated with one star ☆

This signifies that the material may be difficult to find or identify with confidence. These entries are:

Appleton-Le-Moors – "High Cross"
Appleton-Le-Moors – "Low Cross"
Aysgarth – St Andrew's Church
Birdforth – St Mary's Church
Buttercrambe – "Aldby Park"
Carlton-In-Cleveland – St Botolph's Church
Cawood – All Saints Church
Cawood – Castle
Conistone – St Mary's Church
Crayke – St Cuthbert's Church
Danby – St Hilda's Church
Duggleby- Howe
East Ayton – Church Of St John The Baptist
East Barnby – Wade's Stone
Ebberston – King Aldfrith's Shelter
Ebberston – St Mary The Virgin Church
Filey – St Oswald's Church
Giggleswick – St Alkelda's Church
Gilling East – Holy Cross Church
Goldsborough – Wade's Stone
Harrogate – Royal Pump Room Museum
Hawes – Dales Countryside Museum
Helmsley – All Saints Church
Hemingbrough – Church Of St Mary The Virgin
High Hawsker – Abbey or Boiling Well
Hinderwell – St Hilda's Well
Kellington – St Edmund's Church

Kirby Grindlaythe – St Andrew's Church
Kirkby Overblow – All Saints Church
Kirkbymoorside – All Saints Church
Lastingham – St Cedd's Well, St Chad's Well, St Ovin's Well
Levisham – St Mary's Church
Linton-In-Craven – St Michael and All Angels Church
Middlesbrough – Dorman Museum
Over Silton – St Mary's Church
Pickering – Castle
Ripon – Abbot Huby's Wall
Ripon – Prison and Police Museum
Scarborough – Castle and Roman Signal Station
Sherburn In Elmet – All Saints Church
Skelton – Old Church
Skipton – Craven Museum
Tadcaster – St Mary's Church
Upper Helmsley – St Peter's Church
Warthill – Moat
Weaverthorpe – St Andrew's Church
West Heslerton – Site of A-S Village
Wharram Percy – Deserted Medieval Village
Yarm – St Mary's Church

53 Sites Have Been Rated With Two Stars ✫✫

This signifies that the material can be found and identified but it is not particularly well looked after or a "good example". These entries are:

Amotherby – St Helen's Church
Bolton Percy – All Saints Church
Coverham – Holy Trinity Church
Cropton – St Gregory's Church
Drax – St Peter and St Paul's Church
Easby – St Agatha's Church
East Hauxwell (Hauxwell) – St Oswald's Church
Eryholme – St Mary's Church
Folkton – St John The Evangelist Church
Gilling West – St Agatha's Church
Great Ayton – All Saints Church
Hornby – St Mary's Church
Hunmanby – All Saints Church
Kildale – St Cuthbert's Church
Kirby Knowle – St Wilfred's Church
Kirby Misperton – St Laurence's Church
Kirkby (In Cleveland) – St Augustine's Church
Kirkby Malham – St Michael The Archangel Church
Kirkleatham – Old Hall Museum

Levisham – St John The Baptist's Church
Long Preston – St Mary's Church
Low Bentham – Church of St John The Baptist
Low Hawsker – Cross-shaft
Malton – Museum
Middleham – St Mary and St Alkelda's Church
Muston – All Saints Church
Newton-Under-Roseberry – St Oswald's Church
Normanby – St Andrew's Church
North Otterington – St Michael's Church
Nunnington – All Saints and St James's Church
Old Byland – All Saints Church
Ormesby – St Cuthbert's Church
Osmotherley – St Peter's Church
Oswaldkirk – St Oswald's Church
Patrick Brompton – St Patrick's Church
Pickhill – All Saints Church
Picton – St Hilary's Church
Ryther- All Saints Church
Saxton – All Saints Church
Scarborough – Millennium Experience
Spennithorne – St Michael and All Angels Church
Spofforth – All Saints Church
Stainton – St Peter and St Paul's Church
Staveley – All Saints Church
Stillingfleet – St Helen's Church
Thorganby – St Helen's Church
Thornton Watlass – St Mary's Church
Topcliffe – St Columba's Church
West Rounton – St Oswald's Church
West Tanfield – St Nicholas's Church
Whitby – Abbey
Whitby – St Mary's Church and Caedmon's Cross
[See also the entries in private ownership after the star rating index.]

31 sites have been rated with three stars ☆☆☆

This signifies that the material can easily be found and identified. These entries are:

Bedale – St Gregory's Church
Bulmer – St Martin's Church
Crambe – St Michael's Church
Crathorne – All Saints Church
Croft-On-Tees – St Peter's Church
Easington – All Saints Church
East Marton – St Peter's Church

Finghall – St Andrew's Church
Forcett – St Cuthbert's Church
Fylingdales Moor – Lilla Cross
Gargrave – St Andrew's Church
Great Edstone – St Michael's Church
Kildwick – St Andrew's Church
Kirby Hill – All Saints Church
Kirkby Wharfe – St John's Church
Leake – St Mary's Church
Masham – St Mary's Church
Melsonby – St James's Church
Middlesmoor – St Chad's Church
Monk Fryston – St Wilfred's Church
Murton – Yorkshire Museum of Farming
North Grimston – St Nicholas's Church
Pickering – Church of St Peter and St Paul
Skelton – All Saints Church
Stanwick St John – St John's Church
Terrington – All Saints Church
Thirsk – Museum
Wath – St Mary's Church
West Witton – St Bartholomew's Church
Whitby – Whitby Museum and Pannet Art Gallery
[See also the entries in private ownership after the star rating index.]

16 sites have been rated with four stars ✰✰✰✰

This signifies that the material can easily be found and identified and provides good examples. These entries are:

Bilton In Ainsty – St Helen's Church
Burnsall – St Wilfred's Church
Coxwold – Newburgh Priory
Cundall – St Mary and All Saints Church
Ellerburn – St Hilda's Church
Hutton-Le-Hole – Ryedale Folk Museum
Lastingham – St Mary's Church
Lythe – St Oswald's Church
Northallerton – All Saints Church
Sherburn – St Hilda's Church
Sinnington – All Saints Church
Skipwith – St Mary's Church
Stonegrave – Minster (Holy Trinity Church)
Wensley – Holy Trinity Church
Wharram-Le-Street – St Mary's Church
Whitby – Cholmley House Visitor Centre

10 sites have been rated with five stars ☆☆☆☆☆

This signifies that the material can easily be found and identified, providing excellent examples that are full of interest. These entries are:

Appleton-Le-Street – All Saints Church
Brompton-In-Allertonshire – St Thomas's Church
Hackness – St Peter's Church
Hovingham – All Saints Church
Kirk Hammerton – St John's Church
Kirkdale – St Gregory's Minster
Kirklevington – St Martin's Church
Middleton – St Andrew's Church
Ripon – Cathedral (Minster)
Thornton Steward – St Oswald's Church

ANGLO-SAXON STONEWORK IN PRIVATE OWNERSHIP (NO ACCESS)

SECTIONS OF STONEWORK FROM AN A-S CROSS-SHAFT   Rating: ☆☆☆

These three sections of stonework from a 9C A-S cross-shaft have been cemented together and cemented onto a 12-Ins/30 Cms H concrete support that stands on a plinth about 6 Ins/15 Cms H. Together these sections of stonework stand about 33 Ins/83 Cms H.

The lower section of stonework measures 12 Ins/30 Cms H, by 15½ Ins/39 Cms W, by 13½ Ins/34 Cms D. The middle section measures 10 Ins/25 Cms H, by 15 Ins/38 Cms W, by 13 Ins/33 Cms D. The upper section tapers 14½ Ins/36 Cms to 11½ Ins/29 Cms H, by 15 Ins/38 Cms W, by 12 Ins/30 Cms D.

The decoration on all four sides of each of these sections of stonework is in the "Breedon" style, with long-legged and long-necked animals as well as figures and plait work and scroll designs. Although weathered the decoration is easily identified. Most of this cross-shaft is now in St Mary and All Saints Church, Cundall (see the entry for Cundall, North Yorkshire).

SECTION OF STONEWORK FROM AN A-S CROSS-SHAFT   Rating: ☆☆

The section of stonework measures 9½ Ins/24 Cms H, by 18¼ Ins/46 Cms W, with 2 Ins/5 Cms of its depth exposed. It is clearly decorated on the west side but due to weathering the design is indistinct. Apparently the decoration is supposed to represent a crouching animal in relief. There does appear to be an animal clasping (?) a large bone that runs diagonally across the lower part of the section of cross-shaft. None of the other sides is decorated. The east side is now not possible to view.

AMOTHERBY
St Helen's Church
SE 751734   Rating: ✮✮✮

Turn off the B1257 as directed by the "Kirkbymoorside 10¼" direction sign and head north along the minor road (there is no street sign) that runs through Amotherby. Less than 170 Yds/155 M along this road, take another minor road which heads in an easterly direction (it is a no-through road). There is a "church" directional sign opposite the junction. About 70 Yds/64 M along this road the churchyard gates can be seen directly to the east (the road continues in a south-easterly direction).

On the site of an earlier A-S church, the present structure incorporates Norman and 16C fabric but mostly dates from the substantial rebuilding in 1871. During the reconstruction in 1871 several burials were discovered under the church, these included A-S burials.

Internally, on the ledges on the internal east and west walls of the south porch there are a variety of sections of stonework of different sizes, ages and condition.

Internally, on the ledge on the east side of the south porch there are:

1.   A section of stonework from a 9C A-D crosshead comprising three arms and the central section. It is located mostly outside the south porch with one of its arms protruding 3 Ins/7 Cms into the porch through the woodwork surrounding the doors into the porch. It is 35 Ins/88 Cms up from the ground. It has been cemented on top of a large medieval gravestone. The section of stonework measures 15 Ins/38 Cms H, by 19 Ins/48 Cms W, by 5 Ins/12 Cms D. On the west face it is decorated with large circles in the centre of each arm and the centre of the central section. The other three sides are too weathered and damaged for any decoration to be identifiable.

2.   A section of stonework from a 9C A-D wheel head cross comprising most of three arms and the central section. It is located 3½ Ins/8 Cms north of the woodwork surrounding the doors into the porch and 38 Ins/96 Cms up from the ground. It has been cemented on top of a large medieval gravestone. The section of stonework measures 8 Ins/20 Cms H, by 18 Ins/45 Cms W, by 8 Ins/20 Cms D. It is heavily weathered and apart from the central boss the only decoration that can be identified are incised lines outlining the shape of the arms on the west face. The other three sides are too weathered and damaged for any decoration to be identifiable.

3.   A section of stonework from a circular crosshead/grave slab that may be A-S. It is located 23 Ins/58 Cms north of the woodwork surrounding the doors into the porch and 38 Ins/96 Cms up from the

ground. It has been cemented on top of a large medieval tombstone. The section of stonework measures 11 Ins/27 Cms H, by 15½ Ins/39 Cms W, by 2½ Ins/6 Cms D. On the west face it is decorated with a circular foliated design. The other three sides are too weathered and damaged for any decoration to be identifiable.

4.   A section of stonework from a circular crosshead/grave slab that may be A-S. It is located 40 Ins/101 Cms north of the woodwork surrounding the doors into the porch and is 38 Ins/96 Cms up from the ground. It has been cemented on top of a large medieval tombstone. The section of stonework measures 7 Ins/17 Cms H, by 9 Ins/22 Cms W, by 3½ Ins/8 Cms D. On the west face it is decorated with a circular foliated design. The other three sides are too weathered and damaged for any decoration to be identifiable.

Internally, on the ledge on the west side of the south porch there are:

5.   A section of stonework from a memorial cross that could possibly be A-S. It is located 5 Ins/12 Cms north of the woodwork surrounding the south door into the porch and 42 Ins/106 Cms up from the ground. It has been cemented onto a later medieval tomb slab. The section of stonework measures 10 Ins/25 Cms H, by 10 Ins/25 Cms W, by 3½ Ins/8 Cms D. The east face is decorated with a circular design. The other three sides are too weathered and damaged for any decoration to be identifiable.

6.   A damaged section of stonework from a memorial slab that could possibly be A-S. It is located 19½ Ins/49 Cms north of the woodwork surrounding the south door into the porch and 44 Ins/111 Cms up from the ground. It has been cemented onto a later medieval grave slab. The section of stonework measures 12 Ins/30 Cms H, by 13 Ins/33 Cms W, by 7 Ins/17 Cms D. The east face is decorated with a foliated design. The other three sides are too weathered and damaged for any decoration to be identifiable.

7.   A section of stonework from a grave slab that could possibly be A-S. It is located 46 Ins/116 Cms north of the woodwork surrounding the south door into the porch and 16½ Ins/41 Cms up from the ground. It has been cemented onto the ledge on this side of the porch. The section of stonework measures from 12 to 18 Ins/30 to 45 Cms H, by 21½ Ins/54 Cms W, by 6 Ins/15 Cms D. The east face is clearly decorated with a large cross. The other three sides are too weathered and damaged for any decoration to be identifiable. A later section of medieval structural stonework has been cemented on top of this section of stonework from a grave slab.

8.   A section of stonework from a grave slab that could possibly be A-S. During the reconstruction of the church in 1871 this slab was found

under the church covering the burial of an A-S woman. It is located mostly inside the south porch with a 15 Ins/38 Cms section protruding through the woodwork surrounding the doors into the porch. It is 15½ Ins/39 Cms up from the ground. It has been cemented onto the ledge on the west side of the porch. The section of stonework measures 23 Ins/58 Cms to 29½ Ins/74 Cms H (W), by 64 Ins/162 Cms W, by 6 Ins/15 Cms to 9 Ins/22 Cms D (H). The east face has a carving of human face and the upper part of the body although this is very weathered and damaged. There is some suggestion of decoration on the top and north sides; the south side is too weathered and damaged for any decoration to be identifiable.

Externally, there is a round, undecorated bowl of a font that could possibly be A-S. It is located 21½ Ins/54 Cms south of the south wall of the nave and 21½ Ins/54 Cms west of the west wall of the south porch. The font has been cemented onto some 14 Ins/35 Cms H stonework of a more recent date. The font has a diameter of 29 Ins/73 Cms and has a depth of 8 Ins/20 Cms.

APPLETON-LE-MOORS
(1) "Low Cross"
SE 734883   Rating: ☆

The section of stonework from a cross-shaft known as "Low Cross" is located just to the north of Appleton-Le-Moors amidst the grass verge 176 Ins/447 Cms east of the east side of the "main" road running north/south through the village. It stands on a low, stone platform mostly covered by vegetation. It is located about 15 Yds/13 M north of the road junction where a road heads off in an easterly direction towards Cropton and Rosedale. (On the grass verge on the west side of the road, just south of this road junction, there is a directional sign indicating Cropton and Rosedale.)

The section of stonework measures 48 Ins/121 Cms H, by 30 Ins/76 Cms W, tapering 12 Ins/30 Cms to 7 Ins/17 Cms D. It is very weathered and no decoration survives on any of the sides. It seems there was provision for a rectangular plaque on the south side of the stonework, but this plaque is now missing. Low Cross has a distinctive hole through its north and south sides.

Additionally, there are three smaller sections of stonework that may have been broken off from Low Cross. These stand on the same low, stone platform as Low Cross. They are all very weathered with no decoration surviving on any of their sides. The first is located 2 Ins/5 Cms southwest of the southwest corner of Low Cross. This section of stonework measures

8½ Ins/21 Cms H, by 19 Ins/48 Cms W, and between 8 Ins/20 Cms and 18 Ins/45 Cms D. The second is located 3 Ins/7 Cms northwest of the northwest corner of Low Cross. This section of stonework measures 8 Ins/20 Cms H, by 9½ Ins/24 Cms W, by 12½ Ins/31 Cms D. The third is located partially abutting the north side of Low Cross. This section of stonework measures 15 Ins/38 Cms H, by 20 Ins/50 Cms W, by 12½ Ins/31 Cms D.

APPLETON-LE-MOORS
(2) "High Cross"
SE 733885   Rating: ✰

The section of stonework from a cross-shaft known as "High Cross" is located on the grass verge, 84 Ins/213 Cms west of the west side of the "main" road running north/south through the village, and about 350 Yds/320 M north of Low Cross. The section of stonework has been slotted onto a base that measures 28 Ins/71 Cms H, by 35 Ins/88 Cms W, by 25½ Ins/64 Cms D. This base stands on a low, stone platform. The section of stonework measures 38½ Ins/97 Cms H (protruding from the base), by 12½ Ins/31 Cms W, by 10 Ins/25 Cms D. The section of cross-shaft leans in a southerly direction. Due to weathering there is no decoration surviving on any of the sides.

Both "High" and "Low" Crosses are marked on the Ordnance Survey maps and are boundary markers probably connected with Lastingham monastery that lasted from the 7C to the 9C.

APPLETON-LE-STREET
All Saints Church
SE 734735   Rating: ✰✰✰✰✰

Whilst the church is relatively easy to identify in the western part of the village, a route to the church has now been signposted. Immediately behind a stone wall running parallel to the north side of the B1257 there is a freestanding wooden directional sign "All Saints Church". Turn south off the B1257 as directed and proceed along a minor, un-signposted, road* (there is no street sign) for about 59 Yds/53 M until reaching another freestanding wooden directional sign. This sign includes the direction "All Saints Church". To reach the church, as directed, turn off this minor road and take another minor road that leads uphill in a westerly direction. After about 101 Yds/92 M there is another freestanding wooden directional sign "Church Car Park". This sign directs you up a track which heads in a northwest direction towards the church. After about 18 Yds/16 M this track reaches the churchyard gate (the church is now in view).

The church tower can be seen from the B1257 and there is a footpath leading diagonally uphill from the south side of the B1257 towards the church. Using this footpath the churchyard gates are reached after about 47 Yds/42 M. There is no signpost or notice by this footpath and its location is not obvious. It is about 87 Yds/79 M to the west of the minor road off the B1257 referred to in the text above at *.

The church dates from the early 11C. Alterations and additions were undertaken in the 12C, 13C and 14C.

Internally, the east and west walls of the nave, and the eastern part of the north wall of the nave above the later inserted aisles retain A-S material but this is obscured by plaster on both sides of the wall. The foundations of the re-built chancel are also A-S.

Internally, the plain, round font may be A-S. It is located on a low, stepped plinth in the northwest corner of the tower. The font has a diameter of 24 Ins/60 Cms and a height also of 24 Ins/60 Cms.

APPLETON-LE-STREET
All Saints Church. Typical Anglo-Saxon tower.

The tower is a particularly good example of an A-S tower and it now seems that it may have been attached to an earlier nave now in part surviving rather than it being the sole survivor from a complete earlier structure. Its features are best appreciated externally. The tower is typically A-S in its construction with roughly dressed stonework, with side alternate quoining and two projecting string courses dividing the tower into three stages. The original entrance to the tower at ground level on the west face is now blocked by a later inserted window. Also at ground level a former doorway on the south face is now also blocked. There are signs of blocked windows in the north, west and south faces at first floor level (still below the first string course).

Double belfry windows in both the second and third stages of the tower

Projecting string courses separating each of the three stages of the tower

Roughly dressed stonework used throughout the tower

Blocked window

Side Alternate Quoining

Blocked west entrance with later inserted window

Blocked south doorway

However, the most impressive features of the tower are the four double belfry windows on each of the four faces of the tower in the second and third stages. The lower stages of the tower date from the early 11C whilst the third stage, with its smaller belfry windows, appears to date from around the mid 11C.

Externally, the northwest and southwest quoins of the A-S nave are preserved for about 12 Ins/30 Cms on either side of the tower. These quoins indicate the size of the original A-S nave.

AYSGARTH
St Andrew's Church

SE 012885   Rating: ☆

About 880 Yds/804 M east of Aysgarth take the minor road off the A684 and head in a northerly direction down towards Aysgarth Falls. Opposite the appropriate junction there is a signpost, which includes the direction "Aysgarth Falls ¼". About 200 Yds/182 M along this road the entrance to the large churchyard is located on the east side of the road.

Possibly on the site of an A-S church, the present structure dates mainly from the restoration in 1866 although some material from the 14C does survive.

Internally, there used to be a virtually complete 10C decorated A-S crosshead. It was located on a table close to the southern face of the fourth pillar on the south side of the nave. Unfortunately this crosshead was stolen in July 1996 and has not been recovered.

BEDALE
St Gregory's Church

SE 265884   Rating: ☆☆☆

The church is easily located on the northern fringes of Bedale adjacent to the east side of the A684.

On the site of a 9C A-S church most of the present fabric dates from the 13C and 14C.

Internally, A-S fabric is now hardly discernible, but some exists at the western corners of the nave. The whitewashing on the north and south walls of the nave and walls of the chancel prevents other A-S material being identified, but it seems certain that there is some there.

Internally, the original A-S western wall of the nave can be identified above the eastern arch into the tower and below the angled roofline (now incorporated into an enlarged west wall) extending towards the north and south walls of the nave.

Internally, there is a section of stonework from a 10C A-S cross-shaft. It is located standing on some small fragments of stonework lying on the floor level with the tower not the nave (there is a step down to the floor of the nave), and 1½ Ins/3 Cms north of the north-east angle of the pillar supporting the arch on the south side of the tower. (Close to the head of the effigy of the recumbent knight – probably Thomas de Sheffield.) The section of stonework measures 24 Ins/60 Cms H, by 15 Ins/38 Cms W, by 11 Ins/27 Cms D. It is almost cylindrical in shape and decorated with interlace design on all four sides.

Internally, there is a section of stonework from an early 10C hogback grave cover; this is the "Weland Carving". It is located sitting on top of a floor-standing 17 Ins/43 Cms H wooden table. Both section of stonework and the table are situated standing beneath the west arm of the westernmost arch on the north side of the nave and 5 Ins/12 Cms east of the west wall of the nave. There is a notice "Weland Carving" attached to the nave walling behind the section of stonework from this hogback grave cover. The section of stonework measures 14 Ins/35 Cms H, by 22 Ins/55 Cms W, by 14 Ins/35 Cms D. Although damaged, the south-east side is decorated with the depiction of Weland the Smith on his flying machine. The fan-shaped tail and one wing of the machine, as well as the feet, legs, body and head of Weland can be identified. On the end of the section of stonework, the side facing north-east, there is what looks like a Madonna and Child nativity scene (three heads can be identified). On the north-west side there is some suggestion of a tegulated roof below which there is clearly knot work decoration. The fourth side is damaged without any decoration as it has been broken off from the rest of the hogback grave cover (now missing).

BILTON IN AINSTY
St Helen's Church

SE 476504   Rating: ★★★★   Access is possible

The churchyard is situated adjacent to the southeast corner of the crossroads involving the B1224 and the minor road that leads southwards to the main part of Bilton.

Most of the structure of the present church dates from the reconstruction in 1869 although it does incorporate some material from its A-S predecessor, the mid 12C and early 15C.

Internally, there are three separate floor-standing sizeable sections of stonework from A-S cross-shafts. These are located at the east end of the south aisle, between 21 Ins/53 Cms and 23 Ins/58 Cms from the south wall of the chancel. There are descriptive notices for each section of stonework.

1. The easternmost section of stonework from a cross-shaft. It measures 27 Ins/68 Cms H, tapering from 11 Ins/27 Cms to 6 Ins/15 Cms W, by 6 Ins/15 Cms D. This section of stonework dates from 800. On its south face the decoration on the top half is knot work design and on the bottom half the decoration depicts the Biblical scene of Abraham preparing to sacrifice Isaac. On the west edge it depicts what appears to be Moses striking the rock. The north face and east side are decorated with interlace and knot work design.

2. The middle section of stonework from a cross-shaft. It measures 19 Ins/48 Cms H, by 16 Ins/40 Cms W, by 6 Ins/15 Cms D. This section of stonework is probably part of the base from a cross-shaft. It dates from around the late 10C to early 11C. The top, chamfered edge, of this section of cross-shaft dates from a later time when it was reused during rebuilding/restoration. The decoration on the south face depicts the Biblical scene of three figures that represent three children in the fiery furnace. The north face is decorated with knot work design and the west and east sides are undecorated.

BILTON IN AINSTY: St Helen's Church. An Anglo-Saxon wheel head crosshead decorated with the figure of the Holy Rood on each arm.

3. The westernmost section of stonework from a cross-shaft. It measures 29 Ins/73 Cms H, by 21 Ins/53 Cms W, by 11 Ins/27 Cms D. This section of cross-shaft is part of the base of an exceptionally large A-D cross-shaft. It too dates from the late 10C to early 11C. It is decorated on all four sides with coarse interlace design. It is much weathered.

There is a piece of stonework incised with an A-S Mass Dial that can be viewed from the south aisle. It is located on the south face of the square piece of chancel walling situated 15 Ins/38 Cms north-west of westernmost section of cross-shaft "3" above. The hole for the missing gnomon is 46 Ins/116 Cms up from the floor. The distinctive lines radiating outwards from the gnomon hole can be identified.

Internally, there is a decorated A-S wheel head cross, complete in its original form. It is attached to a plinth protruding from the west wall of the nave, beneath the west window surround. There is a descriptive notice underneath. The wheel head measures 18 Ins/45 Cms in diameter. The east face of the wheel head cross is decorated with the figure of the Holy Rood on each arm. The ends of each arm are decorated with interlace design. The west face is undecorated. (This wheel head cross was not originally attached to any of the cross-shafts in the south chapel.)

Internally, there is an undecorated, round, A-S font standing on a plinth, supported by a later pillar of stonework. It is located 146 Ins/370 Cms east of the west wall of the nave.

Internally, there is an A-S window. It is the only window in the west wall of the south aisle. It was reconstructed in the 19C, and is better preserved externally in its original state.

Externally, on the west wall of the north aisle, the top of an A-S window and some associated material can be detected incorporated into the fabric of the wall. It is about 129 Ins/327 Cms up from the ground, below a number of well-worn heraldic shields, and 88 Ins/223 Cms from the north end of the wall.

Externally, there is a small, round A-S window in the centre of the west wall of the nave. It is about 60 Ins/152 Cms above the larger, later lower window.

BIRDFORTH
St Mary's Church

SE 486757   Rating: ☆   Access is possible.

The small church is under 40 Yds/36 M from the east side of the A19. Turn east off the A19 as directed by the "Birdforth Only" sign, and, in fewer than 15 Yds/13 M, turn south and proceed along the old road running parallel to the A19. The churchyard entrance is located on the east side of this road after less than 40 Yds/36 M.

Most of the present structure of the church dates from the restoration in 1897, but it does incorporate earlier 16C, 12C and possibly A-S material.

Internally, the undecorated font could be A-S. It is located 48 Ins/122 Cms from the west end of the nave, on a stepped plinth.

Externally, incorporated into the fabric of the south wall of the nave, there is the distinctive outline of a narrow A-S window, now blocked. It is located 4 Yds/3 M east of the south door, between the two windows on the south side of the nave, and 72 Ins/182 Cms up from the ground.

BOLTON PERCY
All Saints Church

SE 532413   Rating: ★★

The church is easily located on the west side of Bolton Percy, on the west side of the more westerly minor road that runs north/south through the village (there is no street sign).

The present church on this site dates from the early 15C. This replaced the earlier A-S church with Norman additions that stood on this site.

Internally, sitting on the floor in the north-west corner of the church there are:

1.   A section of stonework on which there is an Anglo-Saxon Mass Dial. It is located towards the west end of the nave. It is adjacent to the north end of the most easterly pew (the third one) east of the organ, and adjacent to the east end of the wooden glass-topped display stand. In the centre of the top side of this section of stonework the radiating lines and the centre of this Mass Dial can easily be identified despite weathering and damage to the stonework. The Mass Dial has a 7 Ins/17 Cms diameter. There is no other decoration on any of the other sides of this section of stonework.

Affixed to the top of this section of stonework, to the north of the Mass Dial, there is a notice: "This later and more accurate Anglo-Saxon Mass Dial showing the service hours was recovered from the churchyard's wall 1936. It was part of the earlier building on this site." The section of stonework on which the Mass Dial is incised measures 5½ Ins/13 Cms H, by 21 Ins/53 Cms W, between 9 Ins/22 Cms and 10 Ins/25 Cms D.

2.   A section of stonework on which there is an Anglo-Saxon Mass Dial. It is located in the north aisle. It is adjacent to the north side of the wooden glass-topped display stand and adjacent to the eastern end of the wooden surround to the westernmost pillar in the north aisle. Towards the west end of the top side of this section of stonework the radiating lines and the centre of this Mass Dial can be identified despite weathering and damage to the stonework (they are not so clearly defined as "1" above). The Mass Dial has a 7 Ins/17 Cms diameter. There is no other decoration on any of the other sides.

Affixed to the top of this section of stonework, to the west of the Mass Dial, there is a notice: "This Mass Dial probably Anglo-Saxon and belonging to the earliest building on this site was recovered from the churchyard wall 1936." The section of stonework on which the Mass Dial is incised measures 6½ Ins/16 Cms H, between 16 Ins/40 Cms and 16¾ Ins/42 Cms W, by 11 Ins/27 Cms D.

Note: none of the other sections of stonework displayed in the vicinity, whether displayed in the glass-topped cabinets or not, appear to be A-S in origin.

Externally, there is a section of stonework from what is described as an A-S cross – it is a finial. It is located sitting on top of a square plinth about 15 Ins/37 Cms H and 15 Ins/37 Cms W and D that stands on top of the apex of the roof at the east end of the chancel. The cross measures about 16 Ins/40 Cms H, by 23 Ins/58 Cms W, by 6 Ins/15 Cms D. A Crucifixion scene can be identified on the east side and on the west side there is the depiction of the Virgin and Child (this is difficult to view from ground level). There is no other decoration on any of the other sides. There is both weathering and damage to the cross.

BROMPTON-IN-ALLERTONSHIRE
St Thomas's Church

SE 373963   Rating: ✩✩✩✩✩   Access is possible.

In the north-western part of Brompton, the church is situated adjacent to a small green on the west side of "Northallerton Road" (there are street signs). It is easily located.

A church probably existed on this site in the 7C but the present structure dates from the 12C and 14C and the restorations in the 17C and in 1867.

Internally, there are three excellent, complete examples of A-D hogback grave covers dating from the 10C. These are located on the floor at the east end of the nave, 19 Ins/48 Cms west of the west wall of the chancel and just to the north of the chancel arch. The two westernmost hogbacks measure 16 Ins/40 Cms H, by 8 Ins/20 Cms W, by 44 Ins/111 Cms W L. The easternmost hogback measures 21 Ins/53 Cms H, by 8 Ins/20 Cms W, by 44 Ins/111 Cms L. All three are decorated with distinctive bears at each end. All three are also decorated with different knot work, interlace and other abstract designs.

Internally there are sections of stonework from two other hogback grave covers. These are located on the floor 6 Ins/15 Cms south of the north wall of the north aisle and between 4 Ins/10 Cms and 65 Ins/165 Cms west of the east end of the north aisle. The section of stonework closer to the east end measures 17 Ins/43 Cms H, by 7 Ins/17 Cms W, by 23 Ins/58 Cms L. Although the end of this section of stonework is broken the surviving stonework includes the clear decoration of the paws of the bear and knot work and other designs. The section of stonework farther away from the east end measures 17 Ins/43 Cms H, by 8 Ins/20 Cms W, by 36 Ins/91 Cms L. This end section of stonework is very weathered but decoration comprising large knot work design can be identified.

Internally, there is a section of stonework from a late 10C A-S cross-shaft and its complete crosshead. They are located next to the three complete A-D hogback grave covers, 5 Ins/12 Cms west of the north end of the chancel arch. In total they stand 43 Ins/109 Cms H. The crosshead measures 18 Ins/45 Cms W, by 6 Ins/15 Cms D, and the section of stonework from the cross-shaft measures 11½ Ins/29 Cms W, by 9 Ins/22 Cms D. Both the crosshead and the section of stonework from the cross-shaft are decorated with knot work design.

Internally, there is another well-preserved section of stonework from an A-S cross-shaft with most of its crosshead. They are located on the south side of the chancel, in a blocked alcove (formerly the priests' door). In total they stand some 61 Ins/154 Cms H. The crosshead measures 15 Ins/38 Cms W, by 5 Ins/12 Cms D. The section of stonework from the cross-shaft measures 12 Ins/30 Cms W, by 9 Ins/22 Cms D. The crosshead is decorated with knot work design. The section of stonework from the cross-shaft is decorated with both knot work and abstract designs.

Internally, there are three sections of stonework from 10C A-S crossheads and two 14C grave slabs. These are located in the western part of the nave, to the north of the south door, standing on the plinth that surrounds the font.

1. Part of a wheel head cross comprising part of the central section and two arms, and the connecting wheel between these two arms. It is located standing by the northwest corner of the plinth. It measures 11 Ins/27 Cms H, by 12 Ins/30 Cms W, by 5 Ins/12 Cms D. It is decorated with knot work design on both the faces and ends of the arms.

2. Part of another wheel head cross comprising the central section, two arms and part of a broken third arm, and the connecting wheel between the two complete arms. It is located standing close to the northwest corner of the plinth, immediately behind (i.e. south-east of) "1" above, between "1" and the base of the font. It measures 13 Ins/33 Cms H, by 15 Ins/38 Cms W, by 5 Ins/12 Cms D. It is decorated with knot work design on both the faces and ends of the arms (clearer on the faces than the ends).

3. Most of a wheel head cross comprising part of the central section, three arms and the upper connecting wheels between these arms. It is located standing in the centre of the eastern part of the plinth. It measures 11 Ins/27 Cms H, by 14 Ins/35 Cms W, by 6 Ins/15 Cms D. It is weathered but no decoration can be identified apart from knot work decoration on the north-west face.

Internally, the appropriately described 9C "Cock Shaft" section of stonework from a cross-shaft is located freestanding, 4 Ins/10 Cms to the west of the westernmost pillar on the north side of the nave. The Cock Shaft stands some 30 Ins/76 Cms H, by 10 Ins/25 Cms W, by 8 Ins/20

Cms D. It is decorated with both human, animal and interlace designs. The south face is divided into three panels. The top two panels are each decorated with a bird (hence the "Cock Shaft") and the lowest panel is decorated with zoomorphic figures in combat that have cone-like heads and legs like a horse. The eastern face is decorated with a figure, possibly St John, holding a book. The north face is decorated with the figure of a praying angel and the western face is decorated with interlace design. (The decoration of the south and west faces are the best preserved.)

Externally, there are three sections of A-S stonework incorporated into the fabric of the church. These are:

4.   A section of stonework decorated with interlace pattern. It has been incorporated into the east wall of the chancel. It is located 28 Ins/71 Cms to the south of the east window, 132 Ins/335 Cms up from the ground. This section of stonework measures some 7 Ins/17 Cms H by 13 Ins/33 Cms W.

5.   A section of stonework decorated with interlace pattern. It has been incorporated into the east wall of the chancel. It is located 8 Ins/20 Cms north of the east window some 109 Ins/276 Cms up from the ground. This section of stonework measures 8 Ins/20 Cms H by 15 Ins/38 Cms W.

6.   A section of stonework decorated with a diagonally linked circles design. It has been incorporated into the external fabric of the south wall of the chancel. It is located 26 Ins/66 Cms east of the top of the small, narrow window at the west end of the chancel (15 Ins/38 Cms west of the drainpipe). This section of stonework measures 7 Ins/17 Cms H by 10 Ins/25 Cms W.

From Brompton additional sections of A-S/A-D stonework are now housed in the "Monks Dormitory" in Durham Cathedral. These are:

7.   Two crossheads.

8.   Part of an 11C A-S crosshead decorated with the figure of Christ crucified.

9.   Part of a late crosshead.

10.   Part of a late 10C/early 11C A-D cross-shaft decorated with figures of a stag and a backward looking beast (on the back a crude figure was added at a later date).

11.   Part of a 10C cross-shaft decorated with a figure of a saint under an arch holding a scroll. It may be a copy of an earlier cross at Brompton.

12.   Six hogback grave covers with bear figures at each end.

[Originally eleven late 10C A-D hogback grave covers, either in whole or in part, were found in the church; six are now in the

Monks' Dormitory in Durham Cathedral (see the entry for the Monks' Dormitory, Durham Cathedral, in the Durham and Northumberland gazetteer) and five are in this church. Brompton seems to have been a manufacturing centre for this type of memorial.]

BULMER
St Martin's Church

SE 699676   Rating: ✩✩✩

Near the centre of Bulmer, the church is adjacent to the south side of the minor road running through the village.

A good proportion of the nave walls date from the 11C but most of the church dates from the 12C, 14C and 15C and the restoration in 1898.

BULMER: St Martin's Church. Anglo-Saxon window, herring-bone masonry and blocked doorway.

Anglo-Saxon tall, narrow, round headed window

Anglo-Saxon blocked doorway

Round headed arch with plain typaneum and lintel below

Herring-bone masonry

Herring-bone masonry

Side
Alternate
Side
Alternate

Side

Alternate

Side

Alternate

Door jambs laid in side alternate fashion

Internally, incorporated into the fabric of the north wall of the nave, there is:

1.   Most of an A-S doorway apart from the top rounded arch. It is now blocked. It is located almost diagonally opposite (to the west) of the present south door incorporated into the north wall of the nave. Its A-S origin is more clearly evident externally where the top rounded arch also survives.

2.   The complete head of an A-S wheel head cross. It is located 10½ Ins/26 Cms above the blocked A-S north doorway "1" above. It sits on top of a modern support protruding from the north wall. The wheel head cross measures 15½ Ins/39 Cms H, by 18 Ins/45 Cms W, by 8 Ins/20 Cms D. Although very weathered the west and east facing edges of the cross clearly have some distinctive decoration but it is difficult to identify the design. The south face is very weathered and consequently it does not appear to have any surviving decoration: the north face is in a similar condition.

3.   A tall, narrow, round-headed A-S window. It is located incorporated into the north wall of the nave 87 Ins/220 Cms east of the blocked A-S north doorway "1" above. This can also be identified externally.

Internally, there are single-splayed A-S windows incorporated into the fabric of the south wall of the nave 15 Ins/38 Cms west of the south door and 46 Ins//116 Cms east of the south door. These can also be identified externally.

Externally, very distinctive A-S herring-bone masonry can be seen in the south wall of the nave and in the north wall of the nave adjacent to the blocked north doorway.

Externally, the blocked A-S north doorway comprises a round-headed arch, with a plain, semi-circular typaneum, with a flat lintel underneath supported by jambs laid in side alternate fashion.

BURNSALL
St Wilfred's Church

SE 032615   Rating: ★★★★

In the northern part of Burnsall the church is easily located on the north-eastern side of the B6160.

There is a tradition that St Wilfred (634-709) preached hereabouts (there is a rock on the edge of the River Wharfe still known as "St Wilfred's Pulpit") and that a wooden church was built in the vicinity before 700. This wooden church may have been replaced by a stone church around 970. The present church contains fabric from the rebuilding in 1150 and 1520. It was restored in 1858.

Internally, there is what could possibly be an A-D font. It is located at the western end of the nave, standing on an octagonal plinth in the centre of the floor under the eastern arch of the tower. The font has a square base plinth and the tub changes from square to round in shape. The font measures 26½ Ins/67 Cms square. There are conflicting arguments about the date of the font. Some say it may date from the time of St Wilfred, others that it dates from the 12C. The date of 1150 may be more accurate. It is decorated with animals, roll mouldings and chevron design that indicate a later rather than earlier date.

Internally, there is a section of stonework from what could be an A-S window head. It is located at the western end of the nave, sitting on the floor underneath the centre of the tower, 71 Ins/180 Cms west of the octagonal plinth at the base of the font. (There are two other unrelated sections of stonework nearby.) The window head measures 8 Ins/20 Cms H (D), by 21½ Ins/54 Cms W, by 12 Ins/30 Cms D (H).

Internally, there is an exhibition entitled "Vikings in Burnsall" situated in the western end of the south aisle, by the adjacent south and west walls of the south aisle. The exhibition comprises illustrated notices and sections of A-S/A-D stonework. These are:

1.	A section of stonework from an A-S crosshead with part of its attached cross-shaft and two sections of stonework from A-S cross-shafts. Alternately separating the three original sections of stonework, there are two modern reproductions of sections of cross-shafts. They are located 59 Ins/149 Cms west of the south door into the church and affixed to the south wall of the south aisle. In total they stand 69 Ins/175 Cms H. The section of stonework from a crosshead with part of its attached cross-shaft sits on a wall bracket. The separate sections of original and reproduction stonework from the cross-shaft stand together on a floor standing modern plinth that measures 6¼ Ins/15 Cms H, by 13¾ Ins/34 Cms W, by 8¾ Ins/22 Cms D.

The top part of this display comprises of a section of stonework with a crosshead (only part of the top arm is missing) and part of its attached cross-shaft. Together they measure 22½ Ins/57 Cms H. They bear more traces of the original A-S red lead paint than any other similar stonework in Yorkshire.

The crosshead measures 10½ Ins/26 Cms H, by 13¼ Ins/33 Cms W, by 8 Ins/20 Cms D. Apart from on the north and south faces the large protruding central bosses, and a line running parallel to the shape of the crosshead, there is no decoration on any of the sides due to weathering and damage.

The cross-shaft measures 12½ Ins/31 Cms H, tapering 7½ Ins/19 Cms to 6½ Ins/16 Cms W, tapering 5½ Ins/13 Cms to 4¾ Ins/12 Cms D. It is decorated on all four sides with knot work design.

Beneath this crosshead and part of the attached cross-shaft there is a modern reproduction piece of a cross-shaft.

Beneath this modern reproduction piece there is a section of stonework from a cross-shaft. This section of stonework measures 8¾ Ins/22 Cms H, by 10½ Ins/26 Cms W, by 6½ Ins/16 Cms D. It is decorated on all four sides with knot work design.

Beneath this section of stonework from a cross-shaft there is a modern reproduction piece of a cross-shaft.

Beneath this modern reproduction piece there is another section of stonework from a cross-shaft. This section of stonework measures 8¼ Ins/20 Cms H, by 11 Ins/27 Cms W, by 7½ Ins/19 Cms D. It is decorated with knot work design on the north and south sides only; the two other sides are too weathered and damaged for any decoration to survive.

[Note: The lower two original sections of stonework in this display may be from the same cross-shaft but it is not certain. They date from the late 9C or early 10C.]

2.   A section of stonework from an A-N hogback grave cover. It is located 78½ Ins/199 Cms east of the west wall of the south aisle and 2½ Ins/6 Cms north of the south wall of the south aisle. It sits on a floor standing modern plinth that measures 6 Ins/15 Cms H, by 14 Ins/35 Cms W, by 31½ Ins/80 Cms L. The section of stonework measures 10½ Ins/26 Cms to 13½ Ins/34 Cms H, tapering 10¾ Ins/27 Cms to 9¼ Ins/23 Cms W, by 26½ Ins/67 Cms L. Although on the top side there is an indication of the traditional bear associated with such grave covers, there is no distinctive decoration on any of the sides due to weathering and damage. It dates from the 10C.

3.   Two sections of stonework from two A-S crossheads and a section of stonework from an A-N cross-shaft. Separating the two sections of stonework from the two crossheads from the section of stonework from a cross-shaft is a modern reproduction of a section of the cross-shaft. They are located affixed to the south wall of the south aisle 1¾ Ins/4 Cms east of the west wall of the south aisle. In total they stand 83 Ins/210 Cms H. The two sections of stonework from crossheads sit on separate wall brackets. The sections of original and reproduction stonework from a cross-shaft stand together on a floor standing modern plinth that measures 6 Ins/15 Cms H, by 19½ Ins/49 Cms W, by 11½ Ins/29 Cms D.

The large, early 10C A-S crosshead, with only its lower arm missing, measures 18 Ins/45 Cms H, by 24½ Ins/62 Cms W, by 6½ Ins/16 Cms D. Apart from the large protruding central bosses on the north and south faces, and the small cross in the centre of the north face, there is no decoration on any of the sides due to weathering and damage.

Beneath this crosshead there is a section of stonework from an end of an arm from a different crosshead. This section of stonework measures 6½ Ins/16 Cms H, by 13 Ins/33 Cms W, by 4 Ins/10 Cms D. On both the north and south faces there is line decoration outlining the shape of the arm.

Beneath this crosshead there is a modern reproduction piece of a cross-shaft.

Beneath this modern reproduction piece there is a section of stonework from a cross-shaft. This section of stonework measures between 41¾ Ins/106 Cms and 43½ Ins/110 Cms H, tapering 15 Ins/38 to 14 Ins/35 Cms W, tapering 9 Ins/22 Cms to 5 Ins/12 Cms D. It is decorated with Ringerike design on the north and south faces and Ringerike can just about be identified on the west side – the east side is too weathered for any decoration to survive.

[Note: None of the original sections of stonework were originally together.]

4.   A section of stonework from an early 11C A-N hogback grave cover. It is located adjacent to the west wall of the south aisle. It sits on a floor standing modern plinth that measures 6¼ Ins/15 Cms H, by 14 Ins/35 Cms W by 67 Ins/170 Cms L. The section of stonework measures 17 Ins/43 Cms H, tapering 9 Ins/22 Cms to 5½ Ins/13 Cms W, by 59 Ins/149 Cms L. It is very weathered with no distinctive decoration on any of the sides. However, the two ends do have an indication of the traditional bear associated with such grave covers. At one time this section of stonework was used as a lintel for the porch.

5.   A section of stonework from a crosshead comprising the central section, two of the horizontal arms and the truncated parts of the two vertical arms. It has been attached to the east face of the west wall of the south aisle. It sits on a wall bracket and measures 8½ Ins/21 Cms H, by 15 Ins/38 Cms W, by 7 Ins/17 Cms D. It has no decoration on any of its sides.

6.   A section of stonework from an A-N crosshead with its lower vertical arm missing and two sections of stonework from an A-N cross-shaft joined back together. Separating these two sections of stonework is a modern reproduction piece comprising the lower vertical arm of a crosshead and its attached cross-shaft. They are located attached to the east face of the walling supporting the western arch on the south side of the tower. In total they stand 69 Ins/175 Cms H. They stand on a floor standing modern plinth that measures 6 Ins/15 Cms H, by 12 Ins/30 Cms W, by 6½ Ins/16 Cms D.

The crosshead with its lower vertical arm missing measures 14¾ Ins/37 Cms H, by 16 Ins/40 Cms W, by 6½ Ins/16 Cms D. The east face is decorated with ring chain design and, despite the damage; there are also traces of ring chain design on the west face. There is no decoration on the other two sides due to weathering and damage. It dates from the early 11C.

Beneath the crosshead is a modern reproduction piece comprising the lower vertical arm of a crosshead and its attached cross-shaft.

Beneath this modern reproduction piece there are two sections of stonework from a cross-shaft that have been joined back together. They measure 40¾ Ins/103 Cms H, tapering 9 Ins/22 Cms to 6¼ Ins/15 Cms W, tapering 6½ Ins/16 Cms to 6 Ins/15 Cms D. They are decorated on all four sides with Borre design. They date from the early 11C.

7.   An almost complete (the ends of the two bears are missing) A-N hogback grave cover that has been broken in two but placed back together. It is located in the centre of the floor in this part of the south aisle, 66 Ins/167 Cms east of the west wall of the south aisle. It sits on a floor standing modern plinth that measures 6 Ins/15 Cms H, by 16 Ins/40 Cms W, by 59 Ins/149 Cms L. The hogback measures 18 Ins/45 Cms H, by

10 Ins/25 Cms W, by 53 Ins/134 Cms L. The traditional bears associated with such grave covers can be identified: the one at the west end is better preserved, the one at the east end is damaged. The tegulated roof design with the central dividing ridge can also be identified. There is no other decoration that can be identified due to weathering.

8.   A solid, complete wheel head crosshead. It has been attached to the south face of the walling supporting the eastern arch on the south side of the tower. It sits on a wall bracket that is 67 Ins/170 Cms up from the floor. The crosshead measures 15 Ins/38 Cms H, by 16 Ins/40 Cms W, tapering 6 Ins/15 Cms to 4½ Ins/11 Cms D. Although very weathered the distinctive cross shape can easily be identified on both the north and south faces. No other decoration can be identified on any of the sides.

BUTTERCRAMBE
"Aldby Park"
SE 733584   Rating: ☆

This private house in Aldby Park is located up, and along, a gated drive on the north-west side of the "main" road running southwest/northeast through the village, 300Yds/273 M from where the road crosses the River Derwent. The house is not open to the public.

Aldby Park is an 18C manor house on the site of an A-S palace of King Edwin of Northumbria. King Harold apparently spent the evening here prior to the Battle of Stamford Bridge in 1066 (see the entry for Stamford Bridge, East Yorkshire).

CARLTON-IN-CLEVELAND
St Botolph's Church
NZ 506045   Rating: ☆

The church is easily located towards the northern end of Carlton-In-Cleveland on the west side of the road (there are no street signs) running north/south through the village.

The church was built 1896-97.

In the churchyard, 133 Ins/337 Cms south of the southeast corner of the south aisle there is a section of stonework from an A-S cross-shaft. Both the section of stonework and the plinth on which it stands lean at an angle towards the south. The plinth measures between 7 Ins/17 Cms and 12 Ins/30 Cms H, by 27 Ins/68 Cms W, by 25½ Ins/64 Cms D. The section of stonework measures between 15½ Ins/39 Cms and 18 Ins/45 Cms H, by 12 Ins/30 Cms W, and between 4¼ Ins/10 Cms to 6 Ins/15 Cms D. The four corners of the section of stonework appear to be rounded. No decoration can now be identified on any of the sides.

CAWOOD
(1) All Saints Church
SE 577378   Rating: ☆   Access is possible.

In the north-eastern part of Cawood, the church is located adjacent to the western side of "Church End" (there is a street sign) under 400 Yds/365 M north-east of its junction with the B1223, "Thorpe Lane" (there is a street sign).

On the site of an A-S church the present structure principally dates from 1150 and the restoration in 1887.

Internally, incorporated into the north wall of what is now the vestry on the north side of the chancel, one "medieval" grave cover can be seen to the west of the westernmost window, above the oil tank.

Internally and in the vestry, another "medieval" grave cover can be seen adjacent to the east of the easternmost window, about half way up the height of the window.

A further "medieval" grave cover is located inside the church in the south wall of the south aisle. It is 72 Ins/182 Cms up from the floor and 24 Ins/60 Cms east of the west wall arch.

Also inside the church there is a stone on which a sundial has been incised. Although the markings are now rather warn there is a hole for the missing gnomon in the centre of the appropriate stone. It has been incorporated into the south wall of the south aisle, 72 Ins/182 Cms west of the font, and over 48 Ins/121 Cms up from the floor.

The grave covers and the sundial have been described as "Saxon" although they seem of later date.

CAWOOD
(2) Castle
SE 547377   Rating: ☆

At the crossroads of the B1222 and B1223 in the centre of Cawood take the B1223 which heads in a south-easterly direction. About 50 Yds/45 M from the crossroads the distinctive gatehouse and adjoining former banqueting house (restored) are located under 40 Yds/36 M from the south side of the road.

A manor house was built around 920 on this site and subsequently fortified. As thanks for his victory at Brunanburgh in 937, King Athelstan gave the manor house to the see of York. It became the residence of the archbishops of York and was used by them as such up until the 13C when they moved into their new palace at Bishopthorpe. The castle was mostly demolished in 1646 when some of the material was used in the building work at Bishopthorpe Palace. Since the original manor house at Cawood was "royal" it is sometimes referred to as a "palace" of King Athelstan.

The surviving gatehouse and banqueting house date from the mid-15C.

The Landmark Trust now owns the gatehouse.

CONISTONE
St Mary's Church
SD 981675   Rating: ✫

At the northern end of Conistone, the church is located on the west side of the minor road that follows the east bank of the River Wharfe to link Conistone to Kettlewell. The church is 100 Yds/91 M north of the road junction with the road that crosses the River Wharfe. At this junction there is a free-standing directional sign with "Grassington 3" on one arm and "Kilnsey ½" and "Kettlewell 3¾" on the other.

Although restored in 1846 and in 1957, the church does contain 12C, 13C and possibly A-S fabric.

Internally, the two most western arches of the nave and the supporting stonework in the pillars may be A-S in origin.

Internally, the bowl of the font may be A-S in origin. It is located 108 Ins/274 Cms north of the south door and 72 Ins/182 Cms east of the east face of the west wall. The plain, square-shaped font bowl sits on a more recent square column which itself stands on a square plinth.

The double triangular window in the north wall of the vestry may be A-S in origin as well. (Although the vestry is kept locked this window can be easily viewed externally.)

Externally, some of the stones incorporated into the fabric of the south wall, and possibly the arch of the south doorway, may also be A-S in origin.

COVERHAM
Holy Trinity Church
SE 103864   Rating: ✫✫

The church is located 150-Yds/137 M northwest from the bridge over the River Cover in Coverham. It is easily identified set back from the south side of the road running in a south-westerly/north-easterly direction which leads to Middleham 1½ miles away.

On the site of its A-S predecessor, the present church dates from the 13C with additions and alterations in the 14C, 16C and 17C. It was restored in 1854 and in 1878.

Internally, there is a section of stonework from an A-S cross-shaft. It has been shaped to form the lintel above the south doorway into the church (on the inside, north side, of the south doorway). The section of stonework measures between 56½ Ins/143 Cms and 54 Ins/137 Cms L by 13 Ins/33 Cms W. It is decorated with a possible Crucifixion scene. 12½ Ins/31 Cms east of the west end of the section of stonework, three figures with raised arms standing side by side can be identified: the central figure is the largest. The remaining part of the section of stonework is decorated with interlace design. Only one face of the stonework can be viewed.

COXWOLD
Newburgh Priory
SE 543764   Rating: ☆☆☆☆

880 Yds/804 M south of Coxwold, on the east side of the minor road that links Coxwold to Oulston, there is an ornamental iron gateway on which there is a notice board "Newburgh Priory etc". Proceed through the gateway and up the drive to reach the Priory in about 100 Yds/91 M.

The Priory was founded as an Augustinian House in 1145. It was Dissolved in 1538 and converted into a private residence. The Priory is basically a Tudor building with 18C alterations. The original fabric is now difficult to detect. The Priory contains reputedly the tomb of Oliver Cromwell whose remains were brought here by his third daughter Mary.

Externally, attached to the ground floor fabric of the exterior west wall of the east wing, there is a section of stonework from an A-D grave cover protected by a glass cover. It is located 48 Ins/122 Cms up from the ground, and 7 Yds/6 M from the north end of the wing. The section of stonework is about 24 Ins/61 Cms square and is decorated with two figures, possibly depicting St Mark and St Matthew. It dates from around 1050 and comes from an A-D church that once stood on this site.

CRAMBE
St Michael's Church
SE 733648   Rating: ☆☆☆

In the northern part of Crambe, the church is easily located on the east side of the "no-through road" (there is no road sign to this effect or a street sign), which leads to the village.

The church dates from the 11C and it was extended in the 12C, 13C and 14C. An extensive restoration was undertaken in 1886-87.

The eastern two-thirds of the nave is 11C and the nature of the construction suggests A-S workmanship. On each side of the nave there is an original A-S window.

Internally, the blocked south doorway entrance is A-S and the chancel arch may either be A-S or Saxo-Norman.

Externally, incorporated into the fabric of the south wall of the nave, there is a much weathered section of stonework from what may either be part of a 10C hogback grave cover or a cross-shaft. It is located 12 Ins/30 Cms below the easternmost window on the south side of the nave. The section of stonework is about 12 Ins/30 Cms W and no more than 6 Ins/15 Cms H. It is very weathered and difficult to identify.

Externally, incorporated into the fabric of the south wall of the nave, there is simple 11C Mass Dial. It is 48 Ins/122 Cms up from the ground, and incised on the western jamb of the blocked south doorway. The hole for the missing gnomon can easily be identified with a number of straight lines radiating from it. Part of the bottom arch of the enclosing circle can also be identified.

Externally, the joins in the south nave wall between the 11C and 13C masonry can easily be identified.

CRATHORNE
All Saints Church

NZ 443075   Rating: ✰✰✰   Access is possible.

Close to the eastern edge of Crathorne the churchyard is adjacent to the north side of the road that runs east/west through the village (there are no street signs).

The present church on the site dates from the 12C and the restoration in 1887-88.

Inside the south porch, there is a large, curved section of stonework from a 9C A-D hogback grave cover. It has been incorporated into the fabric of the south wall of the nave immediately above the lintel over the south door. It measures 11½ Ins/29 Cms H by 71 Ins/180 Cms W. The upper part has been decorated with a large scroll-like design and the lower part has been decorated with interlace design.

During the restoration and rebuilding of the church in 1887 about seventeen A-S and medieval sections of stonework were found amongst the stonework comprising the west wall of the nave and the walls of the chancel. Part of two 10C grave covers found are now housed in the

Monks' Dormitory in Durham Cathedral and were the only ones found not now incorporated into the rebuilt church.

Internally, most of the sections of stonework found during the 19C restoration are medieval grave covers and are easily identified protruding from the north wall (five stones – one of these does not protrude from the wall) and south wall (four stones) of the tower, and the west wall of the nave (one on the north side and one on the south side of the tower). Among these there is a section of A-S stonework incorporated into the south wall of the tower. It is the most easterly of the four sections of stonework. It is located 71 Ins/180 Cms east of the west wall of the tower and 66½ Ins/168 Cms up from the floor. The section of stonework measures 13 Ins/33 Cms H, between 4¾ Ins/12 Cms and 6¼ Ins/15 Cms W, by 1¼ Ins/3 Cms D – the part that can be seen protruding from the wall. Despite weathering and damage it is clearly decorated on its north side with a distinctive cross with a square design underneath, and part of another, incomplete design, underneath that. There is no decoration on any of the other sides.

Internally, there is a section of 10C A-S stonework giving the appearance of one wider section of stonework placed upon a narrower section but they are in fact both part of the same section of stonework. It has been affixed to the window ledge of the window on the north side of the nave (there is only one window). In total the section of stonework stands 13 Ins/33 Cms H. The top section of stonework measures 6¼ Ins/15 Cms H, tapering 9¾ Ins/24 Cms to 9 Ins/22 Cms W, tapering 8 Ins/20 Cms to 7¼ Ins/18 Cms D. The south face is decorated with scroll design. The other three sides are decorated with knot work design and no decoration can now be identified on the top. The lower section of stonework measures 6¾ Ins/17 Cms H, tapering 8¾ Ins/22 Cms to 8¼ Ins/20 Cms W, tapering 7 Ins/20 Cms to 6¾ Ins/17 Cms D. The south face is decorated with the depiction of a dragon. The north face is decorated with the depiction of a figure, but since there is no halo around the head this does not appear to represent St John the Evangelist as has been claimed. The other two sides are decorated with knot work design.

CRAYKE
St Cuthbert's Church
SE 560706   Rating: ☆

In the centre of Crayke take the minor road "Church Hill" (there is a street sign) which is signposted "Oulston 3, Coxwold 5" and heads uphill in a north-westerly direction. Just over 100 Yds/91 M along Church Hill, the church is located close to the north side of the road.

A monastery was founded on this site in the 7C. It extended over the area covered by the present 14C church and churchyard.

Two fragments of stonework from a decorated late 8C crosshead were found on this site and these are now on display in the Yorkshire Museum in York (see the entry for the Yorkshire Museum, York).

CROFT-ON-TEES
St Peter's Church

NZ 288098   Rating: ✭✭✭   Access is possible.

The church is situated on the north side of the A167 just before it crosses the River Tees to reach the east bank of the river.

Whilst evidently on the site of an earlier 11C structure, the present church dates mainly from the 14C although it was restored in 1876.

Internally, there are:

1.   A section of stonework from a 9C cross-shaft. It is located in the Millbanke Chapel, which is situated at the eastern end of the north aisle. The section of stonework is standing on the fifth step up from the floor of the north aisle, by the south-west corner of the Millbanke Tomb Chest. The section of stonework and the Millbanke Tomb Chest are enclosed by iron railings on the third step up from the floor in the north aisle. The section of stonework is 24½ Ins/62 Cms east of the iron railings.

The section of stonework measures 18 Ins/45 Cms H, by 12 Ins/30 Cms W, by 6½ Ins/16 Cms D. Its north-west and south-east faces are decorated with birds, animals and vine scroll design ("inhabited vine scroll"). The south-west side is decorated with ring chain design. What decoration survives on the north-east side is vine scroll design.

2.   A section of stonework from an A-S cross-shaft. It is located standing on the floor leaning against the north wall of the north aisle 19½ Ins/49 Cms west of the north doorway. It stands on the floor sandwiched between some piping and the north wall. The section of stonework measures 35 Ins/88 Cms H, tapering 17 Ins/43 Cms to 14 Ins/35 Cms W, by 5½ Ins/13 Cms D. It is decorated with knot work design on all four sides.

CROPTON
St Gregory's Church

SE 756893   Rating: ✭✭

At the northern end of Cropton, turn off the "main" road running in a south-west/north-east direction through the village and take the minor, un-named road that runs in a north-westerly direction. (The turning is

108 Ins/274 Cms north of the easily identifiable wall enclosing the site of the old village well that retains its winding gear.) The church is located at the end of this road, about 100 Yds/91 M from the main village road.

The present church dates from 1844 replacing earlier structures on the site.

Internally, there is an A-S font. It is located in the western part of the nave 63 Ins/160 Cms north of the south door, sitting on a 19 Ins/48 Cms H, shallow, single stepped, and circular plinth. The font measures 19 Ins/48 Cms H with a 27 Ins/68 Cms diameter. There is no decoration on the font.

Externally, there is a section of stonework from a cross-shaft. It is located standing on a 11 Ins/27 Cms H circular plinth, 12 Yds/10 M south of the south door into the church. The section of stonework measures 30½ Ins/77 Cms H, tapering 11¼ Ins/28 Cms to 10 Ins/25 Cms W, tapering 8½ Ins/21 Cms to 7½ Ins/19 Cms D. The section of stonework is weathered with no decoration surviving on any of the sides. However, each of the four corners is chamfered and the stonework has been alternately cut and left to provide spaced protruding pieces of stonework. It dates from the 10C.

CUNDALL
St Mary and All Saints Church

SE 423731   Rating: ☆☆☆☆   Access is possible.

440-Yds/402 M northwest of the minor crossroads in the centre of Cundall, locate a drive (there are no identifying signs) on the east side of the road running in a south-easterly/north-westerly direction through the village. (The entrance to the drive is situated diagonally opposite the south entrance to Cundall Manor Preparatory School.) The drive runs in a north-easterly direction alongside the grounds of a substantial property, almost hidden by trees and vegetation. The church is situated about 125 Yds/114 M from the road, and this drive ends at the churchyard gates.

The church mostly dates from 1852.

Internally, there is a section of stonework from an A-S cross-shaft that dates from around 800. It is located between 5½ Ins/13 Cms and 7 Ins/17 Cms north of the south wall of the tower. It measures 60 Ins/152 Cms L (H), tapering 14 Ins/35 Cms to 11 Ins/27 Cms W, tapering 12¼ Ins/31 Cms to 10 Ins/25 Cms D. The section of stonework is decorated on all four sides in the "Breedon" style with long-legged and long-necked animals as well figures and plait work and scroll designs. The decoration on all four sides is clear. At one time this section of stonework was used as a lintel for a door and probably this is why part of the edge of the present top side and north side have been removed.

Sitting on top of the western end of this section of stonework, there is another small section of stonework broken off from the top of the south face. This small section of stonework measures 7½ Ins/19 Cms L (H), by 9½ Ins/24 Cms W, by 5 Ins/12 Cms D. It too is decorated in the "Breedon" style.

DANBY
St Hilda's Church
NZ 696063   Rating: ☆   Access is possible.

The church is in an isolated position some two and three quarter miles south-west of the village of Danby – from the railway station. It can be reached by taking the minor road at the west end of Ainthorpe that heads in a south-westerly direction (there are no street signs). At the junction between this road and the road that runs west to east to the northern part of Ainthorpe, there is a signpost with two directional signs "Botton" and "Danby Church". Proceed along the minor road as directed by the Danby Church sign. About 1600 Yds/1463 M along this road, the church comes into view, and the road then takes a sharp right angled turn. At this point there is an easy to identify driveway that leads off the west side of the road in the general direction of the church. Proceed along this driveway, it curves on the way, to reach the church after about 90 Yds/82 M.

The present structure is on the site of an A-S church that was rebuilt by the Normans. Whilst some Norman stonework remains, most of the fabric of the church dates from the extensive building work undertaken in the 15C, late 18C and mid 19C. The church was restored 1901-03.

Internally, the central key stone on the west side of the chancel arch is said to be part of an A-S cross. This stone measures approximately 18 Ins/45 Cms H by 26 Ins/66 Cms W. The cross lies on its side with its circular shaped head at the north end and the short, narrow, cross-shaft at the south end. The crosshead has a central cross surrounded by an interlocking circular design. Given the position of this stone so high up it can be difficult to identify with confidence; on either side of this stone there are stones decorated with chevron designs (not A-S).

DRAX
St Peter and St Paul's Church
SE 676263   Rating: ☆☆   Access is possible.

In the centre of Drax village, the church is adjacent to the north side of "Main Road" (there is a street sign).

The fabric of the church does include some A-S material, but it mostly dates from the 12C.

Internally, there is an A-S font with a plain bowl. It is located 72 Ins/182 Cms from the north door, and in the north aisle on a plinth. There is also another font, not A-S, in the south aisle.

Internally, the chancel arch is late A-S.

DUGGLEBY
Howe
SE 880669   Rating: ☆

300 Yds/274 M south-east of the most southerly crossroads in Duggleby, locate the distinctive small hillock comprising the Howe. It is situated in the next but one field adjacent to the east side of the B1253, less than 100 Yds/91 M from the side of the road.

This long barrow contained artefacts from the Neolithic Age (from around 3000 BC) and the remains of a Bronze Age (from around 1800 BC) nobleman. Reputedly it was also used as a burial ground for a Norse giant.

EASBY
St Agatha's Church
NZ 185003   Rating: ☆☆

The churchyard is adjacent to the east side of Easby Abbey and the north-west side of the road leading to the site of the abbey.

The present church on the site dates mainly from the 13C and the restoration in 1869.

Internally, there is a replica of part of an A-S cross-shaft. It is located 36 Ins/91 Cms from the north wall of the chancel, and 72 Ins/182 Cms west of the communion rail. The free-standing replica stands 84 Ins/213 Cms H. It is decorated with Christ and the Twelve Apostles, animals and interlace. The more impressive original of both the cross-shaft and crosshead is in the Victoria and Albert Museum in London. The original dates from 800-825.

EASINGTON
All Saints Church
NZ 744180   Rating: ☆☆☆   Access is possible.

The church is easily located in the centre of Easington, adjacent to the south side of the A174.

The church was built 1888-89.

Internally, on the floor in the north aisle there are five sections of stonework, four of which are of A-S/Viking interest – the fifth is of a later date. Moving from west to east, those of A-S/A-D interest are:

1.   A section of stonework from a 9C A-D cross-shaft. It is located 17 Ins/43 Cms south of the north wall of the north aisle. The section of stonework measures 10½ Ins/26 Cms H (W), by 16½ Ins/41 Cms W (H), by 5½ Ins/13 Cms D. It is decorated in the Jellinge style on three sides, the fourth side, facing the floor, has been rendered so no decoration survives.

2.   A section of stonework from a 9C A-D crosshead comprising most of the central section and two arms. It is located 10½ Ins/26 Cms south of the north wall of the north aisle. The section of stonework measures between 5½ Ins/13 Cms and 8½ Ins/21 Cms H, by 21 Ins/53 Cms W, and between 4¾ Ins/12 Cms and 6 Ins/15Cms D. It is decorated with a centre circle and line decoration on the southwest face. It is decorated with a centre circle, line decoration and knot work design on the northeast face. The southeast side has a simple line outlining the shape of the end of the crosshead. The northwest side is too weathered for any decoration to be identified.

[Note: There are two small fragments of stonework of indeterminate date, origin, and purpose. One of these fragments supports the section of stonework identified at "2" above, and the other lies on the floor between the north wall of the north aisle and "3" below.]

3.   A section of stonework from a 10C hogback grave cover. It is located 15 Ins/38 Cms south of the north wall of the north aisle. The section of stonework measures 15½ Ins/39 Cms H, between 4½ Ins/11 Cms and 9 Ins/22 Cms W, by 35 Ins/88 Cms L. A snakes-head rather than the more usual bear can be identified at the western end of the hogback. The top stone ridge can also be identified. The north and south faces are decorated with knot work design. The fourth side has been broken off from the missing remainder of the hogback.

[Note: There is a large, later medieval, section of stonework standing between "3" above and "4" below.]

4.   An almost complete wheel head crosshead, only part of one of its arms missing, with a section of stonework from its attached cross-shaft. They are located 16½ Ins/41 Cms south of the north wall of the north aisle. In total the crosshead and its attached section of cross-shaft, measure 28 Ins/71 Cms H. The crosshead measures 19 Ins/48 Cms H, by 17½ Ins/44 Cms W, and between 7¼ Ins/18 Cms to 4 Ins/10 Cms D. The section of stonework from the cross-shaft measures

9 Ins/22 Cms H, by 10½ Ins/26 Cms W, by 8¾ Ins/22 Cms D. Due to weathering, damage and rendering, decoration is indistinct on all four sides of both the crosshead and the section of stonework from the cross-shaft.

Externally from the main body of the church, but internally in what is known as "the boiler room". The boiler room is located underneath the west end of the north aisle and it is entered down some steps. Inside there are stored a variety of sections of stonework, three of which appear to be A-S/A-D. These are:

5.   A section of stonework from an A-D cross-shaft. It is located lying flat on iron rails, 6½ Ins/16 Cms south of the north wall, and 43½ Ins/110 Cms west of the east wall of the boiler room. The section of stonework measures 6 Ins/15 Cms H (D), tapering 13¾ Ins/34 Cms to 11 Ins/27 Cms W, and between 19 Ins/48 Cms and 13½ Ins/34 Cms D (H). Although weathered, its top face and west side are decorated with interlace design. The other two sides are too weathered and damaged for any decoration to be identified.

6.   A section of stonework from an A-S cross-shaft. It is located standing on iron rails, 20 Ins/50 Cms south of the north wall, and 8 Ins/20 Cms west of the east wall of the boiler room. The section of stonework measures between 5 Ins/12 Cms and 6 Ins/15 Cms H, by 10 Ins/25 Cms W, by 10 Ins/25 Cms D. The south side is decorated with interlace design. The other three sides are too weathered and damaged for any decoration to be identified.

7.   A section of stonework comprising the central section and two arms from an A-S crosshead. It is located sitting on breeze blocks that lie on the floor 5½ Ins/13 Cms west of the east wall and 6 Ins/15Cms north of the south wall of the boiler room. The section of stonework measures between 6 Ins/15 Cms and 8½ Ins/21 Cms H, by 19¾ Ins/50 Cms W, by 6¾ Ins/17 Cms D. Apart from traces of the central roundel on the west side, no other decoration can be confidently identified on any of the sides due to weathering and damage.

Externally, lying on the ground in the churchyard, there are a variety of assorted sections of stonework partially hidden by the grass. These are located between 60 Ins/152 Cms and 100 Ins/254 Cms, and between 190 Ins/482 Cms and 205 Ins/520 Cms, west of the tower. There are some sections of stonework amongst them of A-S/A-D interest. These are:

8.   A section of stonework from a cross-shaft base that could be A-S. It comprises three sides and the bottom, including the socket for the base of the cross-shaft. It is located 60 Ins/152 Cms west of the tower. The section of stonework stands between11½ Ins/29 Cms and 13½ Ins/34

Cms H, between 18 Ins/45 Cms and 22½ Ins/57 Cms W, by 22½ Ins/57 Cms D. It is too weathered for any decoration to be identified on any of the sides.

9.   A section of stonework from a hogback grave cover. It is located 190 Ins/482 Cms west of the tower and 6 Ins/15 Cms east of a wall in the churchyard. The section of stonework measures 9 Ins/22 Cms H, by 11 Ins/27 Cms W, by 27 Ins/68 Cms L. Although weathered, on the east side there is some outline of a triangular design typical of some hogback grave cover roofs. On the west face, hidden by the grass, there is some very faint knot work decoration that can be identified. The two other sides are too weathered for any decoration to be identified.

10.   A section of stonework from a hogback grave cover that may be part of the hogback identified at "9" above. It is located 195 Ins/495 Cms west of the tower, 2½ Ins/6 Cms east of a wall in the churchyard, and 7 Ins/17 Cms north of the hogback identified at "9" above. The section of stonework measures between 3 Ins/7 Cms and 5 Ins/12 Cms H, by 8½ Ins/21 Cms W, by 8 Ins/20 Cms L. Although weathered, on the east side there is some line decoration. The other three sides are too weathered for any decoration to be identified.

EAST AYTON
Church of St John the Baptist

SE 991849   Rating: ☆   Access is possible.

Towards the western end of East Ayton, the church is easily identified on the north side of the A170, "Racecourse Road" (there is a street sign). It is diagonally opposite the junction of the A170 and the B1261.

The present structure dates from the early 12C, 13C and 14C. Major repairs were made in 1721 and 1883.

Internally, the two large, flat stones either side of the base of the tower arch could be A-S. Both of these stones are chamfered with the higher part being the larger and the lower part being the smaller.

1.   The stone on the south side of the base of the tower is 42 Ins/106 Cms up from the floor. It measures 6 Ins/15 Cms H, by 27 Ins/68 Cms W, and up to 19¾ Ins/50 Cms D – three sides can be viewed. There are two grooves running around the exterior of this flat stone dividing the surface into roughly three equal parts.

2.   The stone on the north side of the base of the tower is 43 Ins/109 Cms up from the floor. It measures 5½ Ins/13 Cms H, by 25 Ins/63 Cms W, and up to 24½ Ins/62 Cms D – three sides can be viewed. There are

two grooves running around the exterior of this flat stone dividing the surface into roughly three equal parts.

Internally, the font may be A-S, although a later date has been ascribed to it. It is located directly under the centre of the tower arch sitting on an 11 Ins/27 Cms H wooden plinth. The font stands 25 Ins/63 Cms H and has a 34 Ins/86 Cms diameter. The circumference of the font is decorated with a series of interlocking arches, with their supporting pillars and their bases similar in style to an A-S chancel arch.

EAST BARNBY
Wade's Stone
NZ 830129   Rating: ☆

At the northern edge of East Barnby, on the east side of the road that runs north/south through the village, locate the first field gate north of the last property in the village. From this field gate Wade's Stone can clearly be identified standing in a field.

Pass through the field gate and into the adjacent field. Proceed in an easterly direction towards the next field gate, keeping alongside the adjacent field fence. The second field gate is about 180 Yds/164 M east of the first. Pass through this gate and into the field containing Wade's Stone. From this second field gate proceed for about 70 Yds/64 M directly across the field in a general easterly direction to reach Wade's Stone.

Wade's Stone is a single, irregular shaped section of stonework that leans in a northerly direction. It measures up to 84 Ins/213 Cms H, by up to 31 Ins/78 Cms W, by up to 23 Ins/58 Cms D. It is weathered and has no decoration on any of its sides.

The stone is connected with the legend of the late 8C Saxon giant Wade who at one time owned Mulgrave Castle and was reputedly buried at this spot. Archaeologists did find buried at the base of this stone the body of an A-S warrior. Apparently, originally there were two stones marking the site of the grave. See the Goldsborough, North Yorkshire entry for another "Wade's Stone" connected with the Saxon giant.

EAST HAUXWELL (HAUXWELL)
St Oswald's Church
SE 165931   Rating: ☆☆

The church is situated in an isolated position, separate from the village, 880 Yds/804 M to the south of East Hauxwell. At a crossroads a sign "Hauxwell Church" directs you in a north-westerly direction and up a gated drive. 105 Yds/96 M along this drive the church is located near to the south-west side of the drive.

The church mostly dates from the early parts of the 12C, 13C and the 14Cs and the restorations in 1860-61 and 1962. However, the church does incorporate some 11C fabric.

Internally, the much altered chancel arch dates from the 11C.

Externally, distinctive, large, 11C herring-bone masonry can be seen in the walling east of the south porch; above, below and between the windows in the south walls of the nave; between the windows in the south wall of the chancel; and in the north wall of the nave between the easternmost window and the vestry.

Externally, part of an A-S window survives in the south side of the nave. It comprises the solid top headstone with the curve of the top of a single headed window in the middle of its bottom edge. It is located incorporated into the walling of the south side of the nave, 10 Ins/25 Cms east of the top of the westernmost window in the south side of the nave and 149 Ins/378 Cms up from the ground.

Externally, there is a section of stonework from an early 11C A-S cross-shaft. It is located incorporated into the fabric of the north wall of the nave. It has been used as a lintel over the blocked-up north doorway. The doorway is situated between the easternmost buttress on the north side of the tower and the westernmost window in the north side of the nave. The section of stonework measures 4½ Ins/11 Cms H by 36½ Ins/92 Cms W. It is decorated with chain work design.

EAST HAUXWELL: St Oswald's Church. An Anglo-Danish cross-shaft with the lower part of its attached crosshead. Interlace and "cats cradle" design can be identified.

In the churchyard there is a section of stonework from a late 10C A-D cross-shaft and a section of stonework from its connected, probably wheel head cross (the section of wheel head is very broken). There is a wire fence separating the "maintained" from the "unkempt" part of the churchyard. The section of stonework from a cross-shaft and section of stonework from the crosshead are to the south of this wire fence in the "unkempt" part of the churchyard. They are located to the south of the church, 18 Yds/16 M south of the westernmost window on the south side of the nave.

The section of stonework from a cross-shaft and the section of stonework from the crosshead stand on a plinth 24 Ins/60 Cms H, by 18½ Ins/47 Cms W, by 13 Ins/33 Cms D. Together they stand 47½ Ins/120 Cms H.

The section of stonework from the crosshead measures 5 Ins/12 Cms H, by 12 Ins/30 Cms W, by 5 Ins/12 Cms D. Although weathered, interlace design decoration can be identified on the remains of the west and east sides.

The section of stonework from the cross-shaft measures 42½ Ins/107 Cms H, tapering 12½ Ins/31 Cms to 9½ Ins/24 Cms W, by 5½ Ins/13 Cms D. Although weathered, interlace and "cats cradle" design decoration can easily be identified on all four sides. Apparently a panel on the east face of the cross-shaft was incised with an inscription "Crux Sancti Jacobi" (the words can no longer be read but the outline of the panel remains).

The crosshead and cross-shaft were attributed to James the Deacon but stylistically they date from the 10C. (James accompanied Paulinus to Northumbria in 625. James died sometime after 664.)

EAST MARTON
St Peter's Church

SD 908507   Rating: ☆☆☆

Towards the western end of East Marton turn south off the A59 (T) along "Church Lane" (there are street signs). Proceed along Church Lane for about 350 Yds/320 M until the road runs out by the entrance to the churchyard.

Although the tower dates from the 12C most of the church dates from the 19C.

Internally, there is a section of stonework from an A-N cross-shaft. It is located at the west end of the nave, to the south of the entrance into the tower. It sits on a purpose built wooden floor-standing plinth that stands 29 Ins/73 Cms H. The section of stonework measures 22 Ins/55 Cms H, tapering 10 Ins/25 Cms to 8 Ins/20 Cms W, tapering 8½ Ins/21 Cms to 6½ Ins/16 Cms D. There is a socket-hole on the top of the section of cross-shaft. It is decorated in the Jellinge style on all four sides. On the top half of the east face it is decorated with a dragon and a Christianised figure of Thor.

Internally, there is a large undecorated A-S tub font. It is located at the western end of the nave, immediately to the east of the middle of the arch into the tower. It stands 18½ Ins/47 Cms up from the floor sitting on a thin mill-wheel supported by three circular stone pillars. The font measures 27 Ins/68 Cms H, by 24½ Ins/62 Cms W, by 25½ Ins/64 Cms D.

EBBERSTON
(1) King Aldfrith's Shelter
SE 898833   Rating: ☆

At the crossroads in the centre of Ebberston take the minor road which heads north off the A170 into "Netherby Dale" (marked on Ordnance Survey maps: there are no directional or street signs for this road). About 150 Yds/137 M from the A170, amidst woodland, 9 feet/274 Cms from the west side of the minor road, in the grass verge, there is a free-standing, vertical "Public Footpath" directional sign. 72 In/182 Cms in front (to the south) of this sign there is another sign about "Chafer Wood", a nature reserve.

Proceed as directed by the public footpath sign in a westerly direction and along a well-defined track as it winds its way uphill through the woodland. After 350 Yds/320 M, with the track now heading in a general northerly direction, the woods temporarily clear and King Aldfith's Shelter comes into view some 50 Yds/45 M farther away to the north-east atop a small knoll. The Shelter is reached by taking the separate, well-trodden path leading up to it.

The Shelter is shaped like a round bee-hive and has an open entrance on its south side (the side first viewed from the track). It stands 144 In/365 Cms H, has an open roof and one small window. It is easy to identify. There is no plaque or information notice.

The shelter was erected in 1790 as a monument to King Aldfrith of Northumbria who was stabbed during a battle with his father King Oswy at Scamridge Dykes to the north of Ebberston (centred SE 895855). Wounded, King Aldfrith took refuge in a cave said to be beneath the floor of the stone shelter. Dying later of these wounds, King Aldfrith was buried at the monastery at Little Driffield (now St Peter's Church: there is a marble tablet in the chancel commemorating his burial within the chancel – see the entry for Little Driffield, East Yorkshire).

EBBERSTON
(2) St Mary The Virgin Church
SE 892832   Rating: ☆

The church is set back about 200 Yds/182 M from the north side of the A170. The entrance to the gateway to a path which leads up to the churchyard can easily be identified by the "St. Mary's Church Ebberston "12th.Century"" sign affixed to a stone gatepost in front of the walling by the north side of the A170.

A church was first built on this site in the 11C. There was substantive rebuilding and alteration in the 12C, 13C, 14C, and 16C. It was restored in 1869.

Internally, there is a plain, round font that may be A-S. It is located on a stepped plinth, under the westernmost arch in the north wall of the nave.

Externally, the rounded arch (not the spiral shafts) of the south doorway may also be A-S.

ELLERBURN
St Hilda's Church

SE 841842   Rating: ☆☆☆☆

The church is easily located on the north side of the minor road that runs into Ellerburn from the south-west.

Although heavily restored during 1904-11 the church is of A-S origin of around 1050.

Internally, A-S material can be identified:

1.   The two stones forming the internal arch over the south door in the nave are A-S.

2.   Two arches and part of their supports from the former A-S chancel arch. These are located incorporated into the north wall of the nave. They have been picked out from the surrounding whitewash. The former chancel arch is located 85 Ins/215 Cms east of the west wall of the nave 90 Ins/228 Cms (west support) and 87½ Ins/222 Cms (east support) up from the floor. The whole arch measures 68 Ins/172 Cms W and 21 Ins/53 Cms H maximum.

3.   Both the north and south sides of the current chancel arch may be supported by A-S stonework. This stonework comprises:

(i)   Circular columns attached to the west faces of both sides of the chancel arch.

(ii)   The through stones at the top of both of the columns referred to at (i) above. The top stone on the north side of the chancel arch is decorated with a simple cross at the northern end of its west face. On its south face it is decorated with a coiled snake design at its western end (south-west facing corner) and with a feather shape enclosing a zigzag design along the rest of this face. (Is this feather depicting the "tufa" the symbol of kingship?) The top stone on the south side of the chancel is decorated with a coiled snake design on its west face. At the western end of its north face (north-west facing corner) it is decorated with a design reminiscent of a crosier head (not dissimilar from the coiled snake design on the west face). (Is this crosier depicting the crosier of St Hilda?) The rest of this north face is decorated with lines, possibly the staff supporting the crosier head.

(iii)   The stones at the bottom of both of the columns referred to at (i) above. At the base of the column on the north side of the chancel the stone support has some enigmatic carving on its west facing and south-west facing corner. These stones may date from the 9C.

Internally there is an 11C tub font. It is located 23 Ins/58 Cms east of the west wall of the nave. The font is supported by a stone column standing 15 Ins/38 Cms H that stands on an 11½-Ins/29 Cms H stepped plinth. The font measures 19 Ins/48 Cms H and 29½ Ins/74 Cms in diameter. There is no decoration on it.

The church contains, but does not display, a 10C A-S sundial. The stone on which the sundial is scratched clearly has the central hole for the missing gnomon and the divisions indicating the time.

Externally, there are a number of sections of 9C/10C stonework incorporated into the fabric of the church. These are:

4.   A section of stonework from a crosshead comprising the central section and most of three arms. It is located incorporated into the exterior south wall of the south porch, 10 Ins/25 Cms west of the gate into the south porch, and 66½ Ins/168 Cms up from the ground. The section of stonework measures 16 Ins/40 Cms H by 22 Ins/55 Cms W. It has been suggested that the shape of the crosshead is reminiscent of a swastika or Thor's hammer. It is too weathered for any decoration to be identified.

5.   A section of stonework from a 10C A-S crosshead comprising the central section, two arms and part of a third arm. It is located incorporated into the exterior south wall of the south porch in the south-eastern corner of the south wall 52½ Ins/133 Cms up from the ground. The section of stonework measures 15½ Ins/39 Cms H, by 11 Ins/27 Cms W, by 6½ Ins/16 Cms D. It is decorated with interlace design on both its south face and east side.

6.   A section of stonework from a 10C A-D hogback grave cover with one end protruding from the stonework. It is located incorporated into the exterior east wall of the south porch. It is situated adjacent to the north side of the extended south wall of the south porch and 82 Ins/208 Cms up from the ground. It measures 11½ Ins/29 Cms H by 9½ Ins/24 Cms W and is decorated with some lines and a ridge design.

7.   A section of stonework from a 10C A-D hogback grave cover with one end protruding from the stonework. It is located incorporated into the

exterior east wall of the south porch. It is situated 11 Ins/27 Cms north of the extended south wall of the south porch and 82½ Ins/209 Cms up from the ground. The section of stonework measures 12 Ins/30 Cms H by 12½ Ins/31 Cms W. It is decorated with some lines and a ridge design.

8.   A section of stonework from a mid 10C A-S wheel head crosshead comprising the central section and most of three arms and two arches linking the arms together to form the wheel. It is located incorporated into the exterior east wall of the south porch. It is situated 9 Ins/22 Cms south of the south wall of the nave and 77 Ins/195 Cms up from the ground. The section of stonework measures 15 Ins/38 Cms H by 10½ Ins/26 Cms W. It is too weathered for any decoration to be identified although it was originally decorated with a kilted figure of Christ.

9.   An A-D ring head crosshead and a section of stonework from its attached cross-shaft. The ring head crosshead comprises the central section, most of two arms and part of a third arm, and three arches linking the arms together to form the ring. The ring head crosshead and the section of stonework from its attached cross-shaft have been incorporated into the exterior south wall of the nave. They are located 42 Ins/106 Cms east of the east wall of the south porch, and 86 Ins/218 Cms up from the ground. Together they measure 29 Ins/73 Cms H. The section of crosshead measures 18½ Ins/47 Cms H by 14 Ins/35 Cms W. The section of stonework from the cross-shaft measures 10½ Ins/26 Cms H tapering 11 Ins/27 Cms to 10 Ins/25 Cms W. The crosshead is clearly decorated with interlace design. The section of stonework from the cross-shaft appears to be decorated in Jellinge style with part of the body and head from an entwined animal.

10.   A section of early 11C A-S stonework. It is located incorporated into the fabric of the south wall of the chancel. It is situated 38½ Ins/97 Cms west of the blocked doorway and 60 Ins/152 Cms up from the ground. The section of stonework measures 7 Ins/17 Cms H by 11½ Ins/29 Cms W. Although heavily weathered it is clearly decorated with two figures: the western figure is without a head, the better-preserved eastern figure is with a head. According to the church guide this depicts a skull and a rabbit.

11.   A section of 9C A-S stonework; a round shaft. It is located incorporated into the fabric of the south wall of the chancel. It is situated 13½ Ins/34 Cms west of the blocked doorway and 60 Ins/152 Cms up from the ground. The section of stonework measures 10½ Ins/26 Cms H by 11½ Ins/29 Cms W. In the centre it is decorated with a rope-patterned design with a border each side.

12.   A section of A-S stonework. It is located incorporated into the fabric of the south wall of the chancel. It is situated 18½ Ins/47 Cms above the eastern arm of the blocked doorway. The section of stonework measures 15½ Ins/39 Cms H by 8½ Ins/21 Cms W. The lower half is decorated with a design involving squares and concentric circles.

13.   A door headstone, possibly of A-S origin. It is located incorporated into the fabric of the east wall of the chancel. It is situated about 56 Ins/142 Cms above the apex of the window and about 56 Ins/142 Cms below the apex of the east wall of the chancel. The door headstone measures about 12 Ins/30 Cms H by 21 Ins/53 Cms W. It is incised with two semi-circles and a plain cross.

14.   A section of stonework from a cross-shaft. It is located incorporated into the fabric of the east wall of the chancel. It is situated 16 Ins/40 Cms south of the southern arm of the top of the east window and about 171 Ins/434 Cms up from the ground. The section of stonework measures about 14 Ins/35 Cms H by 12 Ins/30 Cms W. It is apparently decorated with the carving of a deer, but this is difficult to identify.

15.   A section of stonework from a cross-shaft. It is located incorporated into the fabric of the north wall of the vestry. It is situated 29 Ins/73 Cms west of the east end of the vestry and about 39 Ins/99 Cms up from the ground. The section of stonework measures 11 Ins/27 Cms H by 11½ Ins/29 Cms W. It is decorated with interlace design and it may be part of the cross-shaft for the crosshead at "5" above.

ERYHOLME
St Mary's Church
NZ 321090   Rating: ☆☆

The gated entrance to the drive leading to the churchyard is located on the west side the road running south-west/north-east through Eryholme. The entrance can be identified close to where a typical small freestanding church notice board stands to a height of 70 Ins/177 Cms. Pass through the gate and proceed up a gravel driveway to reach the gated churchyard entrance after 86 Yds/78 M.

The present structure dates from the 13C.

Incorporated into the internal east and west walls of the south porch, there are a number of sections of stonework of varying ages, sizes, conditions and purpose.

The south porch contains a section of stonework from an A-S cross-shaft. It is located incorporated into the internal east walling of the porch, 7 Ins/17 Cms south of the north wall of the porch and 51½ Ins/130 Cms up from the floor. The section of stonework measures 15½ Ins/39 Cms H tapering 19 Ins/48 Cms to 15½ Ins/39 Cms W. Recessed in this section of stonework is a distinctive three-quarter length figure with a clear face. Weathering has removed any trace of decoration.

Although the church is kept locked access is not necessary since the section of stonework from the cross-shaft is in a porch kept open at all times.

FILEY
St Oswald's Church
TA 118811   Rating: ☆

In the northern part of Filey, a signpost "St. Oswald's Church" directs you south off "Church Cliff Drive" (there are street signs) along an un-named (there are no street signs) drive that leads to the church. The church is about 150 Yds/137 M from Church Cliff Drive.

The present structure was built 1180-1230, and has 13C and 15C additions. It was restored in 1885.

Internally, the church contains a 9C section of stonework forming a step near the top of the tower. It is apparently decorated with plait work design. Access to the tower is not readily available and this section of stonework could not be viewed.

FINGHALL
St Andrew's Church
SE 191902   Rating: ☆☆☆   Access is possible.

The church is located about 880 Yds/804 M north-east of Finghall. 250 Yds/228 M south of where the minor road from Finghall joins the A684, close to the south bank of the "Leeming Beck", turn off the road and head in a south-easterly direction along a gravel drive. At the junction of the road and drive there is a directional sign "St. Andrews Church Finghall" attached to the wooden fencing on the south side of the drive. There is also a freestanding wooden "Public Footpath" directional sign by the fencing with the church sign. Proceed along this drive for about 450 Yds/411 M to reach the churchyard containing this small, tower-less church.

The church dates from the 13C.

Internally, there are sections of A-S stonework that comprise:

1.   A section of stonework from a wheel head crosshead comprising the central section and three arms with two of the connecting "wheels". It is located sitting on the window ledge of the westernmost window on the south side of the chancel. It is situated 28 Ins/71 Cms east of the west end of the window ledge and measures 9½ Ins/24 Cms H, by 14 Ins/35 Cms W, by 4½ Ins/11 Cms D. Although weathered a centre circle and some lines outlining the shape of the cross can be identified on both faces

and two of the ends of arms of the crosshead: the third end of arm is too damaged for any decoration to survive.

2.   A section of stonework from an arm from a wheel head cross with parts of two of its connecting "wheels". It is located lying on the floor in the chancel by the eastern end, and in front (to the south) of the choir stall on the north side of the chancel. It is in front (to the west) of the step up to the altar. The section of stonework measures 5 Ins/12 Cms H (D), by 9 Ins/22 Cms W (H), by 7 Ins/17 Cms D (W). Although weathered and damaged traces of knot work decoration can be identified on both of the faces and one side of the arm: the fourth side is the part of the arm broken off from the rest of the crosshead.

3.   A section of stonework from a wheel head cross comprising the central section and most of three arms. It is located lying flat and sitting on the window ledge of the easternmost window on the south side of the chancel. It is situated in the middle of the window ledge – the other sections of stonework on this window ledge are unrelated and are of a later date. The section of stonework measures 10 Ins/25 Cms D (H), by 11 Ins/27 Cms W, by 4 Ins/10 Cms H (D). On the top face some line decoration can be identified, particularly in the central section. The three other sides and the ends of the arms are too weathered or damaged for any decoration to survive.

4.   A section of stonework from a crosshead comprising the central section and an arm. It is located incorporated into the fabric of the south wall of the chancel, 2 Ins/5 Cms west of the east wall of the chancel and 87 Ins/220 Cms up from the floor. The section of stonework measures 15 Ins/38 Cms H by 12 Ins/30 Cms W. It is clearly decorated with the head, body and outstretched right arm of Christ in a Crucifixion scene.

FOLKTON

St John the Evangelist Church

TA 053797   Rating: ☆☆   Access is possible.

The church is located on the west side of the road running in a general north/south direction through Folkton, less than 300 Yds/274 M north of the A1039.

The present structure dates from the early 12C. However, there may be some A-S material incorporated into the fabric of the west wall of the tower but this cannot now be easily identified.

Internally, there is a section of stonework from a 10C cross-shaft. It is located sitting at the northern end of the window ledge of the west window of the tower. The section of stonework measures 12 Ins/30 Cms

H, by 16 Ins/40 Cms W, by 4 Ins/10 Cms D. The decoration on the southeast face includes knot work and animal design. The other three sides are similarly decorated and include two figures but due to damage and weathering the decoration is not clear.

FORCETT
St Cuthbert's Church
NZ 175123   Rating: ✰✰✰

In the south-western part of Forcett St Cuthbert's Church is easily located adjacent on the west side of the B6274.

The present structure dates from the 12C and was mostly restored in 1859.

Internally, there are a number of sections of stonework from 11C A-S/A-D crossheads and cross-shafts incorporated into the interior fabric of the south porch in a haphazard fashion, interspersed with fragments of stonework from later periods. All the sections of stonework are weathered and some are partially obscured by verdigris. Those that can be identified are:

Incorporated into the west wall:

1.   A section of stonework from an A-S crosshead comprising the central section and two arms. It is located 58 Ins/147 Cms up from the ledge forming a seat alongside the west wall, and 6 Ins/15 Cms south of the south door into the church. The section of stonework measures 13 Ins/33 Cms H by 11 Ins/27 Cms W. Although weathered some circular and knot work design can be identified.

2.   A section of stonework from an A-S cross-shaft. It is located 23½ Ins/59 Cms up from the ledge forming a seat alongside the west wall, and 26 Ins/66 Cms north of the south wall of the porch. This section of stonework measures 21 Ins/53 Cms H by 8 Ins/20 Cms W. It is decorated with various designs including, a cross and, in the bottom half, the figures of two men.

3.   A section of stonework from an A-S cross-shaft. It is located 57 Ins/144 Cms up from the ledge forming a seat alongside the west wall, and 20 Ins/50 Cms north of the south wall of the porch. This section of stonework measures 10 Ins/25 Cms H by 12 Ins/30 Cms W. It has been incorporated into the fabric horizontally rather than vertically. It is decorated with a human figure, minus the head, and knot work design.

4.   A section of stonework from an A-S cross-shaft. It is located 60 Ins/152 Cms up from the ledge forming a seat alongside the west wall, and one inch/2 Cms east of the south wall of the porch. This section of

stonework measures 8 Ins/20 Cms H by 11 Ins/27 Cms W. It appears to be decorated with a human figure as well as knot work design.

Incorporated into the east wall, in the recess behind the recumbent knight:

5.   A section of stonework from an A-S cross-shaft. It is located abutting the north side of the central later medieval grave cover, 25 Ins/63 Cms up from the recumbent knight, 18 Ins/45 Cms south of the north end of the recess. This section of stonework measures 21 Ins/53 Cms H by 13 Ins/33 Cms W. It is decorated with a large cross whose upper arm is surrounded by three animals, and knot work design.

6.   A section of stonework from an A-S crosshead, one of whose arms is complete while the other two are broken. It is located 23 Ins/58 Cms up from the recumbent knight and is shaped to fit in the southern curve of the recess. This section of stonework measures 12 Ins/30 Cms H by 20 Ins/50 Cms W. It is decorated with knot work design.

Externally, there are three much-weathered decorated sections of A-S stonework incorporated into the east wall of the south porch:

7.   An almost complete A-S crosshead. It is located 28 Ins/71 Cms north of the buttress at the south end of the porch, and 48 Ins/121 Cms up from the ground. The crosshead measures 14 Ins/35 Cms H by 19 Ins/48 Cms W. Although weathered, knot work decoration can just about be identified.

8.   A section of stonework from an A-S cross-shaft. It is located 53 Ins/134 Cms south of the south wall of the nave and 61 Ins/154 Cms up from the ground. The section of stonework measures about 7 Ins/17 Cms square. It is decorated with knot work design.

9.   A section of stonework from an A-S cross-shaft. It is located 34 Ins/86 Cms south of the south wall of the nave, and 44 Ins/111 Cms up from the ground. The section of stonework measures 21 Ins/53 Cms H by 12 Ins/30 Cms W. It is partially decorated with a circular design.

FYLINGDALES MOOR
Lilla Cross

SE 889986   Rating: ✫✫✫

The assassination attempt on King Edwin of Deira took place in 626 at his palace near the River Derwent at either Malton or Buttercrambe. Lilla put himself between the king and the assassins' double-edged poisoned dagger. Bede wrote about this event in his "History of the English Church and People". Lilla was buried in an existing Bronze Age round barrow which has since been known as "Lilla Howe". Lilla's Cross, dating from A-S times, was placed on the Howe some time later. As the notices referred to in the text below indicate, the cross was removed from the site in 1952 and moved temporarily to a safer place alongside the Whitby to Pickering road, but was restored to its original position in 1962. Excavations on the site in the 1920s revealed pieces of jewellery of A-D provenance some 200 years later than Lilla's recorded death.

Locate "Eller Beck" at SE 858983. Between the two bridges at Eller Beck, on the east side of the A169, there are two separate signs. The more northerly is a Borough of Scarborough sign affixed to a piece of stone walling and the more southerly is a low, free-standing sign "Welcome to Ryedale".

At Eller Beck leave the A169 and head east for just over 90 Yds/82 M along a rough, un-surfaced road to reach a field gate and adjacent stile. Between the A169 and the field gate there are two free-standing MOD signs "MOD Property No Admittance For Vehicles or For Parking" and "MOD Property No Cars Beyond This Point" and a free-standing North York Moors National Park notice.

Pass through the field gate and proceed along the rough un-surfaced road in a general easterly direction. This rough road ceases after about 440 Yds/402 M. Continue in the same direction all the time keeping close to the public side of the MOD field fence.

About 190 Yds/173 M from the end of the rough road and about 630 Yds/576 M from the field gate there is a small hut with a corrugated roof. Continue past this hut for about 250 Yds/228 M until reaching a vertical white post without any sign attached to it (all the time following the line of the MOD field fence and heading in a general easterly direction).

From this point head across country gently uphill using as aiming points the vertical white posts which all now have signs attached to them (the white posts and their signs can all easily be identified).

Continue for about 120 Yds/109 M to the next post with the sign attached: "MOD Property Keep Out Military Lands Bye-Laws In Force". Posts with the same sign attached are then spaced at the following approximate intervals in Yds/M: 170/155, 170/155, 180/164, 150/137, 190/173, 390/356, 220/201, 168/153, 124/113, 175/160, 138/126, and 70/64.

8 Yds/7 M farther east from this last sign there is another free-standing post with a sign attached: "This is a prohibited place within the meaning of the Official Secrets Act any unauthorised person entering the area will be arrested and prosecuted" and another sign attached underneath: "Caution, non-ionizing radiation" with a triangular symbol. These last two signs are by the south side of a well-defined track way that emerges from the prohibited MOD lands.

Follow this well-defined track way as it heads in a general easterly direction (i.e., not on prohibited land) for about 244 Yds/223 M until reaching another vertical post on which there are the MOD notices "This is a prohibited place" etc and "Caution, non-ionizing" etc.

Continue on this well-defined track way for another 240 Yds/219 M, passing a fallen MOD sign on the way, until reaching a junction with another well-defined track way that runs in a north/south direction.

Cross this well-defined track way running north/south and continue in a general easterly direction up towards Lilla Cross that now becomes clearly visible on a small knoll ahead. On the way there is a 36 In/91 Cms H wooden post on which there is an arrow indicating the way to the cross.

After 300 Yds/274 M cross another well-defined track way that heads in a north/south direction. Continue in a general easterly direction for another 55 Yds/50 M to reach the cross.

FYLINGDALES MOOR: Lilla Cross. An Anglo-Saxon cross. It commemorates the death of Lilla in 626 in saving the life of King Edwin of Deira.

The easily identifiable cross, comprising both crosshead and cross-shaft, is situated on the top of a small knoll and is surrounded by a low circle of stones. The cross-shaft is approximately 48 In/122 Cms H by 24 In/61 Cms W at its base and 12 Ins/30 Cms D. The square crosshead, which is integral to the cross-shaft, is approximately 24 Ins/61 Cms H by 24 Ins/61 Cms W by 12 Ins/30 Cms D. The crosshead and cross-shaft are weathered and neither has any decoration surviving on any of their sides. However, incised on the crosshead and the higher part of the cross-shaft, there is some writing, including the date 1894, on its south-west face, a large letter "G" for Goathland on its north-west face, and on its south-east face the letter "C" and a cross.

At the base of the knoll, 12 Yds/10 M from the north-west face of the cross, a large boulder has two descriptive notices attached to it.

The first notice reads: "Lilla Cross Erected about A.D. 626 over the reputed grave of Lilla, an officer of the court of Edwin, king of Northumbria, who died saving the life of the king. Believed to be the oldest Christian memorial in the north of England. Originally erected on moors between Pickering and Robin Hood's Bay, re-set in 1933 by the North Riding County Council. Removed in 1952 by Royal Engineers to avoid destruction from gunfire on artillery ranges."

The second notice underneath reads: "Lilla Cross was re-set here in 1962 by 508 Field Squadron Royal Engineers Territorial Army of Horden Co. Durham in conjunction with the Whitby Rural District Council."

GARGRAVE
St Andrew's Church
SD 932539   Rating: ☆☆☆

In the centre of Gargrave turn south off the A65 (T) as directed by the sign "Parish Church 180 Yds" and proceed along "Church Street" (there is a street sign). The church is easily located after 180 Yds/164 M on the east side of Church Street at its junction with "Church Lane" (there is a street sign).

Apart from the tower that dates from 1521, the present structure dates from the rebuilding in 1851-52.

Internally, there is a display comprising eight sections of stonework of varying sizes and dates. The display is located in the south aisle immediately to the east of the south door. This display stands in a sectioned-off part of the floor, 69 Ins/175 Cms W by 99½ Ins/252 Cms L. The display contains:

1.   A section of stonework from a late 10C/early 11C A-S cross-shaft. It is located 43 Ins/109 Cms north of the south wall of the south aisle and 25 Ins/63 Cms west of the westernmost pew in the south aisle. The section of stonework measures 22 Ins/55 Cms H, tapering 16 Ins/40 Cms to 14 Ins/35 Cms W, by 6½ Ins/16 Cms D. Although the section of stonework is weathered the two faces are decorated with a "hammer head" shaped cross and scroll design and the two other sides are decorated with plait work design.

2.   A section of stonework from a late 10C/early 11C A-S crosshead comprising the central section, a complete arm, and part of two other arms. It is located 74 Ins/187 Cms north of the south wall of the south aisle and 16 Ins/40 Cms west of the westernmost pew in the south aisle. The section of stonework measures 14 Ins/35 Cms H, by 18 Ins/45 Cms W, by 7 Ins/17 Cms D. It is very weathered and any decoration is difficult to identify.

3.   A section of stonework from a late 10C/early 11C A-S wheel head cross comprising an arm and the two sections of stonework forming

part of the wheel connecting it to the other arms. It is located 69 Ins/175 Cms north of the south wall of the south aisle and 31 Ins/78 Cms west of the westernmost pew in the south aisle. The section of stonework measures 9 Ins/22 Cms H, by 14 Ins/35 Cms W, by 6 Ins/15 Cms D. Although the section of wheel head is very weathered the two "eyes" between the arms of the cross can be identified on both faces as can the line decoration outlining the circular shape of the crosshead. No other decoration can be identified.

4.   A section of stonework from a late 10C/early 11C A-S wheel head cross comprising the central section, an arm, part of another arm, the section of stonework forming the wheel connecting them and part of another section of the wheel connecting one of the arms to a missing arm. It is located 84 Ins/213 Cms north of the south wall of the south aisle and 52 Ins/132 Cms west of the westernmost pew in the south aisle. The section of stonework measures 12 Ins/30 Cms H, by 16½ Ins/41 Cms W, by 5½ Ins/13 Cms D. Although this section of stonework is weathered, knot work decoration can be identified on both of the faces. The ends of the arms of the wheel are weathered and no decoration survives.

[There are four other sections of stonework on the display area that are not A-S/A-D. Three are small, nondescript pieces and the largest, oblong-shaped, appears to be part of a later medieval grave slab.]

According to the church guidebook there is another section of stonework from a 10C cross-shaft at the bottom of the tower steps. Apparently this can no longer be identified.

GIGGLESWICK
St Alkelda's Church
SD 812641   Rating: ☆

Less than 400 Yds/365 M west of where the old A65(T) crosses the River Ribble, turn off the A65(T) and proceed in a south-westerly direction along an un-named minor road as directed by the separate signs "Giggleswick" and "Giggleswick School". This minor road reaches a "T" junction in about 150 Yds/137 M. At this junction take the fork to the west and proceed for about another 150 Yds/137 M until reaching the easily recognisable church situated on the north side of the road.

Most of the present structure dates from the late 15C and the restoration in 1890-92, although there is some evidence of earlier material including 12C work. Apparently there may be some A-S stonework surviving in the east end of the church although this cannot be readily identified.

The church is dedicated to Alkelda the Saxon princess murdered by the Danes in 800: see the entry for Middleham, North Yorkshire.

GILLING EAST
Holy Cross Church
SE 616768   Rating: ☆

The church is easily identified situated in the centre of Gilling East set back from the east side of the B1363.

The present structure includes A-S material dating from the 11C. Subsequent building work was undertaken in the 12C, 14C, 16C and 19Cs.

Internally, on both sides of the nave, between the westernmost piers and the tower, and the easternmost piers and the chancel, the walling is apparently A-S, but plaster obscures too much to be certain.

Internally, there is a round font with its base broken and part of its side missing. (A circular section of unrelated stonework has been placed inside the font.) The font is located in the south aisle, sitting on the floor by the steps up to the south doorway and 44 Ins/111 Cms north of the south wall of the south aisle. The font measures 19½ Ins/49 Cms H by 28 Ins/71 Cms in diameter. It is too weathered and worn for any decoration to be identified. It is clearly of some antiquity and just may be A-S or Norman.

Externally, there is a virtually complete A-S crosshead and part of its attached cross-shaft. It is located 138 Ins/350 Cms south of a doorway (not in use) in the south aisle. The crosshead and section of stonework from its cross-shaft both lean at an angle of 45 degrees. The section of stonework from the cross-shaft has been broken at some time and fixed back together with the assistance of iron struts. In total the crosshead and section of stonework from the cross-shaft stand 66 Ins/167 Cms H. The crosshead measures 18 Ins/45 Cms H, by 20 Ins/50 Cms W, by 6 Ins/15 Cms D. The section of stonework from the cross-shaft measures 50 Ins/127 Cms H, tapering 16 Ins/40 Cms to 14 Ins/35 Cms W, tapering 7½ Ins/19 Cms to 6½ Ins/16 Cms D. All four sides of both the crosshead and section of stonework from the cross-shaft are very weathered and there is no trace of any decoration on any of their sides.

GILLING WEST
St Agatha's Church
NZ 182052   Rating: ☆☆   Access is possible, but the sections of stonework can only be viewed by prior arrangement with the vicar.

The church is located 90 Yds/82 M west of the B6274 towards the centre of Gilling West. It is reached by passing through a gated entrance and proceeding along a driveway for 83 Yds/75 M to reach the churchyard entrance. There is a "St Agatha's Church" directional sign by the side of the B6274 opposite the gated entrance.

Although material from the 12C does survive, most of the present church dates from the mid 19C restoration.

There are a number of sections of A-S stonework currently placed inside the tower on the ground floor in the stairwell. They have either been placed next to or on top of each other and are consequently it is difficult to view and identify confidently all the salient features. These sections of stonework are:

1.   Part of an arm from a 10C A-S crosshead. It measures 6 Ins/15 Cms H, by 6 Ins/15 Cms W, by 5 Ins/12 Cms D. Although weathered, interlace decoration can be identified on the end of the arm and the front and rear faces.

2.   Part of an arm from a 10C A-S crosshead. It measures 8 Ins/20 Cms H, by 6 Ins/15 Cms W, by 5 Ins/12 Cms D. Although weathered, knot work decoration can be identified on the end of the arm and the front and rear faces.

3.   An early 11C A-S crosshead comprising the central section, including the central boss, and an arm. It measures 10 Ins/25 Cms H, by 18 Ins/45 Cms W, by 5 Ins/12 Cms D. It is very weathered but some interlace decoration can be identified on the two faces of the crosshead.

4.   An almost complete late 10C A-S wheel head crosshead. It measures 15 Ins/38 Cms H, by 19 Ins/48 Cms W, by 6 Ins/15 Cms D.

GILLING WEST: St Agatha's Church. A former display of stonework, including seven items of Anglo-Saxon interest – these are now stored elsewhere in the church.

Items including parts of Anglo-Saxon crossheads and cross-shafts

Anglo-Saxon crosshead

Anglo-Saxon wheel head crosshead

Although very weathered, interlace decoration can be identified on the two faces of the crosshead and the end of the vertical arm. No decoration can be identified on the ends of the other arms.

5.   Part of a late 10C A-S crosshead comprising the central section, two arms and part of the third arm. It measures 14½ Ins/36 Cms H, by 16 Ins/40 Cms W, by 5½ Ins/13 Cms D. It is decorated with a large cross on both the front and rear faces. No other decoration on any of the other sides survives due to weathering and damage.

6.   A section of stonework from a late 10C A-S cross-shaft which probably formed part of the cross-shaft supporting the crosshead at "5" above. It measures 15 Ins/38 Cms H, by 7½ Ins/19 Cms W, by 6 Ins/15 Cms D. It is decorated with knot work design that can just about be identified on all four sides.

7.   A section of stonework from an A-S cross-shaft dating 950-975. It measures 23 Ins/58 Cms H, by 9 Ins/22 Cms W, by 6 Ins/15 Cms D. It is decorated in Ringerike design that can just about be identified on all four sides.

These sections of A-S/A-D stonework are stored here and it is intended that they should be properly displayed sometime in the future.

GOLDSBOROUGH
Wade's Stone
NZ 829144   Rating: ☆

On the west side of the minor road linking East Barnby to Goldsborough (the road crosses the A174), 440 Yds/402 M to the south-west of Goldsborough, locate the entrance drive to "Brockrigg Farm" (there is a sign identifying it as such attached to the fencing on the north side of the relevant drive).

Wade's Stone is situated in the field adjacent to the minor road, about 300 Yds/274 M west of the road, and about 90 Yds/82 M south of the driveway leading to Brockrigg Farm.

Wade's Stone is a single, irregular shaped section of stonework that leans in a north-westerly direction. It measures up to 60 Ins/152 Cms H, by up to 27 Ins/68 Cms W, by up to 19 Ins/48 Cms D. It is weathered and has no decoration on any of its sides, although there is some graffiti.

The stone is connected with the legend of the late 8C Saxon giant Wade who at one time owned Mulgrave Castle and was reputedly buried at this spot. Apparently, originally there were two stones marking the site of the grave. See the entry for East Barnby, North Yorkshire for another "Wade's Stone" connected with the Saxon giant.

GREAT AYTON
All Saints Church
NZ 557108   Rating: ☆☆

In the centre of Great Ayton, at the northern end of the bridge over the River Leven, turn west off the A173 as directed by the freestanding directional sign "12th Century All Saints Church" (the sign also directs to "Captain Cook Schoolroom Museum and "Tour""). Proceed along the road "Low Green" (there is a street sign). After about 65 Yds/59 M, on the north side of Low Green, there is another freestanding directional signpost "12th Century All Saints Church". Turn north off Low Green as directed and proceed along an un-named drive. This drive terminates at the entrance to the churchyard, 54 Yds/49 M north of Low Green.

The present structure of the church dates from the early 12C with later additions particularly in the 13C, 14C and 15Cs and around 1788 and 1880.

Internally, there are four sections of A-S stonework displayed sitting on the ledge of a blocked-up window in the north wall of the nave 20½ Ins/52 Cms west of the east wall of the nave/west wall of the chancel. They comprise:

1.   A section of stonework from an 8C crosshead comprising the central section, two arms and some of the two other arms. It is easily located abutting the western end of the ledge. The section of stonework measures 12½ Ins/31 Cms H, by 19½ Ins/49 Cms W, by 5½ Ins/13 Cms D. The southeast face is decorated with a foliate design outlining the shape of the crosshead and its centre. The two sides are too weathered for any decoration to be identified. The northwest face has a central boss and no other decoration.

2.   A section of stonework from an 8C decorated cross-shaft. It is easily located 24 Ins/61 Cms east of the western end of the ledge. The section of stonework measures 4½ Ins/11 Cms H, by 13½ Ins/34 Cms W, by 5½ Ins/13 Cms D. The southeast face and the southwest side are decorated with knot work design. The other sides are too weathered for any decoration to be identified.

3.   Two sections of stonework from the same large 9C crosshead comprising the central section and two arms (the western arm has been broken in two; hence there are now two sections). They are located 4 Ins/10 Cms west of the east end of the ledge. The larger of these two sections of stonework measures 7 Ins/17 Cms to 10 Ins/25 Cms H, by 18 Ins/45 Cms W, by 6½ Ins/16 Cms D. The southwest face is clearly decorated with a human torso (including arms) the head and legs are

missing. The northeast face is decorated with line and circle design and the end of the unbroken arm is decorated with knot work design. Lying next to (to the west) of this section of crosshead there is a smaller section of stonework obviously broken off from its western lateral arm. This broken-off section of stonework from the crosshead measures 6 Ins/15 Cms to 9 Ins/22 Cms H, by 8½ Ins/21 Cms W, by 7½ Ins/19 Cms D. The southwest face is clearly decorated with a human hand and part of an arm. The northeast face is decorated with line design and the end of the arm is decorated with knot work design.

4.   A section of stonework from an 8C A-S crosshead or cross-shaft (it is not possible to determine which with confidence). It is located 3 Ins/7 Cms west of the east end of the ledge (behind "3" above). The section of stonework measures 5½ Ins/13 Cms H, by 7 Ins/17 Cms W, by 5½ Ins/13 Cms D. The south face and east side have some decoration but it is not possible to identify a design. The other face and side are too weathered and damaged for any decoration to be identified.

GREAT EDSTONE
St Michael's Church
SE 705840   Rating: ✩✩✩

The small church is situated in the centre of Great Edstone set back from the road. The churchyard entrance is located on the west side of the road that runs in a general north/south direction through the village, close to where the road takes a right angled turn. There is a church notice behind the churchyard wall.

The present church dates mainly from the early 13C church although it does have 18C and 19C additions.

Externally, incorporated into the south wall of the nave there is an A-D sundial. It is easily identified on the face of a large oblong section of stonework (almost plaque-like) distinctly different from the surrounding smaller pieces of stonework 4 Ins/10 Cms directly above the apex of the south doorway. The oblong section of stonework measures 20 Ins/50 Cms H by 48 Ins/121 Cms W.

Although the gnomon is missing, the hole for it and the semi-circle with the incised lines indicating the time are clearly indicated in the top, central part of the section of stonework. In addition, on the western part of the oblong section of stonework, beneath the sundial, an inscription can easily be identified "Othan me prohtea" (Othan has wrought me). The eastern part of the oblong section of stonework is too weathered for any inscription to survive.

HACKNESS
St Peter's Church

SE 968905   Rating: ★★★☆☆

Towards the eastern end of Hackness, the church is easily identified on the south side of the road linking Hackness to Suffield.

Abbess Hild of Whitby had built a monastery at Hackness in 680, the year of her death. The Danes around 869 probably plundered it when they destroyed Whitby Abbey. Stones from the monastery may have been incorporated into St Peter's. The present structure incorporates material from the 8C and the later additions to the church in the 12C, 13C and 16C.

Internally, A-S material survives in the south wall of the chancel in the section of stonework that extends for 120 Ins/304 Cms east of the nave and 120 In/304 Cms H. A-S material also survives in virtually the whole wall containing the chancel arch. The A-S chancel arch survives intact and on the northern impost (where the arch begins) there is a decorative carving, part bird part beast, which dates it to the late 8C. The through-stone jambs of the chancel arch are laid in "Escomb" fashion.

Internally, the fabric of the nave includes material from the late 8C. Incorporated into the fabric of the south wall of the nave there are two A-S windows, most of whose outline survives. One can be identified on the west side of the west arch and one on the east side of the east arch (the outer face of the eastern window can be seen from the south aisle). There is the outline of another A-S window in the north wall of the nave above the easternmost arch. The window in the north wall is difficult to identify and is best viewed from the north aisle.

Internally, either side of the tower the original side alternate quoining of the nave can be identified; similar quoining can also be identified in the northeast corner of the nave (view from the north aisle).

Although there is no indication inside the church today, buried beneath the altar of St Peter's is Reinfrid, formerly one of William I's knights who took part in the "Harrying of the North" during 1069-70. Reinfrid followed the refugees from the Harrying to Evesham in Worcestershire. There he became a monk at Evesham Abbey. Inspired by the writings of Bede, in 1073-74 Reinfrid, accompanied Prior Aldwin and Elfwy the Deacon both from Winchcombe Abbey Gloucestershire, journeyed to the north to revive the monasteries at Jarrow, Wearmouth and Whitby. Reinfrid died (no later than 1086) in an accident on a bridge being built over the River Derwent nearby.

Internally, there are two sections of stonework from the same A-S cross-shaft dating from around 720. These sections of stonework are located 48 Ins/122 Cms west of the east wall in the south aisle, standing on top of a floor standing plinth 24 Ins/61 Cms H. The two sections of stonework have been cemented together and their overall height is now 57 Ins/144 Cms H, by 19 Ins/48 Cms reducing to 13 Ins/33 Cms square. Despite their weathered appearance the sections of cross-shaft are clearly decorated (figures, animals and interlace). On their south, east and northern sides there is lettering both in futhorc and Latin including the name of Abbess Æthelburga, great-niece to Abbess Hild. The cross-shaft dates from around 720.

HARROGATE
Royal Pump Room Museum
SE 298554 Rating: ☆

In the centre of Harrogate, the entrance to the Museum is on the north side of "Royal Parade", 20 Yds/18 M east from its junction with "Valley Drive" (there are street signs). Outside the Museum entrance there is a low, free-standing "Royal Pump Room Museum" notice board.

As with all museums, the displays and the exhibits they contain may be changed, re-sited, removed from display and/or put in store, or loaned to other museums or suitable repositories. Before visiting a museum it is worth checking in advance whether the displays listed in the gazetteer are still in place in the same location(s) set out in the text. Individual exhibits may have been rearranged in terms of their display, the order in which they are displayed and their relationship to other exhibits, some exhibits may have been removed from display.

The Museum building was originally built in 1842. It comprises an octagonal pump room, built to enclose the Old Sulphur Well, and a cast iron annexe built in 1913.

The Museum at one time displayed a 9C/10C grave cover measuring about 12 Ins/30 Cms H by 24 Ins/61 Cms L and incised in runic lettering "suna", meaning son of. The section of stonework was found at Pippin Castle in Heverah Park that has now been submerged under Scargill Reservoir. It is now in store.

HAWES
Dales Countryside Museum
SD 876899 Rating: ☆

The Museum is situated in the "Goods Warehouse" in the old railway station yard in the north-eastern part of Hawes. It is located about 100 Yds/91 M north of the A684. Proceed along a minor road (there is no street sign) as directed by the signpost "Dales Countryside Museum". There is a Museum sign on the relevant building. The Museum is well-signposted in Hawes.

As with all museums, the displays and the exhibits they contain may be changed, re-sited within the museum, removed from display and/or put in store, or loaned to other museums or suitable repositories. Before visiting a museum it is well worth checking beforehand that the displays referred to in the text below are still in place and whereabouts they are in the museum.

Based on local history the Museum includes a separate section showing the Dales through the ages, including A-S and A-D times. The exhibits include a King Offa (757-796) penny.

HELMSLEY
All Saints Church
SE 612838   Rating: ☆

In the centre of Helmsley, the church is located on the north side of the junction of "Church St" and an un-named road linking Church Street to "Market Place" (there are street signs).

The present structure originates from the 12C and the virtual complete rebuilding in 1849.

The church contains a late 10C hogback grave cover. It is located sitting on the floor in the south porch, 6½ Ins/16 Cms north of the south wall and between 3 Ins/7 Cms and 4½ Ins/11 Cms west of the east wall of the south porch. The hogback measures 14 Ins/35 Cms H, between 8½ Ins/21 Cms and 11½ Ins/29 Cms W, by 49 Ins/124 Cms L. The top face is clearly decorated with key design. All the other sides and ends are too weathered for any decoration to be identifiable.

Internally, on the east wall of the south transept "The Columba Chapel", the 19C murals and glass depict a stylised account of the coming of Christianity to northern England with a knight slaying a dragon, the life of St Columba, scenes from Bede including St Oswald's victory at the battle of Heavenfield (634), and St Aidan.

HEMINGBROUGH
Church of St Mary the Virgin
SE 674306   Rating: ☆   Access is possible.

The church is situated near the centre of the western part of Hemingborough. With its distinctively tall spire the church is easily located on the west side of "Main Street" (there is a street sign) 10 Yds/9 M north of its junction with "Finkle Street" (there is a street sign).

The present structure dates mainly from the 13C and the restorations in 1883-86 and 1988-92.

Internally, A-S material has been incorporated into the present fabric in the walls on both sides of the nave, particularly towards the eastern end and surrounding the two most eastern arches on either side of the nave.

HIGH HAWSKER
Abbey or Boiling Well
NZ 937069   Rating: ✰

1320 Yds/1207 M south east of High Hawsker, the well is easily located 6 feet/182 Cms Yds from the east side of the B1447. The well is contained in a distinctive structure in the shape of a small house, standing 72 Ins/182 Cms H, 96 Ins/243 Cms D by 108 Ins/274 Cms L.

Affixed to the brickwork on the western side of the structure there is a sign "Boiling Well. This spring served the local community from the 12th century. In early 19th century, its waters were carted to a reservoir at Whitby Abbey, then piped to Whitby houses east of the Esk."

On the eastern side of this structure there is a door that opens to reveal the well, with water.

The well is marked "T'awd Abba Well" on Ordnance Survey Maps. Local legend says this well was used by Abbess Hild (Abbess of Whitby 657-680).

HINDERWELL
St Hilda's Well
NZ 791171   Rating: ✰

Take the minor, un-named (there are no street signs) road which heads north off the A174 at the northern end of Hinderwell, as directed by the directional sign "Port Mulgrave ½". 120 Yds/109 M from the A174, the churchyard of St Hilda containing the well is easily located on the west side of the road.

Once inside the churchyard, pass through a wooden gate in the fencing attached to the north-east corner of the church to enter the northern part of the churchyard. Set into, but clearly protruding from, the ground, the well is some 20 Yds/18 M from the north wall of the church and is reached by descending a flight of steps.

The well is in a stone enclosure 72 Ins/182 Cms square and 36 Ins/91 Cms H. There is a sign affixed to the inner stonework "St Hilda's Well restored by Hilda Palmer of Crinkle Park 1912". Legend recalls that St Hilda, Abbess of Whitby 657-680, had a "cell" on this site which she used as a retreat when Abbess of Whitby, alternatively, she used the well when travelling in the area.

The fabric of the church dates from the late 18C.

HORNBY

St Mary's Church

SE 222937   Rating: ✩✩

The church is adjacent to the south side of the road that runs west/east through Hornby and is located close to the centre of the village.

An earlier church on this site comprised an A-S nave and chancel; a tower was added in the 11C. The present structure dates from the 11C A-S tower, the rebuilding of the nave and chancel 1180-9, and the rebuilding of the north aisle early in the 14C and the building of the south chapel late in the 15C. There was a comprehensive restoration of the church in 1887-8.

Internally, the tall narrow tower arch is probably Norman rather than A-S given its large overall construction.

Internally, there is an oval shaped shallow font that is probably Norman rather than A-S. It is located at the south-east end of the south aisle 18¾ Ins/47 Cms west of the chapel screen and 8¾ Ins/22 Cms north of the south wall of the south aisle. The bowl of the font is supported by a 17 Ins/43 Cms H stone pillar that stands on a 6½ Ins/16 Cms H plinth. The oval shaped font measures 10 Ins/25 Cms H, by 35 Ins/88 Cms W, by 25 Ins/63 Cms D. It has no decoration on any of its sides.

The three lower stages of the tower are A-S – the fourth stage dates from the late 15C. The A-S distinct features in the tower that can be viewed externally are:

1.   the double belfry openings on all four sides of the third stage

2.   a single window on the south side only of the second stage

3.   a single windows on the north and south sides only of the first stage

4.   the west door, in particular the solid stone lintel and blank typaneum

HOVINGHAM
All Saints Church
SE 666757   Rating: ☆☆☆☆☆

In the middle of Hovingham, take the minor road "Church Street" (there is a street sign, but not at its junction with the B1257) which heads in a south-westerly direction off the B1257. (At the appropriate junction there is a nearby ford.) About 150 Yds/137 M along Church Street the church is located adjacent to the west side of the road.

Despite an extensive rebuilding of the church in 1860, it retains its mid 11C A-S tower. Some of the material in the nave walls may also date from the 11C.

Internally, the east wall of the tower retains its characteristic A-S features: fabric comprising irregular shaped stones; there is a single course of large A-S herring-bone masonry; a small doorway (easily identified off centre to the north (right) immediately below the present frame supporting the roof); the quoins supporting the arch into the tower; and the arch itself which has no central key stone.

Internally, there is a weathered 8C A-S rectangular stone. It is located in the Lady Chapel in the south aisle, by the east window, behind the altar and set in the wall. The stone measures 24½ Ins/62 Cms H, by 63 Ins/160 Cms W, by up to 6 Ins/15 Cms D. The west face is decorated with eight figures sculptured in high relief depicting a scene from the Annunciation (the figures at either end are angels). There is no decoration on any of the other sides.

Internally in the middle of the chancel, there is a well preserved 10C decorated A-D crosshead and a section of stonework from its attached cross-shaft. They are located behind the altar, and on a free-standing iron frame. Together they stand 39½ Ins/100 Cms H. The crosshead measures 20 Ins/50 Cms H, by 15¾ Ins/40 Cms W, by 6¾ Ins/17 Cms D. The section of stonework from the cross-shaft measures 19½ Ins/49 Cms H, tapering 11½ Ins/29 Cms to 10½ Ins/26 Cms W, tapering 9 Ins/22 Cms to 7¾ Ins/19 Cms D. The crosshead is decorated on all four sides with knot work design. The section of stonework from the cross-shaft is decorated similarly on all four sides but with the heads and tails of intertwining beasts identifiable. (Note: the eastern sides of both the crosshead and section of stonework from the cross-shaft are weathered and damaged.)

Externally, the tower retains its characteristic A-S features: fabric comprising irregular shaped stones, large side alternate quoining on the corners (the north-west and south-west corners are the best), two projecting string courses separating each of the three stages of the tower,

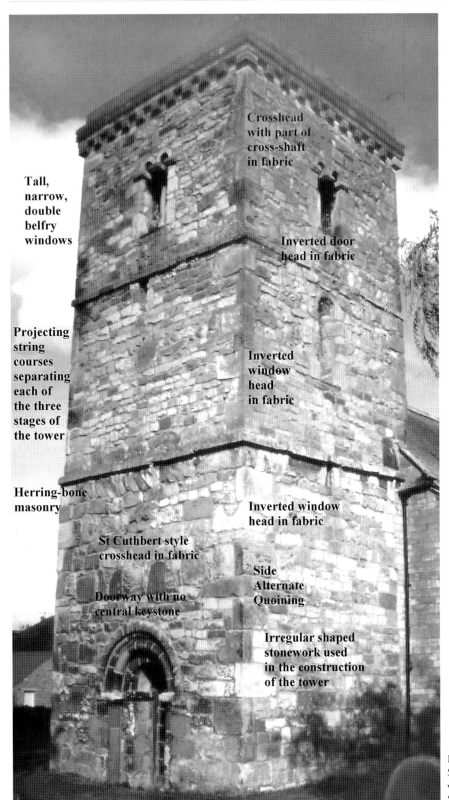

Crosshead
with part of
cross-shaft
in fabric

Tall,
narrow,
double
belfry
windows

Inverted door
head in fabric

Projecting
string
courses
separating
each of
the three
stages of
the tower

Inverted
window
head
in fabric

Herring-bone
masonry

Inverted window
head in fabric

St Cuthbert style
crosshead in fabric

Side
Alternate
Quoining

Doorway with no
central keystone

Irregular shaped
stonework used
in the construction
of the tower

HOVINGHAM: All
Saints Church. Tower
with characteristic Anglo-
Saxon features.

the tall, narrow double belfry windows in the third stage on all four sides, the fact that the tower has three stages and the fact that arch over the west doorway has no central keystone. [It is difficult to date the oblong openings in the second stages on the west and north sides and the first stage on the south side. The window in the second stage on the south side is not A-S.]

On the external western face of the tower, there is a single course of large A-S herringbone masonry, underneath the first level stringcourse. Beneath this herring-bone masonry in the next but one course of stonework there is a distinctive St Cuthbert style carved cross about 21 Ins/53 Cms square. It is easily identified protruding from the stonework in the centre of the wall in line with the top of the former west doorway. The cross dates from the 9C.

Externally, there is a 10C crosshead cross and a section of stonework from its attached cross-shaft. It has been incorporated into the fabric of the south face of the tower. Identify the second course of stonework above the centre of the top (third stage) belfry opening, and the second course of stonework beneath the ornamentation supporting the top of the tower. The central section of the crosshead has slight traces of its central boss but no decoration can now be identified on either the crosshead or its attached section of stonework from its cross-shaft.

The fabric of the tower incorporates stonework from one door head and four window heads from earlier A-S structures on the site. All apart from "4" below have been inverted. They are located:

1.   A door head that has been re-used as a quoin. It is located on the south face of the tower and has been used as part of the quoining on the southwest corner of the tower. It is the quoin immediately above the second stringcourse.

2.   A window head that has been re-used as a quoin. It is located on the west face of the tower and has been used as part of the quoining on the southwest corner of the tower. It is the third quoin above the first stringcourse.

3.   A window head that has been re-used as a quoin. It is located on the west face of the tower and has been used as part of the quoining on the southwest corner of the tower. It is the third quoin below the first stringcourse.

4.   Most of a window head. It is located on the west face of the tower adjacent to a "long" quoin. It is adjacent to the south (right) of the fifth quoin (stone) up from the ground in the northwest corner of the tower. It is 12 Ins/30 Cms south of the northwest corner of the tower. This particular window head has not been inverted and has been placed the correct way up.

5.   A window head that has been re-used as a quoin. It is located on the north face of the tower and has been used as part of the quoining on the northwest corner of the tower. It is the fourth quoin below the first stringcourse.

HUNMANBY
All Saints Church

TA 095775   Rating: ★★☆

Towards the northern end of Hunmanby, the church is easily located adjacent to the east side of the road "Church Hill" (there are street signs).

On the site of an A-S church, the present structure, which dates from the early 12C and the restoration in 1845, incorporates material from its 11C predecessor.

Internally, in the south porch there is a damaged coffin that may be A-S (there is no socket for the head). It is located lying between the north and south walls of the south porch and 2 Ins/5 Cms west of the east wall. The coffin measures between 13½ Ins/34 Cms and 17 Ins/43 Cms H (W), by 70 Ins/177 Cms L, by 23 Ins/58 Cms D. The side now lying on the floor has a large section missing towards its northern end.

Externally, there are windows in the tower that may date from the 11C. The first is located in the west face of the tower, at second storey height, and consists of a single narrow, round-headed window. The second is located in the south face of the tower, again at second storey height, and consists of a double window with a central column and round head. Also located in the south face of the tower, the single narrow round headed windows to the east and below the double windows at first and second storey level may also be A-S.

Externally, incorporated into the fabric of the north aisle to the east of the easterly-most window there are sections of stonework of various dates, sizes and purpose. Amongst these there are:

1.   A section of stonework from an A-S crosshead, comprising the central section, a complete arm and most of two other arms. It is located adjacent to, and less than 1 inch/2 Cms east of the easternmost window in the north aisle, and 77 Ins/195 Cms up from the ground. It measures 9 Ins/22 Cms H, by 6 Ins/15 Cms W, and between 2½ Ins/6 Cms and 3 Ins/7 Cms D. It is very weathered and consequently it is not possible to identify any decoration.

2.   A section of stonework from an A-S crosshead, comprising the central section and most of four arms. It is located 8 Ins/20 Cms east

of the easternmost window in the north aisle and 78 Ins/198 Cms up from the ground. It measures 9½ Ins/24 Cms H, by 12½ Ins/31 Cms W, by 2½ Ins/6 Cms D and is decorated with incised lines outlining the shape of the cross and there are circular lines in the centre of the central section.

3.   A section of stonework from a crosshead and a section of stonework from its attached cross-shaft. They may be A-S. They are located 27 Ins/68 Cms east of the easternmost window in the north aisle and 79 Ins/200 Cms up from the ground. They measure 8½ Ins/21 Cms H by 11 Ins/27 Cms W (it is incorporated "flat" into the wall). The section of stonework from the crosshead is decorated with the outline of a cross in a circular surround. The section of stonework from the cross-shaft is decorated with two roughly parallel lines in the centre.

4.   A section of stonework from a crosshead and a section of stonework from its attached cross-shaft. They may be A-S. They are located 40 Ins/101 Cms east of the easternmost window in the north aisle and 79½ Ins/201 Cms up from the ground. They measure 8½ Ins/21 Cms H by 14 Ins/35 Cms W (it is incorporated "flat" into the wall). The section of stonework from a crosshead is decorated with the outline of a cross in a circular surround with a hole in each arm and the centre. Due to weathering and damage no decoration can now be identified on the section of stonework from the cross-shaft.

5.   A section of stonework from a circular headed grave slab. It may be A-S. It is located 24 Ins/60 Cms east of the easternmost window in the north aisle and 67½ Ins/171 Cms up from the ground. It measures 11 Ins/27 Cms H by 11 Ins/27 Cms W (it is incorporated "flat" into the wall). It is decorated with the outline of a cross in a circular surround.

6.   A section of stonework from a circular headed grave slab. It may be A-S. It is located 35½ Ins/90 Cms east of the easternmost window in the north aisle and 68½ Ins/174 Cms up from the ground. It measures 10½ Ins/26 Cms H by 9 Ins/22 Cms W (it is incorporated "flat" into the wall). It is decorated with a foliated cross design.

7.   A section of stonework from a circular headed grave slab. It may be A-S. It is located 45½ Ins/115 Cms east of the easternmost window in the north aisle and 69 Ins/175 Cms up from the ground. It measures 10½ Ins/26 Cms H by 8½ Ins/21 Cms W (it is incorporated "flat" into the wall). It is decorated with the outline of a cross in a circular surround.

Externally, there is a very weathered section of stonework that is probably later medieval rather than A-S. It has been incorporated into the fabric of the west wall of the tower, 90 Ins/228 Cms up from the ground and 24 Ins/61 Cms north of the south wall. The section of stonework includes an incised petal or star.

HUTTON-LE-HOLE
Ryedale Folk Museum
SE 705900   Rating: ✰✰✰✰

The Museum is easily identified situated on the east side of the more easterly of the two roads that run south-east/north-west through Hutton-le-Hole. Attached to the north, south and east sides of the appropriate building housing the entrance to the Museum, there are "Ryedale Folk Museum" signs.

As with all museums, the displays and the exhibits they contain may be changed, re-sited, removed from display and/or put in store, or loaned to other museums or suitable repositories. Before visiting a museum it is worth checking in advance whether the displays listed in the gazetteer are still in place in the same location(s) set out in the text. Individual exhibits may have been rearranged in terms of their display, the order in which they are displayed and their relationship to other exhibits, some exhibits may have been removed from display. The text in the gazetteer reflects the descriptions and/or accompanying notices to the exhibits at the time of visiting. These too may have been revised, amended, added to or removed.

The Open Air Museum contains a number of reconstructed historic buildings which house displays of crafts and local industries, period shops and workshops, farming and rural life.

The Museum contains A-S and A-D sections of stonework displayed from the "Hayes Archaeological Collection". These are located on the first floor of the Wagon Shed, which is situated towards the north-eastern end of the site.

Six sections of stonework are displayed in an area with a raised wooden platform and sectioned off by a wooden barrier at the north-eastern end of the first floor, adjacent to the north wall of the Wagon Shed. They comprise:

1.   A section of stonework comprising most of an A-S wheel head cross, apart from the section of stonework joining it to the cross-shaft. It is located at the western (left) end of the display. It sits on top of a stand 69 Ins/175 Cms tall. The section of stonework measures 12 Ins/30 Cms H, by 12 Ins/30 Cms W, by 6½ Ins/16 Cms D. On the two faces of the section of stonework it is decorated with interlace design with a central roundel in the centre of the wheel head. There is no surviving decoration on the ends of the arms.

2.   A section of stonework from an A-S wheel head cross, comprising most of the central section, the vertical arm, part of two other arms, and

most of one and part of another "wheel" connecting the arms together. It is located towards the western (left) end of the display, to the east (right) and next to "1" above. It sits on top of a stand 49 Ins/124Cms tall. The section of stonework measures 13 Ins/33 Cms H, by 13½ Ins/34 Cms W, by 7 Ins/17 Cms D. It is decorated with knot work and circular design on both faces. There is no decoration surviving on the ends of the arms.

3.   A section of stonework from an A-S cross-shaft. It is located towards the eastern (right) end of the display, to the east (right) and next to "2" above and to the west (left) and next to "4" below. It sits on top of a stand 36½ Ins/92 Cms tall. The section of stonework measures 11Ins/27 Cms H, by 10½ Ins/26 Cms to 12 Ins/30 Cms W, by 7 Ins/17 Cms D. It is decorated with the face and the "stumpy" body of a man on the south (front) face. The figure of a "squashed up" "Ryedale" dragon decorates the north (rear) face. It is also decorated on the other two sides with ring chain design.

4.   Two sections of stonework, now joined together, from an A-S cross-shaft. They are located at the eastern (right) end of the display, to the east (right) and in front of "3" above. They sit on top of a stand 29½ Ins/74 Cms tall. Together the sections of stonework measure 18½ Ins/46 Cms H, by 6 Ins/15 Cms to 10½ Ins/26 Cms W, by 5 Ins/13 Cms D. They are decorated with a "crab shaped" human figure with elbows raised and legs astride on the south (front) face. The figure of a "Ryedale" dragon decorates the north (rear) face. It is also decorated on the two other sides with interlace design.

5.   A section of stonework from an A-S cross-shaft. It is the more eastern (right) of the two sections of stonework situated in the front of the display. It sits on top of a stand 7 Ins/17Cms tall. The section of stonework measures 28 Ins/71 Cms H, by 9 Ins/22 Cms to 13 Ins/33 Cms W, by 7 Ins/17 Cms D. On the top third of its south face the lower part of a human figure, both legs and feet, and a sword can just be made out. This south (front) face is also decorated with knot work design. (The warrior portrait on the south (front) face is similar to those on the cross-shafts housed in St Andrew's Church Middleton (see the entry for Middleton, North Yorkshire and entries "1", "4" and "5" in particular). The north (rear) face is now too weathered to identify any particular decoration. The two other sides are decorated with a sort of key design.

6.   A section of stonework from an A-S cross-shaft. It is the western (left) of the two sections of stonework situated in the front of the display. It is sits on top of a stand 7½ Ins/19 Cms tall. The section of stonework measures 15½ Ins/39 Cms H, by 12 Ins/30 Cms to 13 Ins/33 Cms W, by 9 Ins/22 Cms D. It is decorated on its south (front) face and the west and east sides with the "Ryedale" dragon. On these three sides there is an

indication of scroll design similar to that found on Ringerike design. The north facing (rear) face has no decoration that can now be identified.

[Numbers "1" to "5" above came from All Saints Church, Kirkbymoorside (see the entry for Kirkbymoorside, North Yorkshire), and Number "6" above came from St Mary's Church, Levisham (see the entry for Levisham, North Yorkshire)].

In a separate display at the north-western end of the first floor, and adjacent to the west wall of the Wagon Shed, there are:

7.   Two sections of stonework from an A-D hogback grave cover now joined together. They are located beneath a 12C lintel and sit on top of a stand 7½ Ins/19 Cms tall. The sections of stonework together measure 6½ Ins/16 Cms H, by 25½ Ins/64 Cms W, by 9½ Ins/24 Cms D. They are decorated with knot work design on their top face and north sides but no other decoration can now be identified on any of the other sides. [It also came from St Mary's Church, Levisham – see the entry for Levisham, North Yorkshire.]

KELLINGTON
St Edmund's Church

SE 547245   Rating: ☆   Access is possible.

The church is separate from Kellington, about 400 Yds/365 M south-west of the village. It is set back from the west side of a minor, un-signposted, road that runs in a south-easterly/north-westerly direction.

Although on the site of an A-S church, the present structure dates from 1100. There were subsequent additions and alterations in the 13C, 14C, and 15C's and 1867-70.

Excavations in and around the church took place during 1990/91. In advance of the work to stabilise the structure of the church to prevent subsidence likely through future mine workings in the area.

The excavations revealed an early, pre-10C metalworking tunnel furnace and a graveyard comprising some 20 burials dating from around 550-750 AD. The excavations also revealed under the present chancel indications of some sort of wooden structure, possibly an oratory connected with the graveyard. A-S pottery shards were found under the present tower. The foundations of an A-S church built mainly in timber were discovered under the floor of the eastern half of the present nave. There is now no visible evidence of the location of these discoveries.

Internally, on the floor at the east end of the north aisle, there is a display of some of the artefacts found during the excavations none of which appear to be of A-S or A-D origin.

KILDALE
St Cuthbert's Church
NZ 604096   Rating: ☆☆   Access is possible.

In the centre of Kildale, turn off the road that runs south-west/north-east through the village, and take the minor road that heads in a north-westerly direction. Opposite the appropriate junction there is a free-standing signpost on which there is a directional indication "Kildale Stn".

Continue on this road for about 400 Yds/365 M. On the way there is a gated track that heads off north down to Kildale Station (there is a large free-standing British Rail sign "Kildale" with the British Rail logo) – ignore this track and keep on the road. After about 66 Yds/60 M past the track to Kildale Station the road passes through an opening in a wall to reach a farm. Immediately before this opening, proceed directly north off this road alongside the wall down to a gated footpath about 18 Yds/16 M away. This gated footpath bridges the railway line; the gate on the other side of this bridge forms the entrance to the churchyard. (The location of this footpath with its two gates is obvious despite the surrounding trees and vegetation.)

The present church on this site dates from 1868. It is on the site of an earlier church where the body and coffin of St Cuthbert (died 687) rested during the journey from Lindisfarne (875) to Chester-le-Street (883) to Durham (995).

Internally, there is a plain and simple, undecorated tub font of indeterminate date. It is located under the tower, 4½ Ins/11 Cms east of the west wall. The font stands on a 8 inch/20 centimetre H floor standing stone column from an earlier church on the site. Now stored in the tub of this font there are two sections of stonework. These are:

1.   A section of stonework from a circular shaped A-S crosshead. It has been placed at the top of the tub on top of "2" below. The section of stonework measures 8 Ins/20 Cms H, by 10½ Ins/26 Cms W, by 4 Ins/10 Cms D. The top and bottom faces are clearly decorated with part of a cross. The other sides and edges are too weathered or damaged for any decoration to be identified.

2.   A section of stonework from an A-S grave slab. It has been placed at the bottom of the tub under "1" above. The section of stonework measures 12 Ins/30 Cms H, by 9½ Ins/24 Cms W, by 4½ Ins/11 Cms D. The top face is clearly decorated with the outline of a simple cross. The other sides are too weathered or damaged for any decoration to be identified.

Internally, under the tower, there are:

3.   A section of stonework from the end of an arm from an A-S crosshead. It is located sitting on the floor 14½ Ins/36 Cms south of the north wall and 2 Ins/4 Cms east of the west wall of the tower. The section of stonework measures 13 Ins/33 Cms H, by 9½ Ins/24 Cms W, by 8 Ins/20 Cms D. Both the east and west faces have clear line markings denoting the arm of the cross and subdividing the arm. The other sides are too weathered or damaged for any decoration to be identified.

4.   A circular shaped crosshead that could be A-S. It is located sitting on the floor diagonally across the northwest corner of the tower touching both the west and north walls of the tower. The crosshead measures 15 Ins/38 Cms H, by 14½ Ins/36 Cms W, by 4 Ins/10 Cms D. Both the southeast and northwest faces are clearly decorated with a cross. On both these faces there is also line decoration in the centre and in the spaces between the spandrels of the cross design. The other sides are too weathered or damaged for any decoration to be identified.

5.   A section of stonework from a circular shaped A-S crosshead. It is located sitting on the floor leaning against the north wall and 18 Ins/45 Cms east of the west wall of the tower. The section of stonework measures 9½ Ins/24 Cms H, by 16½ Ins/41 Cms W, by 5 Ins/12 Cms D. Both the south and north faces are clearly decorated with an ornate scroll-like cross. The other sides are too weathered or damaged for any decoration to be identified.

6.   A section of stonework from a circular shaped A-S crosshead. It is located sitting on the floor 10 Ins/25 Cms south of the north wall and 13 Ins/33 Cms east of the west wall of the tower. The section of stonework measures 8½ Ins/21 Cms H, by 7 Ins/17 Cms W, by 3½ Ins/8 Cms D. On both its top and bottom faces the lines of a cross can be identified. The other sides are too weathered or damaged for any decoration to be identified.

KILDWICK
St Andrew's Church

SE 012458   Rating: ☆☆☆   Access is possible.

In the centre of Kildwick, the church is prominently situated set back from the north side of the junction of "Main Road/Priest Bank Road" and "Skipton Road" (there are street signs). It is under 250 Yds/228 M north of the A629 (T).

On the site of an A-S church, the present church includes some material from the 12C but mostly dates from the early 14C, mid 15C, early 16C and the restoration in 1901.

Internally, on a raised part of the floor, there is a display of twelve sections of stonework of varying ages, shapes and sizes. The display is located to the east of the south aisle, 60 Ins/152 Cms west of what is known as the "Choir Vestry". The display measures 90 Ins/228 Cms by 66 Ins/167 Cms. In the display area there is a descriptive notice relating to the sections of stonework that numbers those of A-S interest 1 to 6. The A-S sections of stonework that date from the 10C are:

1.   A section of stonework from an A-S cross-shaft. It is located 12 Ins/30 Cms north of the south wall of the church and 11 Ins/27 Cms west of the east end of the display. The section of stonework measures 32 Ins/81 Cms H, by 13½ Ins/34 Cms W, by 10 Ins/25 Cms D. The northwest face and the northeast side are decorated with vine scroll design. The other face and side have no identifiable decoration. It is numbered "1" by the descriptive notice by the display.

2.   A section of stonework from what appears to be part of an A-S cross-shaft. It is located 45 Ins/114 Cms north of the south wall of the church and 14 Ins/35 Cms west of the east end of the display. The section of stonework measures 13 Ins/33 Cms H, by 8½ Ins/21 Cms W, by 7 Ins/17 Cms D. The northwest face is decorated with a man with raised arms with an animal on each side (it is not very clear). The decoration on the other face and sides are very weathered and with difficulty some knot work and plait work decoration can just about be identified. It is numbered "5" by the descriptive notice by the display. The notice describes this as a part of a crosshead (an arm) but this seems unlikely since if this were so the depiction of Christ would not be in a vertical position.

3.   A section of stonework from an A-S cross-shaft. It is located 27 Ins/68 Cms north of the south wall of the church and 41 Ins/104 Cms west of the east end of the display. The section of stonework measures 17 Ins/43 Cms H, by 11 Ins/27 Cms W, by 7 Ins/17 Cms D. It is clearly decorated on all four sides with knot work design. It is numbered "4" by the descriptive notice by the display.

4.   A section of stonework from the central part of an A-S crosshead. It is located 49 Ins/124 Cms north of the south wall of the church and 41 Ins/104 Cms west of the east end of the display. It measures 7 Ins/17 Cms H, by 11 Ins/27 Cms W, by 9 Ins/22 Cms D. The central, circular boss is evident on the two faces and some knot work decoration can just about be identified despite the poor state of this section of stonework. There is no decoration on any of the other sides due to weathering and damage. It is numbered "6" by the descriptive notice by the display.

5.   A section of stonework from an A-S cross-shaft. It is located 13 Ins/33 Cms north of the south wall of the church and 59 Ins/149 Cms

west of the east end of the display. It measures 27 Ins/68 Cms H, tapering from 10½ Ins/25 Cms to 9 Ins/22 Cms W, by 8½ Ins/21 Cms D. Knot work decoration can be identified on the lower part of the north-eastern face (the best preserved) and on the two sides. Tooling has destroyed the decoration on the south-western face. It is numbered "2" by the descriptive notice by the display.

6.   A section of stonework from an A-S cross-shaft. It is located 43 Ins/109 Cms north of the south wall of the church and 64 Ins/162 Cms west of the east end of the display. The section of stonework measures 18½ Ins/47 Cms H, tapering from 11 Ins/27 Cms to 9 Ins/22 Cms W, by 6 Ins/15 Cms D. The northeast face is decorated with a man holding an object below. (If the figure is supposed to represent Christ in a Resurrection Scene then the depiction is unlike most others, there is no halo, arms are not outstretched.) The other face and the southeast side are decorated with knot work design. Tooling has removed the decoration on the north-west side. It is numbered "3" by the descriptive notice by the display.

KIRBY GRINDLAYTHE
St Andrew's Church

SE 903674   Rating: ☆

In the centre of Kirby Grindlaythe, at the minor crossroads, take the minor, no-through road westwards (there is no street sign but there is a no-through road sign). Continue along this road for just under 200 Yds/182 M. Before the road passes through an open farm gate, take the drive which heads north uphill. The churchyard gates are reached after 40 Yds/36 M. The church, with its steeple, is easy to locate.

Despite the virtual rebuilding of the church in 1872 fabric survives from the 12C and 14C.

The interior walls of the tower contain two sections of stonework from cross-shafts and a section of stonework from a crosshead. Although these sections of stonework are undoubtedly A-S, and more appropriate to the 10C or 11C, they have been dated as late as the early 12C. These are:

1.   A section of stonework from a cross-shaft. It is located incorporated into the fabric of the south wall, 59 Ins/149 Cms up from the floor, and situated in the southeast corner of the tower. The section of stonework measures 8 Ins/20 Cms H by 19 Ins/48 Cms W. It is decorated with basket-plait design.

2.   A section of stonework from an arm from a crosshead. It is located incorporated into the fabric of the north wall, 99 Ins/251 Cms

up from the floor and 31 Ins/78 Cms west of the east wall of the tower. The section of stonework measures 9 Ins/22 Cms H by 6 Ins/15 Cms W. It is decorated with tree-scroll design.

3.   A section of stonework from a cross-shaft. It is located incorporated into the fabric of the north wall, 99 Ins/252 Cms up from the floor and 42 Ins/106 Cms east of the west wall of the tower. The section of stonework measures 10 Ins/25 Cms H by 5 Ins/12 Cms W. It is decorated with tree-scroll design.

Externally, material may survive from before the 12C in the lower stages of the tower, including the lowest window on the south face, and the quoining, particularly on the northwest corner of the tower.

Access to the tower has to be arranged: contact the Malton Tourist Information Centre, 58 Market Place, Malton, North Yorkshire, YO17 7LW.

KIRBY HILL
All Saints Church

SE 393686   Rating: ☆☆☆   Access is possible.

The church is situated at the eastern end of Kirby Hill. In the centre of Kirby Hill turn off the B6265 and proceed in an easterly direction along "Church Lane" (there is a street sign). Opposite the junction on the west side of the B6265 there is an "Ancient Church ¼" directional sign. Underneath this sign there is a directional sign "Helperby, Easingwold". Continue along Church Lane for about 528 Yds/482 M to reach the church which is easily located in the fork of a "Y" junction of two minor roads that lead north-east and east out of the east end of Kirby Hill.

Despite the rebuilding in 1870, 9C/10C, 11C, 12C, 13C and 15C material work can be easily identified in the present structure.

Internally, incorporated into the external fabric of the south wall of the nave, and now enclosed and forming the internal north wall of the south porch, there are:

1.   A section of stonework from an A-S impost stone. It is located 73 Ins/185 Cms up from the floor and 5½ Ins/13 Cms east of the south doorway into the church. Two sides of the section of stonework can be viewed. It measures 11 Ins/27 Cms H, by 26 Ins/66 Cms W, by 13½ Ins/34 Cms D. Both sides are decorated with interlace design. [In both the north wall of the porch (south wall of the nave) and the internal east wall of the porch the surrounding stonework has been cut away so that the section of stonework can be viewed.] Although dating from the 8C it was not until the 11C that this section of stonework was brought from Ripon and put in its present position.

2.   A section of stonework from an A-S cross-shaft. It is located 108 Ins/274 Cms up from the floor and 11 Ins/27 Cms west of the internal east wall of the porch. The section of stonework measures 15 Ins/38 Cms H and 12 Ins/30 Cms W. Although weathered, knot work design can be identified.

3.   A section of stonework comprising part of three arms from an early 10C A-S crosshead. It is located 25 Ins/63 Cms above the centre of the arch above the south doorway into the church. The section of stonework measures 10 Ins/25 Cms H, by 10 Ins/25 Cms W. Although weathered, knot work design can be identified as can seven balls in the centre circle.

Incorporated into the internal western wall of the south porch there are:

4.   A section of stonework from an A-S cross-shaft. It is located 40 Ins/101 Cms up from the floor and 9 Ins/22 Cms north of the internal south wall of the porch. The section of stonework measures 10 Ins/25 Cms H, by 10½ Ins/26 Cms W. It is decorated with knot work design.

5.   A section of stonework comprising a baluster shaft (this may be Roman?). It is located 81 Ins/205 Cms up from the floor and 15½ Ins/39 Cms west of the north wall of the porch. The section of stonework measures 11 Ins/27 Cms H, by 4½ Ins/11 Cms W. There is no decoration but the baluster shaft is distinctive due to its shape.

Internally, lying on the floor under the tower, there are:

6.   A section of stonework from an early 11C A-D cross-shaft. It is located leaning against the west wall of the tower, 16 Ins/40 Cms south of the north wall of the tower. The section of stonework measures 24 Ins/60 Cms H, tapering 13½ Ins/34 Cms to 10½ Ins/26 Cms W, by 5 Ins/12 Cms D. It is decorated with knot work design on all four sides.

7.   A section of stonework from an A-S crosshead comprising the central section and parts (small) of two arms and a section from its connected cross-shaft. It dates from circa 800. They are located leaning against the north wall of the tower, and 1 inch/2 Cms east of the west wall of the tower. In total they measure 38½ Ins/97 Cms H. The section of stonework from the crosshead measures 9 Ins/22 Cms H, by 12½ Ins/31 Cms W, by 6 Ins/15 Cms D. Although weathered some knot work decoration can be identified on all four sides. In the centre of one of the faces there are four balls. The section of stonework from the cross-shaft measures 29½ Ins/74 Cms H, by 11½ Ins/29 Cms W, by 6 Ins/15 Cms D. Although weathered some knot work decoration can be identified on all four sides.

8.   A section of stonework from an A-S crosshead comprising the central section and most of three arms. It dates from circa 900. It is located sitting on top of another section of stonework (see entry (9) below) in the north-east corner of the tower 1½ Ins/3 Cms west of the east wall of the tower. The section of stonework measures 13½ Ins/34 Cms H, by 21½ Ins/54 Cms W, by 8 Ins/20 Cms D. Although weathered some knot work decoration can be identified on all four sides. On the west face there appears to be the arms, body and head of Christ in a Crucifixion scene.

9.   A section of stonework from an A-S cross-shaft. It dates from circa 1000. It is located supporting the section of crosshead at (8) above. The section of stonework measures 11 Ins/27 Cms H, by 20 Ins/50 Cms W, by 7 Ins/17 Cms D. Due to the weathering it is difficult to identify the nature of the decoration surviving but apparently on one face there is the outline of a large animal.

Internally, under the centre of the tower, there is a plain, A-S font standing on a plinth.

Internally, incorporated into the interior south wall of the nave there is:

10.   A section of stonework from an A-S cross-shaft. It is located 128 Ins/325 Cms up from the floor and 30 Ins/76 Cms east of the arch over the current south door. The section of stonework measures 8½ Ins/21 Cms H by 29 Ins/73 Cms W. It is decorated with knot work design.

Internally, incorporated into the interior north wall of the nave there is:

11.   A section of stonework from an A-S cross-shaft. It is located in the north-west corner of the nave, 40 Ins/101 Cms above the top of the capital from which the western arm of the westernmost arch springs. The section of stonework measures 20 Ins/50 Cms H by 24 Ins/60 Cms W. Its eastern end has been cut into by the curve of the arch. The eastern third of this section of stonework is decorated with circular knot work design. No other decoration can now be identified.

Internally, A-S stonework, comprising irregular-shaped, large pieces can be identified in the south wall of the nave; in the north wall of the nave above the later inserted arches; in the west wall of the nave and the stonework above the tower arch; and the stonework above the chancel arch in the east wall of the nave. Amongst this stonework there are:

12.   The curved top section of stonework from a single A-S window. It is located incorporated into the fabric of the south wall of the nave 17 Ins/43 Cms above the arch over the current south door and 6 Ins/15 Cms east of the centre of this arch.

13.   The curved top section of stonework from a single A-S window. It is located incorporated into the fabric of the south wall of the nave 29 Ins/73 Cms east of the easternmost window on the south side of the nave, 163 Ins/414 Cms up from the floor.

14.   The curved top section of stonework from a single A-S window. It is located incorporated into the fabric of the north wall of the nave, 25 Ins/63 Cms east of the centre of the pillar separating the two arches in the nave and 37 Ins/93 Cms above the easternmost arch.

A-S quoining can be identified internally in the north-west (the better example) and north-east corners of the nave, and externally in the south-west and south-east corners of the nave.

Externally, incorporated into the south wall of the nave there is:

15.   The curved top section of stonework from a single A-S window. It is located incorporated into the fabric of the south wall of the nave, 26 Ins/66 Cms east of the eastern end of the south porch, and 150 Ins/381 Cms up from the ground. It is in a large monolithic block of stonework that has been inverted and incorporated into the fabric of the south wall. It measures 22 Ins/55 Cms H by 44 Ins/111 Cms W.

KIRBY KNOWLE
St Wilfred's Church

SE 468873   Rating: ✫✫✩

The church is easily located on the north side of the road that runs south-west/north-east through Kirby Knowle.

The church dates mostly from 1873-74.

Internally, there are:

1.   A section of stonework from part of an arm from an A-S crosshead. It is located sitting on the floor 1½ Ins/3 Cms north of the south wall of the nave, immediately east of the stonework surround for the south doorway. The section of stonework measures 8 Ins/20 Cms H, by 8½ Ins/21 Cms W, by 7 Ins/17 Cms D. Despite weathering, knot work decoration can be identified on the two faces; on one of the sides there is well-defined vine scroll decoration, including grapes (the other side is broken away from the crosshead and so not decorated).

2.   A section of stonework from what may be part of an arm from an A-S crosshead. It is located sitting on the floor 1½ Ins/3 Cms north of the south wall of the nave and 4½ Ins/11 Cms east of the stonework surround for the south doorway. The section of stonework measures 10½

Ins/26 Cms H, by 7 Ins/17 Cms W, by 7 Ins/17 Cms D. Although there is clearly some decoration on the sides it is difficult to precisely identify what because of the weathering.

[Note: Whether these sections of stonework are from the same crosshead is uncertain.]

Externally, in the churchyard, there are:

3.   A mutilated but complete circular shaped A-S crosshead. It is located 7 Yds/6 M south of the westernmost buttress on the south side of the nave. It sits on a section of stonework, possibly from a cross-shaft, which stands on a plinth 23 Ins/58 Cms H, by 28 Ins/71 Cms W, by 23½ Ins/59 Cms D. The section of stonework, possibly from a cross-shaft, measures 17 Ins/43 Cms H, by 14 Ins/35 Cms W, by 10 Ins D. The crosshead measures 14½ Ins/36 Cms H, by 16 Ins/40 Cms W, by 9½ Ins/24 Cms D. Weathering has worn away any decoration on any of the sides of both these section of stonework.

4.   A section of stonework from an A-S cross-shaft. It is located 10 Yds/9 M south of the westernmost buttress on the south side of the nave. It stands on a plinth 10 Ins/25 Cms H, by 27½ Ins/69 Cms W, by 24½ Ins/62 Cms D. The section of stonework measures 33 Ins/83 Cms H, by 14 Ins/35 Cms W, by 10½ Ins/26 Cms D. Weathering has worn away any original decoration on any of its sides.

KIRBY MISPERTON
St Laurence's Church
SE 778795   Rating: ☆☆

The church is located in the north-western part of Kirby Misperton. It is situated close to the north side of the minor road that approaches the village from the north-west from the neighbouring village of Little Barugh.

An A-S church existed on this site in the 9C but the earliest surviving fabric dates from the 15C. The church underwent some rebuilding in 1838 and 1875.

Internally, the plain, octagonal font may be Saxo-Norman. It is located on a splayed octagonal base on a plinth 62 Ins/157 Cms east of the west wall of the south aisle. The font has a diameter of 21 Ins/53 Cms and a height of 13½ Ins/34 Cms.

Externally, there are three sections of 9C A-S stonework incorporated into the fabric of the south wall of the chancel 17 Ins/43 Cms west of the westernmost buttress supporting the south wall of the chancel (immediately to the west of a drainpipe). These are:

1.   A section of stonework from an A-S cross-shaft. It is located 7½ Ins/19 Cms west of the drainpipe and 48 Ins/121 Cms up from the base of the church. The section of stonework measures 6½ Ins/16 Cms H by 16½ Ins/41 Cms possibly 18 Ins/45 Cms W. It is decorated with a row of small crosses above which there is lettering that does not enable anyone or anything to be identified with confidence.

2.   A section of stonework from an A-S cross-shaft. It is located 13½ Ins/34 Cms west of the drainpipe and 54 Ins/137 Cms up from the base of the church. The section of stonework measures 11 Ins/27 Cms H by 17½ Ins/44 Cms W. It is decorated with a row of small crosses below which there are two rows of lettering that do not enable anyone or anything to be identified with confidence.

3.   A section of stonework from an A-S cross-shaft. It is located immediately behind and to the west of the drainpipe and 54 Ins/137 Cms up from the base of the church. The section of stonework measures 11 Ins/27 Cms H by 17 Ins/43 Cms W. It is decorated with two rows of lettering, some of which are hidden behind the drainpipe. The lettering in the lower line identifies the individual "Tatburg".

Externally, incorporated into the fabric in the north wall of the vestry there are a variety of sections of stonework of varying ages, sizes and purpose. They are all well weathered and some can only be identified with difficulty: not all are A-S/A-D. Those that may be from A-S/A-D crossheads and cross-shafts are located in a row.

(A) Between 7½ Ins/19 Cms east of the easternmost drainpipe in the north wall of the vestry and 23 Ins/58 Cms west of the east wall of the vestry, and between 66½ Ins/168 Cms and 68 Ins/172 Cms up from the base of the church. None of the sections of stonework exceed 10 Ins/25 Cms in height. From east (left) to west (right) they are:

4.   A section of stonework measuring 12 Ins/30 Cms W. It is decorated with simple, small crosses.

5.   A section of stonework measuring 14 Ins/35 Cms W. It is decorated with a single small cross – it is very weathered.

6.   A section of stonework measuring 11 Ins/27 Cms W. It is decorated with concentric circles surrounding a cross.

7.   A section of stonework measuring 8½ Ins/21 Cms W. It is decorated with a foliated design with four circles surrounding a smaller circle inside which there is a cross.

8.   A section of stonework measuring 12 Ins/30 Cms W. It is decorated with a single small cross.

9. A section of stonework measuring 9 Ins/22 Cms W. It is decorated with a series of pierced tiny circles.

(B) Between 1 inch/2 Cms west of the easternmost drainpipe in the north wall of the vestry and 51 Ins/129 Cms east of the door into the vestry, and between 64 Ins/162 Cms and 69 Ins/175 Cms up from the base of the church. None of the sections of stonework exceed 10 Ins/25 Cms in height. From east (left) to west (right) they are:

10. A section of stonework measuring 17½ Ins/44 Cms W. It is decorated with a single, small cross – it is very weathered.

11. A section of stonework measuring 14 Ins/35 Cms W. It is decorated with a foliated design with four circles surrounding a smaller circle inside which there is a cross.

12. A section of stonework measuring 14½ Ins/36 Cms W. It is decorated with concentric circles surrounding a cross.

13. A section of stonework measuring 14½ Ins/36 Cms W. It is decorated with concentric circles surrounding a cross.

14. A section of stonework measuring 16 Ins/40 Cms W. It is decorated with a foliated design with four circles surrounding a smaller circle inside which there is a cross.

KIRK HAMMERTON
St John's Church

SE 465555   Rating: ★☆☆☆☆   Access is possible.

In the centre of Kirk Hammerton the church is located set back from the north side of the road which runs west/east through the village.

The nave and chancel of the A-S church, now the south aisle and chapel, may be earlier than 9C in origin. The tower dates from around 950 and has design similarities with A-S church towers in Lincolnshire. The larger Victorian nave and chancel were added in 1890-91 onto the north walling of the A-S church. The church also has some 12C fabric.

An almost complete A-S church with tower, nave and chancel has been preserved within the present structure of this church. The fabric comprises large blocks of roughly squared stone laid in courses with large blocks of stone forming side alternate quoining. The upper stage of the tower has double belfry windows on each of its sides.

The A-S chancel arch has on the eastern face of the inner arch (the southern half) discernible traces from a later medieval rather than A-S wall painting.

Note: The surviving windows in the nave and chancel are not Anglo-Saxon

KIRKBY (IN CLEVELAND)
St Augustine's Church

NZ 538061   Rating: ☆☆   Access is possible.

The church is located 150 Yds/137 M north of the crossroads in the centre of Kirkby. At the crossroads there is a road sign "Stokesley 2, Stockton 12". Take the road as directed (there are no street signs) that heads in a north-westerly direction towards Stokesley. The church is easily located on the east side of this road.

The original church was probably 50 Yds/45 M north of the present structure. The present church dates mainly from 1815, although a new chancel was built in 1905.

Internally, there are sections of decorated A-S stonework in a niche in the east wall of the south aisle, 28 Ins/71 Cms north of the south wall in the south aisle and 93 Ins/236 Cms up from the floor. These are:

1.   A damaged section of stonework from an A-S wheel head cross comprising most of the central section, a complete arm, part of another arm, and the connecting "wheel" between the two arms. It sits at the northern end of the ledge in the niche. The section of stonework measures 14 Ins/35 Cms H, by 13 Ins/33 Cms W, by 6 Ins/15 Cms D. It is decorated with knot work design on both its west and east sides, and the end of the arm. There is also a central boss on the west side and the remains of a central boss on the east side. All the other sides are too weathered or damaged for any decoration to survive.

2.   A section of A-S stonework possibly from the end of an arm from a crosshead. It sits at the southern end of the ledge in the niche and "3" below has been placed on top of it. This section of stonework measures 9 Ins/22 Cms H, by 8 Ins/20 Cms W, by 6¼ Ins/15 Cms D. It is decorated on its west side with knot work design. All the other sides are too weathered or damaged for any decoration to survive.

3.   A section of A-S stonework possibly from an arm of a crosshead. It has been placed on top of "2" above at the southern end of the ledge in the niche. This section of stonework measures 7 Ins/17 Cms H (W), by 6½ Ins/16 Cms W (H), by 5 Ins/12 Cms D. It is decorated on its west side but the nature of the design is not clear. All the other sides are too weathered or damaged for any decoration to survive.

Internally, incorporated into the east wall of the south aisle 9½ Ins/24 Cms below the niche referred to above there are:

4.   A circular crosshead that is probably 12C rather than A-S. It is located 34½ Ins/87 Cms north of the south wall in the south aisle and 72½ Ins/184 Cms up from the floor. The crosshead measures 11 Ins/27 Cms H by 11¼ Ins/28 Cms W. Apart from the distinctive arms of the cross there is no other decoration.

5.   A section of stonework from a cross-shaft that is probably later medieval rather than A-S. It is located 24 Ins/60 Cms north of the south wall in the south aisle and 61 Ins/154 Cms up from the floor. The section of stonework measures 23 Ins/58 Cms H by 9½ Ins/24 Cms W. It is decorated with a tall, standing figure.

6.   A section of stonework from an A-S cross-shaft. It is located 9½ Ins/24 Cms north of the south wall in the south aisle and 66 Ins/167 Cms up from the floor. The section of stonework measures 18 Ins/45

Cms H by 14 Ins/35 Cms W. It is decorated with the figure of a warrior on horseback.

KIRKBY MALHAM
St Michael the Archangel Church
SD 894610   Rating: ☆☆

In the southern part of Kirkby Malham, at the minor crossroads close to the north bank and bridge over the "Kirkby Beck", take the minor road west. There is no street sign but on the opposite side of the crossroads there is a signpost "Hanlith (only) ½" (there is also a no-through road sign attached to this signpost). On proceeding westwards the church soon comes into view on the north side of the road; the church is about 60 Yds/54 M from the road junction.

On the site of an 8C/9C A-D church, the present structure dates from the 15C and the restoration in 1879-81.

Internally, the font has a 9C/10C A-D bowl. It is located 67 Ins/170 Cms east of the west end on the south aisle. The 3 Ins/7 Cms square base of the font supporting the bowl, sits on supports that stand 19¾ Ins/50 Cms H which themselves stand on a 7 Ins/17 Cms H plinth. The bowl of the font itself is almost circular with a triangular foot at each corner of the square base. The bowl measures 14½ Ins/36 Cms H, by 21 Ins/53 Cms W, by 19 Ins/48 Cms D. The top half of the bowl has no decoration. Above the diagonal shaped feet the stonework has been carved to form two rows giving the appearance of something similar to tegulated roof tiles. Above this roof-tile-like decoration the stonework has been carved so that there are three separate, protruding, narrow sections of stonework around the circumference of the bowl.

Externally, in the churchyard, there is a section of stonework from an 8C/9C A-S missionary cross-shaft. It is located 23 Yds/21 M south-east of the south porch, 87 Ins/220 Cms south of the nearby footpath. The section of stonework stands on a large irregular shaped circular plinth measuring approximately 7 Ins/17 Cms H with a diameter of 62 Ins/154 Cms. The section of stonework measures 43½ Ins/110 Cms H, by 9½ Ins/24 Cms W, by 9 Ins/22 Cms D. There is no decoration on any of its sides due to weathering.

KIRKBY OVERBLOW
All Saints Church
SE 324492   Rating: ☆

In the southern part of Kirkby Overblow, the church is adjacent to the north side of "Swindon Lane", some 60 Yds/54 M west of the junction with "Barrowby Lane". There are street signs to both lanes at their junction. From the north side of Swindon Lane proceed along an unnamed minor road running by the side of the churchyard wall. The churchyard entrance is reached in under 40 Yds/36 M.

The present structure dates mostly from the late 18C.

Externally, there is the distinctive outline of as A-S doorway, now blocked. It is located some 108 Ins/274 Cms east of the tower, and beneath the first window in the north side of the nave. The outline of the doorway is situated immediately beneath the present window ledge and the base of the nave wall.

KIRKBY WHARFE
St John's Church
SE 506411   Rating: ✩✩✩   Access is possible.

The entrance to the churchyard is at the northern end of the Kirkby Wharfe, 16 Yds/14 M east of a drive with entrance pillars either side. On these entrance pillars there are the signs "Strictly Private" and "No Through Road".

The present church is probably on the site of its A-D predecessor. The church dates mostly from the extensive restoration in 1860 although some the late 12C material does survive.

Internally, this church contains three fonts two of which may even be A-S. One font, not A-S, is located near the southwest corner of the nave. A font that may be A-S is located standing on a stepped stone plinth in the northwest corner of the nave. This second font is tub-shaped, undecorated and has a 30 inch/76 centimetre diameter. A second font that may be A-S is located standing on a stone plinth just north of the nave in the southwest corner of the north aisle and 23½ Ins/59 Cms east of the west wall of the north aisle. This third font is also tub-shaped and undecorated and has a 27 inch/68 centimetre diameter.

Internally, there are three sections of A-S stonework standing on the floor at the west end of the north aisle adjacent to the second possible A-S font referred to above. These are:

1.   A section of stonework from a late 9C A-S crosshead comprising the central section and an arm, and a section of stonework from its attached cross-shaft. They are located 28 Ins/71 Cms north of the nave and 40 Ins/101 Cms east of the west wall of the north aisle. Together they stand 49 Ins/124 Cms H. (Note: cement has been used to secure the section of stonework from the crosshead to the section of stonework

Crosshead with
attached cross-shaft

Two tub-shaped fonts
that may be Anglo-Saxon
- both undecorated

Crosshead

There is knot work
design showing on
the faces of these
crossheads and
cross-shafts

Cross-shaft

from the cross-shaft, and to unite the sections of stonework from the cross-shaft now joined together as one.)

KIRKBY WHARFE: St John's Church. A display of Anglo-Saxon stonework.

The section of stonework from the crosshead measures 12½ Ins/31 Cms H, by 12 Ins/30 Cms W, by 4 Ins/10 Cms D. Both faces are decorated with knot work design. The two other sides are too heavily weathered and damaged to identify any particular design.

The section of stonework from the cross-shaft measures 36½ Ins/92 Cms H, tapering 11½ Ins/29 Cms to 7½ Ins/19 Cms W, tapering 5 Ins/12 Cms to 4 Ins/10 Cms D. The east face is decorated with knot work design and two of the sides are decorated with chain work design. The west face is decorated with two figures standing either side of a cross-shaft and beneath the arms of a crosshead.

2.   A section of stonework comprising the central section and most of two arms from an A-S crosshead. It is located 43 Ins/109 Cms north of the nave and 41 Ins/104 Cms east of the west wall of the north aisle (to the north of "1" above). The section of stonework measures 12 Ins/30 Cms H, by 17 Ins/43 Cms W, by 4½ Ins/11 Cms D. The two faces are

decorated with knot work design. The two other sides are too weathered and damaged for any decoration to be identified.

3.   A section of stonework from an A-S cross-shaft. It is located 61 Ins/154 Cms north of the nave and 39 Ins/99 Cms east of the west wall of the north aisle (to the north of "2" above). The section of stonework measures 14½ Ins/36 Cms H, by 10½ Ins/26 Cms W, by 5 Ins/12 Cms D. The two faces are decorated with knot work design; the east face is the clearer. The two other sides are decorated with chain work design.

These crossheads and cross-shafts date from the 9C to the mid-10C.

KIRKBYMOORSIDE
All Saints Church
SE 697866   Rating: ☆

In the centre of Kirkbymoorside, turn off "Market Place" and head in a north-easterly direction along "Church Street" (there are street signs). After some 54 Yds/49 M the entrance to the churchyard is on the north side of Church Street. There are nine steps up to the churchyard gate and on the gate there is a notice about church services.

On the site of a pagan temple, an 8C church was destroyed by the Vikings in the 9C and then rebuilt only to be destroyed again in the 10C. The oldest part of the present structure dates from the 13C. There were additions in the 14C and 15C. The church was restored in 1873-75.

During the 19C restoration two A-S cross-heads and three sections of stonework from A-S cross-shafts were discovered and these are now displayed in Ryedale Folk Museum in Hutton-le-Hole (see the entry Hutton-le-Hole, North Yorkshire). Internally, there is a notice, with photographs, relating to the A-S crossheads and cross-shafts. The notice is located on a board hanging against the south pillar supporting the arch into the tower.

There apparently remains a fragment of an A-S sundial incorporated into a window surround. This cannot be easily identified internally on the remains of the walls on the south side of the nave or in the external walls of the south aisle.

KIRKDALE
St Gregory's Minster
SE 676857   Rating: ☆☆☆☆☆

About 1050 Yds/960 M east of Beadlam, turn east off the A170 and along a minor road signposted "St Gregory's Minster Kirkdale, Skiplam". After about 1230 Yds/1124 M along this road there is a signpost "St.

Gregory's Minster" which directs you northwards along another, poorer quality, minor road. Proceed along this road as directed. The church is easily identified after about 180 Yds/164 M set back from the north-east side of this road.

A church probably existed on this site in the 8C but the earliest surviving fabric dates from around 1060, "Orm's Church". The present church on the site also includes fabric from the 12C, 13C and 15C. Substantial structural changes were made to the church in the 19C and a general restoration was undertaken 1907-09.

A-S fabric survives from Orm's church in the south and west walls of the nave and those parts of the east wall of the nave that survived the later addition of the chancel. His work survives in the archway/doorway into the tower in the west wall of the nave. The west side of this doorway contains the surviving shafts and capitals and has no central stone in the doorway arch itself. The east side of this doorway has a central stone in the arch indicating it has been restored at some later date. His work also survives in the jambs, angle-shafts, bases and capitals of the present chancel arch. Externally, there is A-S quoining in the southwest and northwest corners of the nave

The famous sundial with its inscription is contained within the south porch. It has been incorporated into the fabric of the exterior wall of the nave 18 Ins/45 Cms above the top of the south doorway into the church. The inscription fixes a building period for the church of between 1055 and 1065. The sundial is incised on a single stone slab divided into three sections in total measuring 92 Ins/233 Cms L (W) by 20 Ins/51 Cms H. The westernmost (left-hand) section measures 28½ Ins/72 Cms W, the middle section measures 34½ Ins/87 Cms W, and the easternmost (right-hand) section measures 29 Ins/73 Cms W. The three sections each have writing in Old English:

> The central section contains the sundial. Above the sundial are the words, translated: "This is the day's sun-marker at every hour." Below the sundial are the words, translated, "Hawarth made me: and Brand (was) the priest".

> The western (left) section is incised with the words filling the whole of the section, translated: "Orm the son of Gamel acquired St. Gregory's church when it was completely ruined".

KIRKDALE: St Gregory's Minster. Typical Anglo-Saxon internal doorway: tall and narrow, round headed arch, with through stones laid in "Escomb fashion" in this example.

The eastern (right) section is incised with the words filling the whole of the section, translated: "and collapsed, and he had it built anew from the ground to Christ and to St Gregory, in the days of king Edward and in the days of earl Tostig".

Internally, there are a number of sections of stonework affixed to the stonework left exposed in the north wall of the north aisle (i.e. not plastered). Those of A-S/Viking interest are, from west to east:

1. A section of stonework from an 11C A-S crosshead comprising the central section and part of an arm, and a section of stonework from its attached cross-shaft. They are affixed vertically to the stonework left exposed in the north wall of the north aisle and sit on the stone ledge attached to the north wall of the north aisle. They measure in all 27 Ins/68 Cms H. The section of stonework from the crosshead measures 16 Ins/40 Cms H, by 16 Ins/40 Cms W, by 8 Ins/20 Cms D. The section of stonework from the cross-shaft measures 11 Ins/27 Cms H, by 13 Ins/33 Cms W, by 8 Ins/20 Cms D. Both the sections of stonework are very weathered and damaged and only indistinct decoration survives on their south sides.

2. A section of stonework from a 10C wheel head cross comprising the central section, two arms and part of a third arm. It is located between the two windows in the north wall of the north aisle and 51 Ins/129 Cms up from the floor. This section of stonework measures 11 Ins/27 Cms H, by 20 Ins/50 Cms (maximum) W, by 6 Ins/15 Cms D. The south side is decorated with a circular design. All the other sides are too damaged or weathered for any decoration to be identified confidently.

3. A section of 11C A-S stonework that may possibly be from an arm of a crosshead. It is located 10 Ins/25 Cms below "2" above and 29 Ins/73 Cms up from the floor. This section of stonework measures 11 Ins/27 Cms H, by 7 Ins/17 Cms W, by 6 Ins/15 Cms D. Despite weathering it is decorated with a circular design on all four sides (the east side is damaged).

[Note: the other sections of stonework affixed to this walling are not of A-S/Viking interest.]

Internally, on the north side of the nave, there are:

4. A large A-S tomb slab that has been broken in two but put back together. It is located underneath the easternmost arch of the nave, on a floor standing stone plinth that stands 14 Ins/35 Cms H. The tomb slab measures 6 Ins/15 Cms H, by 21 Ins/53 Cms W, by 67 Ins/170 Cms L. It is decorated with plait work design on its top and widely spaced diagonal lines sometimes known as "ringworm design" on its side edges. It has been associated with Bishop Cedd who died in 664 and who is associated with the monastery at Lastingham (now St Mary's Church, see the entry for St Mary's Church, Lastingham).

5.   Another large A-S tomb slab. It is located underneath the middle arch of the nave, on a floor standing stone plinth that stands 14 Ins/35 Cms H. The tomb slab measures 4 Ins/10 Cms H, by 21 Ins/53 Cms W, by 69½ Ins/176 Cms L. It is decorated with a large cross and scroll work design on its top. All the side edges appear to have been rendered so no decoration survives. It has been associated with King Ethelwald of Northumbria who died in 765.

The dating of both of these tomb slabs has varied over the years ranging from the 8C to the 10C, as has the veracity of the associations with Cedd and Ethelwald.

Internally, there is a stone quern or "hand mill". It is located on the floor in the north-east corner of the nave, 8 Ins/20 Cms south of the foot of the easternmost pillar on the north side of the nave and 5 Ins/12 Cms west of the east wall of the nave. The stone quern stands 19½ Ins/49 Cms H, by 15 Ins/38 Cms W, by 14 Ins/35 Cms D. It is rounded irregularly in shape with a hole in the top. Weathering has ensured no decoration now survives. It is of undoubted antiquity and may possibly be the oldest item in the church.

Inside the chancel the wooden altar cross has its central roundel carved from a piece of timber taken from the Coppergate Viking excavations in York (see the entry for Jorvik Viking Centre York).

Externally, a number of sections of A-S stonework have been incorporated into the fabric of the church.

In the south wall of the nave there are:

6.   A section of stonework comprising the central section and most of two arms from a 10C A-S wheel head cross, and a section of stonework from its attached cross-shaft. They are located incorporated horizontally in the south wall of the nave, 52 Ins/132 Cms east of the south porch, and 10 Ins/25 Cms up from the ground. In total they measure 68 Ins/172 Cms L (H). The section of stonework from the crosshead measures 13 Ins/33 Cms H(W) by 20 Ins/50 Cms W(H). The section of stonework from the cross-shaft measures 12 Ins/30 Cms H(W) by 48 Ins/121 Cms W(H). The lower edges of both the section of stonework from the wheel head cross and the section of stonework from the cross-shaft have clearly been rendered to form a straight line. Both sections of stonework are too weathered for any decoration to survive.

7.   A section of stonework comprising the central section and most of three arms from a 10C A-S wheel head cross, and a section of stonework from its attached cross-shaft. They are located incorporated horizontally in the south wall of the nave, 56 Ins/142 Cms west of the buttress at the east end of the nave, and 14½ Ins/36 Cms up from the ground. In total they measure 60 Ins/152 Cms L(H). The section of stonework from the

crosshead measures 20 Ins/50 Cms H(W) by 21 Ins/53 Cms W(H). The section of stonework from the cross-shaft measures 15½ Ins/39 Cms H (W) by 39 Ins/99 Cms W(H). Both the sections of stonework are clearly decorated but the design is difficult to identify because of weathering.

In the centre of the east wall of the chancel there are:

8.　　A distinctive section of A-S stonework. It is located 124 Ins/314 Cms north of the southeast corner of the chancel and 75½ Ins/191 Cms up from the ground. The section of stonework measures 9 Ins/22 Cms H (W) by 28½ Ins/72 Cms W (H). It is decorated with interlace design.

KIRKDALE: St Gregory's Minster. An Anglo-Saxon cross-shaft incorporated into the external fabric of the east wall of the chancel. It is decorated with interlace design.

9.　　A very weathered section of stonework that may be A-S. It is located adjacent to the south end of the stonework identified at "8" above. It is situated 102 Ins/259 Cms north of the southeast corner of the chancel and 80 Ins/203 Cms up from the ground. The section of stonework measures 5 Ins/22 Cms H(W) by 17 Ins/43 Cms W(H). It is too weathered for any decoration to be identified confidently.

In the west wall of the nave there are:

10.　　A section of stonework comprising most of the central section and two arms, and a complete third arm from an 10C A-S crosshead, and a section of stonework from its attached cross-shaft. They are located incorporated horizontally into the fabric of the west wall of the nave and abutting the north wall of the tower. They are 99 Ins/251 Cms up from the ground. In total they measure 50 Ins/127 Cms W(H). The section of stonework from the crosshead measures 17 Ins/43 Cms H(W) by 12 Ins/30 Cms W(H). The section of stonework from the cross-shaft measures 14 Ins/35 Cms H(W) by 38 Ins/96 Cms W(H). Both sections of stonework are decorated with scroll pattern but the design is difficult to identify because of weathering.

Excavations have revealed that in the field north of the church there was a cemetery containing graves from the 8C and 9C, and an area of industrial or craft activity of a similar or later date. Excavations also revealed outside the west end of the church more graves including a stone sarcophagus dating from 10C. (Finds from these excavations are in the care of York University).

KIRKLEATHAM
Old Hall Museum

NZ 592216   Rating: ☆☆   Arrangements can be made at the Museum to view these items in store.

200 yards from its junction with the A174, turn east off the A1042 along the minor road (there is no street sign) signposted "Kirkleatham Village, Kirkleatham Museum". About 250 yards along this road, the Museum is easily located situated in its own grounds adjacent to the north side of the road. Attached to the walling by the entrance to the grounds of the Museum there is a sign "Kirkleatham, Old Hall Museum etc".

As with all museums, the displays and the exhibits they contain may be changed, re-sited, removed from display and/or put in store, or loaned to other museums or suitable repositories. Before visiting a museum it is worth checking in advance whether the displays listed in the gazetteer are still in place in the same location(s) set out in the text. Individual exhibits may have been rearranged in terms of their display, the order in which they are displayed and their relationship to other exhibits, some exhibits may have been removed from display. The text in the gazetteer reflects the descriptions and/or accompanying notices to the exhibits at the time of visiting. These too may have been revised, amended, added to or removed.

In a Queen Anne period mansion built in 1709, the Museum houses exhibits and displays relating to farming, trades, crafts, industries, domestic life, transport and maritime history, geology, natural history and archaeology in the locality.

On the second floor of the Museum, locate the room in which there are exhibits entitled "Kirkleatham The story of a village". On entering the room, in the first display case, there are two items of A-S interest. These are numbered in the display:

"No 5. Clay loom weights (3), probably Anglo-Saxon of the 7th century A.D. Used to weight down threads on a weaving loom. Found at Kirkleatham.

No 6. Fragment of late 6th century Anglo-Saxon coloured bead from Gisborough Priory."

Currently stored in the Museum there are four sections of stonework of A-S and A-D interest, all of which come from the Old Church at Upleatham. These are:

1.   A section of stonework from an arm from a crosshead. It measures 11 Ins/27 Cms H, between 6 Ins/15 Cms and 8½ Ins/21 Cms W, by 5¼ Ins/13 Cms D. It is decorated with interlace design on both faces. There is no decoration on any of the other sides.

2.   A section of stonework from a cross-shaft. It measures between 6 Ins/15 Cms and 9 Ins/22 Cms H, by 8¾ Ins/22 Cms W, by 4½ Ins/11 Cms D. It is decorated with Borre design on all four sides.

3.   A section of stonework from a hogback grave cover. It measures 14¾ Ins/37Cms H, by 10 Ins/25 Cms W, by 15½ Ins/39 Cms L. The face of one of the bears can be identified along with some tegulated roof design on two sides. No other decoration can be identified on any of the other sides due to weathering and damage.

4.   A section of stonework comprising the central section and three of the arms from a crosshead. It measures 14 Ins/35 Cms H, by 19 Ins/48 Cms W, by 6 Ins/15 Cms D. There is no decoration on any of the sides that can now be identified – it has also been rendered.

KIRKLEVINGTON
St Martin's Church

NZ 432098   Rating: ★★★★★

The church is located in eastern part of Kirklevington. Turn off the A67 and proceed in a westerly direction along the minor road "Forest Lane" (there are street signs). Forest Lane runs through Kirklevington on an east/west axis. About 250 Yds/228 M west of the A67, and on the south side of Forest Lane, there is a pair of gates by which there is a church notice board. Pass through these gates and follow the footpath until it reaches the church after about 70 Yds/64 M.

Although possibly on the site of a 9C church, the earliest surviving structural material dates from the late 12C. The church was rebuilt in the 13C and restored in 1882-3. It was during the 19C restoration that the sections of A-D stonework were found which date from between 850 to 1100. These sections of stonework are occasionally moved around and so may not be precisely in the locations identified below. One day it is intended that the various sections of stonework be formally displayed.

Internally, there are three sections of A-D stonework in the south porch on the ledge by the window in the east wall. These are:

1.   Broken sections of stonework from a cross-shaft – the two pieces have been correctly placed back together. They are located 2 Ins/5 Cms north of the southern end of the ledge. The section of stonework

measures 8¼ Ins/20 Cms H, by 14¾ Ins/37 Cms W, and between 5 Ins/12 Cms and 6 Ins/15 Cms D. It is decorated with interlace design on the southwest face and the northwest and southeast sides. The northeast face is too weathered and damaged for any decoration to survive.

2.   A section of stonework from a cross-shaft. It is the middle of the three sections of stonework located on this ledge. The section of stonework measures between 6 Ins/15 Cms to 12 Ins/30 Cms H, by 18 Ins/45 Cms W, by 3¼ Ins/8 Cms D. It is decorated on its south west face with the figure of a man (his legs are missing) holding a cross or an axe – it is not clear which. There is no decoration on any of the other three sides due to weathering.

3.   A section of stonework probably from a cross-shaft. It is located abutting the northern end of the ledge. The section of stonework measures between 6 Ins/15 Cms and 6½ Ins/16 Cms H (D), between 2 Ins/5 Cms and 5 Ins/12 Cms W, and between 10 Ins/25 Cms to 12½ Ins/31 Cms D (H). Despite damage there is interlace decoration on the top and some indistinct decoration on the side facing the north wall of the ledge. The two other sides are too damaged for any decoration to survive. It dates from around 850.

4.   A section of stonework that could be from an arm of a crosshead. It is located sitting on the floor beneath the northern end of the window ledge and 2 Ins/5 Cms west of the east wall of the south porch. The section of stonework measures between 4½ Ins/11 Cms and 8 Ins/20 Cms H, between 5 Ins/12 Cms and 5½ Ins/13Cms W, by 11 Ins/27 Cms D. On the north and south faces there is some indistinct decoration. Due to weathering and damage there is no decoration on any of the other sides.

Internally, there are two sections of A-D stonework in the south porch on the ledge by the window in the west wall. These are:

5.   A section of stonework comprising the central section and part of an arm from a crosshead. It is located at the northern end of the ledge. The section of stonework measures between 11½ Ins/29 Cms and 14 Ins/35 Cms H, between 6 Ins/15 Cms and 9½ Ins/24 Cms W, and between 3½ Ins/7 Cms and 4¼ Ins/10 Cms D. It is decorated a linear design on both its southeast facing and northwest sides. There is no decoration on any of the other sides.

6.   A virtually complete ring head crosshead. It is located at the southern end of the window ledge. The ring head crosshead measures 11 Ins/27 Cms H, by 11¼ Ins/28 Cms W, by 4½ Ins/11 Cms D. There are clearly defined central circular "holes" with similar size circular holes separating the arms of the cross on both its southwest and northwest faces. These two faces are also decorated with a circular linear design. There is no decoration on any of the other sides.

(There is an illustrated descriptive notice about the sections of stonework found in the church below the window ledge, and attached to the internal west wall of the south porch.)

Internally, there are two sections of A-D stonework in the south porch standing on the floor by the west wall. These are:

7.   An almost complete wheel head crosshead. It is located 42 Ins/106 Cms north of the south wall of the porch. The wheel head crosshead measures 13 Ins/33 Cms H, by 18 Ins/45 Cms W, and between 5½ Ins/13 Cms and 6½ Ins/16 Cms D. On the top facing arm of the crosshead interlace decoration can be identified. Due to weathering and damage no other decoration can be identified on any of the other sides.

8.   A section of stonework from a cross-shaft. It is located 69 Ins/175 Cms north of the south wall of the porch. It measures between 5 Ins/12 Cms and 10 Ins/25 Cms H, by 9 Ins/22 Cms W (D), by 9 Ins/22 Cms D (W). On the east and south sides it is decorated with interlace design. The north side is decorated with a loosely formed interlace design. The west side is too weathered and damaged for any decoration to survive.

Internally, standing on the floor and leaning against the west wall of the nave there is:

9.   A section of stonework from an A-D cross-shaft. It is located 84 Ins/213 Cms south of the north wall of the nave. The section of stonework measures 31¾ Ins/80 Cms H, by 9½ Ins/24 Cms W, by 7½ Ins/19 Cms D. On its east face there are two complete and two incomplete decorative panels. The top complete panel contains interlace design and the lower complete panel contains the depiction of the figure of Odin and his two ravens "Thought" and "Memory", or alternatively, Christ and two doves. It is not possible to identify with certainty the decoration contained within the two incomplete panels. There is some interlace decoration on the south side. On the west face and the north side, it is not possible to identify any surviving decoration due to weathering and damage. The section of stonework dates from 950.

Internally, near the west end of the nave and standing on the floor near the north wall of the nave, there are four sections of stonework, two of which are of A-S/A-D interest. These are:

10.   A section of stonework from a cross-shaft. It is located sitting on the floor 14 Ins/35 Cms east of the west wall of the nave and 4¼ Ins/10 Cms south of the north wall of the nave. The section of stonework measures 22 Ins/55 Cms H, tapering 12 Ins/30 Cms to 10½ Ins/26 Cms W, between 7 Ins/17 Cms and 7½ Ins/19 Cms D. On the north face it is decorated with two human figures, but with bear-like heads, confronting each other. No decoration survives on any of the other sides due to weathering and damage.

[The two large sections of stonework immediately to the east of this section are not A-S/A-D.]

11.   A section of stonework from a cross-shaft. It is located standing on the floor and leaning against the north wall of the nave, 58½ Ins/148 Cms east of the west wall of the nave. The section of stonework measures 28¾ Ins/73 Cms H, tapering 12¼ Ins/31 Cms to 10½ Ins/26 Cms W, by 8 Ins/20 Cms D. On its south face it has two complete decorative panels; the upper panel contains interlace design and the lower panel contains the depiction of two figures with swords. Below the panel containing the two figures there is an incomplete panel – it is not possible to identify any decoration. The east side is decorated with ring chain design. There is interlace decoration on the west side and some surviving interlace decoration on the otherwise weathered north face.

Internally, sitting on the floor behind the final pew at the back of the north side of the nave, there are:

12.   An A-S ring head crosshead complete apart from its lower vertical arm. It is located, 13 Ins/33 Cms south of the north wall of the nave. The crosshead measures 17½ Ins/44 Cms H, by 18 Ins/45 W, by 5 Ins/12 ms D. On its west face it is decorated with the face, upper body, arms and hands of Christ Crucified – there is also some interlace decoration on the vertical arm above the head. On the east face and the ends of the three arms it is decorated with interlace design. The crosshead dates from 900.

13.   A section of stonework comprising the central section, part of two arms, a complete third arm from an A-D crosshead and part of its attached cross-shaft dating from around 1000. They are located 33 Ins/83 Cms south of the north wall of the nave. In total they measure 14 Ins/35 Cms H (W), by 16½ Ins/41 Cms W (H), and between 3½ Ins/8 Cms and 5½ Ins/13 Cms D.

The crosshead measures 9½ Ins/24 Cms H, by 13½ Ins/34 W, by 6 Ins/15 Cms D. On its west face it is decorated with linear design. On its east face it is decorated with part of an arm, a hand, and part of the legs and feet from a Crucifixion scene. There is no other decoration on any of the other sides due to weathering and damage.

The section of stonework from the cross-shaft measures 6½ Ins/16 Cms H, by 9½ Ins/24 W, between 5¼ Ins/13 Cms and 6 Ins/15 Cms D. On its west face it is decorated with two figures with distinctive animal heads confronting each other. On its east face there is no decoration due to weathering and damage. The top facing and floor sides are decorated with interlace design.

14.   A section of stonework from an A-S cross-shaft. It is located 57 Ins/144 Cms south of the north wall of the nave. It measures 10½ Ins/26

Cms H (W), by 18½ Ins/46 Cms W (H), by 8 Ins/20 Cms D. On both the west and east faces interlace decoration can be identified. There is no decoration on any of the other sides due to weathering and damage.

Internally, there are two sections of A-D stonework incorporated into the north wall of the vestry beneath the easternmost window. These are:

15.   A section of stonework from a cross-shaft. It is located 19 Ins/48 Cms west of the east wall in the vestry, 31 Ins/78 Cms up from the floor and 19 Ins/48 Cms beneath the window ledge. The section of stonework measures 14½ Ins/36 Cms H by 8 Ins/20 Cms W. It is decorated with a hunting scene depicting a hart being chased by a wolf. The section of stonework dates from 900.

16.   A section of stonework from a cross-shaft. It is located 28½ Ins/72 Cms west of the east wall in the vestry, 32 Ins/81 Cms up from the floor and 26 Ins/66 Cms beneath the window ledge. The section of stonework measures 8 Ins/20 Cms H by 6 Ins/15 Cms W. It is decorated with the figure of a saint, minus his head, holding palms. This section of stonework dates from 1000.

(Note: Both these sections of stonework from cross-shafts at "15" and "16" above are obscured from view by the chest of drawers standing immediately in front of them. There are also a number of other later sections of stonework of various sizes, shapes and dates incorporated into the walling of the vestry.)

LASTINGHAM
(1) St Cedd's Well
SE 729905   Rating: ☆

St Cedd's Well is located in the centre of Lastingham, on the north side of the road running west/east through the village (there are no street signs, but this part of the road is known as "Front Street"), and 25 Yds/22 M south of a junction with a no-through road that heads uphill in a northerly direction (there are no street signs, but this road is known as "High Street").

The well is enclosed in a substantial "Georgian style" enclosure, 75½ Ins/191 Cms north of the north side of the road. The enclosure measures 102 Ins/259 Cms H, by 55½ Ins/140 Cms W, by 52½ Ins/133 Cms D. On the road-facing side of the enclosure there is a wooden notice on which there are words in Latin commemorating St Cedd AD 654. The well retains a "tap" for obtaining water.

St Cedd founded the monastery at Lastingham in 654 with land given to him by Æthelwold, king of Deira. At the time St Cedd was bishop of the East Saxons and the affairs of the monastery were administered through his representatives. While on a visit to Northumbria in 664 Cedd died. St Cedd is mentioned by the Venerable Bede in his History of the English Church and people completed in 731.

LASTINGHAM
(2) St Chad's Well
SE 729906   Rating: ☆

St Chad's Well is located in the centre of Lastingham, on the east side of the no-through road that heads uphill in a northerly direction (there are no street signs, but this road is known as "High Street") and 96 Yds/87 M north of a junction with a road running west/east through the village (there are no street signs, but the westerly arm of this part of the road is known as "Front Street" and the southerly arm is known as "Ings Lane").

The well is incorporated within a stretch of stone walling that is easy to identify set back from the east side of the road. The enclosure surrounding the well can be identified by the two stone pillars supporting a rounded arch with a triangular head that protrudes from the walling – vegetation is in evidence. The enclosure measures 86 Ins/218 Cms H, by 69 Ins/175 Cms W, by 69½ Ins/176 Cms D. On the road-facing side of the enclosure, the words "St Chad" can just about be identified carved into the centre of the arch. The well retains a rusted water pump with an accompanying water trough – no water was apparent when this well was visited.

St Chad became abbot of Lastingham after Cedd's death in 664. In 669 he was appointed bishop to the Mercians and established the see (throne of a bishop) at Lichfield. He died on 2 March 672. St Chad is mentioned by the Venerable Bede in his History of the English Church and people completed in 731.

LASTINGHAM
(3) St Mary's Church
SE 727904   Rating: ☆☆☆☆

In the western part of Lastingham, the church is easily located on the side of a hill on the apex of a minor road junction. It is adjacent to the south-west side of the road but partially obscured by trees.

A monastery was founded on this site by St Cedd in 659. When he died in 664 he was buried by the altar in the crypt to the church. The monastery was apparently abandoned sometime in the 9C but with the examples of 9C and 10C stonework in the crypt there must be some doubt as to what actually did happen. Much of the present fabric in the church dates from the rebuilding of the monastery from 1078. The church also has 13C and 14C alterations and additions. It was subject to restorations in 1828 and 1879.

The crypt is entered from inside the church through a gate and down steps in the centre of the western end of the nave. It dates from 1078 and may well have A-S stonework incorporated into its fabric as it was built on the foundations of an earlier A-S church. (In particular the pillars may be A-S in origin.)

In the crypt, in the south aisle, there are:

1.   What an accompanying notice describes as a "Viking hog-back tombstone". It is sitting on the floor in the middle of the south aisle, 35 Ins/88 Cms north of the south wall. This 10C grave cover measures 16 Ins/40 Cms H, by 11 Ins/27 Cms W, by 48 Ins/122 Cms L. Although weathered, some decoration of a bear with a bar across its mouth does survive.

2.   What an accompanying notice describes as "A cross shaft from the 10th century. The shaft combines both Saxon and Viking designs". It is standing on the floor, 39 Ins/99 Cms east of the west wall and 36 Ins/91 Cms north of the south wall of the south aisle. This section of stonework from a cross-shaft stands 49 Ins/124 Cms H, by 8½ Ins/21 Cms W, by 8½ Ins/21 Cms D. It is decorated on all four sides with designs including rope work, knot work and key design. Although weathered, its decoration is the clearest of all the pieces displayed.

3.   What an accompanying notice describes as "The Old "Ain Howe" Cross". It is located standing against the south wall, 8 Ins/20 Cms from the east wall of the south aisle. The cross stood on the moors until it fell down in the 19C. It is of uncertain age. The section of stonework from the cross stands 42 Ins/106 Cms H, by 17 Ins/43 Cms W, by 9 Ins/22 Cms D.

In the crypt, in the north aisle and standing on the floor, there are:

4.   What an accompanying notice describes as "A 9th Century Crosshead. The churchyard cross from which this comes would have stood 24 ft H" (the head alone would have been about 60 Ins/152 Cms H). This large section of stonework from a crosshead comprises the central section and most of two arms and part of the top vertical arm. It stands vertically on the floor in the middle of the north aisle, 46 Ins/116 Cms south of the north wall of the north aisle. It measures 21 Ins/53 Cms to 23 Ins/58 Cms H, by 58 Ins/147 Cms W, by 9 Ins/22 Cms D. Although weathered, circular motif decoration can be identified on both the south and north sides of the central section and arms, and on the ends of each of the complete arms. However, the western arm now affixed to the central boss appears to come from another crosshead given

its different knot work decoration and its smaller size in comparison with the eastern arm.

5.   There is a group of three decorated sections of stonework. The associated notice describes them as "The doorposts of the Saxon monastery" (only two of these sections of stonework are from door jambs, the other section of stonework is from a cross-shaft). They stand 27 Ins/68 Cms south of the north wall and 24 Ins/61 Cms west of the east wall of the north aisle. They comprise:

(i)   The section of stonework nearest the north wall. This section of stonework apparently comes from an 11C cross-shaft but, conceivably it may comprise the central boss and an arm from a crosshead. It stands 24 Ins/61 Cms H, tapering from 11 Ins/27 Cms to 8 Ins/20 Cms W, by 6 Ins/15 Cms D. It is weathered but is decorated on all four sides with "key" pattern.

(ii)   The section of stonework nearest to the east wall. This section of stonework is a door jamb from the 9C monastery. It stands 18 Ins/45 Cms H, by 13 Ins/33 Cms W, by 7 Ins/17 Cms D. It is weathered, but on its southern face it is decorated with some sort of circular motif. The other sides have either been rendered or damaged and consequently no decoration can now be identified with certainty.

(iii)   The most westerly of the three sections of stonework. This section of stonework is a door jamb from the 9C monastery. It stands 27 Ins/68 Cms H, by 8 Ins/20 Cms W, by 8 Ins/20 Cms D. It too is weathered and is clearly decorated with some abstract design on its southern face. The other sides have either been rendered or damaged and consequently no decoration can now be identified with certainty.

(The crypt also contains four assorted medieval and later grave covers.)

In the north wall of the north aisle of the crypt there is an iron gate blocking the way to a passageway. On the floor behind this iron gate there are more sections of assorted stonework (they are sometimes moved around so their exact position changes from time to time). These sections of stonework include:

6.   What the guidebook describes as "small "vesicular windows" again from the pre-Conquest monastery". The "windows" lie on the floor about 26 Ins/66 Cms to the north of the iron gate. They comprise four pieces of broken stonework with a circular design indicating that they were originally all joined together forming a square. Together they measure 5 Ins/12 Cms H (D), by 14 Ins/35 Cms by 16 Ins/40 Cms.

7.   A section of stonework comprising the central section from a late 8C/early 9C crosshead. It lies on the floor about 42 Ins/106 Cms

to the north of the iron gate. The section of stonework is decorated with "cat's cradle" design. It is about 8 Ins/20 Cms in diameter. Its associated arm is now detached, and difficult to identify with certainty among the jumble of stones kept in the dark behind this locked iron gate.

(Note: The accompanying notices to some of the sections of stonework referred to above are not always displayed or identified with the correct section of stonework.)

The upper and lower decorated stone end from an 8C chair which formed part of the Abbot's throne and found at Lastingham is now in the Yorkshire Museum in York (see the entry for the Yorkshire Museum, York) .

Externally, there is an A-S Mass Dial. It is easily located east of the south porch on the south face of the first buttress on the south wall. The Mass Dial has been incised on the more western (left-hand) of the two sections of stonework forming the south face of the buttress. It is 94 Ins/238 Cms up from the ground. The hole for the missing gnomon can be identified and some of the scratches to indicate the time.

Externally, a section of A-S stonework has been incorporated into the buttress supporting the west end of the south aisle. It is the fourth stone down from the top on the south face of the buttress. It is decorated with five lines forming a quarter circle design.

Externally, according to the guidebook, there is apparently a section of A-S stonework incorporated into the fabric of the north wall of the north aisle above the pointed head of the doorway. It is difficult to identify with any certainty.

LASTINGHAM
(4) St Ovin's Well
SE 739904   Rating: ☆

St Ovin's Well is located in the centre of Lastingham, on the east side of the road running west/east through the village – it temporarily follows a north/south direction at this point – (there are no street signs, but this road is known as "Low Street"). The well is 23 Yds/21 M south of the junction with the no-through road that heads uphill in a northerly direction (see the entry for St Chad's Well, "2" above) and the road that runs west/east through the village (see the entry for St Cedd's Well, "1" above).

The well is incorporated within a stretch of stone walling 22 Ins/55 Cms east of the east side of the road. The enclosure surrounding the well can be identified by the two stone pillars supporting a rounded arch with a triangular head that protrude from the walling – vegetation is in evidence. The enclosure measures 76 Ins/193 Cms H, by 55 Ins/139 Cms W, by 28½ Ins/72 Cms D. There is now no evidence of a tap or water pump – no water was apparent when this well was visited.

There is no commemorative notice or carving on the stonework. However, the walling forms part of the garden wall to the property that has a plaque "Ovins Well House" on the wall above and to the south (right) of the main entrance doorway.

Ovin accompanied Æthelthryth from Ely in Cambridgeshire to the north for Æthelthryth's marriage to king Ecgfrith of Northumbria in 659. When Æthelthryth joined the monastery at Coldingham in 670 Ovin joined the monastery at Lastingham as a novice. He became a trusted companion of Bishop Chad and accompanied him on a mission to the Mercian monastery at Lichfield. Ovin eventually returned to his home at Haddenham, near Ely and died there in 675. Æthelthryth had returned in 673 to Ely and founded the monastery there. (The base of a cross raised in memory of Ovin by Æthelthryth is now in Ely Cathedral.) Æthelthryth is mentioned by the Venerable Bede in his History of the English Church and people completed in 731.

LEAKE
St Mary's Church
SE 433906   Rating: ☆☆☆

This isolated church is easily located on the east side of the A19, about 4 miles south of the junction of the A19 and A684. To reach the church take the un-signposted, but obvious, drive that winds its way to approach the church from a south-westerly direction. The church is about 170 Yds/155 M from the A19.

Possibly on the site of an A-S church, the present structure includes work from the 13C to the 15C.

Externally, there is a much-weathered A-S sundial incorporated into the fabric of the south wall of the south aisle. It is located 44½ Ins/113 Cms east of the east wall of the south porch, 62 Ins/157 Cms up from the base of the church. The stone on which the sundial is scratched measures 18 Ins/45 Cms H by 19 Ins/48 Cms W. It is possible to identify the hole and retaining piece of iron for the missing gnomon and a large semi-circular groove 7 Ins/17 Cms below the hole for the gnomon (where the indications of time would be). There are no other distinguishing markings. (Immediately next to (east of) this sundial there is a better-preserved section of later medieval stonework decorated with a beast.)

Externally, there is a distinctive "St Cuthbert-style" A-S crosshead incorporated into the fabric of the west face of the tower. It is located about 24 Ins/61 Cms above the large window in the centre of the west face of the tower. The crosshead measures about 24 Ins/61 Cms square. It is weathered but there are slight traces of decoration in the central section.

LEVISHAM

(1) St John the Baptist Church

SE 833905   Rating: ☆☆

The small, aisle-less church is easily located adjacent to the west side of the main (un-named) road running north/south through Levisham by a junction with another minor road which heads off in a westerly/north-westerly direction.

The present structure dates from 1884 which was built on the site of an earlier church whose date of origin is unknown.

Internally, in the north porch there are:

1.   A section of stonework from an A-D grave cover. It is located standing on the floor of the porch 8 Ins/20 Cms south of the north wall and leaning against the east wall of the porch. The section of stonework measures 16 Ins/40 Cms H, by 24½ Ins/62 Cms W, by 6 Ins/15 Cms D. It is decorated on the west face with Jellinge design; all the other sides are too damaged for any decoration to survive.

2.   A section of stonework from an A-D grave cover. It is located standing on the floor of the porch 1 inch/2 Cms north of the south wall and leaning against the east wall of the porch. The section of stonework measures 18 Ins/45 Cms H, by 24½ Ins/62 Cms W, by 7½ Ins/19 Cms D. It is decorated on the west face with Jellinge design; all the other sides are too damaged for any decoration to survive.

3.   A section of stonework from an A-D grave cover. It is located lying on the floor of the porch beneath "1" above. It has clearly been broken off the southern end of "1" above. This section of stonework measures 3½ Ins/8 Cms H, by 7½ Ins/19 Cms W, by 6 Ins/15 Cms D. It is decorated on the west face with Jellinge design; all the other sides are too damaged for any decoration to survive.

Internally, there is an 11C "tub" font. It is located in the west end of the nave, 50 Ins/127 Cms south of the door into the north porch. The font sits on a supporting circular base standing on a floor standing plinth. The font measures 18 Ins/45 Cms H by 29 Ins/73 Cms in diameter. (The supporting circular base is 16 Ins/40 Cms H standing on top of a 10 inch/25 Cms H plinth.) On the eastern face of the font there is a much-weathered carving of a cross and a bishop's crosier.

LEVISHAM
(2) St Mary's Church
SE 833901   Rating: ☆

From the "Levisham" village sign (affixed to an old circular millstone) at the southern end of the village, proceed downhill along the "main" road out of Levisham in a general southerly direction. Continue along this road as it takes a sharp bend to follow an easterly route.

After about 240 Yds/219 M from the village sign, locate a vertical, free-standing wooden signpost on the south side of the road. Incised on both arms of this signpost is the word "Link" and a directional arrow. Proceed in a south-westerly direction off the road downhill along the rough track as directed by one of the "Link" signpost arms.

From this signpost, and as you proceed down along the rough track, the ruins of the church, partially surrounded by trees, can be identified farther down the valley.

About 170 Yds/155 M from the "Link" signpost, the rough track reaches a junction with other rough tracks. Take the rough track leading off in a south-easterly direction. (This track clearly leads to the church.) About 115 Yds/105 M along this track there is a gate into the churchyard containing the ruined church.

Attached to this churchyard gate there is an information notice about St Mary's Church. (The two parts of a Saxon gravestone with a distinctive dragon design referred to are the sections of stonework now in the porch of St John the Baptist Church, Levisham – see the entry "1" above.)

The church was largely re-built in 1802 and the tower was added in 1897 to commemorate 60 years of Queen Victoria's reign.

Internally, the ruins incorporate what was considered to be a distinctive A-S chancel arch. However, with apparently 12C material found at a lower level in the structure, there must be some doubt, even after allowing for the re-use of good quality building material. Fabric of a similar age may have been incorporated into some of the other parts of the building although this cannot now be easily identified.

The village in the vicinity of the church was abandoned after the Black Death 1348-49.

LINTON-IN-CRAVEN
St Michael and All Angels Church
SE 005632   Rating: ☆

As soon as the B6265 reaches the west bank of the River Wharfe turn off the B6265 and take the minor road south as directed by the signs

"Linton ¾, Burnsall 3" and "Linton Parish Church XllC". (There is also a "Youth Hostel ¾" sign.)

Continue along this minor road for about 700 Yds/640 M and then turn off and proceed along another minor road ("Church Road") in a north-easterly direction as directed by the sign "Linton Parish Church XIIC". At the road junction there is a street sign "Church Road Leading to Linton Falls" and a no-through road sign.

Proceed along Church Road for about 500 Yds/457 M until the road runs out at the entrance to the churchyard. (On the way ignore all the signs to Linton Falls.)

Although a major restoration of the church took place in 1861, material does survive from around 1150 and 1250 and the early 14C.

Internally, there is a large, plain, tub-shaped font possibly of A-S vintage. It is located 72 In/182 Cms west of the south door, and to the east of the west window in the south aisle, on a stepped plinth.

Internally, there is a framed photograph and a plaque underneath commemorating the 9C/10C brass crucifix, "The Linton Crucifix", which was on display before it was stolen in 1980. The photograph is located below the top of the west face of the first free-standing pillar west of the chancel, (supporting the arch separating the south side of the nave from the south aisle).

LONG PRESTON
St Mary's Church
SD 837581   Rating: ☆☆

The church is situated in the south-eastern part of Long Preston. Just under 200 Yds/182 M northwest of the junction of the A65 and the A682, take the minor road off the A65 which heads in a north-easterly direction (there is no street sign). The church is easily located 150 Yds/137 M along this road on its northeast side just before the road turns to follow a northwest direction.

On the site of an A-S church the present structure dates from the late 14C and the partial rebuilding in 1869. Fabric from the earlier churches on the site appears to be incorporated into the walling of the nave (internally) and the tower (both internally and externally).

Internally, there is a gravestone that has been described as A-S but seems more typically later medieval. It is located incorporated into the flooring of the chancel, adjacent to the base of the wall separating the chancel from the north aisle, and between the organ and the choir stalls. The gravestone measures 65 Ins/165 Cms L tapering 16½ Ins/ 41 Cms to 9 Ins/22 Cms W. It is clearly decorated with a cross surrounded by a circle from which two parallel lines run the length of the gravestone, and shears.

Internally, there is another gravestone that has been described as A-S but seems more typically later medieval. It is located in the "Hammerton" Chapel, adjacent to the south side of the chancel. The gravestone has been incorporated into the low north wall separating the chapel and the chancel. It is situated adjacent to the west end of the base of the pillar supporting the eastern arm of the easternmost arch separating the chapel and the chancel (the small arch to the east is discounted). It measures 40 Ins/101 Cms L by 16½ Ins/41 Cms W. Although very weathered four roundels and parallel lines can be identified.

Internally, there is a hexagonal-shaped 11C A-S font. It is located in the centre of the floor in the south aisle 93 Ins/236 Cms east of the west wall of the south aisle. The font stands on a separate 7 Ins/17 Cms H hexagonal-shaped section of stonework that itself stands on a modern 6 Ins/15 Cms H plinth. The font measures 29 Ins/73 Cms H, by 25 Ins/63 Cms W, by 23 Ins/58 Cms D. It is decorated with an irregular design.

Externally, there is a weathered, but distinctive, A-S finial. It is located sitting on top of the apex of the roof of the south porch 5 Ins/12 Cms north of the southern end of the south porch. The crosshead measures about 14 Ins/35 Cms H, by 10 Ins/25 Cms W, by 5 Ins/12 Cms D. Although weathered there are distinctive lines separating the "arms" from each other and from the central section. There is no other decoration.

LOW BENTHAM
Church of St John the Baptist
SD 644693   Rating: ⭐⭐

On the western edge of Low Bentham, the church is located about 100 Yds/91 M west of where the B6480 crosses the River Wenning. The churchyard is adjacent to the south side of the B6480.

The Scots destroyed a church on this site in 1340 and the present tower survives from the subsequent rebuilding. However, most of the present structure dates from the rebuilding work undertaken in 1822 and 1876.

Internally, there is a section of A-S stonework that could be part of a cross-shaft or from the central section of a large crosshead. It is located in the south aisle at the eastern end of the window ledge of the second window from the west end of the south aisle. The section of stonework measures 17½ Ins/44 Cms H, by 18 Ins/45 Cms W, by 10 Ins/25 Cms D. It is decorated on its northwest face with the Crucifixion scene in relief. The other three sides are too weathered or damaged for any decoration to survive.

Internally, there is a section of stonework from an A-S crosshead comprising the central section, an arm and part of another arm. It is located in the south aisle leaning against the east wall of the window ledge of the second window west of the east end of the south aisle (south of the font). It is the most easterly of the three sections of stonework on this window ledge. The section of crosshead measures 12 Ins/30 Cms H, by 10 Ins/25 Cms W, by 3½ Ins/8 Cms D. On the northwest face it is decorated with a head in relief in the centre and knot work decoration. The southeast face has a central, circular boss. Due to weathering the other sides have no surviving decoration.

LOW HAWSKER
Cross-shaft

LOW HAWSKER: Anglo-Saxon Cross-Shaft. Weathering will one day remove all trace of decoration.

NZ 922074   Rating: ☆☆

Proceeding south from Whitby along the A171 take the minor road (there is no street sign) that heads in a south-westerly direction off the A171 indicated by the first "Low Hawsker ¼" directional sign. After about 400 Yds/365 M the distinctive section of stonework from an A-S cross-shaft can easily be identified standing on a plinth at the western end of a walled allotment on the north side of the road.

The section of stonework measures 76 Ins/193 Cms H, tapering 15½ Ins/39 Cms to 11 Ins/27 Cms W, tapering 12½ Ins/31 Cms to 7 Ins/17 Cms D. The plinth on which the section of stonework stands measures between 11 Ins/27 Cms and 13 Ins/33 Cms H, by 40 Ins/101 Cms W, by 33 Ins/83 Cms D. The section of stonework is very weathered. However, chain pattern decoration can be identified on both the southwest and southeast faces. There is a hint of chain pattern design surviving on the northwest face but the weathering on the northeast face has removed all trace of decoration. The decoration at one time included various forms of interlace design and animals, possibly including birds.

The section of stonework dates from the 10C. It is all that survives from a chapel that apparently once stood in the vicinity.

LYTHE
St Oswald's Church
NZ 850132   Rating: ✰✰✰✰

The church is situated 200 Yds/182 M to the east of the village of Lythe. It is easily located on the north side of the A174.

The original church was built on the site of a Viking burial ground dating from around 950. It is for this reason that when the church was extensively restored in 1910 sections of A-S/Viking stonework were discovered concealed in the walling. The present church dates mostly from 1910 although there is some earlier fabric surviving from the 12C and the restorations in 1819 and 1870.

Internally, the church displays the sections of stonework discovered during the 1910 restoration. Most of these are displayed at the west end of the church under the tower but some are stored in the basement of the tower and can only be viewed by appointment with the vicar. The sections of stonework are occasionally moved around and so may not necessarily be precisely in the locations indicated below. One day it is intended that they be formally displayed.

Those sections of stonework, which can be definitely attributable to the A-S/A-D from around 950 to 1050, are numbered 1 to 30. They come from various A-S/A-D grave slabs, crossheads and cross-shafts, and A-D hogback grave covers. The faces of the sections of stonework displayed outwards are usually the best decorated. Many of the sections of stonework are weathered and damaged but some decoration can usually be identified.

Those sections of stonework numbered (i) to (x) are of later medieval origin and include grave slabs and architectural features from the church fabric. The order of the numbers 1 to 30 and (i) to (x) is sequential and the two types of numbering are intermingled to reflect as accurately as possible the positions of the sections of stonework.

Internally, on the ledge against the north wall of the tower there are:

1.   A section of stonework comprising the central section and an arm and part of another arm from a crosshead. It is located 1½ Ins/3 Cms west of the east end of the ledge and it leans against the north wall of the tower. The section of stonework tapers 11½ Ins/29 Cms to 9 Ins/22 Cms H, by 17 Ins/43 Cms W, tapering 9½ Ins/24 Cms to 5½ Ins/13 Cms D. It is decorated in the centre with a head, possibly representing Christ, and some worn knot work design on the south face. It is has a central boss on the north face and there is knot work design on the east side. It is too weathered and damaged for any other decoration to survive on the other sides.

2.　A section of stonework from a grave marker. It is located 19½ Ins/49 Cms west of the east end of the ledge. This section of stonework measures 11½ Ins/29 Cms H, by 12¼ Ins/31 Cms W, by up to 3¾ Ins/9 Cms D. It has lines in the shape of a cross incised on its south face. There is no other decoration on the other damaged sides.

3.　An almost complete crosshead apart from the section joining it to its cross-shaft. It is located 37½ Ins/95 Cms west of the east end of the ledge and it leans against the north wall of the tower. The crosshead measures 6½ Ins/16 Cms H, by 10¾ Ins/27 Cms W, by 4 Ins/10 Cms D. Apart from incised lines forming a "V" separating the arms of the cross on both faces of the crosshead there is no other decoration.

4.　A section from of stonework from a grave marker. It is located 44½ Ins/113 Cms west of the east end of the ledge and it is adjacent to the north wall of the tower. The section of stonework measures 8 Ins/20 Cms D (H), by 9 Ins/22 Cms W, by 4½ Ins/11 Cms H (D). Apart from incised lines forming a "V" separating the arms of the cross on both faces of the crosshead there is no other decoration.

5.　An almost complete crosshead apart from the section joining it to its cross-shaft. It is located 50 Ins/126 Cms to the west of the east end of the ledge. The crosshead measures 8 Ins/20 Cms H, by 14¼ Ins/36 Cms W, by 6 Ins/15 Cms D. Apart from incised lines forming a "V" separating the arms of the cross on both faces of the crosshead there is no other decoration.

6.　A virtually complete wheel head cross. It is located 65¾ Ins/169 Cms west of the east end of the ledge. The wheel head cross measures 14¾ Ins/37 Cms H, by 16 Ins/40 Cms W, by 6 Ins/15 Cms D. It is very weathered and no decoration can be positively identified on any of the sides.

7.　A section of stonework from an A-D hogback grave cover. It is located 89 Ins/226 Cms west of the east end of the ledge. The section of stonework measures between 8 Ins/20 Cms and 9½ Ins/24 Cms H, by 10½ Ins/26 Cms W, by 11¼ Ins/28 Cms D. Although weathered, one of the bears and some knot work decoration can be identified. No other decoration can be identified on any of the other sides due to weathering.

8.　Two sections of stonework now placed back together, from the cross-shaft known as "The Wrestlers". (They are separated by pieces of woodwork to hold them in place.) The sections of stonework are located at the westernmost end of the ledge. Together they measure 29 Ins/73 Cms H, by 13½ Ins/34 Cms W, by 7 Ins/17 Cms D.

On the top section of stonework, on the southeast face, the lower body and the legs of two men wrestling can be identified beneath which the top half of the body and head of a horse or dragon can clearly also be identified. The northwest face is too weathered and damaged for any decoration to be identified with certainty. On both the other two sides some knot work decoration can be identified.

On the lower section of stonework the legs of a horse or dragon can be identified on the southeast face. Due to weathering and damage no other decoration can be identified with certainty on the other sides of this lower section of cross-shaft.

[Also on this ledge there are an additional five fragments of stonework all of which are too small to be able to identify their origin and purpose with certainty. There are also some notices about the stonework affixed to the side of the ledge and on the ledge itself.]

Internally, on the floor beneath the ledge against the north wall of the tower there are:

9.   An almost complete crosshead, apart from some damage to one of the arms, and a section of stonework from its attached cross-shaft. They are located below the western end of the ledge, abutting some west walling of the tower. Together they measure 25½ Ins/64 Cms H, by 12 Ins/30 Cms W, by 5 Ins/12 Cms D. Apart from incised lines forming a "V" separating the arms of the cross on both faces of the crosshead there is no other decoration.

10.   A section of stonework from an A-D hogback grave cover. It is located 1½ Ins/3 Cms south of the ledge and 13¾ Ins/34 Cms east of some nearby west walling. The section of stonework measures between 11 Ins/27 Cms and 13½ Ins/34 Cms H, by 13½ Ins/34 Cms W, by 27 Ins/68 Cms L. It is decorated with a tegulated roof and with knot work design on both its east and west faces. The other sides are too weathered and damaged for any decoration to be identified.

Internally, on the floor to the east of a door opening into the north wall of the tower there is:

11.   A complete crosshead with a section of stonework from its attached cross-shaft. In total they measure 21 Ins/53 Cms H, by 13½ Ins/34 Cms W, by 5 Ins/12 Cms D. Apart from incised lines forming a "V" separating the arms of the cross on both faces of the crosshead there is no other decoration.

Internally, in rows on the floor close to the west wall of the tower there are:

(i)   A section of stonework from a later medieval grave cover. It is located 1½ Ins/3 Cms east of the west wall and 5½ Ins/13 Cms south of the north wall of the tower. The section of stonework stands 27 Ins/68 Cms H, by 10 Ins/25 Cms W, by 6 Ins/15 Cms D. It is decorated with an incised cross and the number B15 has been added later.

12.   A section of stonework from a grave cover. It is located 17 Ins/43 Cms east of the west wall and 2 Ins/5 Cms south of the north wall of the tower. The section of stonework measures 31 Ins/78 Cms L, by 15 Ins/38 Cms W, by 8 Ins/20 Cms D. Despite weathering, knot work design can be identified on the top and the top stone "ridge" survives. The other sides are too damaged or worn for any decoration to be identified.

13.   A section of stonework from a hogback grave cover currently standing vertically on end. It is located 3½ Ins/8 Cms east of the west wall and 20 Ins/50 Cms south of the north wall of the tower. The section of stonework measures 20½ Ins/52 Cms H (L), by 10 Ins/25 Cms W, by 9 Ins/22 Cms D (H). Although weathered it is decorated with knot work and a half circle design on its two faces – the bear is missing.

14.   A complete crosshead with a section from its attached cross-shaft. They are located 19½ Ins/49 Cms east of the west wall and 23½ Ins/59 Cms south of the north wall of the tower. Together they measure 24¾ Ins/62 Cms L (H), by 11 Ins/27 Cms (crosshead) and 7¼ Ins/18 Cms (cross-shaft) W, by 5 Ins/12 Cms D. Apart from incised lines forming a "V" separating the arms of the cross on both faces of the crosshead there is no other decoration.

(ii)   A section of stonework from a later medieval grave cover. It is located 1 inch/2 Cms east of the west wall and 34 Ins/86 Cms south of the north wall of the tower. The section of stonework measures 18½ Ins/47 Cms L, by 9 Ins/22 Cms W, by 7 Ins/17 Cms D and is decorated with an incised cross and a circular motif design.

15.   A section of stonework from a hogback grave cover. It is located 23 Ins/58 Cms east of the west wall and 45 Ins/114 Cms south of the north wall of the tower. The section of stonework measures up to 11¾ Ins/29 Cms H, by 11½ Ins/29 Cms W, by 18¾ Ins/47 Cms L. Although weathered some knot work decoration and tegulated roof design can be identified.

16.   A section of stonework from a hogback grave cover currently standing vertically on end. It is located 1 inch/2 Cms east of the west wall and 60 Ins/152 Cms south of the north wall of the tower. The section of stonework measures 24½ Ins/62 Cms H (L), by 10 Ins/25 Cms W, by 10½ Ins/26 Cms D (H). Although weathered a distinctive central ridge separating the tegulated roof design as well as knot work design can be identified.

17.   A section of stonework from a hogback grave cover. It is located 19 Ins/48 Cms east of the west wall and 63 Ins/160 Cms north of the south wall of the tower. The section of stonework measures between 9½ Ins/24 Cms and 10 Ins/25 Cms H, by 7½ Ins/19 Cms W, by 27 Ins/68 Cms L. Although weathered, it is decorated with the face of a bear. The roof ridge is very oblong and it is decorated with key pattern design.

18.   A section of stonework from a hogback grave cover. It is located 4 Ins/10 Cms east of the west wall and 43½ Ins/110 Cms north of the south wall of the tower. The section of stonework measures between 8½ Ins/21 and 11¾ Ins/29 Cms H, by 11 Ins/27 Cms W, by 22 Ins/55 Cms L. It is decorated with a tegulated roof and knot work design.

19.   A section of stonework from a hogback grave cover. It is located 21½ Ins/54 Cms east of the west wall and 35½ Ins/90 Cms north of the south wall of the tower. The section of stonework measures 8½ Ins/21 Cms H, by 10½ Ins/26 Cms W, by 22 Ins/55 Cms L. It is decorated with a tegulated roof and knot work design. The sides are badly damaged.

20.   A section of stonework from a cross-shaft. It is located 35 Ins/88 Cms east of the west wall and 37 Ins/93 Cms north of the south wall of the tower. The section of stonework measures 15 Ins/38 Cms H (W), by 22¾ Ins/57 Cms W (H), by 9 Ins/22 Cms D. Although weathered it is decorated on the east face with knot work design and on its top side with a large stepped square design. The other sides are too damaged for any decoration to be identified.

(iii)   A section of stonework from a grave cover incised with a cross typical of later medieval rather than A-S/A-D design. It is located 52 Ins/132 Cms east of the west wall and 37 Ins/93 Cms north of the south wall of the tower. The section of stonework measures by 6 Ins/15 Cms H, by 20 Ins/50 Cms W, by 15 Ins/38 Cms D.

21.   A section of stonework from a cross-shaft. It is located leaning up against the west wall 30½ Ins/77 Cms north of the south wall of the tower. The section of stonework measures 25 Ins/63 Cms H, by 10¾ Ins/27 Cms W, by 6 Ins/15 Cms D. Despite the weathering some knot work decoration can be identified on its west face. The other sides are either rendered or too weathered for any decoration to survive.

22.   A section of stonework from a cross-shaft. It is located 14 Ins/35 Cms east of the west wall and 15½ Ins/39 Cms north of the south wall of the tower. The section of stonework measures 10½ Ins/26 Cms H (W), by 23¾ Ins/60 Cms W (H), by 6½ Ins/16 Cms D. Although weathered it is decorated with knot work design on all four sides with line design on two of its edges.

23.   A section of stonework from a cross-shaft. It is located 38 Ins/96 Cms east of the west wall and 19½ Ins/49 Cms north of the south wall of the tower. The section of stonework measures 21½ Ins/54 Cms H, tapering 15 Ins/38 Cms to 11½ Ins/29 Cms W, by 8½ Ins/21 Cms D. It is clearly decorated with knot work design on both faces and line decoration on the northwest side. There is no decoration on the fourth side due to weathering and damage.

24. A section of stonework from a hogback grave cover. It is located 63 Ins/160 Cms east of the west wall and 15 Ins/38 Cms north of the south wall of the tower. The section of stonework measures 8½ Ins/21 Cms H, by 11½ Ins/29 Cms W, by 18½ Ins/46 Cms L. Part of the central ridge and knot work design can be identified on the top, all the other sides are too weathered and damaged for any decoration to survive.

Internally, on the floor and close to the south wall of the tower there are:

(iv) A section of stonework comprising a Norman typaneum, broken but now put back together. It is located standing on the floor in the southwest corner of the tower. It is 2 Ins/5 Cms north of the south wall and 3 Ins/7 Cms east of the west wall of the tower. The section of stonework in total measures 20 Ins/50 Cms H, by 30 Ins/76 Cms W, by 5½ Ins/13 Cms D. It is decorated with Adam, the Tree of Knowledge, a column and an animal.

25. A section of stonework from a cross-shaft (a nondescript, unrelated, fragment of stonework has been placed on top). It is located 5 Ins/12 Cms north of the south wall and 28½ Ins/72 Cms east of the west wall of the tower. The section of stonework measures 19 Ins/48 Cms H, by 12 Ins/30 Cms W, by 6 Ins/15 Cms D. It is decorated with knot work design on all four sides.

26. A section of stonework from a hogback grave cover. It is located 1½ Ins/3 Cms north of the south wall and 51 Ins/129 Cms east of the west wall of the tower. The section of stonework measures 17 Ins/43 Cms H, by 12 Ins/30 Cms W, by 10½ Ins/26 Cms L. It is decorated with a tegulated roof and knot work design.

27. A section of stonework from a hogback grave cover. It is located leaning against the south wall 72 Ins/182 Cms east of the west wall of the tower. The section of stonework measures 17½ Ins/44 Cms H, by 9 Ins/22 Cms W, by 16½ Ins/41 Cms L. It is decorated with a tegulated roof and knot work design.

28. A section of stonework from a hogback grave cover. It is located 2½ Ins/6 Cms north of the south wall and 88½ Ins/224 Cms east of the west wall of the tower. The section of stonework measures between 8 Ins/20 Cms and 10¼ Ins/25 Cms H, by 12 Ins/30 Cms W, by 22½ Ins/57 Cms L. It is decorated with a tegulated roof and knot work design.

29. A complete crosshead and a section of stonework from its attached cross-shaft. They are located 1 inch/2 Cms north of the south wall and 104 Ins/264 Cms east of the west wall of the tower. Together they measure 26 Ins/66 Cms L (this would be height when standing), by 10 Ins/25 Cms W, by 5 Ins/12 Cms D. Apart from incised lines forming

a "V" separating the arms of the cross on both faces of the crosshead there is no other decoration.

(v)   There are also odd, small fragments of stonework lying on the floor supporting and lying amongst the sections of stonework from cross-shafts and hogback grave covers. These fragments are too small to identify their origin and purpose.

(vi)   A section of later medieval stonework. It is located at the western end of the window ledge on the south wall of the tower. The section of stonework measures 8 Ins/20 Cms H, by 14 Ins/35 Cms W, by 7½ Ins/19 Cms D. It is decorated with a winged head with leaf design, the "Green Man". (There is also another section of later medieval stonework on this ledge, part of a capital.)

Additional sections of stonework of varying dates, sizes and purpose are stored in the basement of the tower. They stand in an upright position in a row close to the east wall of the basement of the tower. They include:

(vii)   A low, squat section of stonework that does not appear to be A-S/A-D. It is located 28 Ins/71 Cms north of the south wall of the basement of the tower. The section of stonework measures 26 Ins/66 Cms H (W), by 11 Ins/27 Cms W (D), by 10 Ins/25 Cms D (H).

30.   A damaged section of stonework from a hogback grave cover. It is located 46 Ins/116 Cms north of the south wall of the basement of the tower. The section of stonework measures 27 Ins/68 Cms H (W), by 12 Ins/30 Cms W (D), by 4½ Ins/11 Cms D (H). Some tegulated roof decoration can just about be identified.

(viii)   A section of stonework from a grave cover that appears to be later medieval rather than A-S/A-D. It is located 65 Ins/165 Cms north of the south wall of the basement of the tower. The section of stonework measures 28 Ins/71 Cms H (W), by 13 Ins/33 Cms W (D), by 7½ Ins/19 Cms D (H). Apart from the thin protruding "ridge" of stonework on the top (now vertical) edge no decoration can be identified.

(ix)   A section of stonework from a grave cover that appears to be later medieval rather than A-S/A-D. It is located 80 Ins/203 Cms north of the south wall of the basement of the tower. The section of stonework measures 35 Ins/88 Cms H (W), by 11 Ins/27 Cms W (D), by 11 Ins/27 Cms D (H). Apart from the thin protruding "ridge" of stonework on the top (now vertical) edge no decoration can be identified.

(x)   A section of stonework from a grave cover that appears to be later medieval rather than A-S/A-D. It is located 93 Ins/236 Cms north of the south wall of the basement of the tower. The section of stonework measures 28 Ins/71 Cms H (W), by 10 Ins/25 Cms W (D), by 5 Ins/12 Cms D (H). No decoration can be identified.

[There are other sections of stonework also stored in the basement of the tower but these all appear to be later medieval in origin mostly comprising church architectural features.]

Externally, the buttresses supporting the north aisle of the church apparently contain more section of A-S/A-D stonework.

Externally in the churchyard, there is a Norman, but possibly A-S stone coffin. From the north end of the chancel proceed along the pathway running in an easterly direction for 525 Ins/1333 Cms. Leave the pathway and head across the graveyard in a northerly direction heading towards the northern churchyard wall. After about 600 Ins/1523 Cms the coffin is located lying on the ground 168 Ins/426 Cms south of the northern churchyard wall. The coffin and the surrounding area are much overgrown and some searching is required. The coffin has been broken in two lengthways and the north side is also broken in two, part of its northeast corner is missing. As the coffin is lying broken on the ground the width measurements reflect the greater width than when the coffin was properly put together. The coffin measures 82 Ins/208 Cms L, tapering 36 Ins/91 Cms to 29 Ins/73 Cms W (broken), by 10 Ins/25 Cms H.

MALTON
Museum
SE 786717   Rating: ✰✰

In the centre of Malton, the Museum is located on the north-west side of the Market Place (there are street signs). There is a large "Malton Museum" sign attached to the front of the appropriate building.

As with all museums, the displays and the exhibits they contain may be changed, re-sited, removed from display and/or put in store, or loaned to other museums or suitable repositories. Before visiting a museum it is worth checking in advance whether the displays listed in the gazetteer are still in place in the same location(s) set out in the text. Individual exhibits may have been rearranged in terms of their display, the order in which they are displayed and their relationship to other exhibits, some exhibits may have been removed from display. The text in the gazetteer reflects the descriptions and/or accompanying notices to the exhibits at the time of visiting. These too may have been revised, amended, added to or removed.

The Museum is housed in the former Town Hall that dates from the 18C.

The Museum contains exhibits collected from the local area dating from 8000BC to Medieval times. These include a display about Wharram

Percy Deserted Medieval Village (see entry for Wharram Percy, North Yorkshire). This display is to be expanded in the future. At present the items relating to Wharram Percy are kept in two display cabinets on the first floor. One cabinet displays a necklace of glass and amber beads and two pots. The other display contains a fragment of an ivory purse ring, oyster shells, Niedermendig lava quern fragments, a "Runic" brooch (the runes are scratched on the reverse), animal bones, and a stone column re-used as a mortar. The precise origins and date of these items is not stated in the displays.

Separately, but in the vicinity of the Wharram Percy display cabinets, there is a section of stonework that may be A-S in origin. It is not clear whether it is from a crosshead or cross-shaft or from a building or where it has come from. It sits on a wooden plinth measuring 16 Ins/40 Cms H, by 15 Ins/38 Cms W, by 12 Ins/30 Cms D. The section of stonework measures 8 Ins/20 Cms H, by 8½ Ins/21 Cms W, by 8 Ins/20 Cms D. On the un-damaged side it is incised with an oblong design.

The Museum also houses in a separate room on the first floor a temporary exhibition (it is unlikely that this exhibition will be retained) on the West Heslerton excavations (see the entry for West Heslerton, North Yorkshire). The displays in the Museum include items and artefacts relating to before and during the A-S period. There is a large notice "Lighting up the Dark Ages. The Anglo-Saxons AD 400-850" in the vicinity of the three display cabinets of A-S interest.

1.   A display cabinet that contains an illustrated notice "West Heslerton: plan of the Anglo-Saxon village and its community". The items and artefacts displayed are:

Shield boss.
Spear.
Sword.
Knife.
Buckle.
Girdle hangers and a key.
Wrist clasps.
A beaver tooth and an amber pendant.
An amulet made from a pig's tusk.
Brooches: two annular, one Cruciform and one square headed.

2.   A display cabinet that contains a illustrated notices: "A-S buildings and woollen and linen cloth production" and "A-S cemetery and the village". The items and artefacts displayed are:

Iron shears.
Plant-dyed wool – nettle, woad, ivy berries, cow parsley, brambles, birch, madder.

Spindle whorls of bone, chalk, stone and pottery.
Thread beaters – to keep the weave neat and to unpick mistakes.
Bone weaving tablet – used to make braids.
Bronze and bone needles.
Leatherworking.
Antler working.

3.   A display cabinet that refers specifically to the Middle Saxon period 650-850. This cabinet contains illustrated notices about the village, settlement and activities, and an impression of how the village might have looked in AD 650. The items and artefacts displayed are:

Crucible fragments.
Iron and slag waste from smelting. Iron knives.
Whetstones – two with grooves for sharpening tools.
Two pots one incised with lines.
Bronze fishing hook.
Bone knife.
Middle Saxon stycas and sceattas.
Lyre (musical instrument) bridge.
Bone dice and bone and pottery gaming counters.
7th century strap end with gilded animal ornament.
Bronze brooches.
Bronze and bone cloak fastening pins.
Bone combs including Saxon "whip-handled" combs.

MASHAM
St Mary's Church

SE 226807   Rating: ☆☆☆

The church is easily located in the south-eastern part of Masham. The entrance and the gates to the churchyard are situated at the end of a short drive leading off the south-east corner of the large Market Place/Square. On the walling by the churchyard gates there is a St Mary's Church Notice. The entrance to the churchyard is some 20 Yds/18 M from the Market Place/Square.

The present structure includes A-S material possibly dating from the 9C. However, most of the church dates from building work undertaken in the mid 12C, early 13C and 14C. There were additions in the 15C additions and the church was restored in the late 19C.

Internally, A-S fabric can be seen surviving in a string course that protrudes from the stonework and runs along the former exterior north wall of the nave, now in the north aisle. To locate the string course go into the north aisle and look above the westernmost arch. Two stones decorated with interlace design have been included in this string course and these can also be viewed from the north aisle. One decorated stone is located in the corner of the westernmost end of the nave beneath the modern light and is about 18 Ins/45 Cms W. The other decorated stone is located above the point of the arch of the westernmost arcade arch and is about 9 Ins/22 Cms W. The large, square stones surviving in the fabric above the later inserted openings in the west, north and east walls of the nave probably survive from the A-S church.

Internally there is a large A-S grave marker and an A-S decorated crosshead. These are located on the floor in a recess and under the easternmost window in the north aisle among a variety of other sections of stonework of different sizes, ages and purpose. A descriptive notice hangs on the wall below the window and identifies each section of stonework. The precise position of all these sections of stonework changes from time to time, but two A-S sections of stonework can be definitely identified. They are:

1.   A section of stonework from an arm and the central boss from an A-S crosshead. It dates from the early 9C. It probably formed part of the crosshead for the cross-shaft whose lower section is outside the south porch (see below): However, according to the notice these sections of stonework are not linked. It is located 24 Ins/60 Cms east of the walling forming the west wall to this recess. It leans against the north wall of the north aisle. As it stands at present it measures 23 Ins/58 Cms H, by 13 Ins/33 Cms W, by 4½ Ins/11 Cms D. It is decorated with intricate vine scroll design on both faces. There is no decoration on any of the other sides.

2.   An A-S grave marker. It is located 10½ Ins/26 Cms west of the iron railings surrounding the monument commemorating Sir Marmaduke Wyville and 12½ Ins/31 Cms south of the north wall of the north aisle. It is free-standing. The grave marker measures 17½ Ins/44 Cms H, tapering from 11½ Ins/29 Cms to 7 Ins/17 Cms W, by 3½ Ins/8 Cms D. It is weathered with some indistinct decoration on both faces. There is no decoration on any of the other sides.

3.   There is also a section of stonework from a 12C cross-shaft decorated with a cross in the A-S tradition. It is located 55 Ins/139 Cms east of the walling forming the west wall of this recess. The cross-shaft leans against the north wall of the north aisle.

Externally, A-S quoining can be identified in: the south-east corner of the nave adjoining the east wall of the south aisle; the north-east corner of the tower adjoining the west wall of the north aisle; and, the south-east corner of the tower adjoining the west wall of the south aisle.

Externally, there is part of a weathered A-S stone pillar that formed the lower part of a cross-shaft. (part of the crosshead is preserved inside the church – see "1" above). It is located on a stepped plinth 15 Ins/38 Cms H whose base is some 191 Ins/485 Cms from the step by the south porch of the church. The A-S pillar stands 81 Ins/205 Cms H and is 24 Ins/60 Cms in diameter. It is decorated with four tiers of arcading. The lowest tier is decorated with animals with long necks and a stag. The upper tiers are decorated with human figures that may depict scenes from the Old Testament. The style of the decoration indicates Mercian influence. Unfortunately, the decoration is very weathered. The pillar dates from the early 9C.

The decorative style of this pillar is similar to that on the cross-shaft in St Mary and All Saints Church Cundall, see the appropriate entry in North Yorkshire.

MELSONBY
St James's Church

NZ 202084   Rating: ☆☆☆   Access is possible.

At the crossroads in the centre of Melsonby, take the road (there is no street sign) that heads in a northerly direction. Less than 100 Yds/91 M along this road turn east along "Church Row" (there is a street sign). Continue along this Church Row for about 300 Yds/274 M until reaching the church, located on the north side of the road.

On the site of an A-S church the present structure dates from the mid 12C and was completed in the 13C. It was restored around 1870.

Internally, the opening above the tower arch facing the nave follows the design layout of some A-S churches.

Internally, there are five items of A-S interest. These are:

1.   A section of stonework from a 9C A-S grave cover. It is located near the west end of the nave, 67½ Ins/171 Cms north of the westernmost arch on the south side of the nave. It sits on a purpose built floor-standing support similar in shape to a low chair. The support lifts the grave cover 12 Ins/30 Cms off the floor and stands at its maximum 39 Ins/99 Cms H. The section of stonework measures 30 Ins/76 Cms H, tapering 12 Ins/30 Cms to 10 Ins/25 Cms W, tapering 5 Ins/12 Cms to 3 Ins/7 Cms D. The east face is decorated with a hart and greyhounds (the head of the hart is missing) with a clear border on each side decorated with plait work and vine scroll design. The north side is decorated with a large circular design that apparently depicts a row of human heads. Both the south facing and west sides have been rendered and this action has removed all trace of decoration.

2.   A section of stonework from a 9C A-S grave cover. It is located near the west end of the nave, 58 Ins/147 Cms south of the westernmost

arch on the north side of the nave. It sits on a purpose built floor-standing support similar in shape to a low chair. The support lifts the grave cover 12 Ins/30 Cms off the floor and stands at its maximum 39 Ins/99 Cms H. The section of stonework measures 34 Ins/86 Cms H, tapering 12 Ins/30 Cms to 9 Ins/22 Cms W, tapering 4 Ins/10 Cms to 3 Ins/7 Cms D. The east side is decorated with knot work design and a clear border on each side that is also decorated with knot work design. The south face is decorated with vine scroll design. Both the north facing and west sides have been rendered and this action has removed all trace of decoration.

3.   A section of stonework from what is probably the end of an arm from an A-S crosshead. It is located sitting in the centre of the window ledge of the west window in the tower. The section of stonework measures 9 Ins/22 Cms H, by 8 Ins/20 Cms W, by 5 Ins/12 Cms D. It is decorated with a circular design on its east face. All the other sides are too weathered or damaged for any decoration to be identified.

4.   Two hollow stones that were probably used as oil lamps. They may be A-S in origin. They are located in the north aisle sitting on the window ledge of the second window east of the west wall of the north aisle (the middle window). The more western of these two stones is square in shape and measures 5 Ins/12 Cms H, by 6 Ins/15 Cms W, by 6 Ins/15 Cms D. The more eastern of these two stones is round in shape and measures 6 Ins/15 Cms H with a diameter of just less than 7½ Ins/19 Cms. Both stones are much worn and without any decoration.

MIDDLEHAM
St Mary And St Alkelda Church
SE 126878   Rating: ✰✰

The church is located in the western part of Middleham, to the west of the A6108. The entrance to the drive that leads up to the churchyard is located adjacent to the south side of "Kingsley House". (There is a Kingsley House notice board referring to "Mark Johnston Racing" by the walling by the entrance gate to the house.) The churchyard entrance is reached up this drive, some 78 Yds/71 M west off the A6108.

The present structure dates from 1280 with subsequent rebuilding work in 1340 and 1470. The church was restored in 1878.

Inside the church, there is a section of A-S stonework. It is located in the south-east corner of the nave, just in front (i.e. to the west) of the wooden chancel rail, 24 Ins/60 Cms north of the pillar supporting the south side of the chancel arch. The section of stonework has been incorporated into the fabric of the floor. It measures 28½ Ins/72 Cms W by 16½ Ins/41 Cms D. It is decorated with knot work design. It formed part of the tomb cover for St Alkelda who was a princess murdered by the Danes in 800.

Internally, there is a brass plate on the north face of the easternmost pier on the south side of the nave, 75 Ins/190 Cms up from the floor. The brass plate states: "Near this pillar on the spot indicated by tradition were found during the work of restoration the remains of S. Alkelda Patron Saint of this church." (The exact place where the remains were discovered is not identified). St Alkelda's remains were discovered and then re-buried in 1878 during the restoration of the church.

MIDDLESBROUGH
Dorman Museum
NZ 492191   Rating: ☆

To the west of the centre of Middlesbrough, there are directional signs, "Dorman Museum" in the vicinity of the Museum. It is located on the west side of "Albert Park", situated at the junction of the B1272 "Linthorpe Road" (there is a street sign) on its west side, Park Road (there is a street sign, but not near the Museum) on its north side, and Park Road South (there is a street sign, but not near the Museum) on its east side. (The Museum is behind, to the south of, the large war memorial.) The appropriate building housing the Museum is easy to identify, it has the words "Dorman Memorial Museum" in large letters in the stonework above the entrance doorway.

As with all museums, the displays and the exhibits they contain may be changed, re-sited, removed from display and/or put in store, or loaned to other museums or suitable repositories. Before visiting a museum it is worth checking in advance whether the displays listed in the gazetteer are still in place in the same location(s) set out in the text. Individual exhibits may have been rearranged in terms of their display, the order in which they are displayed and their relationship to other exhibits, some exhibits may have been removed from display. The text in the gazetteer reflects the descriptions and/or accompanying notices to the exhibits at the time of visiting. These too may have been revised, amended, added to or removed.

The Museum contains exhibits and displays relating to the history of Middlesbrough and its people.

On the ground floor of the Museum, among the archaeology exhibits, there are some items of A-S/Viking interest housed in the "Town in Time" Gallery 1 which is on the east (Park Road South) side of the building, entered through a former doorway separating it from the shop and reception area. Above the former doorway there is a sign "Please begin your visit here".

Immediately on entering the Gallery, on the left, attached to the wall, there is an illustrated notice, "What's in a name?" this refers to English and Scandinavian place names in the locality.

In the Gallery, and contained in the second glass cabinet on the left hand side, there are some artefacts of A-S interest. Numbered "18" in the display cabinet and sitting on the rear shelf, at the left hand end, there is an Anglo-Saxon burial urn with line, dot and triangular design. Behind number 18, and affixed to the rear wall of the display cabinet, there is number "19", an Anglo-Saxon necklace comprising coloured beads.

Also in the Gallery, and in a separate display entitled "A Mighty River" there is an illustrated notice "An Ancient River" that includes a map of Anglo-Saxon kingdoms and places.

MIDDLESMOOR
St Chad's Church
SE 092741   Rating: ✫✫✫

Clearly visible from the southern approach to the village, the church is located some 75 Yds/68 M from the east side of the main road which runs north/south through Middlesmoor. It is reached by taking a very minor road (in parts cobbled) that winds its way south, then east, between houses for about 75 Yds/68 M. The entrance to this minor road is under 20 Yds/18 M south of the telephone box (at the time of visit) by the side of the main road.

MIDDLESMOOR: St Chad's Church. An Anglo-Danish hammer-head crosshead with attached cross-shaft.

It is not known when the first church was built on this site but the present structure dates from 1866 when the church was completely rebuilt.

Internally, the font incorporates an A-S bowl. The font is located underneath the centre of the west tower (bell chamber). The bowl of the font is supported by a circular shaft that stands on a low, circular plinth. The bowl measures 33 Ins/83 Cms in diameter. The decoration depicting the Four Evangelists was a later addition to the font.

Internally, there is a complete 11C A-D "hammer-head" crosshead with part of its connecting cross-shaft attached. It is located 11 Ins/27 Cms east of the west wall of the nave and 29 Ins/73 Cms north of the tower arch. The crosshead and part of its cross-shaft has been cemented into a 19 inch/48 centimetre H, roughly-shaped, plinth that sits on the floor. (Leaning against the plinth there is a large fragment from a 17C grave slab.) The crosshead measures 19 Ins/48 Cms H, by 15½ Ins/39 Cms W, by 7 Ins/17 Cms D. The section of stonework from the cross-shaft measures 35½ Ins/90 Cms H, by 15 Ins/38 Cms W, by 7½ Ins/19 Cms D. Both crosshead and section of stonework from the cross-shaft are weathered. On the crosshead, on the upper horizontal arms and the central vertical arm between the upper and lower horizontal arms, it is decorated with large crosses separated by a large circle. A circular design can be identified on the lower horizontal arms of the crosshead. Knot work decoration can be identified on all four sides of the cross-shaft. On the eastern face of the cross-shaft lettering can be identified to the effect "The cross of St Chad". (The words were carved when the cross-shaft was lying horizontally rather than standing vertically.)

MIDDLETON
St Andrew's Church

SE 782854   Rating: ☆☆☆☆☆

Towards the north-western end of Middleton, the church is adjacent to, but set back from, the north side of the A170. It is easy to identify.

On the site of a church dating from the 8C, the present church includes material from the 10C and early 11C. However, most of the church now dates from the early 12C and 13C and the restoration in 1886.

Internally, A-S walling survives surrounding the tower arch into the vestry, the walling above the arches on the present north and south sides of the nave, and the walling at the east end of the nave now separating the nave from the north and south aisles. Large side alternate quoining can be identified in the northeast and southeast corners of the nave. However, much of the A-S material is difficult to identify because of the covering plasterwork.

Internally, there are three substantial sections of stonework from A-D cross-shafts and their associated crossheads. These are located at the eastern end of the north aisle and comprise:

1.   A section of stonework comprising most of a wheel head cross, apart from one horizontal arm, and a section of stonework from its attached cross-shaft. In the notices and guidebooks they are referred to as "Cross B". They date from the 10C.

They are located 25½ Ins/64 Cms west of the east wall of the north aisle and 23 Ins/58 Cms south of the north wall of the north aisle. Together they stand on a 15 Ins/38 Cms H stone plinth of unrelated but old provenance. The section of stonework from the cross-shaft and the wheel head cross stand together 45 Ins/114 Cms H.

The section of stonework from the wheel head cross measures 21 Ins/53 Cms H, tapering 15 Ins/38 Cms to 7½ Ins/19 Cms W, tapering 7 Ins/17 Cms to 5 Ins/12 Cms D. All faces and sides of the stonework are decorated with knot work design.

The section of stonework from the cross-shaft measures 24 Ins/60 Cms H, tapering 11½ Ins/29 Cms to 10 ½ Ins/26 Cms W, tapering 7½ Ins/19 Cms to 6½ Ins/16 Cms D. It is decorated in the Jellinge style. A warrior with a pointed helmet, spear, sword, scramasax (short sword), shield and axe, is depicted on its west face. A dragon bound with ropes is depicted on its east face. The north and south sides of the cross-shaft are decorated with knot work design.

2.   A ring head cross and a section of stonework from its cross-shaft. In the notices and guidebooks they are referred to as "Cross C". They date from the early 11C.

They are located 22 Ins/55 Cms west of the east wall of the north aisle and 56 Ins/142 Cms south of the north wall of the north aisle. Together they stand on a 15½inch/39 Cms H modern stone plinth. The ring head cross and the section of stonework from the cross-shaft stand together 59 Ins/149 Cms H.

The ring head cross measures 16 Ins/40 Cms H, tapering 13½ Ins/34 Cms to 9 Ins/22 Cms W, tapering 8 Ins/20 Cms to 7 Ins/17 Cms D. It is decorated on all four sides with knot work and ring plait designs.

The section of stonework from the cross-shaft measures 43 Ins/109 Cms H, tapering 13 Ins/33 Cms to 9 ½ Ins/24 Cms W, tapering 9 Ins/22 Cms to 7 Ins/17 Cms D. It is decorated with knot work design on the west, east and north sides and on the south side with ring plait design. The bottom 24 Ins/60 Cms of this cross-shaft on all four sides appear too damaged or weathered for any decoration to be identified with confidence.

3.   A wheel head cross and a section of stonework from its attached cross-shaft. In the notices and guidebooks they are referred to as "Cross A". They date from the 10C.

They are located 28 Ins/71 Cms west of the east wall of the north aisle and 22 Ins/55 Cms north of the south wall of the north aisle. Together they stand on a 16 Ins/40 Cms H stone plinth of unrelated but old provenance. The wheel head cross and the section of stonework from the cross-shaft stand together 42 Ins/106 Cms H.

The wheel head cross measures14½ Ins/36 Cms H, tapering 12½ Ins/31 Cms to 9½ Ins/24 Cms W, tapering 5½ Ins/13 Cms to 4 Ins/10 Cms D. All sides are decorated with knot work design.

The section of stonework from the cross-shaft measures 27½ Ins/69 Cms H, tapering 10½ Ins/26 Cms to 9 ½ Ins/24 Cms W, tapering 5½ Ins/13 Cms to 5¼ Ins/13 Cms D. It is decorated in the Jellinge style. A dragon bound with ropes is depicted on its west face. It is decorated on its east face with the figure of a hunter with a spear and scramasax (short sword), two hounds and a stag. The north and south sides are decorated with knot work design.

Internally, there are two sections of stonework from 10C A-D cross-shafts cemented onto the ledge of the window at the east end of the north aisle. They comprise:

4.   A section of stonework from a cross-shaft. It is located at the northern end of the ledge. In the notices and guidebooks it is referred to as "Cross D".

The section of stonework measures 18 Ins/45 Cms H, tapering 12 Ins/30 Cms to 10 Ins/25 Cms W, by 6½ Ins/16 Cms D. On its southwest face it is decorated with a helmeted warrior with a forked beard, a knife and scramasax (short sword). It is very weathered and consequently it is difficult to identify the wavy/circular type decoration on the northwest and southeast sides. The northeast side of the stonework has been attached to the wall and so it is not possible to view.

5.   A section of stonework from a cross-shaft and a separate arm from a crosshead now attached together. (They may be from the same crosshead and cross-shaft.) In the notices and guidebooks it is referred to as "Cross E".

The two sections of stonework together measure 21 Ins/53 Cms H, tapering 9 Ins/22 Cms to 6½ Ins/16 Cms W, by 5 Ins/12 Cms D. On its northwest face it is decorated with the head and shoulders of a warrior. The other face and sides of the section of stonework from the cross-shaft, and the faces and sides of the arm from the crosshead are decorated with knot work design. The southeast side of the section of stonework from the cross-shaft has been attached to the wall and it is not possible to view.

[Note: The other sections and pieces of stonework lying on the floor and on the stone ledge by the north wall of the north aisle are of a later date.]

Externally, A-S fabric comprising large, irregular shaped pieces of stonework can be easily identified incorporated into the west walls of the nave. One section runs north 52½ Ins/133 Cms from the join with the northeast corner of the tower, and the other section runs south 56 Ins/ 142Cms from the join with the southeast corner of the tower. These surviving sections of A-S stonework terminate on each side with large side alternate quoining. In addition, quoining from an earlier (possibly 8C) A-S church can be identified amongst this walling. The northeast and southeast corners of the tower bisect this earlier quoining. This earlier quoining comprises upright stones of irregular height.

Apart from the upper belfry stage, the tower is also A-S and dates from the 10C. Externally the tower displays the following A-S features:

6.   An A-S stringcourse separating the top (belfry) stage and the lower first and second stages of the tower.

7.   Large side alternative quoining can be identified in both the northwest and southwest corners of the tower.

8.   An A-S doorway can be identified in the west face of the tower. It was subsequently blocked in the 12C and a small elliptical-shaped window inserted in its upper part.

9.   A distinctive "St Cuthbert-style" 8C A-S sculptured stone cross (part of the upper vertical arm is missing). It is located 32 Ins/81 Cms above the elliptical-shaped window and directly above a piece of protruding stonework. The cross measures nearly 24 Ins/60 Cms square.

10.   A section of stonework comprising the lower part of a wheel head cross minus most of its two horizontal arms and most of the associated wheel, and a section of stonework from its attached cross-shaft. They date from the early 10C. They have been incorporated into the fabric of the south wall of the tower, horizontally rather than vertically. Together they are located abutting the west wall of the nave, and in line with the bottom of the first floor window in the tower (about 30 Ins/76 Cms east of this window). The section of stonework from the wheel head cross measures 10 Ins/25 Cms H (W) by 30 Ins/76 Cms W (H). The section of stonework from the cross-shaft measures about 20 Ins/50 Cms W by 10 Ins/25 Cms H. It is decorated in the Jellinge style with an entwined beast.

11.   The lower two small, plain windows in the south face of the tower are A-S.

Externally, there is a section of stonework from a 10C A-D cross-shaft. It is located incorporated into the fabric of the north aisle 28 Ins/71 Cms east of the blocked north door and 52 Ins/132 Cms up from the ground. The section of stonework measures 9 Ins/22 Cms H by 20 Ins/50 Cms W. However, it might be alternatively located incorporated into the fabric of the north aisle 19½ Ins/49 Cms east of the blocked north door and 29½ Ins/74 Cms up from the ground. The section of stonework measures 7½ Ins/19 Cms H by 16 Ins/40 Cms W.

This section of stonework is decorated with a carving of an oval face incised with a nose and eyes similar in style to the designs on the cross-shafts inside the church but with a different head shape. Unfortunately, it is rather too weathered to identify with confidence. This information is recorded in the hand held notice boards inside the church.

MONK FRYSTON
St Wilfred's Church

SE 504297   Rating: ✩✩✩   Access is possible.

The church is situated towards the western end of Monk Fryston, close to the south side of the A63(T). The churchyard is separated from the south side of the A63(T) by a lane. The church is clearly visible from the A63(T).

The present structure retains much 11C A-S material despite the alterations in the 13C and 14C and the restoration in 1889-91.

Internally, the origin and nature of the stonework is difficult to determine because the walls have been whitewashed. The four corners of the nave, and the walling above the later inserted arcades in the nave, are apparently A-S. The east walling of the tower with its belfry window in its second stage is A-S.

Externally, the tower is recognisable as A-S and dates from the 11C, apart from the 14C belfry (fourth) stage. Unfortunately later buttressing and later inserted windows obscure much of the A-S material in the first stage, the largest single stage.

The three lower stages of the tower, which are A-S, contain distinctive A-S string courses, A-S windows (in the second stage) and quoining (more easily identifiable higher up the tower where they are not obscured by later buttressing).

MURTON
Yorkshire Museum of Farming

SE 650524   Rating: ✩✩✩

440 Yds/402 M of a mile east of its junction with the A64(T), turn off the A166 and proceed in a northerly direction along a minor road, "Murton Lane"(there is a street sign). Opposite the junction, amongst other signs, there is a directional signpost "Yorkshire Museum of Farming".

After about 470 Yds/429 M, the drive leading to the main entrance to the Museum can easily be identified on the west side of Murton Lane. Affixed to the surrounding fencing, by the entrance drive, close to its junction with Murton Lane, there is a large sign, "Murton Park, Yorkshire Museum of Farming, Houlgate Village, Great Yorkshire Railway".

The Museum contains the site of a reconstructed Danelaw Village ("Houlgate Village"). The village is a reconstruction of a 9C, "Dark Age",

Viking settlement. It contains timber-framed buildings with plank and wattle walls covered with daub (mud and grass), and roofs thatched with wheat or barley straw. Staff in costume endeavour to explain the way of life in the 9C.

MUSTON
All Saints Church

TA 097796   Rating: ✰✰   Access is possible.

The church is located in the centre of Muston. It is on the north side of the A1039, "King Street" (there is a street sign), and near to the west side of the bridge over the watercourse known as "The Dams".

On the site of an A-S church, the present structure dates from 1863.

Internally, there is an A-S altar stone comprising a large flat stone with no distinctive markings. It is located behind the altar's frontal, between an upper and a lower altar table in the east end of the chancel. The altar stone measures 4 Ins/10 Cms H, by just less than 120 Inst/304 Cms W, by 36 Ins/91 Cms D.

NEWTON-UNDER-ROSEBERRY
St Oswald's Church

NZ 569133   Rating: ✰✰   Access is possible.

Towards the northern end of Newton-Under-Roseberry turn off the A173 and head in a north-westerly direction along "Church Lane" (there is a street sign). After about 200 Yds/182 M the church is easily located on the west side of Church Lane.

Probably on the site of an A-S church the earliest fabric survives from the early 12C. Extensive rebuilding work was undertaken in 1857 and 1901.

Externally, there is a section of stonework from an A-S impost block (a through-stone from a doorway or arch). It has been incorporated into the fabric of the south face of the buttress attached to the south-east corner of the tower. The section of stonework is located 43 Ins/109 Cms up from the ground and its western end forms part of the south-west corner of the buttress. The section of stonework measures 11 Ins/27 Cms H, by 40 Ins/101 Cms W, by 8½ Ins/21 Cms D. The south face of the stonework is clearly decorated with a dragon attacking a quadruped. The west face is decorated with what seems to be some sort of winged animal.

NORMANBY
St Andrew's Church
SE 735817   Rating: ☆☆

The small, tower-less church, with an external "Bell Gable", is located near the centre of the village, adjacent to the east side of the road that runs north/south through Normanby. There is a church notice board behind the churchyard wall by the side of the road.

Despite a heavy restoration in 1894-95, material from the 12C and early 18C survives in the present structure.

Internally, there is a section of A-S stonework probably from a grave slab. It is located incorporated into the fabric of the west wall of the nave 41 Ins/104 Cms north of the south wall of the nave and 65 Ins/165 Cms up from the floor. The section of stonework measures 18½ Ins/46 Cms H by 12½ Ins/31 Cms W. It is decorated with a distinctive cross enclosed within a circle with parallel vertical lines extending from the cross.

Internally, there is a section of A-S stonework probably from a grave slab. It is located incorporated into the fabric of the north wall of the north aisle 77 Ins/195 Cms east of the west wall of the north aisle and 67 Ins/170 Cms up from the floor. The section of stonework measures 13 Ins/33 Cms H by 18½ Ins/46 Cms W. It is decorated with a distinctive cross enclosed within a circle.

NORTH GRIMSTON
St Nicholas's Church
SE 842677   Rating: ☆☆☆

The church is situated at the western end of North Grimston, set back from the north side of the B1248.

The present structure dates mostly from the early 12C although there may be some earlier workmanship.

Internally, the "simple" nature of the construction of the tower arch indicates workmanship of A-S inspiration.

Internally, there is a richly decorated large, round font. It is located, in the centre of the west end of the nave, standing on a low, round plinth, 108 Ins/274 Cms east of the tower arch. The font stands 36 Ins/91 Cms H and has a diameter of 36 Ins/91 Cms. Its decoration depicts the Last Supper and Christ's decent from the Cross. The font is older than the church and may be A-S.

Internally in the chancel the two windows in the north wall appear to date from 11C/12C. The chancel arch and the old roofline evident on the east wall of the chancel, suggest a similar date.

NORTH OTTERINGTON
St Michael's Church
SE 362897   Rating: ☆☆   Access is possible.

The church is in an isolated position set back from the west side of the A167. It is about 100 Yds/91 M north of the turning off the A167 to Solberg Hall. The church is screened from the A167 by trees but despite this it is easy to identify.

The present structure dates from the 12C and was restored in the 19C.

Internally, there are a number of sections of 10 C A-S/A-D stonework standing on the floor and leaning against or by the east wall of the south aisle. [Note: The sections of stonework may be moved around and so they may not necessarily be precisely in the locations indicated below.] These are:

1.   A section of stonework from an A-S cross-shaft. It is located 3 Ins/7 Cms south of the south wall of the nave and it leans against the east wall of the south aisle. The section of stonework measures 22½ Ins/57 Cms H, by 12½ Ins/31 Cms W, by 8½ Ins/21 Cms D. Despite damage, it is decorated with chain work design decoration on the west face and knot work design on the north and south sides.

2.   A section of stonework from an A-S cross-shaft. It is located 18 Ins/45 Cms south of the south wall of the nave and 2 Ins/5 Cms west of the east wall of the south aisle. The section of stonework measures 15 Ins/38 Cms H, by 15½ Ins/39 Cms W, by 5 Ins/12 Cms D. Despite damage, interlace decoration can be identified on the west face.

3.   A section of stonework from an A-S cross-shaft. It is located 38 Ins/96 Cms south of the south wall of the nave and 1 inch/2 Cms west of the east wall of the south aisle. The section of stonework measures 12 Ins/30 Cms H, tapering 12 Ins/30 Cms to 11 Ins/27 Cms W, by 6 Ins/15 Cms D. Despite damage, interlace decoration can be identified on the west face and on the south facing edge.

4.   A section of stonework from the end of an arm from an A-S crosshead. It is located 38½ Ins/97 Cms south of the south wall of the nave and 11 Ins/27 Cms west of the east wall of the south aisle. The section of stonework measures 5 Ins/12 Cms H, by 12 Ins/30 Cms W, by

7½ Ins/19 Cms D. Vine scroll decoration can be identified on the west face and on the top face.

5.   A section of stonework from an A-S wheel head cross comprising parts of three arms and the connecting spandrels. It is located 51 Ins/129 Cms south of the south wall of the nave and it leans against the east wall of the south aisle. The section of stonework measures 9½ Ins/24 Cms H, by 16 Ins/40 Cms W, by 5 Ins/12 Cms D. It is decorated with a Crucifixion scene, only the lower torso and legs and the lower part of the arms can be identified on the west face (a good deal of imagination will be required).

6.   A section of stonework from an A-S crosshead comprising the centre and three arms. It is located 68 Ins/172 Cms south of the south wall of the nave and it leans against the east wall of the south aisle. The section of stonework measures 11½ Ins/29 Cms H, by 13½ Ins/34 Cms W, by 5½ Ins/13 Cms D. It is very weathered and does not appear to have any surviving decoration (it was discovered in the bed of nearby River Wiske).

[Note: There are nine sections of stonework standing or lying on the floor close or by the east wall of the south aisle. Only six seem to be of A-S/A-D origin.].

NORTHALLERTON
All Saints Church

SE 366942   Rating: ☆☆☆☆   Access is possible

The church is situated in the north-west part of Northallerton. It is adjacent to the west side of the A167, in the part of the road known as "High Street" (there is a street sign).

The present church is on the site of a 7C wooden A-S church thought to have been established by Paulinus. The 7C church was rebuilt in stone in the 9C. The present structure dates from 1190. It was enlarged and rebuilt in the 15C and restored in 1885.

Internally, scattered about the church there are a number of sections of stonework from various dates, including those of A-S and A-D origin.

In the north transept, sitting on the window ledge in the north wall, there are:

1.   A virtually complete A-S wheel head cross. It is located 4 Ins/10 Cms east of the west end of the window ledge. The wheel head cross measures 14½ Ins/36 Cms H, by 14½ Ins/36 Cms W, by 4 Ins/10 Cms D. The central roundel on both faces of the wheel head and the two horizontal ends of the arms are decorated with knot work design. The

ends of the other two arms are too weathered for any decoration to survive.

2.   A section of stonework from the end of an arm from a crosshead. It is located 19 Ins/48 Cms east of the west end of the window ledge. The section of stonework measures 7 Ins/17 Cms H, by 10½ Ins/26 Cms W, by 4½ Ins/11 Cms D. It is very weathered and damaged and as a consequence it is not possible to identify with certainty any decoration on any of the sides.

3.   A section of stonework from an 11C crosshead comprising the central section, most of two arms and part of a third arm. It is located 22 Ins/55 Cms west of the east end of the window ledge. The section of stonework measures 13½ Ins/34 Cms H, by 14 Ins/35 Cms W, by 5 Ins/12 Cms D. Although weathered and damaged, ring work design can be identified on both faces and the two undamaged ends of the arms. The end of the third arm of the crosshead is too damaged for any decoration to survive.

4.   A section of stonework from probably an arm from a 10C crosshead. It is located 14 Ins/35 Cms west of the east end of the window ledge. The section of stonework measures 10 Ins/25 Cms H, tapering 8 Ins/20 Cms to 5½ Ins/13 Cms W, by 5½ Ins/13 Cms D. It is decorated with knot work design on all four sides.

5.   A section of stonework from an arm from a crosshead. It is located leaning against the wall at the east end of the window ledge. The section of stonework measures 8 Ins/20 Cms H, by 8 Ins/20 Cms W, by 4 Ins/10 Cms D. It is decorated with knot work design on the southwest face and northwest side. The other face and side are too weathered and damaged for any decoration to be identified.

(The other sections of stonework sitting on this window ledge are not A-S/A-D.)

In the north aisle, sitting on the window ledge in the centre of the window ledge of the easternmost window, there is:

6.   A section of stonework from a 10C wheel head cross comprising the central section, two arms, and part of two other arms (damaged). The section of stonework measures 10½ Ins/26 Cms H, by 14 Ins/35 Cms W, by 5 Ins/12 Cms D. Although it is weathered some knot work decoration can be identified on both faces and the ends of the arms of the crosshead.

(There are other sections of stonework on this window ledge that are not A-S/A-D.)

At the west end of the north aisle in the sectioned-off part of the church locate the westernmost window. Sitting on this window ledge, near to its western end, there is:

7.   A section of stonework from an arm from a 10C crosshead. It measures 9 Ins/22 Cms H, tapering 10 Ins/25 Cms to 7 Ins/17 Cms W, by 3½ Ins/8 Cms D. Although it is very weathered some knot work decoration can be identified on the faces of the arm, but it is too weathered for any other decoration to be easily identified.

NUNNINGTON
All Saints and St James Church
SE 666790   Rating: ☆☆

The church is easily located in the southwest corner of Nunnington. It is adjacent to the northeast angle of the junction of the roads skirting the south and west of Nunnington.

Although probably on the site of an A-S church, the present structure dates mainly from the late 13C and the restorations in 1672 and in 1883-84 (some 12C material does survive).

Quoining suggestive of A-S origin survives internally either side of the tower arch and externally in the northwest and southwest corners of the tower.

Internally, there are:

1.   A section of stonework from a 10C A-D cross-shaft. It is located incorporated into the fabric of the west wall of the nave picked out from the surrounding plasterwork. It has cut into the exposed stonework supporting the northern arm of the arch of the tower. It is 86½ Ins/219 Cms up from the floor. The section of stonework measures 7 Ins/19 Cms H by 19½ Ins/49 Cms W. The picking out from the surrounding plasterwork of this section of cross-shaft has clearly damaged its decoration. What remains appear to be chisel marks rather than the step and knot work patterns the illustrated notice attached to the west wall near to "1" suggest.

2.   A section of stonework from a 10C A-D cross-shaft. It is located incorporated into the fabric of the west wall of the nave picked out from the surrounding plasterwork. It is adjacent to the exposed stonework supporting the southern arm of the arch of the tower. It is 88½ Ins/224 Cms up from the floor. The section of stonework measures 6 Ins/15 Cms H by 16 Ins/40 Cms W. The picking out from the surrounding plasterwork of this section of cross-shaft has clearly damaged its decoration. What remains appear to be chisel marks rather than the step and knot work patterns the illustrated notice attached to the west wall near to "1" above suggest.

OLD BYLAND
All Saints Church

SE 551859   Rating: ✰✰

On the east side of the east road that runs north/south through Old Byland, and on the east side of the adjacent green, locate an arched gateway that provides the entrance to the churchyard. (This arched gateway seems part of the garden walling of the adjacent houses.) Behind the walling adjacent to the gateway there is a free-standing wooden sign "All Saints Church". Pass through the wooden gate forming part of the gateway and proceed along a concrete footpath to reach the church about 40 Yds/36 M away.

The present structure dates from the 11C and from 1145 when the monks from the nearby Byland Abbey undertook rebuilding work. (Byland Abbey was then located about a mile east of the village in the vicinity of the present Tylas Farm.)

Internally, there is the round bowl of what the notice describes as a "Saxon font". It is located sitting on the floor in the recess for the now blocked "priest's door" in the south wall of the chancel.

Externally, the south wall of the chancel, including the arched stonework over the later inserted arch in the blocked priest's door, and the north wall of the nave, belong to the 11C A-S church.

Externally, in the east wall of the nave, A-S coping stones from the earlier A-S church have been embedded into the stonework between the roof of the present chancel and the easily identifiable lower roofline of the original nave.

Externally, the quoining on the external south-east corner of the nave may also be A-S.

Externally, there is an A-S sundial. It is located on the east face of one of the south-east cornerstones on the east wall of the south porch. The appropriate cornerstone is 103 Ins/261 Cms up from the ground. The gnomon of the sundial is missing, but the hole for it and the scratch marks of the dial enable the correct stone to be identified. This sundial originally had the dedication "Sumar-Ledan Huscarl me facit" i.e. it was commissioned by "Sumerled the housecarl". (It is clearly not in its original south-facing position.)

In the south porch, there are two distinctive sculptured stones. These have been incorporated into the fabric of the external south wall, 71 Ins/180 Cms up from the ground and on either side of the bottom of the doorway arch. The stones depict a winged horse and staff motif connected with the cult of the 7C St Oswald. The stones might be either A-S or 12C in date.

ORMESBY

St Cuthbert's Church

NZ 531167   Rating: ✩✩   Access is possible.

Ormesby is now a southern suburb of Middlesbrough. The church is located in the western part of Ormesby. Turn off the B1380 and proceed in a southerly direction along "Church Lane" (there are street signs) as directed by the "St Cuthbert's Church" sign opposite the appropriate junction. The churchyard is easily identified on the west side of Church Lane, about 700 Yds/640 M from its junction with the B1380. Pass through the gates to the churchyard and proceed up the path to reach the church after about 50 Yds/45 M.

It is possible that the first church on this site was founded around 883 when the monks carrying St Cuthbert's coffin rested in the vicinity. Excavations in the vestry in 1975 apparently revealed part of a wall that may be A-S – it is now not possible to identify this walling. The present structure dates mostly from 1875 although some early 12C material does survive.

Internally, there is a section of stonework comprising most of the central section with its central boss, two arms and part of a third arm from an A-D crosshead. It is located sitting in the centre of the window ledge by the west window in the tower. This section of stonework measures 10 Ins/25 Cms H, by 18 Ins/45 Cms W, by 4½ Ins/11 Cms D. Slight traces of knot work decoration can be identified on the east face. It is very weathered and no other decoration can confidently be identified on any of the other sides. It dates from 950.

Internally, there is a section of stonework from an A-D hogback grave cover. It is located on the window ledge by the easternmost window in the north wall of the north aisle. The section of stonework measures 8 Ins/22 Cms H, by 14 Ins/35 Cms W, by 33 Ins/83 Cms L. The south face is clearly decorated with a tegulated roof design. It is very weathered and no other decoration can confidently be identified on any of the other sides. It dates from the 10C.

Externally, there are a number of sections of stonework of various ages, sizes and condition incorporated into the fabric of the church. Those of A-S/A-D interest are:

1.   A possible section of stonework from an A-S cross-shaft. It has been incorporated into the fabric of the east wall of the extension built onto the south side of the chancel. It is located 8 Ins/20 Cms south of the south side of the chancel and 129 Ins/327 Cms up from the ground. The section of stonework measures 9 Ins/22 Cms H by 15 Ins/38 Cms W. It is decorated with rope work design.

2.   A possible section of stonework from an A-D cross-shaft. It has been incorporated into the fabric of the south wall of the nave. It is located

33 Ins/83 Cms west of the buttress at the east end of the nave, (this buttress is now attached to the west wall of the extension on the south side of the chancel) and 96 Ins/243 Cms up from the base of the nave near ground level. The section of stonework measures 8 Ins/20 Cms H by 13 Ins/33 Cms W. It is decorated with a horizontal line under which there is a wavy line with the more distinctive Ringerike design beneath.

3.   A section of stonework from an A-D cross-shaft. It has been incorporated into the fabric of the south wall of the nave. It is located 18 Ins/45 Cms east of the easternmost window on the south side of the nave and 106 Ins/269 Cms up from the base of the nave near ground level. The section of stonework measures 7 Ins/17 Cms H by 10 Ins/25Cms W. It is decorated with a Jellinge style design.

Externally, there is a Saxon coffin. It is located sitting on the ground 23 Ins/58 Cms north of the northeast corner of the chancel. The coffin is now used as a flower trough and is much covered with moss. The southwest corner has been broken off but placed back in its rightful position. It measures 72 Ins/182 Cms L, tapering 25 Ins/63 Cms to 16 Ins/40 Cms W, by 9 Ins/22 Cms D. (There is a 22 Ins/55 Cms H unrelated gravestone at the western end of the coffin.)

According to one set of notes about the church there is also a Saxon font in the churchyard. This font could not be identified and it seems it is no longer in that location.

OSMOTHERLEY
St Peter's Church

SE 455972   Rating: ★★

The church is located on the western side of the centre of Osmotherley. Turn off "West End" (there are street signs) that links Osmotherley with the A19(T) and head in a southerly direction along "School Lane" (there is a street sign). The church is reached after 30 Yds/27 M and is on the east side of School Lane.

On the site of an A-S church the earliest surviving fabric dates from the 1190. Further building work was undertaken in the 14C and 15C. The church was restored in 1892.

On the ledges inside the south porch there are sections from 10C A-D stonework.

On the ledge on the east side of the porch there are:

1.   A section of stonework from an A-D cross-shaft. It is located in the south-east corner of the porch. This section of stonework measures 24 Ins/61 Cms H, by 8 Ins/20 Cms W, by 8 Ins/20 Cms D. The west face is clearly decorated with chain plait design. The other sides are very

weathered and worn although some decoration similar to that on the west face can be identified.

2. A mutilated section of stonework from an A-D hogback grave cover (two pieces have been joined back together to form this section of stonework). It is located 26 Ins/66 Cms north of the southern end of the ledge. This section of stonework measures 5 Ins/12 Cms H, by 30 Ins/76 Cms W, by 8 Ins/20 Cms D. Although very weathered, some decoration of a lozenge-type design can be identified on the "roof" and at the southern end a bear can just about be identified.

On the ledge on the west side of the porch there are:

3. A section of stonework from an A-D cross-shaft. It is located in the south-west corner of the porch and measures 26 Ins/66 Cms H, by 11 Ins/27 Cms W, by 9 Ins/22 Cms D. Despite weathering some ring chain decoration can be identified on all three sides on show (the fourth side is affixed to the walling and cannot be seen).

OSMOTHERLEY; St Peter's Church. A display of stonework including items of Anglo-Saxon and Anglo-Danish interest.

4.   A section of stonework from an A-S crosshead comprising the central section, most of three damaged arms and part of a fourth arm. It is located 15 Ins/38 Cms north of the southern end of the ledge. The section of stonework has been placed on top of an un-related 12C section of stonework (a scalloped capital). The A-S section of stonework is affixed to the west wall of the porch. It measures 8½ Ins/21 Cms H, by 11 Ins/27 Cms W, by 3½ Ins/8 Cms D. Apart from a scooped out circle on the east face there is no decoration on any of the sides.

(On the west ledge of the south porch there are other sections of stonework of varying ages and sizes that are not A-S or A-D.)

OSWALDKIRK
St Oswald's Church

SE 621788   Rating: ✩✩   Access is possible.

The church is located near the western end of Oswaldkirk. It is adjacent to the south side of the minor road that leads to Ampleforth. The church is about 350 Yds/320 M west of the junction of this minor road with the B1363 in the centre of Oswaldkirk.

The current church is probably on the site of its A-S predecessor. Despite the restoration in 1886 the church does include material from the 12C.

Inside the south porch on the western ledge there are some sections of stonework of A-S/A-D interest. These are:

1.   An A-S window head. It is located at the southern end of the ledge. The window head measures 12½ Ins/31 Cms D (H), by 21 Ins/53 Cms W, by 5½ Ins/13 Cms H (D).

2.   A section of stonework from an A-S cross-shaft. It is located in the middle of the ledge, next to, and to the north of "1" above. This section of stonework measures 10 Ins/25 Cms H, by 14½ Ins/36 Cms W, by 15 Ins/38 Cms D. The east face is decorated with interlace pattern. The other sides are either too damaged or weathered for any decoration to be identified.

3.   A section of stonework from a 10C A-D hogback grave cover. It is located at the northern end of the ledge. The section of stonework measures 12 Ins/30 Cms H, by 11½ Ins/29 Cms W (D), by 16½ Ins/41 Cms D (W). Its south side is decorated with the representation of the Virgin and the Child. The other sides are too weathered for any decoration to be identified. (There is a modern replica of the representation of the Virgin and the Child affixed to the inner west

wall of the porch about 12 Ins/30 Cms above the section of cross-shaft identified at "2" above.)

There are sections of later stonework on the ledge on the eastern side of the porch that are not A-S/A-D.

Externally, there is a weathered section of stonework from an A-S cross-shaft. It has been incorporated as a long quoin into in the south-west corner of the nave, about 73 Ins/185 Cms up from the ground. The section of stonework measures 77½ Ins/196 Cms (west face) W (H), by 19½ Ins/49 Cms (south face) D (W), and on both faces it measures 7 Ins/17 Cms H (D). There is now no discernible trace of decoration on the two exposed sides of this section of cross-shaft.

OVER SILTON
St Mary's Church

SE 456932   Rating: ☆

The isolated church is about 440 Yds/402 M east of Over Silton. It can easily be identified from the road. To reach the church continue eastwards along the road which runs north-west/south-east through Over Silton for 440 Yds/402 M until reaching a vertical directional signpost "Public Footpath" on the north side of the road. By this signpost there is a grass track that leads to a field gate, adjacent to which is a stile. To reach the entrance to the churchyard, cross the stile and proceed uphill northwards all the time keeping on the west side of the hedge and fence in the adjacent field. The entrance to the churchyard is about 180 Yds/164 M north of the road.

The church dates mostly from the 12C and 14C. It was extensively restored in 1894.

Internally, there is a small, plain, possibly A-S font. It is located 49½ Ins/125 Cms east of the west wall of the nave and 118 Ins/299 Cms north of the south door. It is located sitting on a 13½ Ins/34 Cms H supporting pillar of stonework that stands on a 10¾ Ins/27 Cms H stepped plinth. The bowl of the font measures 16½ Ins/41 Cms square by 9 Ins/22 Cms D. There is no decoration on the font apart from incised parallel lines that run around the circumference and are joined by lines at forty-five degree angles. The parallel lines are located 1½ Ins/3 Cms below the top of the font and are spaced about 1¼ Ins/3 Cms apart.

In the churchyard, there is what is apparently a section of stonework from an A-S boundary cross standing on a plinth. It is located 15 Yds/13 M south of a small door into the south wall of the chancel and 15 Yds/13 M southeast of the southeast corner of the south porch. Both the section of stonework from the boundary cross and the plinth now lean in a westerly direction at an angle of about 70 degrees. The section of stonework from the boundary cross stands between 40½ Ins/102 Cms and 45¾ Ins/116 Cms H, tapering 14 Ins/35 Cms to 13 Ins/33 Cms W, tapering 14 Ins/35 Cms to 5 Ins/12 Cms D. It is weathered, damaged and irregularly shaped – its sides curve inwards – and there is a horizontal bar dividing it into two sections. There is no decoration on any of the sides.

PATRICK BROMPTON
St Patrick's Church
SE 219907   Rating: ☆☆

The church is near the western edge of Patrick Brompton and can easily be identified on the north side of the A684.

The present nave was built on the site of an A-S church. Material from this church may be incorporated into the present structure although this can no longer be identified. The present fabric of the church dates from the 12C, with 14C additions. The church was restored in 1864.

Internally, there is a section of stonework from an A-S wheel head cross comprising most of the central section, three arms and two of the connecting "wheels". It is located in the northwest corner of the north aisle sitting on top of an old font (not A-S) that sits on an unrelated section of stonework (not A-S). [Other items/sections of stonework, not A-S, have also been placed on top of the font and in front of the section of wheel head cross.] The section of stonework sits diagonally across the top of the font and leans against the north and west walls of the north aisle. The wheel head cross measures 14½ Ins/36 Cms H, between 21 Ins/53 Cms and 22 Ins/55 Cms W, and between 3½ Ins/8 Cms and 4 Ins/10 Cms D. Due to weathering no decoration can be identified on any of the sides of the wheel head cross.

PICKERING
(1) Castle (EH)
SE 798845   Rating: ☆

In the central, eastern, part of Pickering, at the junction on the east side of "Market Place" and the road "Burgate" (there are street signs), there is a free-standing signpost with various directions including "Castle". Proceed uphill in a northerly direction along Burgate as directed by the "Castle" signpost ("Burgate" becomes "Castlegate" (there are street signs)). The castle is situated along this road about 440 Yds/402 M north of the Market Place. The entrance to the castle grounds is located on the north side of Castlegate just before the road changes direction westwards.

It is possible that the original mound on which the keep now stands is A-S in origin; it may have been either the site of the local "moot" or the home of the local "thegn". However, building of the castle took place mainly in the last part of the 12C with major additions and alterations in the early 14C.

PICKERING
(2) Church of St Peter and St Paul
SE 798840   Rating: ✩✩✩

In the central, eastern, part of Pickering, at the junction on the east side of "Market Place" locate a building on the north side of the road with the sign "Burgate" attached to it. Adjacent to the east side of this building there is a flight of steps that lead up to the churchyard.

The present church is built on the site of its A-S predecessor. The church includes material from the 12C to 15Cs. It was restored in 1876-79.

Internally, there is a section of stonework from a late 10C A-S cross-shaft. It is located in the south aisle, 36 Ins/91 Cms east of the west wall of the south aisle, on a ledge on the south side of the westernmost pillar of the nave. The section of stonework measures 13 Ins/33 Cms H, by 8½ Ins/21 Cms W, tapering 6¾ Ins/17 Cms to 6 Ins/15 Cms D. Although weathered, knot work decoration can be identified on all four sides.

Internally, there is an A-S font. It is located in the centre of the floor at the west end of the nave 124¼ Ins/315 Cms east of the doorway into the tower. The font sits on what appear to be a series of three circular sections of stonework of different heights, but of similar diameters, that together stands on the floor a 24 Ins/60 Cms H – they are not A-S. The font measures 11½ Ins/29 Cms H by 25 Ins/63 Cms in diameter. There is no decoration on it.

The church houses one of the most complete series of wall paintings in England. These date from the mid 15C and were restored in the 19C, and include the martyrdom of St Edmund, King of the East Angles. He was martyred on the 20th November 870 and was the first patron saint of England. St Edmund is located on the north wall of the nave in the bottom, easternmost painting, in between the last two easternmost arches in the nave. (The painting above it depicts the martyrdom of St Thomas Becket of Canterbury.)

PICKHILL
All Saints Church
SE 347837   Rating: ✩✩

In the centre of Pickhill turn off the road which circles through the village (south-west/north-west) and proceed in an easterly direction along a minor road. (There are no street signs.) This minor road leads up to the church less than 100 Yds/91 M away. The church is situated on the north side of the road on a small hill and is easy to locate. (The churchyard occupies the north-east quadrant near another minor road crossroads.)

The present structure includes material from the 12C, 13C and 16C. The church was restored in 1877.

Internally, there are 17 sections of stonework of various dates and sizes some of which are identified by notices. They are located on a ledge on the north wall of the tower. There are four sections of stonework of A-S/A-D interest. These are:

1.   A section of stonework from a 10C A-D cross-shaft. It is located 128 Ins/325 Cms east of the west wall of the tower. This section of stonework measures 13½ Ins/34 Cms H, by 10 Ins/25 Cms W, by 4½ Ins/11 Cms (maximum) D. It is clearly decorated on the south face with the figure of a man. On the two other unbroken faces it is decorated with interlace design.

2.   A section of stonework from a 10C A-D cross-shaft. It is located 84 Ins/213 Cms east of the west wall of the tower. This section of stonework measures 20 Ins/50 Cms H, by 12 Ins/30 Cms W, by 6 Ins/15 Cms D. It is apparently decorated with "dragon" design on the west side (probably) but the dragon is difficulty to identify because of weathering. Interlace decoration can be identified on two of the other sides.

3.   A section of stonework from a mid 10C A-D hogback grave cover. It is located 41 Ins/104 Cms east of the west wall of the tower. This section of stonework measures 16 Ins/40 Cms H(L), by 6½ Ins/16 Cms W, by 13 Ins/33 Cms D(H) – it presently stands vertically rather than horizontally. It is very weathered and is decorated with the head of an unusual shaped bear (it has been described as more like a rat) and plait work design.

4.   A section of stonework from an end of a 10C A-D hogback grave cover. It is located 52 Ins/132 Cms east of the west wall of the tower. This section of stonework measures 17 Ins/43 Cms H, by 8 Ins/20 Cms W, by 19 Ins/48 Cms L. It is clearly decorated in what is described as "quasi-Jellinge" style including a creature.

PICTON
St Hilary's Church
NZ 419078   Rating: ★★

The future of the church is uncertain. For further information contact the Diocesan Office in York (Diocesan House, Aviator Court, Clifton Moor, York, YO30 4WJ).

The church is situated in an isolated position some 400 Yds/365 M north-east of Picton and some 400 Yds/365 M west of the railway line linking Northallerton and Yarm. The church is easily identified adjacent to the south side of the road.

The small church was built in 1911.

Internally, there is a section of stonework from an A-D cross-shaft found in St Martin's Church, Kirklevington, (see the entry for Kirklevington, North Yorkshire). It has been incorporated into the fabric of the south wall of the chancel. It is located between the window in the south wall of the chancel and the easternmost arch on the south side of the nave. It is 80 Ins/203 Cms up from the floor. The section of stonework measures 14½ Ins/36 Cms H by 9½ Ins/24 Cms W. It is decorated with interlace decoration and what may be either a fish tail or a bird. It dates from 920.

RIPON
(1) Abbot Huby's Wall
SE 316713   Rating: ✫

The walling is located in the centre of Ripon. Opposite the north side of the Cathedral (Minster) and adjacent to the north side of Minster Road (there is a street sign), there is a lengthy section of walling which runs roughly parallel to the Cathedral.

At the junction of Minster Road and St Mary's Gate (to the north-east of the Cathedral) the wall changes direction and heads north along the west side of St Mary's Gate. (The St Mary's Gate street sign is not visible until reaching the north end of the wall that terminates with houses). About 130 Yds/118 M north from the east end of the Cathedral, on the south side (adjacent) of some wrought-iron gates, there is a distinctive plaque affixed to the wall. This plaque records that Abbot Huby of Fountains built the wall circa 1505 on the site of the Saxon Ladykirk.

RIPON
(2) Cathedral (Minster)
SE 314711   Rating: ✫✫✫✫✫

The Cathedral is easily located in the centre of Ripon. It is east of the junction of "Minster Road", "Kirkgate" and "Bedern Bank" (there are street signs).

Apart from St Wilfred's 7C crypt, the Cathedral includes fabric from the 12C and 13C. However, most of the present structure dates from the building undertaken in the 15C, the early 16C and the extensive restoration in 1862-70.

On the site of an earlier mission station, St Wilfred founded a church on this site in 672 and the crypt from his church survives. St Wilfred's crypt is located internally within the present Cathedral in the south-east corner of the nave. A free-standing sign "To the Saxon Crypt" directs you to the entrance at the east end of the south aisle. Proceed as directed down some steps into the crypt which comprises two vaulted chambers. In the passages providing both the present and former entrances and exits to the crypt the roofing apparently incorporates A-S and Medieval grave slabs. However, these slabs are difficult to detect.

Internally, locate the Cathedral Treasury. It is situated to the north of the "Choir", and is entered through a door on the east side of the north transept. The Treasury contains:

1.   "The Ripon Jewel". This dates from the 7C and the design suggests that it was made to adorn a relic casket or cross ordered by St Wilfred. It is located in the glass display cabinet on the south side of The Treasury – i.e. the cabinet closest to the western entrance to The Treasury. The Jewel is displayed towards the northern end of the middle shelf in the display cabinet. The Ripon Jewel was found in 1976. It comprises a small, gold roundel, 1¼ Ins/3 Cms in diameter. The back is a plain gold sheet. The front has settings for gems fashioned with strips of gold. There are four "large" square cells linked around the outer arc by smaller triangular cells. The square cells contain amber and the triangular cells contain garnets. The central setting and the inner arc linking the large square cells are missing. There is a descriptive notice about the similar 7C "Holderness Cross" which was sold in London in October 1999 for £55,000.

2.   A section of stonework from a 9C A-S crosshead comprising the central section and part of two arms. This section of stonework is no longer in the Treasury and appears to have been "lost". It was located on the south side of The Treasury behind two display cabinets standing on the floor by the base of a pillar. It measures 28 Ins/71 Cms H, by 11 Ins/27 Cms square and is decorated with a human head and body surrounded by an abstract decorative design.

3.   A section of stonework from a 10C A-D crosshead comprising part of an arm and a small part of another arm. It is known as the "Sigurd Stone". It is located near to the eastern exit to The Treasury. It protrudes from a floor standing wooden container. The Sigurd Stone is about 10 Ins/25 Cms H, by 10 Ins/25 Cms W by 7 Ins/17 Cms D. The west face of the Sigurd Stone depicts Sigurd sucking his thumb scorched while roasting a slice of the heart of Fafnir the dragon on whose head he rests his feet. The top facing edge and the east side are decorated with vine scroll design. The remaining sides and edges are too damaged for any decoration to survive. The remains of the accompanying crosshead have

been presented to St Wilfred's Church, Mereside, Blackpool. (There is a descriptive notice, "The Sigurd Story", nearby.)

Externally, there are two sections of decorated A-S stonework. They have been incorporated horizontally into the fabric of the buttress-like extension on the west face of the north transept. They are situated about 164 Ins/416 Cms up from the ground and 34 Ins/86 Cms south of the north face of the north transept. The more northerly section of stonework measures about 10 Ins/25 Cms H, by 29 Ins/73 Cms W, by about 21 Ins/53 Cms D. It is decorated with circles containing interlace design. The more southerly section of stonework measures about 10 Ins/25 Cms H, by 29 Ins/73 Cms W, by about 18 Ins/45 Cms D. It is decorated with larger circles containing interlace design.

Externally, on the south side of the Cathedral and on the south side of the Chapter House (towards the south-east corner of the Cathedral) stairs lead down to the Chapel of the Resurrection. The chapel was built in 1080. In this chapel the altar utilises the base of a pillar taken from the 9C A-S church on this site.

Externally on the south side of the Cathedral there is what appears to be a section of stonework from a cross-shaft. It is located 8 Yds/7 M south of the exterior wall of the south aisle, and 20 Yds/18 M east of the west front of the Cathedral. It stands 55 Ins/139 Cms H by 9 Ins/22 Cms square. It is very weathered with no surviving decoration and it is difficult to date.

RIPON
(3) Prison And Police Museum
SE 315713   Rating: ☆

In the centre of Ripon, the Museum is situated on the east side of "St Mary's Gate" (there is a street sign, see the Abbot Huby's Wall entry above). St Mary's Gate is located running in a northerly direction off the eastern end of "Minster Road" (there is a street sign). Minster Road runs along the north side of the Cathedral. On the wall of the Museum there is a large notice board as well as a distinctive police lamp that now has the word "Museum" on its faces.

As with all museums, the displays and the exhibits they contain may be changed, re-sited, removed from display and/or put in store, or loaned to other museums or suitable repositories. Before visiting a museum it is worth checking in advance whether the displays listed in the gazetteer are still in place in the same location(s) set out in the text. Individual exhibits may have been rearranged in terms of their display, the order in which they are displayed and their relationship to other exhibits, some exhibits may have been removed from display.

Housed in the 19C prison building, the Museum depicts the history of law and order in England from A-S times to the 19C.

On the first floor in the former night cells, Room F contains displays relating to "Law & Order in Anglo-Saxon and Medieval Times: Non-Custodial Punishments". The displays refer to the charters granted by the kings in A-S (800-1066) and later Medieval (1066-1485) times to the Charters of the Archbishops of York and the Canons of Ripon Minster.

RYTHER
All Saints Church

SE 555394   Rating: ☆☆   Access is possible.

Towards the eastern end of Ryther, turn off the B1223 and head in a north-easterly direction a long a minor no-through road (there is no street sign). (The junction is at a right-angled bend and there is a no-through road signpost indicating the appropriate road.) This minor no-through road narrows considerably before reaching its destination at the churchyard gates about 200 Yds/182 M away from the B1223.

Although restored in 1898 the church retains A-S, 13C and 14C material.

Internally, the chancel arch is A-S with both the arch and jambs clearly comprising through-stones.

Internally, there is a single stone that is part of an A-S window that protrudes from the whitewashed walling. It is located in the north wall of the nave, 36 Ins/91 Cms east of the top of the westernmost window.

There may be other A-S material incorporated into the fabric of the nave, but if so, it is currently obscured by the whitewash on the walls on the inside of the church.

Externally, the re-used A-S quoining can be identified incorporated into the north-east and south-east corners of the chancel.

Externally, three A-S window heads can be identified which have been inverted and incorporated into the fabric of the north wall of the nave. These are located:

1.   50 Ins/127 Cms west of the westernmost buttress, 145 Ins/368 Cms up from the ground.

2.   17 Ins/43 Cms east of the westernmost buttress, 145 Ins/368 Cms up from the ground. The top, eastern, corner looks as though it might be half of a window head, but there is now another, small stone placed in the aperture.

3.   91 Ins/231 Cms east of the westernmost buttress, 145 Ins/368 Cms up from the ground.

SAXTON
All Saints Church

SE 475368   Rating: ☆☆

The church is situated in the northern part of Saxton. It is located adjacent to the south side of "Dam Lane" (there is a street sign "Dam Lane formerly Silver Street"). It is in the south-west angle of a minor crossroads.

On the site of an A-S church, the present structure dates from the 12C and the alterations in the 13C and 15C.

Internally, there is a section of stonework from a 10C A-S crosshead comprising part of the central section and an arm. It is located in a niche in the north wall of the chancel 5 Ins/12 Cms above the northern end of the altar rail. The section of stonework measures 11 Ins/27 Cms H, by 9 Ins/22 Cms W, by 6 Ins/15 Cms D. It is decorated with ring work design on the two faces. There is no decoration on any of the other sides.

Also, there are five more sections of stonework none of which appear to be A-S or A-D in origin. These are located on the floor in the opening adjacent to the southern side of the chancel arch (the hagioscope or holy view).

SCARBOROUGH
(1) Castle And Roman Signal Station (EH)

TA 049892/051892   Rating: ☆

The castle dominates Scarborough sitting high on the headland separating "North Bay" and "South Bay". There are various "English Heritage" directional signs in the town pointing the way up to the castle. The entrance to the site is through the Barbican Gate that is situated at the eastern end of "Castle Road" (there are street signs).

The extensive, substantial, remains include both inner and outer bailey walling and towers, the barbican and the ruins of the tall keep. The site of the castle, nearest the headland, was first occupied during the Iron Age.

A Roman Signal Station was built in the latter part of the 4C. It originally comprised a tower standing two or three storeys high and about 14 Yds/12 M square. The tower was surrounded by a courtyard 100 feet/30 M square whose perimeter was defended by a wall with a gate, which itself was defended by a ditch. The surviving remains from the station are now situated in the outer bailey of the castle.

Sometime in either the 7C or 8C a monastery was founded in the vicinity of the Roman Signal Station. At the beginning of the 11C a small chapel was built on the site of the watchtower of the Roman Signal Station. King Harald Hardrada of Norway destroyed this chapel, along with the associated monastery, prior to his defeat by King Harold of England at the battle of Stamford Bridge in 1066. The remains of the chapel and associated buildings now in the vicinity of the Signal Station date from the 12C, 14C and 16C.

In 966 a fortified settlement a "burh" was set up by the Viking leaders Kormak and Thorgils. Thorgils was named "Skarthi" (Harelip). The town he helped established became known as "Skarthi's burh" (Scarborough). It is likely that the present castle site covers the site of this burh.

SCARBOROUGH
(2) Millennium Experience
TA 050887   Rating: ☆☆

On the sea front at Scarborough, opposite the eastern end of "Old Harbour", "The Millennium Experience" is housed in the easternmost building in the road known as "Sandside".(The building nearest to the roundabout at the junction of Sandside and "Marine Drive" (there are no street signs)). The appropriate building is easy to identify as it has large "Millennium" signs on both its harbour side and eastern side.

The Millennium Experience involves "time travel" through 1000 years comprising realistic reconstructions with accompanying storytelling of Scarborough's history. You "travel" through a 1930s railway journey: the foundation of modern Scarborough in 966 by Thorgils, the house of the Skarthi family, Edward I in the castle keep, the building of the castle, sieges and weaponry, local trade (including fishing), Scarborough spa waters, the Civil War sieges of the castle, day trippers to Scarborough, the bombardment of Scarborough on 16 December 1914 and the more recent seaside resort of Scarborough.

SHERBURN
St Hilda's Church
SE 959775   Rating: ☆☆☆☆   Access is possible.

Towards the northern end of Sherburn, the church is easily located on the eastern side of St Hilda's Street (there are street signs), just under 880 Yds/804 M north of where this road joins the A64(T).

On the site of an A-S church the church apparently contains some A-S masonry but this cannot be easily identified. The present structure dates from the 11C. There were additions and alterations between the 12C to the 15C. It was extensively rebuilt and restored in 1912.

Internally, there are 21 sections of stonework of varying ages and sizes. These are located on the floor around the walls of the tower. Attached to the north wall of the tower there is a descriptive notice with photographs relating to some of the sections of stonework. Those of A-S/A-D interest are:

1.   A section of stonework from an arm from a crosshead, known as "The Crucifix". This is the easternmost section of stonework lying on the floor by the north wall of the tower. The section of stonework measures 7 Ins/17 Cms H, by 12 Ins/30 Cms W, by 5½ Ins/13 Cms D. Despite weathering the decoration on the top face shows the extended arm of Christ Crucified surrounded by leaves. The other sides are too weathered for any decoration to be identified with confidence. The arm dates from the late 10C.

2.   A section of stonework from a cross-shaft, known as "The Fan Shaft". It is located lying on the floor by the north wall of the tower next to the west side of "1" above. The section of stonework measures 8½ Ins/21 Cms H, by 14 Ins/35 Cms W, by 5½ Ins/13 Cms D. On the top face it is decorated with a fan-shaped design with flanking wings below which there is the halo of a saint. The other face has no identifiable decoration. Some interlace design decoration can be identified on the two sides.

3.   A section of stonework from a grave cover. It is located lying on the floor by the north wall of the tower 91 Ins/231 Cms east of the west wall of the tower. The section of stonework measures 23 Ins/58 Cms L, by 13 Ins/33 Cms W, by 4½ Ins/11 Cms D. It is clearly decorated with knot work design and the lower, longest arm of a cross on the top face. There is no other decoration on any of the other sides.

4.   A section of stonework from a cross-shaft, known as "The Weland Shaft". It is located lying on the floor by the north wall of the tower 73 Ins/185 Cms east of the west wall of the tower. The section of stonework measures 11½ Ins/29 Cms L (H, if it were standing upright), by 9 Ins/22 Cms W, by 7½ Ins/19 Cms D. The top face is decorated with the head and arms of Weland the Smith and the "bird machine" that encloses him. The woman held in the birds' beak is either his wife or the King Nithud's daughter. The other face and two sides are too weathered or damaged for any decoration to be identified with confidence. It dates from the 10C.

5.   A section of stonework from a cross-shaft that may be A-S/A-D although it is described in the notice as "The Norman Gable Cross". It

is located lying on the floor by the north wall of the tower 60 Ins/152 Cms east of the west wall of the tower. The section of stonework measures 22½ Ins/57 Cms H, by 7½ Ins/19 Cms D, by 11 Ins/27 Cms W. It is decorated with interlace and geometrical design on all four sides.

6.   A section of stonework from what may be the arm of an A-S crosshead. It is located lying on the floor by the south wall of the tower 21 Ins/53 Cms east of the west wall of the tower. The section of stonework measures 10 Ins/25 Cms L (H), by 6½ Ins/16 Cms W, by 6½ Ins/16 Cms D. Despite weathering some interlace decoration can be identified on the two faces of the crosshead; there is no decoration on the end of the arm.

7.   A section of stonework from what may be an A-S/A-D cross-shaft. It is located on the floor by the south wall of the tower 45 Ins/114 Cms east of the west wall of the tower. The section of stonework measures 15 Ins/38 Cms L (H), by 8½ Ins/212 Cms W, by 6½ Ins/16 Cms D. On the top face it is partially decorated with what appears to be a face with some leaf and circular design. The other face and sides have no decoration that can be confidently identified.

Externally, there is a section of stonework from an A-S cross-shaft which has connections with the tale of Weland – see the notice attached to the inside north wall of the tower. It has been incorporated into the fabric of the south wall of the chancel and placed horizontally rather than vertically. It is located 24 Ins/60 Cms east of a blocked doorway, 10 Ins/25 Cms up from the ground and behind a drainpipe. The section of stonework measures 12½ Ins/31 Cms H(W) by 45 Ins/114 Cms W(H). Although decoration can be identified the weathering obscures much of the detail. It apparently depicts St John with his eagle with interlace design above. Below St John there is the head and top half of the torso of another evangelist.

SHERBURN IN ELMET
All Saints Church

SE 487336   Rating: ☆

The church is conspicuous on a hill at the western end of Sherburn. The extensive surrounding churchyard is adjacent to the northwest side of the B1222; in the vicinity of the church the road is known as "Church Hill" (there are street signs). At the western end of the churchyard there is an un-named no-through road (there is a no-through road signpost) which leads north off the B1222, (Church Hill), and reaches the churchyard gates nearest to the church in just under 50 Yds/45 M.

On the site of an A-S church the present structure dates from around 1120 with alterations and additions in the 13C and 15C. The church was restored in 1857.

Possibly some A-S material survives incorporated into the present structure but it cannot be easily identified.

Externally, immediately north of the north side of the church, the flat platform of land, now buttressed with a wall and forming part of the graveyard, covers the site of an A-S palace of King Athelstan, the first King of All England, who reigned from 924 to 939. The palace was built around 938 following his victory over a combined Viking and Celtic army at the battle of Brunanburh in 937. From this time until the middle of the 14C Sherburn became the seat of the archbishops of York.

SINNINGTON
All Saints Church

SE 746860   Rating: ☆☆☆☆   Access is possible.

The church is located on the north-eastern edge of Sinnington. In the centre of Sinnington locate the bridge crossing the River Seven (this bridge is easy to identify). From the bridge, follow the minor no-through road (there is a no-through road sign) as it proceeds north along the east bank of the River Seven between the river and the "dry" bridge. After about 176 Yds/160 M take the right fork in the road that heads in a north-easterly direction.

After about 50 Yds/45 M there is a minor road junction where both roads have signs indicating "No-through road" and "No Turning Area". Additionally, underneath the signs for the road running in an easterly direction, there is a wooden directional sign "The Hall", underneath which there is a directional sign "The Church". At this junction take the road that heads uphill in an easterly direction as indicated by "The Church" sign. The entrance to the churchyard is reached after about 176 Yds/160 M along this road from the wooden directional sign at the road junction. (Unfortunately there appear to be no helpful street signs and few directional signs in Sinnington. Despite this the church is not too difficult to find).

The present structure includes fabric from the 12C despite the restoration in 1904. With its sections of A-S and A-D stonework the present structure could be older than some of the identifiable fabric implies.

Internally, incorporated into the fabric of the walling by the west and east edges of the middle window on the south side of the nave there are:

1.   A section of stonework from an A-S cross-shaft. It is located 21 Ins/53 Cms up from the western end of the bottom of the window ledge. It has been used as an edging piece. The section of stonework measures 18 Ins/45 Cms H by 8½ Ins/21 Cms W (maximum). Its eastern face, the only side that can be viewed, is clearly decorated with knot work design.

2.   A section of stonework from an A-S cross-shaft. It is located 23 Ins/58 Cms up from the eastern end of the bottom of the window ledge and 12 Ins/30 Cms southwards towards the window. The section of stonework measures 13½ Ins/34 Cms H by 9 Ins/22 Cms W. Despite weathering some knot work design decoration can be identified on its western face. There is no decoration on its north side – the only other side that can now be viewed.

Internally, there is a section of stonework from an A-S cross-shaft. It is located on the north side of the chancel and has been cemented onto the western end of the window ledge by the western sidewall of the window. The section of stonework measures 21 Ins/53 Cms H, by 10½ Ins/26 Cms W, by 8 Ins/20 Cms D. It is clearly decorated with knot work design on both sides and the face it is possible to view.

Internally, there is a distinctive consecration cross (no date indicated). It is located inset in a 4 inch/10 centimetre square area of plasterwork incorporated into the south wall of the chancel, 53 Ins/134 Cms up from the floor, and 6 Ins/15 Cms west of the south end of the altar rail.

Internally, there are also two distinctive sections of stonework from A-S cross-shafts incorporated into the walling in the blocked former western doorway into the church. These are:

3.   The lower, smaller section of stonework from a cross-shaft is 36 Ins/91 Cms up from the floor, below the small, unrelated, stone plinth protruding from the wall. The section of stonework measures 13 Ins/33 Cms H by 9½ Ins/24 Cms W. It is decorated with knot work design on the only side that can now be viewed.

4.   The higher, larger section of stonework from a cross-shaft is 60 Ins/152 Cms up from the floor and has been cemented onto a small, unrelated, stone plinth protruding from the wall. The section of stonework measures 31 Ins/78 Cms H by 12 Ins/30 Cms W. It is decorated in Jellinge style with a dragon bound with ropes decorating its east face and knot work design on the parts of the other two sides that can now be viewed.

Externally, incorporated into the fabric of the south wall of the nave there are:

5.   A section of re-used A-S stonework. It has been incorporated into the centre of the eastern side of the window nearest the east wall of the south porch. It is located 51 Ins/129 Cms east of the east wall of the south porch and 106 Ins/269 Cms up from the ground. This section of stonework measures 31 Ins/78 Cms H tapering 15 Ins/38 Cms to 9½ Ins/24 Cms W. Although weathered the top part of the section of stonework is decorated with a suggestion of knot work design.

6.   A section of stonework from a late 10C A-S crosshead comprising the central section and three arms and a part of its attached cross-shaft. They have been placed upside down. They are located 71 Ins/180 Cms east of the south porch and 112 Ins/284 Cms up from the ground. The section of stonework measures 20 Ins/50 Cms H by 17 Ins/43 Cms W. It is decorated with knot work design.

7.   A section of stonework from a late 10C A-S crosshead comprising the central section and three arms. It is located 121 Ins/307 Cms east of the south porch and 113 Ins/287 Cms up from the ground. The section of stonework measures 15 Ins/38 Cms H by 17 Ins/43 Cms W. It is clearly decorated with the figure of Christ Crucified (only the lower half of the body is missing) under whose outstretched arms there are what have been described as snakes. There is also some decoration with knot work design.

8.   An A-S sundial. The hole for the central gnomon, now missing, can be identified on a stone 102 Ins/259 Cms west of the buttress at the eastern end of the nave (6 Ins/15 Cms east of the drainpipe) and 52½ Ins/133 Cms up from the ground. The appropriate stone measures 6 Ins/15 Cms H by 12½ Ins/31 Cms W. The stone is very weathered and no incised lines for indicating the time can now be detected. In 1877 the words in Old Englisc "mergen" (morning) and "æfen" (evening – not afternoon as indicated in the church guide), could be identified. (According to the church guide this sundial cannot be now be identified.)

Externally, sections of A-S/A-D stonework have been incorporated into the fabric of the blocked-up former west doorway. Although they are all weathered they can be identified:

SINNINGTON: All Saints Church. Two sections of Anglo-Saxon stonework have been incorporated into the external fabric of the south aisle. The one on the left comprises most of a crosshead with part of its attached cross-shaft, decorated with knot work design. The one on the right comprises most of a crosshead decorated with Christ crucified.

9.   A section of stonework from a cross-shaft. It is located 6½ Ins/16 Cms south of the north end of the former doorway and 24 Ins/60 Cms up from the ground. The section of stonework measures 4½ Ins/11 Cms H by 25 Ins/63 Cms W. It is decorated with interlace design.

10.   A section of stonework from a cross-shaft. It is located 19 Ins/48 Cms south of the north end of the former doorway and 37½ Ins/95 Cms up from the ground. The section of stonework measures 9½ Ins/24 Cms H by 13 Ins/32 Cms W. Although very weathered some circular decoration, possibly the two large eyes of a dragon, can be identified.

11.   A section of stonework from a cross-shaft. It is located 6 Ins/15 Cms north of the south end of the former doorway and 39 Ins/99 Cms up from the ground. The section of stonework measures 5 Ins/12 Cms H by 8 Ins/20 Cms W. It is decorated with a circular design.

12.   A section of stonework from a cross-shaft. It is located 12 Ins/30 Cms north of the south end of the former doorway and 62½ Ins/158 Cms up from the ground. The section of stonework measures 3½ Ins/8 Cms to 9½ Ins/24 Cms H by 24 Ins/60 Cms W. It is decorated with knot work design.

13.   A section of stonework from a cross-shaft. It is located 7 Ins/17 Cms south of the north end of the former doorway and 72½ Ins/184 Cms up from the ground. The section of stonework measures 10½ Ins/26 Cms H by 10½ Ins/26 Cms W. It is decorated with knot work design.

14.   A section of stonework from a cross-shaft. It is located 17½ Ins/44 Cms south of the north end of the former doorway and 92 Ins/233 Cms up from the ground. The section of stonework measures 8 Ins/20 Cms H by 14 Ins/35 Cms W. Although very weathered some indistinct decoration can be identified.

Externally the location of an A-S sundial can be identified on a stone incorporated into the west wall of the nave. The hole for the missing central gnomon can be identified 64 Ins/162 Cms north of the outer edge of the blocked-up former west doorway and 85 Ins/215 Cms up from the ground. The stone containing the gnomon hole measures 11 Ins/27 Cms H by 13½ Ins/34 Cms W. Due to weathering there are no words, lines or any decoration on this stone. (Note: There is another, not A-S/A-D, sundial on a stone incorporated into the west wall of the nave. It is located adjacent to the circular pillar support on the outer north side of the blocked-up former west doorway 33 Ins/83 Cms up from the ground. The gnomon hole contains a screw and the stone has lines indicating the time.)

Externally, incorporated into the fabric of the north wall of the nave there are:

15.   A section of stonework that might be from an A-D hogback grave cover. It is located 14 Ins/25 Cms west of the east end of the nave and 142 Ins/360 Cms up from the ground. The section of stonework measures 10 Ins/25 Cms H by 11 Ins/27 Cms W. It is decorated with knot work design.

16.   A section of stonework from an A-S/A-D cross-shaft. It is located 10 Ins/25 Cms east of the blocked-up former north doorway and 120 Ins/304 Cms up from the ground. The section of stonework measures 8½ Ins/21 Cms H by 9 Ins/22 Cms W. It is decorated with knot work design.

SKELTON
(1) All Saints Church
NZ 660190   Rating: ☆☆☆   Access is possible.

In "Skelton Town Centre" (it is described as such on a roadside sign), the church with its substantial square tower is easily identified on the north side of the "High Street" (there is a street sign).

The church was built in 1884.

Internally, there is a section of stonework on which there is part of an A-D sundial with associated writing. It is located cemented onto the northern end of the window ledge on the east side of the inner south porch. This section of stonework measures 15 Ins/38 Cms H, by 11 Ins/27 Cms W, by 6 Ins/15 Cms. The sundial now faces a south-westerly direction; the lower, southeast quadrant survives together with writing underneath. The letters running horizontally are in Roman script whilst the letters running vertically are Old Norse runes forming an incomplete text that is subject to interpretation. All Saints is the only example where writing on a sundial combines Roman script and Norse runes. The sundial dates from the mid 11C.

SKELTON
(2) Old Church
NZ 652190   Rating: ☆   Access is possible.

The church is located in an isolated position on the western edge of Skelton. It is reached by turning off the A173 and heading in a northerly direction along a drive (there are no street signs). The entrance to the church is 116 Yds/106 M north of the A173. The entrance to the appropriate drive leading to the church is easily located despite the lack of signage.

On the site of two earlier churches the present structure dates mostly from 1785 although the chancel is medieval.

Internally, there are five sections of stonework of various ages and sizes four of which may be A-S/A-D. They are located lying on the floor in the southwest corner of the chancel. They are:

1.   A coffin with a socket for the head. It is located adjacent to the walling in the southwest corner of the chancel. The coffin measures 77 Ins/195 Cms L, tapering 27 Ins/68 Cms to 16 Ins/40 Cms W, by 16 Ins/40 Cms D.

2.   A coffin without a socket for the head. It is located 33 Ins/83 Cms north of the south wall of the chancel. The coffin measures 83 Ins/210 Cms L, tapering 27 Ins/68 Cms to 20 Ins/50 Cms W, by 20 Ins/50 Cms D.

3.   A child's coffin without a socket for the head. It is located 5 Ins/12 Cms north of the south wall of the chancel and 85 Ins/215 Cms east of the west wall of the chancel. The coffin measures 43 Ins/109 Cms L, tapering 15 Ins/38 Cms to 13 Ins/33 Cms W, by 11 Ins/27 Cms D.

4.   A child's coffin lid, although it may be part of a later medieval grave cover. It is located lying on top of "3" above. The coffin lid measures 31 Ins/78 Cms L, by 16 Ins/40 Cms W, by 4 Ins/10 Cms D.

[Note: A fifth section of stonework, decorated with a diamond pattern design has been placed inside the child's coffin "3". This fifth section of stonework is not A-S/A-D.

SKIPTON
Craven Museum
SD 991518   Rating: ☆

In the centre of Skipton, on the east side of "High Street" (there are street signs), Craven Museum is located on the first floor of the Town Hall. The Town Hall is about 30 Yds/27 M south of the small roundabout in front of the churchyard to the distinctive Holy Trinity Church at the northern end of High Street. The Town Hall is on the corner of a junction with High Street and "Jerry Croft" (there is a street sign) that leads to Skipton's main central car park. In the High Street, outside the Town Hall and on the cobbled pavement, there is a freestanding directional signpost that includes the direction "Craven Museum". Also on the cobbled pavement outside the Town Hall there is a freestanding "The Craven Museum" notice board. On the side of the building along Jerry Croft there is a directional notice attached at first floor level "The Craven Museum" etc.

Although on the High Street side of the building there are no signs or notices identifying it as the Town Hall or the Museum, the Town Hall is Palladian in style and looks like a town hall. It dates from 1862. Enter the building from the High Street, and once inside follow the directional signs to the entrance to the Museum that is on the first floor. (On the ground floor keep straight ahead then take the staircase to the left as directed and enter the Museum on the first floor through a door.)

As with all museums, the displays and the exhibits they contain may be changed, re-sited, removed from display and/or put in store, or loaned to other museums or suitable repositories. Before visiting a museum it is worth checking in advance whether the displays listed in the gazetteer are still in place in the same location(s) set out in the text. Individual exhibits may have been rearranged in terms of their display, the order in which they are displayed and their relationship to other exhibits, some exhibits may have been removed from display. The text in the gazetteer reflects the descriptions and/or accompanying notices to the exhibits at the time of visiting. These too may have been revised, amended, added to or removed.

The Museum contains exhibits and displays relating to Skipton and the Craven Dales. The Archaeology display "Craven 400-1700 AD" includes:

1.   An A-S spearhead that dates from around 4-6C. The socket and blade are decorated with circular depressions. It was found near Bolton Priory.

2.   An A-D spearhead from the 11C found in York.

3.   A whetstone made of mica and used between the 10C and 12C. It was found at Askrigg.

SKIPWITH

St Mary's Church

SE 657386   Rating: ☆☆☆☆

On the western edge of Skipworth, before reaching Little Skipworth, the church is situated adjacent to the north side of "Main Street" (there is a street sign) that runs west/east through the village.

The church contains A-S, late 12C, early 14C and 15C fabric. The church was restored in 1877.

The lower part of the tower and the western two bays of the nave date from either the 7C or 8C. The remaining part of the tower, apart from the present belfry stage, dates from the 11C.

Internally, there is a section of stonework on which there is an engraved a picture depicting five men and a boar (a boar hunt). It has been incorporated into the south face of the north wall of the tower, 47½ Ins/120 Cms east of the west wall of the tower and 8½ Ins/21 Cms up from the floor. It is hidden behind a latched wooden cover. The section of stonework measures 14 Ins/35 Cms H by 24½ Ins/62 Cms W.

Externally, A-S fabric, including large stone quoining, is clearly identifiable up to the belfry stage of the tower.

Externally, incorporated into the south face of the tower there is a decorated section of A-S/A-D stonework. Locate the top of the first window up from the ground and look along the line of the top of this window to the west end of the tower. The penultimate stone from the west end of the south face of the tower has a figure of a bear carved into it. Despite weathering the head and snout of the bear can clearly be identified at the eastern end of this section of stonework. It measures about 15 Ins/38 Cms H by 36 Ins/91 Cms W.

SPENNITHORNE
St Michael and All Angels Church

SE 137889   Rating: ★★

In the southern part of Spennithorne the church is easily located adjacent to the east side of the road that runs north/south through the village.

On the site of an A-S church, the earliest surviving fabric in the present structure dates from the 12C and it also includes mostly 14C workmanship. The church was restored in 1871-72.

Internally there is an early 11C A-D grave cover. In the north side of the chancel, enter the vestry through a door just in front (to the west) of the northern end of the altar rail. The grave cover has been incorporated into the fabric of the east wall of the vestry, 9 Ins/22 Cms south of the only window and 34 Ins/86 Cms up from the floor. The grave cover measures 58 Ins/147 Cms H by 18½ Ins/46 Cms W. Although weathered the double-headed cross and knot work design can clearly be identified.

Externally, there is a much-weathered section of stonework from an A-S cross-shaft. It has been incorporated into the fabric of the east face of the chancel, between the north side of the window and the north buttress attached to the north-east corner of the chancel. It is located 5 Ins/12 Cms north of the east window and 79 Ins/200 Cms up from the ground. The section of stonework measures 36 Ins/91 Cms W by 9½ Ins/24 Cms H. Although some decoration can be identified it is not clear whether this is all vine scroll design or includes a scene as some guides suggest.

SPOFFORTH
All Saints Church

SE 364511   Rating: ☆☆   Access is possible.

On the eastern side of Spofforth the church is easily identified on the north side of the A661.

The present structure includes material from the 12C, 13C, 15C despite the extensive rebuilding in 1855.

Internally, there is a section of stonework from a mid 10C A-S cross-shaft. It is located in the south aisle, on the ledge of the third window from the east end of the south aisle. Of the three sections of stonework on this ledge, the section of A-S cross-shaft is that nearest to the western end of the ledge. It measures 23 Ins/58 Cms H, by 12 Ins/30 Cms W, by 6½ Ins/16 Cms D. Knot work decoration can be identified on the face and on the two sides it is possible to view. (The two other, smaller, sections of stonework on this ledge are of later medieval date. One is decorated with a consecration cross of unknown date.)

STAINTON
St Peter and St Paul's Church

NZ 481140   Rating: ☆☆   Access is possible.

The church is located in the central, southern part of Stainton. It is easily identified on the south side of "Hemlington Road" (there is a street sign – but not near the church) linking Stainton to Hemlington. The church is situated at the junction of Hemlington Road and "Thornton Road" (there is a street sign) linking Stainton to Thornton.

On the site of an A-S church the present structure includes material from the early 13C, the late 15C and 18C. The church was gradually restored on various occasions in both the 19C and 20C.

Internally, incorporated, but protruding from, the north wall of the "Parish Room", there are:

1.   A section of stonework comprising the central section and three of the arms from an A-S crosshead. The section of stonework is 7 Ins/17 Cms west of the east wall of the parish room and 95 Ins/241 Cms up from the floor. It measures 18½ Ins/46 Cms H by 29 Ins/73 Cms W (Although it is not now possible to view, the depth is 6 Ins/15 Cms D). Due to weathering the only decoration that can now be identified on the face is linear design. Although it is not now possible to view them, the north face is also decorated with linear design and the ends of the arms are decorated with interlace design.

2.   A section of stonework from a 10C A-D hogback grave cover. The section of stonework is 20½ Ins/52 Cms west of the east wall of the parish room and 120½ Ins/306 Cms up from the floor. The section of stonework measures 8 Ins/20 Cms H, by 12 Ins/30 Cms W, by 15 Ins/38 Cms L. Although weathered, the head and claw of the bear can be identified.

Internally, incorporated into the south wall of the parish room (the former exterior fabric of the north wall of the chancel), there are:

3.   A section of stonework from an A-S cross-shaft. It is located 17 Ins/43 Cms west of the east wall of the parish room and 125 Ins/317 Cms up from the floor. The section of stonework measures 9 Ins/22 Cms H by 15 Ins/38 Cms W and is decorated with knot work design.

4.   A section of stonework comprising the central section, all of one arm and parts of two other arms from an A-S crosshead. It is located 114 Ins/289 Cms west of the east wall of the parish room and 139 Ins/353 Cms up from the floor. The section of stonework measures 14 Ins/35 Cms H by 12 Ins/30 Cms W. Although weathered the decoration includes small individual crossheads surrounded by a circle and lines following the shape of the cross.

Externally, there is an A-S coffin. It is located 45 Ins/114 Cms south of the south-eastern buttress of the chancel. The coffin has been placed on a low plinth. It measures 77 Ins/195 Cms L, by 20 Ins/50 Cms W, by 17 Ins/43 Cms H. There is no socket for a head.

STANWICK ST JOHN
St John's Church

NZ 185119   Rating: ☆☆☆

About 400 Yds/365 M north of Stanwick St John, the church is easily located on the west side of the road, running roughly north/south through the hamlet.

With its oval burial ground suggesting an early Christian site in the "Celtic" monastic tradition, the present structure is on the site of an A-S church. The church retains material from the late 11C (in the tower) and early 13C despite the extensive restorations in the 15C and in 1868.

Internally, under the tower there are four sections of stonework, two of which are definitely A-S/A-D. These are:

1.   The lower part of a crosshead and a section of stonework from its attached cross-shaft and a separate section of stonework from the same cross-shaft. These two sections of stonework have been joined together

and it is clear that at sometime someone tried to cut the stonework into smaller sections. They are located standing on top of a 20 Ins/50 Cms H plinth sitting on the centre of the floor under the tower. Together they stand 50 Ins/127 Cms H, by 10 Ins/25 Cms W, by 7 Ins/17 Cms D. They are decorated in the Jellinge style on all four sides. On the west face a hound can be identified just below the join with the section of crosshead. Also on this west face a hart can be identified just below the join with the section of cross-shaft decorated with the hound. The section of stonework from a crosshead and section of stonework from the cross-shaft date from the late 9C.

2.   A section of stonework probably from an A-S/A-D cross-shaft. It is located leaning against the church pew adjacent to the west wall of the tower. The section of stonework measures 28½ Ins/72 Cms H, by 10½ Ins/26 Cms W, by 4 Ins/10 Cms D. On the two faces it is decorated with knot work design surrounding oblong panels that are now too weathered to reveal any design or words. The two sides are decorated with knot work design.

Internally, there are a considerable number of sections of stonework of different dates, sizes, shapes, condition and purpose incorporated into the south wall of the south aisle, in the section of walling running from the south door into the church to the west wall of the south aisle. The sections of stonework of A-S/A-D interest are:

3.   A section of stonework from a cross-shaft. It is located 1 inch/2 Cms east of the west wall of the south aisle and 22½ Ins/57 Cms up from the floor. It measures 9½ Ins/24 Cms H by 7½ Ins/19 Cms W and is decorated with knot work and Jellinge design.

4.   A section of stonework from a cross-shaft. It is located 16½ inch/41 Cms east of the west wall of the south aisle and 22½ Ins/57 Cms up from the floor. It measures 12½ Ins/31 Cms H by 9 Ins/22 Cms W and is decorated with knot work and Jellinge design.

5.   A section of stonework from a cross-shaft. It is located 26½ inch/67 Cms east of the west wall of the south aisle and 29½ Ins/74 Cms up from the floor and measures 5 Ins/12 Cms H by 4 Ins/10 Cms W. Although weathered there is some decoration of knot work and Jellinge design. This section of stonework could well have been broken off from the section of cross-shaft identified at "4" above.

6.   A section of stonework from a cross-shaft. It is located 8 Ins/20 Cms east of the west wall of the south aisle and 39½ Ins/100 Cms up from the floor. The section of stonework measures 8½ Ins/21 Cms H by 14½ Ins/36 Cms W and is decorated with knot work and Jellinge design.

7.   A section of stonework from possibly a cross-shaft. It is located 1½ Ins/3 Cms east of the west wall of the south aisle and 40 Ins/101 Cms up from the floor. It measures 7 Ins/17 Cms H by 6 Ins/15 Cms W and is decorated with a circular design.

Internally, there are a considerable number of sections of stonework of different dates, sizes, shapes, condition and purpose incorporated into the west wall of the south aisle. The sections of stonework of A-S/A-D interest are:

8.   A section of stonework from a cross-shaft. It is located 33 Ins/83 Cms south of the north wall of the south aisle and 18 Ins/45 Cms up from the floor (it is partially hidden by the south end of the pew). The section of stonework measures 5½ Ins/13 Cms H by at least 4 Ins/10 Cms W (the rest is hidden by the pew). It is decorated with knot work design.

9.   A section of stonework from a cross-shaft. It is located 33½ Ins/85 Cms south of the north wall of the south aisle and 23 Ins/58 Cms up from the floor. (It is adjacent to the south end of the pew.) It measures 10 Ins/25 Cms H by 13½ Ins/34 Cms W and is decorated with knot work design and lines.

10.   A section of stonework from a cross-shaft. It is located 58½ Ins/148 Cms south of the north wall of the south aisle and 23½ Ins/59 Cms up from the floor. The section of stonework measures 5 Ins/12 Cms H by 23 Ins/58 Cms W. It is clearly decorated with the figure of a man and some line design. Note: as the section of stonework has been placed horizontally rather than vertically, the figure is lying on its side.

11.   A section of stonework from possibly a cross-shaft. It is located 72 Ins/182 Cms south of the north wall of the south aisle and 32 Ins/81 Cms up from the floor. It measures 9 Ins/22 Cms H by 13 Ins/33 Cms W and is decorated with a four-legged beast and some lines.

12.   A section of stonework from possibly a cross-shaft. It is located 6½ Ins/16 Cms south of the north wall of the south aisle and 34 Ins/86 Cms up from the floor (it is partially hidden by a pew). The section of stonework measures 7 Ins/17 Cms H at least (the rest is hidden by the pew) by 11 Ins/27 Cms W and is decorated with ring plait design.

13.   A section of stonework from a cross-shaft. It is located 46 Ins/116 Cms south of the north wall of the south aisle and 38½ Ins/97 Cms up from the floor. The section of stonework measures 9 Ins/22 Cms H by 14 Ins/35 Cms W and is decorated with knot work design.

14.   A section of stonework from a cross-shaft. It is located 31 Ins/78 Cms south of the north wall of the south aisle and 38½ Ins/97 Cms up from the floor. It measures 9 Ins/22 Cms H by 13½ Ins/34 Cms W and is decorated with knot work design.

Externally, there are a number of sections of stonework of different dates, sizes, shapes, condition and purpose incorporated into the south wall of the south aisle. They are all very weathered. Those sections of stonework of A-S/A-D interest are:

15.   A section of stonework from a cross-shaft dating from around 800. It is located 119 Ins/302 Cms east of the east wall of the south porch and 20½ Ins/52 Cms up from the ground. The section of stonework measures 8 Ins/20 Cms H by 24 Ins/60 Cms W. It is decorated with an elongated, curving bird design (the bird-like features, including the heads require imagination). The section of cross-shaft has been placed horizontally rather than vertically so the birds are lying on their sides.

16.   A section of stonework from a cross-shaft dating from around 800. It is located 173 Ins/439 Cms east of the east wall of the south porch and 22 Ins/55 Cms up from the ground. It measures 6 Ins/15 Cms H by 24 Ins/60 Cms W and is decorated with an elongated, curving bird design (the bird-like features, including the heads require imagination). The section of cross-shaft has been placed horizontally rather than vertically so the birds are lying on their sides.

[Note: The decoration on "15" and "16" above are similar but not the same.]

Externally, standing in the churchyard there is a section of stonework from an early 9C A-S cross-shaft. It is located 194 Ins/492 Cms east of the east wall of the south aisle. The section of stonework stands on a plinth 13 Ins/33 Cms H, by 23 Ins/58 Cms W, by 21 Ins/53 Cms D. The section of stonework measures 28 Ins/71 Cms H, by 12 Ins/30 Cms W, by 6½ Ins/16 Cms D. Although the section of stonework from the cross-shaft is moss-covered, decoration can be identified. On the west face there is some line decoration suggesting oblong panels. The east face is too weathered but no doubt decoration similar to that on the west face at one time existed. Interlace decoration can be identified on the other two sides. Apparently the upper part of this cross-shaft is the section of cross-shaft inside the church under the tower identified at "2" above.

Externally, there are two coffins that may possibly be A-S/A-D. These are:

1.   A coffin with a socket for a head. The coffin is lying on its side and raised off the ground by a variety of unrelated sections of stonework. It is located at the base of the southern end of the west wall of the tower. The coffin measures 85 Ins/215 Cms L, tapering 26 Ins/66 Cms to 20 Ins/50 Cms W, by 14 Ins/35 Cms D.

2.   A coffin without a socket for a head. This seems to be the older of the two coffins and is located sitting on the ground beneath the

westernmost window in the north side of the nave. The coffin measures 77 Ins/195 Cms L, by 27 Ins/68 Cms W (the eastern end is missing), by 19 Ins/48 Cms D.

STAVELEY
All Saints Church
SE 362627   Rating: ✫✫

The church is easily located near the western edge of Staveley, on the north side of the road that runs west/south-west through the village.

The church was built in 1864.

Internally, there is a section of stonework from an early 11C A-D cross-shaft with the lower part of its attached crosshead. It is located under the tower 12½ Ins/31 Cms south of the north wall and 62 Ins/157 Cms east of the west wall of the tower. It stands on a stepped plinth that measures14½ Ins/36 Cms H, by 28½ Ins/72 Cms W, by 28½ Ins/72 Cms D. The cross-shaft, with the bottom "fan" of its "fan-shaped" crosshead, stands 33 Ins/83 Cms H in total.

The section of stonework from the crosshead measures 5½ Ins/13 Cms H, by 15½ Ins/39 Cms W, by 6½ Ins/16 Cms D. It is decorated in "Ringerike" style on its south side. All the other sides, and the ends of the arms, are too weathered or damaged for any decoration to survive.

The section of stonework from the cross-shaft measures 27½ Ins/69 Cms H, tapering 11 Ins/27 Cms to 9 Ins/22 Cms W, by 6¾ Ins/17 Cms D. On the south and west sides it is decorated in "Ringerike" style. On the east side, despite the weathering, it is just about possible to identify two figures, one with a hound and another below with a spear. Both figures are towards the southern edge of the east side. The upper figure is the better preserved with the head, eyes and legs just about identifiable. The top of the spear held by the lower figure stands below the northernmost foot of the upper figure. The legs and feet of the lower figure can just about be identified. The north side is too weathered for any decoration to be positively identified.

STILLINGFLEET
St Helen's Church
SE 593411   Rating: ✫✫

The church is located close to the east side of the B1222 in the northern part of Stillingfleet.

It dates from the mid 12C and was altered and extended in the 13C, 14C and 15Cs.

The present church is famous for its wooden south door (formerly the main entrance) on which the iron work depicts a Viking ship. The door is at least 12C in date and, given its subject, there is some debate as to whether it dates from the 10C or 11C and whether it came from another site. This original door is now situated internally behind the new south main door and kept in the open position. (The new door is now kept locked and entrance to the church is through the north door.)

STONEGRAVE
Minster (Holy Trinity Church)
SE 656778   Rating: ☆☆☆☆

On the western edge of Stonegrave turn off the B1257 and head in a westerly direction down a minor road (there is no street sign). (On a small green at the road junction there is a sign "Stonegrave Minster founded before A.D.757".) The church is easily identified and the churchyard entrance is about 106 Yds/96 M from the B1257. After about 35 Yds/32 M leave this minor road and proceed in a north-westerly direction along the obvious pathway leading to the church.

A Minster church on this site had already been established by 757. The present structure includes both A-S and 12C material although the comprehensive restoration in 1863 has obscured much of the earlier material. The lower two stages of the tower are A-S in origin and may date from the 10C (the lowest stage) and the 11C (the second stage).

Internally, A-S fabric dating certainly from the 10C but possibly some dating from the 8C survives in the west wall of the nave. The centrally placed tall, narrow doorway with its distinctive irregular sized jambs and rounded arch is A-S. (Unfortunately it is obscured by plasterwork and whitewash and best seen from inside the tower.) A blocked A-S doorway also survives in the second stage of the internal east wall of the tower.

Internally A-S fabric may survive above and between the later inserted 12C arches in the north and south walls of the nave but again, plasterwork obscures the detail.

Internally, the following items of mostly 10C A-S/A-D stonework can be identified:

1.   A section of stonework from a wheel head cross head comprising the central section and two arms, most of one other arm and two of the connecting "wheels", and a section of stonework comprising most of its attached cross-shaft. They date from around 920.

They stand on a 10 Ins/25 centimetre high 13C coffin lid sitting on the floor. They are located in the south aisle 110 Ins/279 Cms north from the south door into the church. They are situated underneath the eastern arm of the westernmost arch on the south side of the nave, and 13 Ins/33 Cms west of the eastern pillar supporting this westernmost arch. The section of stonework from the wheel head cross and section of stonework from the cross-shaft stand in all 68½ Ins/174 Cms H.

The section of stonework from the wheel head cross measures 16½ Ins/41 Cms H, by 21 Ins/53 Cms W, by 5½ Ins/13 Cms D. The west and east faces are decorated with lines outlining the shape of the arms of the crosshead with the inner lines entwined at the end of each arm. The north and south sides are too weathered for any decoration to survive.

The section of stonework from the cross-shaft measures 52 Ins/132 Cms H, tapering 15½ Ins/39 Cms to 10½ Ins/26 Cms W, tapering 8½ Ins/21 Cms to 6½ Ins/16 Cms D. All four sides of this section of stonework are richly decorated with plait and key pattern design although the east face suffers from weathering. In addition on the west face the decoration from the bottom of the cross-shaft upwards includes:

(i)   A figure of a Celtic priest with a book-satchel around his neck (at the bottom of the cross-shaft). The priest has his feet carved sideways pointing the same way and he has a round head with a Celtic tonsure.

(ii)   A representation of a standing cross with both crosshead and cross-shaft (above and separate from (i) above).

(iii)   A seated, praying figure with a book held aloft as commonly depicted in monuments where the Celtic form of Christianity prevailed (above and separate from (ii) above).

2.   A section of stonework from a 10C/11C A-D grave cover. It has been incorporated into the floor of the church immediately to the west of the 13C coffin lid that acts as a plinth to the section of stonework from an A-S wheel head cross and the section of its attached cross-shaft at "1" above. The section of stonework measures 21½ Ins/54 Cms (W) by 19 Ins/48 Cms (D). It is decorated with the figure of an archer shooting a stag.

3.   A section of stonework from the block that originally formed part of the base for the section of stonework from the wheel head cross head and the section of stonework from the cross-shaft at "1" above. It is located sitting on the floor 20 Ins/50 Cms south of "1" above and 4 Ins/10 Cms west of the wooden bench on which there are seven sections of A-S/A-D stonework [see "4" to "10" below].

The section of stonework from part of the base for the entry at "1" above measures between 7½ Ins/19 Cms to 11 Ins/27 Cms H, by 23 Ins/58 Cms W, by 9 Ins/22 Cms D. The south face is decorated with a lamb with a dove on its back, key pattern and cable moulding design.

The three other sides are too weathered and rendered for any decoration to survive.

Internally, sitting on two shelves of a wooden bench there are seven sections of A-S/A-D stonework. The bench is located in the south aisle 8½ Ins/21 Cms south of the central pillar on the south side of the nave.

On the top shelf there are:

4.   A section of stonework from a cross-shaft. It is located at the north end of the shelf. The section of stonework measures 14½ Ins/36 Cms H, by 11½ Ins/29 Cms W, by 6½ Ins/16 Cms D. The four sides are decorated with knot work design.

5.   A section of stonework probably from part of the cross base at "3" above. It is located next to, and to the south of "4" above. The section of stonework measures 8 Ins/20 Cms H, by 12½ Ins/31 Cms W, by 7 Ins/17 Cms D. The west face is decorated with a dog resembling a greyhound with another greyhound on its back. The three other sides are too weathered and rendered for any decoration to survive.

6.   A section of stonework from a cross-shaft. It is located next to, and to the south of "5" above. The section of stonework measures 12 Ins/30 Cms H, by 9½ Ins/24 Cms W, by 9½ Ins/24 Cms D. The west face is decorated with interlace design. The face currently facing southwards is decorated with a human figure comprising the face and part of the upper torso (the face and torso are upside down). The north side is too damaged, weathered and rendered for any decoration to survive. The east side appears to have been curved to form part of an arch and consequently any decoration has been removed.

7.   A section of stonework probably from part of the cross base at "3" above. It is located at the south end of the shelf, next to, and to the south of "6" above. The section of stonework measures 12½ Ins/31 Cms H, by 8½ Ins/21 Cms W, by 8 Ins/20 Cms D. The west face is decorated with key pattern and cable moulding design. The three other sides are too damaged or rendered for any decoration to survive.

On the lower shelf there are:

8.   A section of stonework from a cross-shaft. It is located at the north end of the shelf. The section of stonework measures 12 Ins/30 Cms H, by 11 Ins/27 Cms W, by 8 Ins/20 Cms D. The west face and the north side are decorated with interlace design. The two other sides are too damaged or rendered for any decoration to survive.

9.   A section of stonework probably from part of the cross base at "3" above. It is located next to, and to the south of "8" above. The section of stonework measures 13 Ins/33 Cms H, by 15½ Ins/39 Cms W, by 5

Ins/12 Cms D. The west face is decorated with key pattern and cable moulding design. The three other sides are too damaged or rendered for any decoration to survive.

10.   A section of stonework probably from a cross-shaft. It is located at the south end of the shelf. The section of stonework measures 15 Ins/38 Cms H, tapering 11 Ins/29 Cms to 7½ Ins/19 Cms W, by 5 Ins/12 Cms D. The two faces are decorated with interlace design and the two other sides are decorated with geometric patterns including straight lines on the edges.

Externally, apart from the fabric itself, the following A-S features can easily be identified in the tower:

11.   The two lower stages are separated from each other and the third stage of the tower by protruding A-S stringcourses.

12.   The distinctive A-S side alternate quoining on the southwest and northwest corners of the tower.

13.   The A-S window. It is easily identified on the south face of the second stage of the tower immediately above the first stringcourse.

14.   An A-S sundial comprising the central hole for the missing gnomon and some of the markings indicating the time. It can be identified on the south face of the tower by counting 10 corner stones (on the south-west corner) down from the first string course and then identifying the first adjacent stone to the east. The sundial is 9 Ins/22 Cms east of the southwest corner of the tower. The stone on which the sundial has been scratched measures about 14 Ins/35 Cms H by 22 Ins/56 Cms W.

15.   Part of the original A-S external western doorway into the tower. Some material from the doorway survives despite it being blocked and partially filled with a later inserted window.

The church guide refers to a Saxon font being buried at the time of the restoration in 1863. There is no indication of whether this font is still buried or where it was buried.

TADCASTER
St Mary's Church

SE 486435   Rating: ☆   Access is possible.

In the centre of Tadcaster, the church is located set back from the north side of "Kirkgate" (there is a street sign) by the junction of Kirkgate and "Westgate" (there is a street sign).

The church dates from around 1150 and includes late 13C, late 14C and 15C fabric. The church was restored during 1875-77.

Internally, there is a section of stonework from the end of an arm from an A-S crosshead. It is located incorporated into the fabric of the west wall of the south aisle of the church. Adjoining and surrounding this section of stonework, and also incorporated into and protruding from the stonework in the west wall there are a number of later, but more distinctive and more richly decorated, sections of stonework.

The section of stonework from the end of an arm from a crosshead is located 106 Ins/269 Cms north of the south wall of the south aisle and 55½ Ins/140 Cms up from the floor. (It is above the two small memorial plaques to Alfred Walker and William S. Oxtoby.) The section of stonework measures 4 Ins/10 Cms H by 6½ Ins/16 Cms W. Despite some damage it is clearly decorated with interlace design.

The church guide refers to a child's coffin, possibly of Saxon date, under the tower. There is now no child's coffin under the tower and there is now no knowledge of the coffin.

TERRINGTON
All Saints Church
SE 672707   Rating: ☆☆☆

In the centre of Terrington turn off the road that runs west/east through the village and proceed in a northerly direction up a minor road. At the appropriate road junction there is a street sign "Church Lane Leading to North Back Lane" and a large separate sign "Terrington Hall Preparatory School" etc. The church is less than 100 Yds/91 M along this road and is adjacent to the east side of the road.

The present structure mostly dates from the 12C with 14C and 15C additions. The church was restored in 1868.

Internally, there is a single-splayed A-S window in the south wall of the nave. It is located 42 Ins/106 Cms east of the south door and 101 Ins/256 Cms up from the floor. The exterior face of this window come now be viewed from the south aisle.

Internally, a section of stonework from an A-S grave slab has been re-used to provide the window head for the external face of the A-S window in the south wall of the nave. It has been inserted at a forty-five degree angle and has been reworked to provide a semi circular shape for the top of the window opening. The section of stonework can be identified from the south aisle. It measures 24 Ins/60 Cms H by 22 Ins/55 Cms W. Due to the fact that it is now at angle, the top corner of the section of stonework is 21 Ins/53 Cms above the top of the window opening. It is decorated with knot work design.

Internally, there is some very distinctive 11C A-S herring-bone masonry to almost the full height and width of what remains of the south face of the south wall of the nave. This can now be viewed from the south aisle.

THIRSK
Museum

SE 428822   Rating: ☆☆☆

In the centre of Thirsk, the Museum is located on the east side of "Kirkgate" (there are street signs) – the B1448, 75 Yds/68 M north of its junction with the north-west corner of Market Place. Hanging from the first floor of the appropriate building over the pavement there are signs "Thirsk Museum" and a silhouette of a drover with a pot of ale in one hand and a stick in the other with the word "Museum".

Just above the lintels to the adjacent doorways into numbers 14 and 16 Kirkgate there is a plaque that records "Here lived Thomas Lord Born in Thirsk, November 23rd, 1755. He established the first ground known as Lords. The home of the M.C.C. in Dorset Square, St. Marylebone in 1787 subsequently removing its turf to Regent's Park in 1811 and finally to St. John's Wood in 1814."

As with all museums, the displays and the exhibits they contain may be changed, re-sited, removed from display and/or put in store, or loaned to other museums or suitable repositories. Before visiting a museum it is worth checking in advance whether the displays listed in the gazetteer are still in place in the same location(s) set out in the text. Individual exhibits may have been rearranged in terms of their display, the order in which they are displayed and their relationship to other exhibits, some exhibits may have been removed from display. The text in the gazetteer reflects the descriptions and/or accompanying notices to the exhibits at the time of visiting. These too may have been revised, amended, added to or removed.

The Museum contains artefacts depicting the history of life in Thirsk, including displays relating to Thomas Lord and cricketing memorabilia, a Victorian kitchen, sitting room and bedroom and shop-fronts formerly in the Thirsk vicinity.

Downstairs in the Museum there is a section of stonework from an arm of a 9C/10C A-S crosshead. It is displayed in a glass cabinet by the window looking onto Kirkgate, in the more northerly front room of the Museum, i.e. not in the room where the public entrance is. The section of stonework measures 5 Ins/12 Cms H, by 11 Ins/27 Cms W, by 6 Ins/15 Cms D. Although weathered, knot work decoration can just about be identified on both faces of the arm of the crosshead. The end of the arm is too weathered for any decoration to survive. It was found in a garden rockery in Kirby Wiske in 1999 (there are information notices and a photograph of the garden rockery).

Also downstairs, there is a section of stonework from a 9C hogback grave cover displayed in the room behind the one with the section of stonework from an arm of the crosshead. It stands on a 4½ inch/11 Cms H wooden plinth standing on the floor adjacent to the dividing wall between the front and rear rooms. The section of stonework measures 18 Ins/45 Cms L, by 10 Ins/25 Cms W, by 11 Ins/27 Cms H. It is a typical example of a hogback with its arched profile and its overlapping tile and scroll pattern decoration. The decoration is a stylised representation of a hut with a shingle roof providing shelter for the dead. Like the section of stonework from an arm of a crosshead in the front room of the Museum, it too was found in a garden rockery in Kirby Wiske.

Upstairs in the Museum, in display cabinets in the rear room there are artefacts found at "The Castle Garth Dig". (At the site of the castle in Thirsk there is no information notice or anything to see relating to the excavations. Among the surviving earthworks there is just a squat stone recording the site.)

The central cabinet contains several items of A-S interest including in the upper part of the cabinet, a cruciform brooch, part of an annular brooch, an iron annular brooch, an iron knife, two small pots, brooch fastenings, wrist clasps used for fastening clothing, a strap with an iron buckle, and an ornamental fastener. The pieces are in varying states of preservation and size and some are not easy to identify without the accompanying informative text.

In the lower part of the same display cabinet there are some of the human remains dating from the early 6C found in the A-S cemetery beneath the castle. These are a piece from a skull, a jaw bone with teeth and two thigh bones measuring 20 Ins/50 Cms L indicating that the man was 7 feet/213 Cms tall. From another individual for whom it is impossible to identify the age and sex, there are bones from the lower leg and foot. In this cemetery about ten graves were found, although not all contained human remains. The nearly complete skeletons found included an adult male of 20-30 years of age in whose grave were also found an iron blade and animal bones; an adult male of 20-25 years of age with the suggestion of an old, healed injury to the skull and buried with a small pot near to the skull; a child of about age 10; a child of about age 3; and a male of indeterminate age buried with an iron blade, four copper alloy sleeve clasps and a copper cruciform brooch found under the skull.

An adjacent cabinet displays various pieces of pottery found during the Castle Garth excavation including three small pieces of 6C A-S pottery and two even smaller pieces of 10C A-S pottery.

THORGANBY
St Helen's Church
SE 689417   Rating: ✰✰✰

Towards the southern end of Thorganby, the church is adjacent to the west side of the road that runs north/south through the village.

The present mostly brick structure dates from 1690 although some 12C and 15C material does survive. However, most of the surviving fabric dates from the extensive rebuilding undertaken between 1740 and 1770. Restoration work was undertaken in 1948.

Internally, there is a rounded, wide, but shallow A-S chancel arch.

THORNTON STEWARD
St Oswald's Church
SE 170869   Rating: ✰✰✰✰✰

The church is situated in an isolated position to the southwest of Thornton Steward separate from habitation. It is reached along a no-through road that leads to a gated drive situated at the west end of the village.

At the entrance to the gated drive there is a sign affixed to the adjacent wall "Manor Farm, Road to St. Oswalds Church Only". Pass through the gate and continue along the drive for about 600 Yds/548 M as it heads in a south-westerly direction. Pass through another gate just before reaching the churchyard entrance. The drive ends and the churchyard with its notice board referring to a Pre-Conquest church, is easily located at this point – uphill on the north side of the drive.

The foundations of the church are A-S. Much of the fabric may also be A-S or Saxo-Norman, particularly in the walling of the nave although internally this is obscured by whitewash. It also has material from the 13C and 14C.

Internally, picked-out from the surrounding whitewash there are:

1.   Part of a south doorway comprising the west and east vertical stonework supports. It may be A-S in origin. It is located incorporated into the fabric of the walling on the south side of the nave. The section of walling that formed the western vertical support is located 3 Ins/7 Cms east of the westernmost window on the south side of the nave. It stands 79 Ins/200 Cms H up from the floor. The section of walling that formed the eastern vertical support is located 46½ Ins/118 Cms east of the western vertical support on the south side of the nave. It stands 66½

Ins/168 Cms H up from the floor. The quoining is not clearly defined in either of these supports.

2.   Part of the top arch section of stonework from a window that may be A-S. It is located incorporated into the fabric of the walling on the south side of the nave. It is easily identified above the eastern arm of the westernmost window on the south side of the nave.

3.   Part of the top arch section of stonework from a window and a section from its attached stonework that may both be A-S. It is located incorporated into the fabric of the walling on the south side of the nave. It is easily identified in line with "2" above and 26 Ins/66 Cms west of the easternmost window on the south side of the nave.

4.   Part of the top arch section of stonework from a window that may be A-S. It is located incorporated into the fabric of the walling on the north side of the nave. It is easily identified above the eastern arm of the westernmost window on the north side of the nave.

5.   Part of the top arch section of stonework from a window that may be A-S. It is located incorporated into the fabric of the walling on the north side of the nave. It is easily identified above the western arm of the easternmost window on the north side of the nave.

6.   Part of a chancel arch that may be A-S. It is easily identified above the existing chancel arch in the east wall of the nave (west wall of the chancel).

Internally, on the window ledge of the westernmost window on the south side of the chancel, and above a door, there are five sections of A-S stonework. These are:

7.   A section of stonework from a crosshead comprising the central section and two arms. It is located 2½ Ins/6 Cms west of the wall at the eastern end of the window ledge. The section of stonework measures 15½ Ins/39 Cms H, by 17 Ins/43 Cms W, by 5 Ins/12 Cms D. On the southwest face it is decorated with a seated figure of Christ. On the northeast face it is decorated with a Crucifixion scene with the arms of Christ outstretched. On both faces and on the ends of each of the arms there is knot work decoration.

8.   A section of stonework from a wheel head cross comprising the central section, a complete arm, most of two other arms, and two sections of the connecting "wheel" and part of another section of the connecting "wheel". It is located 12½ Ins/31 Cms west of the wall at the eastern end of the window ledge. The section of stonework measures 13½ Ins/34 Cms H, by 15½ Ins/39 Cms W, by 5 Ins/12 Cms D. On its southwest face it is decorated with the figure of Christ in a Crucifixion scene (because the wheel head is displayed upside down so the figure of Christ is also upside down). The northeast face is decorated with a circle

in the centre and what appears now as some line and abstract design. The end of the undamaged arm is decorated with knot work design. The ends of the other two arms are too damaged for any decoration to survive.

9.   A section of stonework from probably the arm of a crosshead. It is located 13½ Ins/34 Cms east of the wall at the western end of the window ledge. The section of stonework measures 16 Ins/40 Cms H, by 13 Ins/33 Cms W, by 6½ Ins/16 Cms D. On all four sides there is some indication of knot work decoration.

10.   A section of stonework from an arm of a crosshead. It is located abutting the wall at the western end of the window ledge, close to the window and behind (to the south) of '11' below. The section of stonework measures 6½ Ins/16 Cms H, by 10 Ins/25 Cms W, by 4½ Ins/11 Cms D. On its north face it is decorated with three heads above which there is a hand and two splayed legs and feet from what appears to be a running figure. The south face is decorated with knot work design. The west facing and east sides are decorated with circular design.

11.   A section of stonework from an arm of a wheel head cross with a small section of "wheel" attached. It is located 1½ Ins/3 Cms east of the wall at the western end of the window ledge, in front (to the north) of (10) above. The section of stonework measures 9½ Ins/24 Cms H, by 10 Ins/25 Cms W, by 6 Ins/15 Cms D. The north face is decorated with knot work, almost Jellinge, design. On its south face it is decorated with a cross. The ends of the arms are too weathered and damaged for any decoration to survive.

Externally, possible A-S quoining can also be seen at each of the four corners of the nave and the two corners of the east end of the chancel.

Externally, there is a blocked-up north doorway in the north wall of the nave that could be A-S. The long and short quoining survives standing up to the height of the bottom of the westernmost window on the north side of the nave.

Externally, similar top arch sections of stonework from two of the four possible A-S windows identified internally can also be identified. One top arch section of stonework is located above the eastern arm of the westernmost window on the north side of the nave. The other top arch section of stonework is located 26 Ins/66 Cms west of the easternmost window in the south wall of the nave, in line with the top curving section of the more recent window.

Externally in the churchyard, there is a memorial stone commemorating the reburial of some thirty 7C-10C Anglo-Saxons. The memorial stone is located 226 Ins/574 Cms southwest of the southwest corner of the extension on the west end of the nave. The memorial measures 29½ InsIns/74 Cms H, by 18 Ins/45 Cms W. In the centre of the east side there is a plaque: "Here lie the remains of 30 bodies. Uncovered during the laying of a water main in 1996. It is believed that they were originally buried in the 7th-10th century AD. May they rest in peace." Apparently of the thirty bodies found seventeen were mostly complete and there were bones from thirteen others.

THORNTON WATLASS
St Mary's Church
SE 233853   Rating: ☆☆

The church is situated some 200 Yds/182 M south-west from Thornton Watlass and separate from the village. It is adjacent to the west side of the road that runs south-west/north-east through the village.

The present structure dates mainly from the restoration in 1868 although the tower dates from the early14C.

Internally, there are two sections of A-S crossheads incorporated, but protruding from the fabric in the walling of the south porch. These are:

1.   A section of stonework from an early 11C wheel head cross comprising the central section and most of three arms with their connecting spandrels and "eyes" in between. It has been incorporated into the east wall 29½ Ins/74 Cms south of the north wall of the porch and 46 Ins/116 Cms up from the floor. This section of stonework measures 18½ Ins/46 Cms H by 12½ Ins/31 Cms W. It is clearly decorated with the figure of Christ with arms outstretched.

2.   A section of stonework from an early 11C wheel head cross comprising the central section and three arms with their connecting spandrels and "eyes" in between. It has been incorporated into the west wall 32 Ins/81 Cms south of the north wall of the porch and 46 Ins/116 Cms up from the floor. This section of stonework measures 19 Ins/48 Cms H by 11½ Ins/29 Cms W. It has lines around the edges and has what appears to be a spread-eagled figure, the fingers on the ends of outstretched arms can be identified but the head and the top of the cross is missing.

Note: In the churchyard there is no trace of the broken shaft (from an A-S cross-shaft?) referred to in the church guide.

TOPCLIFFE
St Columba's Church
SE 399760   Rating: ☆☆   Access is possible.

The church is situated near the western end of Topcliffe. It is easily identified set back from the north side of the A168(T).

The present structure mostly dates from the restoration in 1855 but it does include some material from the early 14C.

Internally, there is a virtually complete A-S wheel head cross. At present it does not have a permanent location, However, a formal display is planned near to the font at the west end of the nave. The wheel head cross measures 17 Ins/43 Cms in diameter. Apart from a central boss indicated on both faces and the line outline following the shape of the arms of the cross there is no decoration that can now be identified due to weathering.

Internally, part of what may be an A-S font survives. (The bottom of the font is missing.) It is located placed on top of the internal east wall of the south porch in a space between the rafters and the roof. The font measures 18 Ins/45 Cms in diameter and 8 Ins/20 Cms D.

UPPER HELMSLEY
St Peter's Church

SE 695571   Rating: ☆   Access is possible.

The church is situated at the northern edge of Upper Helmsley and is easily identified on the east side of the road.

The present structure dates mostly from the rebuilding in 1888 but it does incorporate artefacts from its 18C and 19C predecessors.

Internally, there is a small, round, undecorated font bowl dating from the 11C. It is located at the west end of the church, and underneath the tower, which sits on a plinth. The font is supported by a round piece of stonework.

Internally, there is a carved stone of probably medieval origin. It has been incorporated into the south wall of the chancel, about 48 Ins/121 Cms up from the floor, and just above the last pew to the west.

WARTHILL
Moat

SE 676553   Rating: ☆

Along the road which runs north/south through Warthill, and opposite St Mary's Church, (i.e., on the east side of the road), there is a large pond. To the north-east of this pond behind a farmhouse, "Hill Farm House" (there is an identifying sign at the entrance to the property attached to a gatepost), there is a small hill, which probably marks the site of an A-S hall.

The hill can best be seen from the rear of the farmhouse. Follow a road cum track for about 100 Yds/91 M as it skirts the southern edge of the pond and continues as a public footpath around the edge of the Hill Farm House and into the countryside in an east, south-easterly direction.

Legend recalls that King Harold used this vantage point as a look-out point prior to the Battle of Stamford Bridge in 1066 (see the entry for Stamford Bridge, East Yorkshire).

WATH
St Mary's Church

SE 325772   Rating: ✫✫✫   Access is possible (the inner vestry is kept locked).

The church is situated at the north-eastern end of Wath, adjacent to the north side of the road that runs south-west/north-east through Wath.

The foundations of an A-S church were found under the nave during the restoration in 1873. The church also contains fabric from the 13C, 14C and 15C.

Internally, there are three sections of A-S stonework that have been incorporated into the fabric of the north wall of the "outer" vestry. The vestry is entered through a door in an arch on the north side of the chancel. A wooden doorway frame cuts in two both sections of stonework from cross-shafts "1"and "2" below, but the complete sections can easily be viewed. The sections of stonework are:

1.   A section of stonework from an A-S cross-shaft. It is located 13 Ins/33 Cms west of the easternmost window in the vestry and 47 Ins/119 Cms up from the floor. (It is immediately above "2" below.) The section of stonework measures 13½ Ins/34 Cms H by 19½ Ins/49 Cms W and is decorated with either a hound or a wolf above a more easily identified hart.

2.   A section of stonework from an A-S cross-shaft. It is located 13 Ins/33 Cms west of the easternmost window in the vestry and 35 Ins/88 Cms up from the floor. (It is immediately below "1" above.) The section of stonework measures 11½ Ins/29 Cms H by 16 Ins/40 Cms W. Despite weathering knot work decoration can be identified.

3.   A section of stonework from an A-S crosshead comprising the central section and arm and part of its connected cross-shaft. It is located 20 Ins/50 Cms east of the easternmost window in the vestry and 53 Ins/134 Cms up from the floor. Together they measure 20 Ins/50 Cms H. The section of stonework from the crosshead measures 9½ Ins/24

Cms H by 17 Ins/43 Cms W. Although weathered in the centre of the crosshead two figures can be identified: their heads are missing. The section of stonework from the cross-shaft measures 10½ Ins/26 Cms H by 9 Ins/22 Cms W. The section of stonework is very weathered and no decoration can be identified.

Internally, there is a A-S crosshead comprising most of the central section and three arms. It is located in the "inner vestry" which is entered from a door in the eastern wall of the "outer" vestry. The crosshead sits on a ledge attached to the north wall of the vestry. It is 61½ Ins/156 Cms west of the east wall of the vestry and 79 Ins/200 Cms up from the floor. The crosshead measures 11½ Ins/29 Cms H, by 13½ Ins/34 Cms W, by 5½ Ins/13 Cms D. Weathering has left the crosshead with little identifiable decoration apart from lines outlining some of the edges.

In the churchyard, there is a section of stonework from an A-S crosshead with part of its attached cross-shaft incorporated into the base of the south face of the churchyard wall. It is located 23 Yds/21 M west of the gateway into the churchyard from which the path leads up to a door in the south wall of the chancel, and 35 Yds/32 M east of the western gateway into the churchyard. Together they measure 22½ Ins/57 Cms H. The section of stonework from the crosshead measures 6½ Ins/16 Cms H by 16 Ins/40 Cms W. It appears to be in the shape of a four-armed star. It is weathered and no decoration can be identified. The section of stonework from the cross-shaft measures 15 Ins/38 Cms H by 9½ Ins/24 Cms W. There is a groove running down the centre. It is weathered and no decoration can be identified.

WEAVERTHORPE
St Andrew's Church
SE 966711   Rating: ☆

The churchyard is adjacent to the east side of a minor road, 600 Yds/548 M north of where this road joins the main west/east road running through Weaverthorpe. It is on the slope of a hill overlooking the village and is some distance from other buildings.

Possibly built on the site of an A-S church, the present structure, although described as being built in the "Saxon" style, dates from the early 12C and includes 14C material. The church was restored 1870-71.

The tower, nave and chancel display some A-S rather than the Norman characteristics which their building date implies, in terms of architectural details, size and proportions. However, the ashlar fabric of the tower is certainly Norman rather than roughly coursed A-S.

Internally, there is an A-S font at the southwest end of the nave. It is decorated with a variety of separate, distinctive abstract designs each one enclosed within a circle.

WENSLEY
Holy Trinity Church
SE 092896   Rating: ✩✩✩✩

The church is situated towards the southern end of Wensley. It is easily located set back from the east side of the A684.

The present structure dates from 1245 and was built on the site of an A-S church. Sub3

d with vine scroll design on three sides (the fourth side is affixed to the wall and cannot be viewed).

Internally, there is a section of stonework from an arm of an A-S crosshead. It is located sitting on the floor in the south aisle, adjacent to the south wall of the south aisle and 45 Ins/114 Cms east of the south door in the south aisle. (It is some 34 Ins/86 Cms south-east of the font.) The location of this section of stonework changes from time to time. It measures 7½ Ins/19 Cms H (D), by 12 Ins/30 Cms W, by 10 Ins/25 Cms D (H). Although weathered and damaged it is decorated with knot work design on all four sides.

Internally, there is a section of stonework from an A-S wheel head cross comprising the central section with the vestiges of a central boss on one side, most of the four arms and two of the connecting "wheels" between the arms. It is located in the vestry, standing on the floor, leaning against a radiator by the west wall of the vestry. It measures 16 Ins/40 Cms H, by 18 Ins/45 Cms W, 5 Ins/12 Cms D. There is no decoration on any of the sides due to weathering.

Internally in the north aisle, there are three small A-S grave slabs protruding from the whitewashed walls. These grave slabs are incorporated into the fabric of the wall in the north aisle, two above and one below. They commemorate three priests.

4.   The grave slab below the other two "5" and "6" below. It is located 123 Ins/312 Cms east of the north doorway in the nave and 39 Ins/99 Cms up from the floor. The grave slab measures 14½ Ins/36 Cms H, by 18 Ins/45 Cms H. It is decorated with a circle of leaves type design. It dates from 792.

5.   The grave slab above and to the left of "4" above. It is located 118 Ins/299 Cms east of the north doorway in the nave and 61½ Ins/156 Cms up from the floor. The grave slab measures 13½ Ins/34 Cms H, by

13 Ins/33 Cms W. It is decorated with a cross and the names of two priests in the spandrels of the cross. In the top two spandrels of the cross, and split by the top vertical arm of the cross, is the name Eadberehct. In the lower two spandrels of the cross, and split by the lower vertical arm of the cross, is the name Aruini. Eadberehct and Aruini were priests in 792.

6.   The grave slab above and to the right of "4" above. It is located 134 Ins/340 Cms east of the north doorway in the nave and 58½ Ins/148 Cms up from the floor. The grave slab measures 16½ Ins/41 Cms H, by 9 Ins/22 Cms W. It is decorated with a cross with birds in the spandrels, and the name Donfrid beneath the cross. Donfrid was a priest in 760.

WEST HESLERTON
Site Of A-S Village
SE 916758   Rating: ☆

In the centre of West Heslerton take the minor road "High Street" (there is a street sign) which heads in an easterly direction off the more easterly of the two minor roads running north/south through the village.

This road becomes a no-through road (there is no initial indication of this fact) and it leads to Rectory Farm (marked on Ordnance Survey maps). The road surface deteriorates as the road progresses. Before reaching the Rectory Farm, but after passing a school, the site is situated in the fields to the north side of the road.

The excavations at this site revealed the existence of a self-sufficient agricultural community in the vicinity. It comprised some 60 houses including large, timber-framed dwellings. The settlement lasted from 450 to 650. There is now no trace of the excavations.

In Malton, the Museum temporarily houses an exhibition of the excavations with examples of the artefacts discovered (see the entry for Malton, North Yorkshire).

WEST ROUNTON
St Oswald's Church
NZ 414034   Rating: ☆☆

The church is situated at the southern end of West Rounton, 20 Yds/18 M east of the road running north/south through the village. To reach the church, turn east off this road and take the no-through road (there is an appropriate road sign but no street sign). The church is easily located on the south side of this road.

The church dates from 1150 although it was extensively restored in 1860.

Internally, there is possibly an A-S font, it may be later in date. On entering the church by the south door it is immediately to the west (left), 18½ Ins/46 Cms north of the south wall of the nave. The bowl of the font sits on a 16 Ins/40 Cms H circular support that stands on a 7 Ins/17 Cms H circular plinth sitting on the floor of the nave.

The font has a diameter of 30 Ins/76 Cms and is 16¾ Ins/42 Cms D – in the places where the font is damaged this measurement is reduced. On the east side of the font, from south to north, it is decorated with a large head, and "The Archer". The Archer is a centaur with the head, arms and top half of the body of a man, pulling a bow and arrow, on top of the lower half of the elongated body of an animal with four legs. The north-west side is decorated with a large four legged cat-like animal with a large head. Due to weathering and damage, other designs on the font are less easy to identify. However, there is an indication of chevron design around the lower third of the font suggesting a design of a later (Norman) date.

WEST TANFIELD
St Nicholas's Church
SE 267787   Rating: ☆☆   Access is possible.

Approach West Tanfield from a south-easterly direction along the A6108. As soon as the road reaches the north bank of the River Ure, turn off the A6108 and head in a westerly direction along a minor no-through road (there is a "no through road" road sign under which there is a "local traffic only" directional sign). Continue along this road for about 110 Yds/100 M before reaching the churchyard entrance on the north side of the road.

The present church dates from the 14C and 15C. It was restored in 1859-60.

Internally, there are two sections of A-S stonework. These are:

1.   A section of stonework from a mid 9C A-S cross-shaft. It is located standing on the floor one inch/2 Cms east of the north door and 6½ Ins/16 Cms south of the north wall of the north aisle. The section of stonework measures 19 Ins/48 Cms H, tapering 12 Ins/30 Cms to 10 Ins/25 Cms W, by 7 Ins/17 Cms D. The top face has been shaped so that the next section of cross-shaft can be slotted in on top, and the bottom face appears to be shaped so that the section of stonework from the cross-shaft below can similarly be slotted in. The two faces of the

section of stonework have been decorated with vine scroll design. The two other sides have been decorated with simple diagonal lines either side of a central straight line.

2.   A section of stonework from a mid 9C A-S cross-shaft. It is located 109 Ins/276 Cms east of the north door and 6 Ins/15 Cms south of the north wall of the north aisle. It is sitting on top of a 10½-Ins/26 Cms H later medieval gravestone lying on the floor. The section of stonework measures 13½ Ins/34 H, by 20 Ins/50 Cms W, by 13 Ins/33 Cms D. Although very weathered animal decoration can be identified on both the west and south sides of the section of stonework. The two other sides are too weathered for any decoration to be identified.

WEST WITTON
St Bartholomew's Church

SE 062885   Rating: ☆☆☆   Access is possible but special arrangements for viewing the grave slab must be made with the churchwardens. (In the first instance contact the Vicar at Holy Trinity Church, Wensley, North Yorkshire.)

The church is situated in the centre of West Witton on the north side of the A684. To reach the churchyard by road turn north off the A684 and along a narrow minor road separating two houses. Attached to the west wall of the house on the east side of the appropriate road there is a weathered wooden sign: "To the Church". The churchyard is located on the east side of this road, about 75 Yds/68 M north of the A684.

Pedestrian access to the church is gained by proceeding along a driveway between two houses leading off the north side of the A684. Attached to the west wall of the house on the east side of the appropriate driveway there is a large directional sign: "To St. Bartholomew's Church etc.…". 16 Yds/14 M from the A684 there is a gated pathway, attached to the gates are church notices. Pass through these gates and proceed along the pathway to reach the south porch of the church. By this route the south porch of the church is about 74 Yds/67 M from the A684.

On the site of the 6C A-S church, the present structure dates mostly from 1875-76 although the tower is 16C.

Inside the church in the vestry there is a small A-S grave marker. The vestry is entered through a door on the north side of the chancel. The grave marker has been incorporated into the south wall of the vestry: in the centre of the walling to the east of the south door into the vestry and 60½ Ins/153 Cms up from the floor. The grave marker measures 17½ Ins/44 Cms H by 16¼ Ins/41 Cms W and is thought to date from the time of Bishop Cedd who died in 664, although given the decoration around the perimeter a late 9C date may be more appropriate.

Other stones of A-S origin were found when the church was restored in 1875 but these are now in Holy Trinity Church Wensley (see the entry for Wensley, North Yorkshire).

The leaflet guide to the church says a small church bell may be A-S but since no other bell from this period survives this is most unlikely.

WHARRAM-LE-STREET
St Mary's Church

SE 864659   Rating: ✰✰✰✰

The church is set back from the west side of the B1248 in the southern part of Wharram-Le-Street. At the crossroads of the B1248 and the minor roads to Birdsall and Duggleby as indicated by the directional signpost, proceed in a north-westerly direction along the B1248. After about 60 Yds/54 M turn off the B1248 and proceed in a westerly direction up a drive that passes between two houses. There is no signpost or notice board at the entrance to this drive but the church can be identified from the beginning of this drive. Proceed up this drive and past two houses; the drive then becomes a track. Continue up this track through an open field gate to reach the churchyard field gate, which is about 84 Yds/76 M west of the B1248.

This A-S church, which may date from before 1050, includes 12C and 14C material. It was restored during 1862-64.

A-S material survives in the tower, parts of the nave and the foundations of the chancel.

Internally, A-S fabric can be identified in the nave despite the plasterwork. This includes:

1.   The east wall of the nave, in particular the material either side of the chancel arch.

2.   The west wall of the nave, in particular either side of the tower arch (view from inside the tower).

3.   The walling above the later inserted arches on the north side of the nave (view from the north aisle).

4.   In the south walling of the nave to the west of the south doorway.

The foundations of the rebuilt chancel are also A-S but this is not possible to verify due to the extensive plasterwork obscuring any early stonework that may survive incorporated into the present structure.

Internally, in the tower there is a A-S blocked round-headed doorway that opened into the nave. This is only visible from the interior of the upper floor of the tower and could not be verified.

Externally, A-S features can be most clearly identified in:

5.   The roughly faced fabric of the A-S tower that has been dated to 1050.

6.   The side alternate quoining on the southwest and northwest corners of the tower, and the external northwest and southwest corners of the nave that extend from the northeast and southeast corners of the tower. Also, side alternate quoining survives in the northeast corner of the nave.

7.   The roughly faced A-S stonework survives in the west wall of the nave. It is located about 32 Ins/81 Cms either side of the tower.

8.   The double windows at the belfry (top) stage on each face of the tower each framed by pilasters.

9.   The chamfered string course below the belfry stage of the tower.

10.   The small windows of the south and west faces below the belfry stage of the tower.

11.   The two larger windows of the south and west faces in the stage below those identified in "10" above.

12.   The former west doorway into the tower, now blocked and converted into a window retains its A-S soffit.

Externally, there is an A-S sundial that can be identified by the hole for the missing gnomon. It is located on the south face of the tower, 26 Ins/66 Cms east of the west wall of the tower and 210 Ins/533 Cms up from the ground.

WHARRAM PERCY
Deserted Medieval Village (EH)
SE 858644   Rating: ☆

Just under 800 Yds/731 M south-east of Wharram-Le-Street, turn off the B1248 and head in a south-westerly direction along a minor road as indicated by the separate directional signs "Thixendale 4", "Burdale 2" and by the English Heritage directional signpost "Wharram Percy Medieval Deserted Village". About 1050 Yds/960 M along this minor road, on the east side of the road, there is a freestanding directional sign

"Medieval Deserted Village (Ancient Monument)". As directed by this sign proceed into the car park on the west side of the road.

In the car park there is a descriptive sketch plan of the site. As directed by the freestanding sign "Wharram Percy Deserted Medieval Village ¾ mile Footpath steep in places", proceed in a general westerly direction, mostly downhill, along a well-defined track. The site of the deserted medieval village is reached after about 1300 Yds/1188 M. On the way on the some of the gateposts there are "Wolds Way" direction indicator signs and yellow direction indicator signs sometimes together, sometimes separately.

On the way to the village pass by a kissing-gate, go through a second kissing-gate with a direction indicator arrow and go down to another third kissing-gate nearby (visible from the second kissing-gate). Pass through this third kissing-gate and immediately go down some steps and across a small bridge. From the bridge head in a westerly direction to another (the fourth) kissing-gate that can be seen once the bridge is crossed. 144 Ins/365 Cms in front of this kissing-gate there is a free-standing Wharram Percy information notice. Pass by this notice and go through the fourth kissing-gate. Proceed along the well-defined path up to the site of the village. The research centre building and the ruined church come into view.

There are descriptive notices in various places on the site. Extensive excavations have provided evidence of continued occupation of this site during the Neolithic period, the Iron and Bronze Ages, Roman and A-S periods, and medieval times until it was deserted around 1500. The earthworks include medieval manor houses, farms, ordinary houses, crofts, a kiln, roads and fields. The buildings range from the A-S period through the 12C and 13C to the 16C and 18C. However the church, now ruined, was used up until 1949.

The surviving fabric of the church is mostly 12C with 13C and 14C additions. Internally, paving slabs in the floor of the present nave mark out the outline of the 10C stone church.

Externally, on the south side of the chancel to this 10C church a group of three A-S grave covers of the local "thegn" and his family – two adults and one child – were found when the site was excavated.

The excavations on the site also revealed the following items of A-S interest:

1.   A corn drying mill in use by 9C. The present pond is a reconstruction of the 14C fish pond, with its dam built over the remains of the A-S mill.

2.   The site of A-S farm buildings among the "North Manor earthworks".

3.   An extensive A-S farmstead to the west of "South Manor" perhaps the home of a thegn.

4.   An 8C smithy.

5.   Two sections of stonework from the arms of different 8C crossheads. One is decorated with interlace design and the other is undecorated.

A-S artefacts found during the excavations included carved bone and antler combs and pins, a copper and iron belt and sword fittings, thousands of shards of pottery and a sceat 700-725. None of the A-S artefacts are displayed on the site, or at present in any museum; they are currently in store. (Enquiries to English Heritage in York.)

WHITBY
(1) Abbey (EH)
NZ 903112   Rating: ✰✰

The Abbey is on the east side of the River Esk in Whitby. From the town centre there are frequent "Whitby Abbey" directional signs with the English Heritage logo directing you along the appropriate roads (Church Street, Green Lane and Abbey Lane – there are street signs) to the Abbey, which is easily identified from a distance. There are also directional signs in the town "Abbey. St. Mary's Church".

On reaching the top of the Abbey Foreland the abbey can now be entered via the Visitor Centre in Cholmley House or through the purpose-built entrance to the south of the abbey by the car park.

The A-S abbey was founded in 657. The Danes destroyed it around 867. Not until 1078 was the monastery re-established by Reinfrid a former Norman knight involved in the "Harrying of the North" in 1069-70, who had become an un-lettered monk at Evesham Abbey in Worcestershire. Excavated evidence survives from the late 11C church on this site. Most of the present Benedictine structure on the site dates from the 1220s with 13C, 14C and 15C additions and rebuilding. The monastery was suppressed in 1539. German warships shelled the abbey ruins on 16 December 1914 when damage was done to the west end.

Excavations in 1924-25 to the north of the present nave and north transept revealed foundations relating to the A-S "double" abbey of nuns and monks founded by Abbess Hild in 657. (She was Abbess 657-680.) These foundations included part of the base of the enclosing wall or bank around the monastic site, six small dwellings and a larger related hall or dormitory. (The area is grassed-over now.)

Incised sections of stonework including sections from crossheads and cross-shafts dating from 657-867 were also found during the excavations 1924-25. These included part of the slab commemorating Abbess Elfled 713-714. Also found during these excavations were coins, brooches, rings, strap-ends, pins, buckles, small pieces of metalwork, glass, bone, jet, loom-weights pottery and three bronze or copper plaques from book covers. Many of these finds are now in the British Museum in London.

Excavations between 1999 and 2000 took place about 250 Yds/228 M south of the southeast corner of the abbey church. They revealed an Anglian enclosure including a cemetery containing more than 1000 graves of men, women and children dating from the 8C and 9C.

Throughout the abbey site there are ten (two are numbered "9") freestanding informative illustrated notice boards. These "Audio Points" also indicate the appropriate numbers for additional information provided by the audio commentary for the site. (The commentary includes actors and actresses speaking the words of Brother William and Saint Æflæd.)

Audio Point:

• Number 1 describes "Two thousand years of history". It is located in the centre of the southern end of the site near the entrance to the car park.

• Number 2 describes "Anglo-Saxon Whitby". Additional information is provided at this point on Abbess Hild, Caedmon the Poet, Early Missionaries and Brother William (a fictional 16C monk providing continuity to the storyline). It is located close to the southern end of the Abbey Pond to the east of the abbey ruins.

• Number 3 describes "Whitby in the Middle Ages". Additional information is provided at this point on Whitby's Saints, Reinfrid, Whitby's Wealth and Brother William. It is located close to the eastern end of the abbey ruins.

• Number 4 describes "The Anglo-Saxon Community". Additional information is provided at this point on Anglo-Saxon Northumbria, The Lost Monastery, The Life of Bede and Brother William. It is located 34 Yds/31 M north of the west end of the nave of the abbey church.

• Number 5 describes "Pilgrims and Patrons". Additional information is provided at this point on Brother William. It is located in the centre of the abbey ruins on the northeast side of the central crossing in the abbey church.

• Number 6 describes "Monastic Life". Additional information is provided at this point on the Medieval Abbey, Benedictine Monks, Closure of the Monasteries and Brother William. It is located southeast of the southeast corner of the south transept of the abbey church.

• Number 7 describes "Whitby and the Cholmley family". Additional information is provided at this point on the Cholmley family, Elizabeth Cholmley, and the Cholmley House and Gardens. It is located to the south of the western end of the abbey ruins and to the east of the "Inner Court" to the north of the Cholmley House Visitor Centre.

• Number 8 describes "Whitby Abbey Headland". Saint Æflæd, abbess of the first monastery on this site, provides additional information at this point. It is located to the south of the western end of the abbey ruins (further south than Number 7 above) and to the east of Cholmley House Visitor Centre.

• Number 9 provides a "Welcome to Whitby Abbey". There are two Audio Points numbered 9 and both are located attached to the walling forming the interior part of the southern entrance to the site by the car park. One is attached to the western end of the walling (this is the first to be seen from entering the site from the car park) and the other is attached to the eastern end of the walling

Externally, there are an assortment of tombstones (some of which are A-S) and stonework from the abbey structure. These are located 341 Ins/866 Cms north of the north wall of the nave in a hollow in the ground. Some are more hidden by the grass than others. There are 13 coffins in this hollow but it is difficult to identify with confidence those of A-S origin. They are all weathered and worn with no trace of decoration and some are broken. They range in size from 88 Ins/223 Cms to 38 Ins/96 Cms L, from 27 Ins/68 Cms to 15 Ins/38 Cms W, standing up to 15½ Ins/39 Cms H off the ground. 3 have the remains of vertical uprights at either the head and/or foot. One of these uprights comprises a wheel head cross measuring 23½ Ins/57 Cms H, by 24 Ins/60 Cms W, by 6 Ins/15 Cms D. On both the west and east faces it is decorated in the centre with a cross radiating out from which there are lines outlining the arms of the cross and the arch of the "wheel". There is no other decoration on any of the sides or edges of the wheel head.

WHITBY
(2) Cholmley House Visitor Centre (EH)
NZ 902112   Rating: ★☆☆☆

The Visitor Centre is housed in Cholmley House which is located to the southwest of the abbey ruins. Cholmley House was completed in 1672.

The Visitor Centre can be entered by two separate routes: (1) From the north and to the west of the abbey ruins. Proceed through the "Outer" and "Inner" Courts and then enter Cholmley House through its north facing entrance. (2) From the east. Leave the western side of the abbey site near to Audio Point Number 8, and then enter Cholmley House through its eastern entrance.

As with all museums, the displays and the exhibits they contain may be changed, re-sited, removed from display and/or put in store, or loaned to other museums or suitable repositories. Before visiting a museum it is worth checking in advance whether the displays listed in the gazetteer are still in place in the same location(s) set out in the text. Individual exhibits may have been rearranged in terms of their display, the order in which they are displayed and their relationship to other exhibits, some exhibits may have been removed from display. The text in the gazetteer reflects the descriptions and/or accompanying notices to the exhibits at the time of visiting. These too may have been revised, amended, added to or removed.

The Cholmley House Visitor Centre has four displays of A-S interest.

1.   An interactive audio-visual display entitled "Saints and Song". It is located freestanding in the upper floor of the display areas, to the north of Display Cabinet identified "2" below. The display provides the visitor with the opportunity to ask three questions of the animated Abbess Hild and Caedmon.

2.   A Display Cabinet titled "Anglo-Saxon Whitby". This cabinet displays:

Numbered 1 and 2: Two mounts used to decorate the covers of Bibles or Prayer Books.

Numbered 3 and 4: Two writing styli.

Numbered 5: A hone stone used for sharpening tools.

Numbered 6 and 7: Two small fragments from hanging bowls. These are made from copper alloy and were probably used to hold oil lamps.

Numbered 8: A section of stonework from an arm of a crosshead. It measures 5 Ins/12 Cms H, by 8 Ins/20 Cms W, by 2½ Ins/6 Cms D and is incised with the words "orate pro" (pray for). It could possibly commemorate Abbess Æfleæd who died in 714. There is no decoration surviving on the other three sides due to weathering and damage. It dates from the late 8C/early 9C.

Numbered 9: A section of stonework from an arm of a crosshead. It measures 6½ Ins/16 Cms H, by 9½ Ins/24 Cms W, by 3½ Ins/8

Cms D. It is incised with letters RhT (the meaning of these letters is unknown). There is no decoration surviving on the other three sides due to weathering and damage. It dates from the late 8C/early 9C.

Numbered 10: A section of stonework from a slab from a stone coffin. It measures 7½ Ins/19 Cms H, by 12½ Ins/31 Cms W, by 4 Ins/10 Cms D. It is decorated with a finely carved quadruped (animal). There is no decoration surviving on the other three sides due to weathering and damage. It dates from the late 8C/early 9C.

3.   A Display Cabinet titled "Anglo-Saxon Spinning and Weaving". This cabinet displays:

Numbered 1 and 2: Spindle whorls, clay weights.

Numbered 3, 4 and 5. Pins, including pins with decorated heads, needles and a pin sharpener.

Numbered 6, 7, 8 and 9: Fragments of glass from glass vessels, window glass, glass beads and a glass bangle.

Numbered 10: A counter.

Numbered 11: A decorated silver strap end dating from the 9C.

Numbered 12: Balance used to weigh small items such as coins.

Numbered 13: Three bone combs.

Numbered 14: A cooking pot.

Numbered 15a, 15b and 15c: Spoons, a bone knife handle and an ivory pendant.

Numbered 16: A copper alloy skillet (a small saucepan).

Numbered 17: Hone stones for sharpening knives and agricultural tools.

Numbered 18: A stone mould for casting ingots.

Un-numbered: Two tweezers and a key.

Un-numbered: A bone-tuning peg comes from a stringed instrument, perhaps a lyre.

Attached to the west end of this display there is a section of stonework from a 7C or early 8C baluster shaft. The section of stonework measures 18½ Ins/47 Cms H, by 10½ Ins/26 Cms W, by 4½ Ins/11 Cms D. It has incised line markings similar in design to sections of baluster shafts found at St Paul's Church, Jarrow and St Peter's Church, Monkwearmouth, (see the entries for Monkwearmouth in the Durham and Northumberland gazetteer).

Attached to the south face of this display there are seven sections of A-S stonework displayed in rows. Some line decoration can be identified on all seven. From the left (west) to the right (east) these are:

(i)   A section of stonework from an end of an arm of a crosshead. It is the section of stonework nearest the western end of the display in the top row. It measures 10½ Ins/26 Cms H, by 11 Ins/27 Cms W, by 4½ Ins/11 Cms D and is decorated with chain work design on the south and west sides. All the other sides are too weathered and damaged for any decoration to survive.

(ii)   A section of stonework from a cross-shaft. It is the section of stonework nearest the western end of the display in the lower row. It measures 16½ Ins/41 Cms H, by 11½ Ins/29 Cms W, by 6 Ins/15 Cms D. It is decorated with incised lines in a triangular pattern on all four sides and it dates from the late 9C/early 10C.

(iii)   A section of stonework from the end of an arm of a crosshead. It is the second section of stonework from the western end of the display in the top row and measures 10½ Ins/26 Cms H, by 8 Ins/20 Cms W, by 4¼ Ins/11 Cms D. It has some incised lines denoting the shape of the cross on the south side. All the other sides are too weathered and damaged for any decoration to survive.

(iv)   A section of stonework from a crosshead (only the lower part) with a section of stonework from its attached cross-shaft. They are located in the middle of the display in the lower row. In total they measure 25 Ins/63 Cms H, by 12½ Ins/31 Cms W, by 5½ Ins/13 Cms D. They have some incised lines denoting the shape of the cross on the south sides. All the other sides on both sections of stonework are too weathered and damaged for any decoration to survive.

(v)   A section of stonework from the end of an arm of a crosshead. It is the second section of stonework from the eastern end of the display in the top row and measures 10 Ins/25 Cms H, by 11 Ins/27 Cms W, by 4½ Ins/11 Cms D. It has some incised lines denoting the shape of the cross on the south side. All the other sides are too weathered and damaged for any decoration to survive.

(vi)   A section of stonework from a cross-shaft. It is the section of stonework nearest the eastern end of the display in the lower row and measures 15½ Ins/39 Cms H, by 11½ Ins/29 Cms W, by 4½ Ins/11 Cms D. It is decorated with an animal on its south side. All the other sides have either been rendered, damaged or weathered for any decoration to survive.

(vii)   A section of stonework from the end of an arm of a crosshead. It is the section of stonework nearest the eastern end of the display in the top row and measures 9½ Ins/24 Cms H, by 11 Ins/27 Cms W, by 4½ Ins/11 Cms D. It has some incised lines denoting the shape of the cross on the south side. All the other sides are too weathered and damaged for any decoration to survive.

4.   On a display on a ledge forming part of the internal south wall of Cholmley House and attached to purpose built stands there are:

(i)   A section of stonework comprising the central section and two arms from a crosshead (broken but put back together) and a section of stonework from its attached cross-shaft. These are the more westerly of the two sections of crosshead and cross-shaft. Together they stand 31 Ins/78 Cms H from the top of the section of stonework from the crosshead to the bottom of the section of stonework from the cross-shaft, by 6½ Ins/16 Cms D (both), by 22 Ins/55 Cms (crosshead)/10½ Ins/26 Cms (cross-shaft) W. They are both plain in decoration apart from incised lining following the shape of the stonework on the north and south sides. All the other sides of both sections of stonework are too damaged or weathered for any decoration to survive. They date from the late 7C/early 8C.

(ii)   A section of stonework comprising the central section, one arm and most of another arm from a crosshead and two sections of stonework attached from the same cross-shaft. These are the more easterly of the two sections of stonework. They stand 54 Ins/137 Cms H from the top of the section of stonework from the crosshead to the bottom of the section of section of stonework from the cross-shaft, by 6¼ Ins/15 Cms D (both), by 24 Ins/60 Cms (crosshead)/11 Ins/27 Cms (cross-shaft) W. They are both plain in decoration apart from incised lining following the shape of the stonework on the north and south sides. All the other sides of both section of stonework are too damaged or weathered for any decoration to survive. They date from the late 7C/early 8C.

(Note: Displayed between "(i)" and "(ii)" above there is a section of stonework comprising a medieval boss, not A-S or Viking in origin.)

WHITBY
(3) St Mary's Church And Caedmon's Cross
NZ 902113   Rating: ☆☆

There are frequent directional signposts in the town on the east bank of the River Esk "Abbey. St. Mary's Church".

Standing in the churchyard of St Mary's, is the distinctive "Caedmon's Cross". It is located at the top of the 199 steps leading up from the town towards the church and abbey, 108 Ins/274 Cms from the north side of the pathway. Both the crosshead and cross-shaft are decorated. The decoration includes:

On the East Side. Figures of Christ, King David, Abbess Hild [with the heads of the five bishops she trained, Aetla, Bosa, John of Beverley, Oftor, the second Wilfred (bishop of York after John)], and Caedmon.

On the West Side. Interwoven vine decoration with four figures representing the bishops trained by Hilda (the second Wilfred is not included). Below this design are the first nine lines of Caedmon's Hymn of Creation in modern English.

On the North Side. A pattern of apple branches interwoven with birds and squirrels. The edges of this side show the first nine lines of Caedmon's Hymn of Creation in A-S "runes".

On the South Side. Wild roses spring from an old "Iona" type cross. The edges of this side show the first nine lines of Caedmon's Hymn of Creation written in the miniscule script used by the monks writing the Lindisfarne Gospels.

The cross stands 25 feet/7 M H from the top of the cross to the bottom of the supporting plinth. This replica of the 7C/8C Ruthwell cross was erected in 1892. Caedmon was a farm worker on abbey lands at the time of Abbess Hild 657-680. History records him as the first vernacular poet.

The present church dating from 1110 was built on the site of its A-S predecessor. It was extended and remodelled in 1170, 1225, 1380 and at various times during the 19C. The church was restored in 1905 and in 1970-75.

Inside the church, on boarding placed on the top of two areas of pews in the north-western part (corner) of the nave, there are a number of items of interest displayed, some with descriptive notices. Those of A-S interest are:

1.   A fragment of clay marked with impressions of wattle work. This fragment has been placed in a glass fronted wooden box 4½ Ins/11 Cms square. The box is attached to a section of wood on which there are attached other items, not A-S.

The box containing the fragment of clay is located on the section of boarding immediately to the north of the main body of the church, between the first and second windows in the west wall. This box has been placed at the southern end of the first group of pews with boarding on top. The box is 56 Ins/142 Cms east of the west wall of the church and 47 Ins/119 Cms west of the east end of the boarding.

The fragment of clay possibly came from farm buildings associated with the A-S monastery 657-870. (There is an accompanying notice "Wattle and Daub from Saint Hilda's Monastery".) It was found near to the Abbey ruins during the excavations in 1922.

2. A "Saxon" (so says the accompanying notice) baby's stone coffin missing only its bottom edge. It is located on the boarding nearest to the north wall 54 Ins/137 Cms east of the west wall of the church and 71 Ins/180 Cms south of the north wall of the church. The coffin measures 21 Ins/53 Cms L, tapering 12 Ins/30 Cms to 8½ Ins/21 Cms W, by 10½ Ins/26 Cms D.

WHITBY
(4) Whitby Museum and Pannet Art Gallery
NZ 894108   Rating: ☆☆☆

The Museum is located on the west side of the River Esk in the centre of Whitby. There are directional signposts "Whitby Museum & Art Gallery Pannett Park " in the town.

Pannet Park can be entered from "Chubb Hill Road" and "Bagdale" (there are street signs). There are a number of easily identifiable signs "Welcome to Pannett Park, Home of The Whitby Museum and Art Gallery" etc in the grounds of Pannett Park. These are visible whichever approach is used. The Museum building is closest to the east side of Chubb Hill Road and is easily located. It can be reached by any one of a number of entrances on the east side of Chubb Hill Road and the footpaths that wind their way uphill through the park. Incised in the stonework above the entrance on the south side of the building are the words "Pannett Art Gallery" beneath which there is a sign "Whitby Museum".

As with all museums, the displays and the exhibits they contain may be changed, re-sited, removed from display and/or put in store, or loaned to other museums or suitable repositories. Before visiting a museum it is worth checking in advance whether the displays listed in the gazetteer are still in place in the same location(s) set out in the text. Individual exhibits may have been rearranged in terms of their display, the order in which they are displayed and their relationship to other exhibits, some exhibits may have been removed from display. The text in the gazetteer reflects the descriptions and/or accompanying notices to the exhibits at the time of visiting. These too may have been revised, amended, added to or removed.

The Museum includes displays on geology, natural history, shipping (including a collection of ships models made from bone by French Prisoners of War during the French Revolutionary/Napoleonic Wars 1793-1815), weapons, Captain Cook, local history and archaeology.

The A-S items of interest are displayed in three cabinets and beneath one cabinet on the ground floor of the Museum about 11 Yds/10 M diagonally southwest from the pay desk.

1.   In a display cabinet entitled "The Anglo-Saxon Monastery" there are:

(1.)   A section of stonework from an end of an arm from a crosshead. It measures 8 Ins/20 Cms H, by 7½ Ins/19 Cms W, by 4½ Ins/11 Cms D. On the front face it is incised "hic re (quiescit) in hoc se" meaning "That is. Here rests in this tomb", the name is lost. It is very weathered and consequently no other decoration survives on any of the other sides. This section of stonework dates from the 8C and was found at Whitby Abbey.

(2.)   A section of stonework from a crosshead comprising the central section, two arms and parts of two other arms. It measures 11 Ins/27 Cms H, by 17 Ins/43 Cms W, by 4½ Ins/11 Cms D. It is too weathered for any decoration to be confidently identified on any of the sides. However, there is the faint trace of an indecipherable inscription on the front face.

2.   On vertical supports behind a second display cabinet there are a number of information notices:

(1)   Whitby Abbey.
(2)   Was there a signal station here in Roman times?
(3)   The Foundation of the Anglian Monastery.
(4)   Whitby Headland: Historic Features.
(5)   An Isolated Spot.
(6)   Reconstruction of lands belonging to the Anglian Abbey of Streanaeshalch.
(7)   Seventh Century Northumbrian Monasteries.
(8)   Archaeology and the Abbey (three notices).

The display cabinet in front of these notices contains:

In the column under the first section of glass entitled "Before the Angles Came":

(1)   Flint scrapers.
(2)   A Roman brooch.
(3)   A Roman melon bead.
(4)   Roman coins.

In the column under the second section of glass entitled "A Royal Monastery":

"(1) A copper alloy cross, silvered. The shape of the cross is characteristic of the A-S monastery at Whitby.

(2)   and (3) Two jet crosses, one has inlaid decoration in white metal. The date of both is uncertain.

(3)   A lead bulla. The seal bears the name of Archdeacon Boniface of the Papal Court in Rome. It would have been sent with a document to Hild or one of her successors and illustrates the allegiance of Northumbria to the Roman Church which was confirmed at the Synod of Whitby in 664.

(4)   A fragmentary inscription on a stone that measures 4 Ins/10 Cms flat (H), by 6 Ins/15 Cms W, by 2 Ins/5 Cms D. The first line reads (C) VNVBVRG (A) – Cyneburg, the wife of King Oswald of Northumbria who died in 541.

(5)   Sceattas: One from the reign of King Aldfrith (c 685-705). Three from the reign of King Eadberht (c737-758). One from the reign of King Eadberht with his brother Archbishop Ecgberht (died 766). One from the reign of King Aethelred I (first reign 774-779) with Archbishop Eanbald (778-796)."

In the column under the un-named third section of glass:

"(1)   Stycas. Two from the reign of King Eanred (c810-841). Two from the time of Archbishop Eanbald II. Four from the reign of King Aethelred II (c841-849). Two from the time of Archbishop Wigmund.

(2)   Moneyer's names. From Aethelred I's second reign (c790-796). The reverse gives the name of the moneyer who struck the coin, a means of quality control. Only three of the four moneyers on the stycas are named: Ceolbald, Cudheard and Tidwulf.

(3)   A copper alloy comb. An openwork cast bronze comb is extremely unusual, it may be a Frankish import."

In the column under the fourth section of glass entitled "A Life Consecrated to God":

"(1)   A copper alloy stylus with interlace design on the blunt end. It was used for smoothing the wax and erasing mistakes.

(2)   A copper alloy stylus with incised zigzag border.

(3)   A bronze/copper alloy chain and mounts. These come from hanging bowls probably used in churches as lamps. The bird shaped piece is an escutcheon and would have been attached to the rim of the bowl.

(4)   A curved bronze/copper alloy rod finished with an animal head. It may be a hook from another escutcheon.

(5)   Bronze/copper alloy mounts for decoration.

(6)   Two lengths of chain.

(7)   One bird shaped escutcheon.

(8)   One curved rod finished with an animal head. It may be the hook from another escutcheon.

(9)   Two other decorative mounts. One is curved and has a fish tail, and the other is decorated with a wavy line design."

In the column under the un-named fifth section of glass:

"(1)   A bone pricker with an iron point. It was used for ruling manuscripts and pricking holes in the parchment to transfer the layout to the next page.

(2)   A copper alloy parchment clip, possibly a bookmark.

(3)   Gilded, copper alloy Book Mounts. The design is made up of two superimposed crosses.

(4)   A small gold collar attached to a similar Book Mounts as at "3" above.

(5)   Three glass mounts for book covers, or other sacred objects such as chalices or reliquaries.

(6)   Two small glass plaques made up of twisted rods of coloured glass. The larger one has gold interlace inlay."

In the column under the un-named sixth section of glass:

An Anglo-Saxon comb with a "runic" inscription. It has an inscription in Latin and Old English "d (æ) usmæus godaluwalu d/oh/e/lipæcy", meaning "My God, God Almighty, help cy-".

3.   The third display cabinet containing items of A-S interest:

In the first column under the un-named first section of glass:

"(1)   Eleven fragments of various shapes and sizes of wattle and daub from the A-S monastery at Whitby.

(2)   A piece of window glass from the Whitby monastery site.

(3)   Illustrated notice about the 1920's excavations of Whitby's A-S monastery."

In the second column under the first section of glass entitled "None Rich, None Needy":

"(1)   A pair of copper alloy tweezers.

(2)   Three small copper alloy spoons.

(3)   Four penannular brooches (one has lost its pin). A safety pin and an annular brooch.

(4)   Four dress pins. The first two have ring and dot ornament on the heads that are faceted. The others have round heads.

(5)   Six copper alloy finger rings, although some may be penannular brooches that have lost their pins.

(6)   Six strap ends including a different type of strap end with its rivets still in place. Two hooked tags.

(7)   Four copper alloy keys.

(8)   Jewellery: A rock crystal sphere mounted in copper alloy. Glass Beads, coloured green, pink and turquoise. A copper alloy pendant with remains of gilding and red enamel. A broken brooch or ring with a bezel enamelled red and white.

(9)   A lead mount with egg and dot ornament. A lead mount with vine scroll ornament. A silver disc with an animal biting its hind food. A gilt bronze stud in the form of a dragon."

In the third column under the first section of glass entitled "A Disciplined Life":

"(1)   A small saucepan (skillet) in copper alloy; the handle was mended in Saxon times.

(2)   Two spoons made from bone.

(3)   A pot boiler stone.

(4)   A wooden peg from a harp or lyre."

In the first column under the second section of glass entitled "Industry":

"(1)   A round jet bead.

(2)   A faceted jet bead.

(3)   A jet finger ring. Medieval rather than A-S?

(4)   A partly worked piece of jet with a figure of eight scratched upon it.

(5)   Five part worked jet discs showing marks of the point of a lathe. They could be unfinished spindle whorls.

(6)   Two whetstones.

(7)   A bone spindle whorl decorated with ring and dot ornament.

(8)   An antler buckle shaped like two horses heads back to back; the serrated edge represents the mane.

(9)   Four glass fragments. These include a green glass rod that is not a finished product suggesting that glass making took place at Whitby. A blue glass fragment from a bracelet. The two other fragments are not specifically mentioned.

(10) Six bronze copper alloy rings of uncertain function."

In the second column under the second section of glass entitled "Textiles":

"(1) Two large needles made of bone.

(2) Twenty-nine pins.

(3) Iron shears used as scissors.

(4) A fragment of textile comprising brown wool with a loose weave, probably from a shroud."

In the third column under the second section of glass entitled "Spinning" and "Weaving":

"(1) Eleven spindle whorls. The one in the modern spindle is jet and has incised lines round it for decoration. Others are made of bone, limestone, lead, fired clay, shale and slate. One has incised chevrons round the sides.

(2) Seven loom weights."

Beneath an unrelated glass topped display cabinet containing models of "The Medieval Abbey" there is an incised section of stonework from an A-S grave cover. It sits on the floor, cushioned by some foam, 1¾ Ins/4 Cms H. The grave cover is probably part of a funerary memorial. It measures 3 Ins/7 Cms H (D), by 20½ Ins/52 Cms W, by 16 Ins/40 Cms D (H). On the top, flat (D), side lettering on two sides of an incised cross has been read as "VI(D) [Bvrg] or as (C) IN [Bvrg]". Either way this could be a female personal name, Widburg or Cynburg. There is no other decoration on any of the sides of this incised section of stonework. It dates from the 9C.

YARM
St Mary's Church
NZ 416129   Rating: ☆   Access is possible.

In the northern part of Yarm the church is located on the west side of the A67. On the south bank of the River Tees, just before the A67 crosses the River Tees, turn off the A67 and head in a westerly direction along "Bridge Street" (there is a street sign). Bridge Street soon changes direction to head in a southerly direction and it then becomes "West Street" (there is a street sign). After about 300 Yds/274 M the church is easily located on the west side of West Street.

On the site of an A-S church the present structure does contain some late 12C, 13C and 15C material. However, most of the present fabric dates from 1730 and the restoration in 1878.

Internally, a number of sections of stonework of varying sizes, ages and states of preservation have been incorporated into the fabric of the south wall of the vestry, either side of the window. Amongst these are:

1.   A section of stonework from an A-D hogback grave cover. It is located on the west side of the window in the vestry. It is 18 Ins/45 Cms west of the recess for the window and 67 Ins/170 Cms up from the floor. The section of stonework measures 8½ Ins/21 Cms H by 30 Ins/76 Cms W. The tegulated decoration on the roof can easily be identified.

2.   A section of stonework from an A-D hogback grave cover. It is located on the west side of the window in the vestry. It is immediately adjacent to the west (right) end of "1" above and it is 69 Ins/175 Cms up from the floor. The section of stonework measures 6½ Ins/16 Cms H by 18 Ins/45 Cms W. The tegulated decoration on the roof can be easily identified.

3.   A section of stonework, broken in two, but clumsily placed back together. It is located on the west side of the window in the vestry. It is 14 Ins/35 Cms east of the west wall of the vestry and 44½ Ins/113 Cms up from the floor. The section of stonework measures 21½ Ins/54 Cms H, by 12 Ins/30 Cms W, with only 5 Ins/12 Cms of its depth protruding from the fabric of the wall. There are some distinctive lines dividing the section of stonework into two and indicating a border surround, and there is also some sort of circular decoration. It is possible that this section of stonework is A-S/Viking.

4.   A section of stonework from a crosshead comprising part of the central section and part of two arms. It is located on the east side of the window in the vestry. It is 13 Ins/33 Cms west of the east wall of the vestry and 53 Ins/134 Cms up from the floor. The section of stonework measures 7½ Ins/19 Cms H, by 10 Ins/25 Cms W, by 5 Ins/12 Cms D (the part that is showing). Due to weathering it is difficult to identify any decoration apart from a curved diamond design in the centre. It is doubtful whether this section of stonework is A-S/Viking.

South Yorkshire

In South Yorkshire 23 sites of Anglo-Saxon & Viking interest have been identified and entered in the text.

5 sites have been entered and rated with one star ☆

This signifies that material may be difficult to find or identify with confidence. These entries are:

Conisbrough – Castle
Kirk Sandall – *St Oswald's Church*
Laughton-En-Le-Morthen – Castle
Rotherham – All Saints Church
Royston – Kirk Cross

10 Sites Have Been Entered And Rated With Two Stars ☆☆

This signifies that material can be found and identified but it is not particularly well looked after or a "good example". These entries are:

Austerfield – St Helen's Church
Bradfield – St Nicholas's Church
Ecclesfield – St Mary's Church
Mexborough – St John's Church
Morthen – A-S cross-shaft
Sheffield – Millennium Galleries
Sprotbrough – St Mary's Church
Thrybergh – St Leonard's Church
Thrybergh – A-S cross-shaft
[See also the entry in private ownership after the star rating index.]

3 sites have been entered and rated with three stars ☆☆☆

This signifies that material can easily be found and identified. These entries are:

Bolton-Upon-Dearne – St Andrew's Church
Doncaster – Museum and Art Gallery
Rotherham – Clifton Park Museum

4 sites have been entered and rated with four stars ✩✩✩✩

This signifies that material can easily be found and identified, and provides good examples. These entries are:

Burghwallis – St Helen's Church
Cawthorne – All Saints Church
Conisbrough – St Peter's Church
Laughton-En-Le-Morthen – All Saints Church

1 site has been entered and rated with five stars ✩✩✩✩✩

This signifies that material can easily be found and identified, providing excellent examples that are full of interest. This entry is:

Sheffield – Weston Park Museum

ANGLO-SAXON STONEWORK IN PRIVATE OWNERSHIP (No Access)

Sections of stonework from crossheads incorporated into walling – all three are in the same ownership. RATING ✩✩

1.   Two arms from the same 10C A-S crosshead. Both arms have now been separated. Each arm measures 17 Ins/43 Cms H (W) and 9 Ins/22 Cms W (H). These two arms probably formed the two horizontal arms and part of the central section from the same crosshead. They are decorated with vine scroll design.

2.   A circular-shaped 10C A-S crosshead. The whole circular crosshead is about 14 Ins/35 Cms "square". Unusually, the fan-shaped cross arms of this crosshead almost touch each other giving the appearance of four "holes". It appears to have been cut in two at some time but it is now back together. There is no decoration.

3.   A section of stonework from an arm of a 10C wheel head cross. The section of stonework measures 14 Ins/35 Cms H (W) by 7 Ins/17 Cms W (H). It has no decoration apart from distinctive line markings outlining the shape of the arm.

AUSTERFIELD
St Helena's Church

SK 662947   Rating: ☆☆☆   Access is possible.

Towards the northern part of Austerfield, the churchyard, and an entrance, is easily identified on the east side of the A614. Easily visible from the side of the road, and behind the churchyard railings, there is a free-standing "St Helena Church" notice board and a separate free-standing illustrated notice. Pass through the churchyard entrance and proceed along the pathway to reach the church. The church is some 65 Yds/59 M away from the A614.

The possibility of an A-S church on this site, or in the near vicinity, stems from the fact that the Synod of the Northumbrian and English churches was held at Austerfield in 702. This synod was ordered by Pope Sergius I to reconcile St Wilfred with King Aldfrith of Northumbria. Wilfred wished to gain acceptance as Bishop of all Northumbria but this was not acceptable to King Aldfrith and he expelled Wilfred. No agreement was reached at this synod.

The present church on the site dates from 1080 and includes fabric and alterations from the 13C. It was restored in 1897-98.

In the south porch the carving on the typaneum over the south door is said to be A-S, although it appears to be of a later date. It depicts a bull although it has been described as a dragon.

BOLTON-UPON-DEARNE
St Andrew's Church

SE 456025   Rating: ☆☆☆   Access is possible.

The church is prominently situated on the west side of the B6098. It is located on the southern corner of the junction of the B6098 and "High Street" (there is a street sign) which heads in a westerly direction.

Although extensively restored in 1854 the present church contains 11C, 14C and 16C material.

The nave of the present structure is on the site of, and incorporates material from, the 11C A-S church on this site.

Internally, A-S fabric can easily be identified in much of the south wall of the nave. In this section of walling there is a complete A-S window (also referred to in "2" below). The fabric in the northeast corner of the nave, now inside the church, is also A-S in origin but this is now difficult to identify.

Internally, there is a section of stonework from part of the end of an arm from an A-S crosshead.

It is located in the north-western corner of the nave on the section of the nave flooring that is raised. It sits on a modern plinth that measures 17½ Ins/44 Cms H, tapering 12 Ins/30 Cms to 9½ Ins/24 Cms W, by 8 Ins/20 Cms D. The section of stonework measures 4 Ins/10 Cms H(D), by 11½ Ins/29 Cms W, by 8 Ins/20 Cms D(H). Both faces are decorated with knot work design. There is no decoration on any of the other sides.

Externally, the south wall of the nave clearly contains A-S material. This includes:

BOLTON-UPON-DEARNE: St Andrew's Church. Anglo-Saxon long and short quoining.

1.   Large long and short A-S quoining. This can be identified in both the southwest and the southeast corners of the nave.

2.   A complete round-headed A-S window (it can also viewed internally and is referred to above). It can easily be identified, almost equidistant between the tops of the two other windows in the south wall (both of later date).

3.   A blocked opening of A-S origin. Its jambs have alternate stones laid flat and upright, and its top is cut off by the insertion in the 14C of a new, westernmost, nave window. It is thought that this opening led to a south porticus rather than forming a doorway itself.

Externally, A-S stonework has been re-used in the north wall of the north aisle. This includes:

4.   Some of the larger sections of stonework incorporated into the fabric of the bases of the two westernmost buttresses supporting the wall of the north aisle may be A-S in origin. (The buttress to the east may also contain A-S material but this is not so certain.)

5.   A-S material used as support for a doorway, now blocked. The doorway is located between the two westernmost buttresses supporting the external wall of the north aisle. Where the lower supporting pillars should be on both sides of the doorway, there is re-used A-S stonework, possibly including long and short quoining.

Externally, quoining from the A-S church is located in the former northwest angle of the nave of the A-S church, between the west wall of the north aisle and the northeast angle of the tower. The A-S quoining can be identified between 55 Ins/139 Cms up from the ground up to the angle of the roof of the north aisle.

BRADFIELD
St Nicholas's Church

SK 267925   Rating: ☆☆

The entrance to the churchyard is located at the north-western end of "Towngate" (there are street signs); about 100 Yds/91 M northwest of the minor road that runs north-south through Bradfield.

The current church on the site includes fabric from the 12C, 14C and the late 15C.

Internally, there is an A-S crosshead with a section of its attached cross-shaft. It is located opposite the south door into the church, almost touching the north wall of the north aisle. It stands on a stepped plinth.

The crosshead and section of cross-shaft measures 48 Ins/122 Cms H by 8 Ins/20 Cms D. The crosshead is 15 Ins/38 Cms W and the cross-shaft 12 Ins/30 Cms W at their maximum. The crosshead is decorated on its south side with a central boss surrounded by four smaller bosses. Due to weathering it does not appear to have any decoration on any of the other sides that can be viewed. The section of stonework from the cross-shaft is weathered and no decoration can now be identified on any of the sides that can be viewed.

In front of, and attached to, the top step of the plinth there is a plaque recording: "This ancient Saxon Cross was found at a place known as "The Cross" Low Bradfield and placed in this church A.D 1886.".

BURGHWALLIS

St Helen's Church

SE 536121   Rating: ☆☆☆☆   Access is possible.

The church is situated in the north-eastern part of Burghwallis, to the south of "Grange Lane" (there are street signs) that runs south-west/ north-east through the village. To reach the church turn off Grange Lane and along a drive heading directly south. Opposite the entrance to this drive there is a free-standing "Church of England" directional sign. By the entrance to the drive there is a free-standing church notice board. The church is located at the end of this drive and is about 110 Yds from Grange Lane.

Apparently on the site of an early British church built in wood, the earliest parts of the present structure, the nave and the chancel, date from the early 11C. The tower is probably Norman rather than A-S. Further building work took place in the late 12C, early 13C, late 14C, and the 17C. The church was restored in 1881.

Internally, because of the extensive use of whitewash on the walls it is difficult to identify fabric of A-S origin positively apart from the blocked doorway in the south wall of the chancel, some 5 Yds/4 M east of the chancel arch.

Externally, fabric of A-S origin can be identified in:

1.   The lower courses of the south walls of both the nave and the chancel; the distinctive "herring-bone" pattern of stonework may also be A-S.

2.   The distinctive side alternate A-S quoining. It has been incorporated into the south-west and south-east corners of the nave, and the south-east corner of the chancel. Similar quoining, although not so

well-preserved, can be identified in the north-west and north-east corners of the north wall of the nave.

3.   A blocked-up A-S doorway in the north wall of the nave. It is situated 144 Ins/365 Cms east of the west end of the nave, half covered by a later attached buttress.

CAWTHORNE
All Saints Church

SE 285079   Rating: ☆☆☆☆   Access is possible.

The church is located in the central, southern part of Cawthorne. It is about 200 Yds/182 M north of the A635. To reach the church turn west off "Church Street" and proceed along "Church Lane" (there are street signs). There are two entrances to the churchyard on the north side of Church Lane, about 30 Yds/27 M and 80 Yds/73 M west of its junction with Church Street.

On the site of an A-S church the present structure mainly dates from the extensive restoration in 1875, although material does survive from the 13C and 15C.

Internally, there is an 11C A-S font. It is situated in the north-east corner of the south aisle, 19¾ Ins/50 Cms south of the north wall of the south aisle and 16½ Ins/41 Cms west of the walling dividing the south aisle from the vestry. The font stands on an assortment of unrelated sections of stonework that raise it 8 Ins/20 Cms off the floor. The font measures 18 Ins/45 Cms H, by 27 Ins/68 Cms W on its west side, tapering 22 Ins/55 Cms to 20 Ins/50 Cms W on its north side, by 23 Ins/58 Cms W on its east side, tapering 25 Ins/63 Cms to 24 Ins/60 Cms W on its south side.

Each side of the font is divided by vertical lines into four rectangular panels. The west side of the font has its two central panels each decorated with a dragon – the head is at the bottom of each panel – while the two outer panels are each decorated with tree scroll design. The decoration on each of the four panels on the north side of the font is tree scroll design. The east side of the font has its two central panels each decorated with tree scroll design, while the two outer panels are each decorated with a crosshead supported by a slender cross-shaft. The south side of the font has its two central panels each decorated with a crosshead supported by a slender cross-shaft, while the two outer panels are decorated with tree scroll design.

Externally, there is a large, very distinctive 11C A-S crosshead. It has been incorporated into the centre of the east wall of the "Lady Chapel" (extending eastwards from the north aisle of the church). It has been

CAWTHORNE: All Saints Church. A large Anglo-Saxon crosshead incorporated into the external fabric of the east end of the north aisle.

"picked out" from the surrounding stonework in the wall. It is located 27½ Ins/69 Cms up from the ground. The complete crosshead measures 35 Ins/88 Cms H by 34 Ins/86 Cms W. The centre and lower vertical arm of the crosshead are decorated with an unusual "D" shape design. Despite the weathering there are other indications of decoration whose design is difficult to determine. There are incised lines outlining the shape of the cross.

Externally, standing on a stepped plinth, there is a large 11C cross comprising both the crosshead and cross-shaft. The crosshead is original whilst the cross-shaft includes mostly "new" sections of stonework with two "original" sections of stonework. The cross is situated about 25 Yds/22 M west of the west door into the tower of the church, and 108 Ins/274 Cms south of a pathway. The cross stands approximately 154½ Ins/392 Cms H in total.

The crosshead measures 30 Ins/76 Cms H, by 19 Ins/48 Cms W, by 7½ Ins/19 Cms D. On the east face there is no decoration apart from the central boss comprising a raised circle within another raised circle. On the west face there are the weathered remains of what appears to be a Crucifixion scene comprising the ends of the arms and fingers of the hands. There are also incised lines outlining the shape of the cross. There is no decoration on any of the other sides.

The cross-shaft measures 124½ Ins/316 Cms H, tapering 15 Ins/38 Cms to 11 Ins/27 Cms W, tapering 19 Ins/48 Cms to 6 Ins/15 Cms D. The cross-shaft incorporates two original sections of stonework.

One original section of stonework comprises a 38 Ins/96 Cms H section of stonework forming the lowest part of the cross-shaft (the part that stands on the stepped plinth). The west face of this section of stonework is decorated with a stylised figure whose two hands, legs and feet can be identified – there is a rectangular design divided into four between the hands and legs. From the remaining design that can be identified it appears that the figure may be standing on top of a crosshead decorated with a circular design. There are also incised lines outlining the shape of the cross-shaft. The south side of this section of stonework is decorated with abstract designs enclosed within separate rectangles. There is also some slight indication of the incised lines outlining the shape of the cross-shaft. There is no decoration that can now be confidently identified on the other two sides.

The other original section of stonework forms a 14 Ins/35 Cms H section of the cross-shaft – the highest part of the cross-shaft that is directly underneath and supports the crosshead. No decoration survives on any of the sides of this section of stonework apart from incised lines outlining the shape of the cross-shaft on the west face.

There is no decoration on any of the modern sections of stonework apart from incised lines outlining the shape of the cross-shaft on its west face.

CONISBROUGH
(1) Castle (EH)
SK 514989   Rating: ☆

The castle dominates the locality in the eastern part of Conisbrough. It is situated adjacent to the west side of the A6023. The entrance to the castle site is on the east side of "Castle Hill" (there are street signs), about 230 Yds/210 M from the A 6023 – 1 mile from the junction of the A6023 and the A630.

The name Conisbrough derives from the Anglo-Saxon "Cyningesburh" meaning the defended burh of the king. This suggests there was a fortified A-S burh in the vicinity. Rather than on the site of the present castle which was first occupied around 1070, it is likely that the burh was situated on the slightly more substantial hill on which the St Peter's Church now stands. (St Peter's would almost certainly have been within the burh.)

CONISBROUGH
(2) St Peter's Church
SK 512987   Rating: ★★★★   Access is possible.

In the eastern part of Conisbrough, the church of St Peter is located on the corner (junction) of "Church Street" and "High Street" (there are street signs).

A preaching cross was first erected on the site of St Peter's and was replaced by a wooden A-S church between 540 and 547. This church was rebuilt in stone around 740 to 750 and in 1050 the chancel of the church was enlarged. The church was considerably enlarged during 1150 to 1200 with further work in 1350, 1450 and 1475. Alterations were undertaken in 1866, 1882/83 and in 1913/14.

Internally there is A-S walling below the later inserted clerestory windows in both the north and south walls of the nave. It may date from the 7C or 8C. Incorporated into the surviving A-S fabric there are:

1.   Part of an A-S window comprising two vertical uprights and their horizontal ties. They are located 7 Ins/17 Cms above the westernmost arch on the north side of the nave, and below the western end and centre of the westernmost clerestory window. Each vertical and horizontal tie stand together 26 Ins/66 Cms H and the two vertical uprights are 31 Ins/78 Cms apart.

2.   Part of an A-S window comprising the rounded head and the supporting vertical stonework – now with inset blocking stonework. It is located about 12 Ins/30 Cms above the central arch on the north side of the nave, slightly off centre, to the east. This face of the window measures 26 Ins/66 Cms H by 14 Ins/35 Cms W. Viewed from the north aisle this window has a rounded head with less distinctive supporting vertical stonework – now blocked in (not inset). This face of the window measures 39 Ins/99 Cms H by 24 Ins/60 Cms W. It is an opening to bring in light from the nave into the upper room of the north porticus that at one time stood on this side of the nave.

3.   Part of an A-S window comprising two vertical uprights and their horizontal ties. They are located 20 Ins/50 Cms above the easternmost arch on the north side of the nave, and below most of the full width of the easternmost clerestory window. Each vertical and horizontal tie stand together 28 Ins/71 Cms H and the two vertical uprights are 30 Ins/76 Cms apart.

4.   Part of a former doorway into the north "lateral" chamber. (This chamber was adjacent to the east side of the north porticus.) The surviving

part of the doorway, now in-filled, comprises a lintel with some of the western side jamb comprising side alternate quoining. This doorway is located on the north-east corner of the nave incorporated into the fabric of the north wall of the nave. The lintel measures 6½ Ins/16 Cms H by 32 Ins/81 Cms W. It virtually abuts the west of the west wall of the chancel and it is 60 Ins/152 Cms up from the floor. The top surviving piece of stonework from the side alternate quoining measures between 8½ Ins/21 Cms and 6½ Ins/16 Cms H by 17 Ins/43 Cms W. It is 8½ Ins/21 Cms west of the west wall of the chancel and 50 Ins/127 Cms up from the floor. (Note: some of the side alternate quoining is missing between this piece and the floor.)

5.   Part of an A-S window comprising a single vertical upright and tie. It is located extending immediately above the eastern arm of the westernmost arch on the south side of the nave, and below the eastern end of the westernmost clerestory window. It is about 75 Ins/190 Cms above the decorated top of the base supporting the arch. The vertical upright and horizontal tie stand together 24 Ins/60 Cms H and together they extend 18 Ins/45 Cms across.

Internally, A-S side alternate quoining can be identified in the south-west and north-west corners of the nave where the west end of the nave joins the walling of the tower. This can be viewed from both the north and south aisles (the better example can be viewed from the south aisle).

Internally, A-S fabric also survives in the south wall of the chancel.

Internally, there is a section of stonework from a 10C A-S cross-shaft. It is located in the south aisle, 32 Ins/81 Cms west of the east wall, and 26 Ins/66 Cms north of the south wall of the south aisle. It sits on the floor beneath a very weathered large grave cover (the grave cover nearest to the south wall) decorated with the protruding carving of two birds; there is no decoration on any of the other sides of this grave cover. This large grave cover measures between 9 Ins/22 Cms and 12 Ins/30 Cms H (D), by 76 Ins/193 Cms L, tapering 23 Ins/58 Cms to 17 Ins/43 Cms D (W), and is thought by some to be A-S.

The section of stonework from an A-S cross-shaft measures between 7½ Ins/19 Cms to 8 Ins/20 Cms H (W), by 20 Ins/50 Cms W (H), and between 8½ Ins/21 Cms to 10 Ins/25 Cms D. On the south side it is decorated with plait work design and there appears to be some indistinct decoration on its top side. There is no decoration on any of the other sides.

Externally, in the churchyard there are the remains of a preaching cross thought by some to be in use up until around 540. It is located 11 Yds/10 M south of the south porch of the church and 78 Ins/198 Cms east of the pathway heading northwards to the south porch. The cross stands 50¼ Ins/127 Cms H, tapering 9¾ Ins/24 Cms to 8½ Ins/21 Cms W, tapering 9 Ins/22 Cms to 7¼ Ins/18 Cms D. It comprises a cross-shaft and part of the lower vertical arm of the crosshead although it now appears to be a single section of stonework. However the top 7 Ins/17 Cms of this stonework can be identified as coming from a crosshead. Due to weathering no decoration can be identified on any of the sides.

DONCASTER
Museum and Art Gallery
SE 579030   Rating: ✰✰✰

In the centre of Doncaster, the Museum is situated on the east side of "Chequer Road" (there are street signs). From the northern end of Chequer Road, where it joins a crossroads with "Wood Street" and other roads (there are single street signs for both Chequer Road and Wood Street only), proceed as indicated by the "Museum & Art Gallery" directional sign in a southeast direction along Chequer Road.

After about 175 Yds/160 M, on the east side of Chequer Road, there is an entrance gateway. The ornamental arching over this entrance gateway includes the words "celebrating 800 years as a borough". There is also a separate, small notice about Museum opening times affixed to the railings on the south side of the gateway. (Before reaching this gateway (to the north), there is also a free-standing "Doncaster Museum and Art Gallery" sign amidst flowerbeds on the pavement on the east side of Chequer Road.) Go through the entrance gateway and the building housing the Museum is clearly evident about 30 Yds/27 M away. The appropriate building has the words "Doncaster Museum and Art Gallery" affixed to the walling near to the entrance.

As with all museums, the displays and the exhibits they contain may be changed, re-sited, removed from display and/or put in store, or loaned to other museums or suitable repositories. Before visiting the museum it is worth checking in advance whether the displays listed in the text below are still in place in the same location(s) set out in the text. Individual exhibits may have been rearranged in terms of their display, the order in which they are displayed and their relationship to other exhibits, some exhibits may have been removed from display. The text in the entry reflects the descriptions and/or accompanying notices to the exhibits at the time of visiting. These too may have been revised, amended, added to or removed.

The Museum on the ground floor contains informative displays and exhibits relating to the local area, including the regimental museum for the King's Own Yorkshire Light Infantry (1757-1968).

The Museum collections include four sections of A-S stonework identified as the "Frickley Cross-Shafts". These sections of stonework from cross-shafts date from between 900-1000 and come from at least two distinct crosses. They are displayed in the "By River and Road" gallery within the medieval section.

The Frickley Cross-Shafts comprise:

1.   A section of stonework from the lower part of a cross-shaft with a socket on top for the next part of the cross-shaft to be slotted in. It measures 22 Ins/55 Cms H, by 11½ Ins/29 Cms W, by 8¼ Ins/20 Cms D. This section of stonework is decorated with ring chain design on all four sides.

2.   A section of stonework from the very top of a cross-shaft that may include the wedge-shaped bottom arm of a crosshead. It measures 17½ Ins/44 Cms H, by 10 Ins/25 Cms W, by 6½ Ins/16 Cms D. This section of stonework is decorated on the two faces with vine scroll design and on the other two sides with knot work design.

3.   A section of stonework from the base of a cross-shaft. It includes the provision of a tenon to fit into the socket of a stone base. The section of stonework measures 25½ Ins/64 Cms H, by 12¾ Ins/32 Cms W, by 5¾ Ins/14 Cms D. There are traces of interlace design but all sides are weathered and damaged and the design on each is indistinct.

4.   A section of stonework from a cross-shaft. It measures 9¼ Ins/23 Cms H, by 9½ Ins/24 Cms W, by 4¾ Ins/12 Cms D. On one face this section of stonework is decorated with the body and hoofed feet of a four-legged animal with its long tail knotted around its feet (the head and neck are missing). There is interlace design on the other sides.

ECCLESFIELD
St Mary's Church

SK 353942   Rating: ☆☆   Access is possible.

In the northern part of Ecclesfield, the church is easily located set back from the west side of the B6087, "Church Street" (there are street signs). It is situated about 550 Yds/502 M south of the junction of the B6087 and the A6135.

The present structure dates from the 14C with some re-used 12C material.

Internally, there is a section of stonework from an 11C A-S cross-shaft. It is located in the south transept, 8½ Ins/21 Cms north of the south wall and 25 Ins/63 Cms east of an exterior door into the south transept. It stands on a large floor-standing flat cross base 1½ Ins/3 Cms north of the south wall of the south transept and 14 Ins/35 Cms east of the exterior door into the south transept. The section of stonework measures 57½ Ins/146 Cms H, tapering 12½ Ins/31 Cms to 11 Ins/27 Cms W, tapering 9 Ins/22 Cms to 7 Ins/17 Cms D. The north side is decorated with a number of crosses, most of which are enclosed within circles. There are two larger central crosses with arms of equal length enclosed within even larger crosses. The whole north side is enclosed within a line border. The other three sides are very weathered and, apart from lines indicating the borders on each side, there is no decoration.

This section of stonework from a cross-shaft has been cemented onto a cross base with what appears two sockets for cross-shafts. The more easterly socket remains empty, the more westerly socket is filled with the section of cross-shaft described above. The cross base has been broken but put back together. It seems to sit on the floor although on closer inspection it partly sits on some small fragments of unrelated stonework. The cross base measures 14 Ins/35 Cms H, by 56½ Ins/143 Cms W, by 25½ Ins/64 Cms D. The cross base is very weathered and apart from lines indicating the borders of each of the sides it has no decoration.

KIRK SANDALL
St Oswald's Church

SE 609082   Rating: ☆   Access is possible.

The church is located in an isolated position in the north-western part of Kirk Sandall. At the crossroads containing the junction of "Sandall Lane" (there are street signs) and "Doncaster Road" (there is a street sign), there is a directional sign "Kirk Sandall Ind. Est." and a separate directional sign attached to a lamppost "St Oswald's Church". Proceed as directed along Sandall Lane in a general westerly direction (crossing over the railway).

After about 500 Yds/457 M turn off Sandall Lane and head in a northwest direction along a minor road (there are no street signs) in the general direction of the large power station cooling towers clearly visible in the distance. Proceed along this minor road up to the small, "squarish" church that comes into view on the way (the road reduces in width and surface quality on the way).

The church is situated on the north side of the junction of minor roads and track ways. (The church is in an area where there is industrial dereliction but new houses are being built in the locality.) The church is about 440 Yds/402 M away from Sandall Lane.

The church mostly dates from the restoration in 1864 although some A-S, 12C, 13C and 14C material does survive.

Internally no A-S fabric can be identified. However, there is a plain, round "tub" font that could be Saxo-Norman. It is located, internally, standing on a two-stepped plinth against the west wall of the south aisle.

Externally, there are sections of A-S herring-bone masonry. This masonry can be identified in separate areas in the west walling of the nave, particularly in the stonework above the west window.

Externally, A-S quoining can be identified in the west wall at the former southwest corner of the nave (the better example) and the former north-west corner of the nave.

LAUGHTON-EN-LE-MORTHEN
(1) All Saints Church
SK 517882   Rating: ★☆☆☆   Access is possible.

The church, with its tall spire and ornate tower, is easily located adjacent to the west side of the road that runs roughly north-west/south-east through the village. At its northern end this road is called "Rotherham Lane" but it becomes "High Street" as it leads south-eastwards (there are street signs).

The present church on this site dates mainly from around 1377, but as well as A-S material it also contains material from the 12C, 13C and 16C. The church was restored in 1895.

Internally, the fabric of the church is clearly of different dates, but at times it is difficult to date precisely. The lower stages of both the east and south walls of the chancel, both internally and externally, may have utilised re-used A-S material.

A-S material can be identified at the west end of the north aisle of the church. This can best be seen externally and comprises:

1.   A 180 inch/457 centimetre stretch of A-S walling. This is easily identified at the west end of the north wall of the north aisle, between the two westernmost buttresses.

2.   A very distinctive A-S hooded doorway. It is located in the centre of the external walling in the north aisle, it is clearly outlined with protruding stonework (A later inserted doorway has destroyed some of the material.) The round, hooded arch has distinctive voussoirs underneath. The style of this A-S doorway is said to denote the transition from a wooden to a stone building.

3.   Large long and short A-S quoining. This is located at the eastern end of this section of external walling in the north aisle. It is adjacent to

the west side of the more eastern of the two buttresses framing the A-S walling. This quoining denotes the surviving northeast corner of an A-S porticus.

4.   A-S material. This is incorporated into the 180 inch/457 centimetre section of the west wall of the north aisle.

LAUGHTON-EN-LE-MORTHEN: All Saints Church. Anglo-Saxon fabric, hooded doorway and quoining surviving from a porticus.

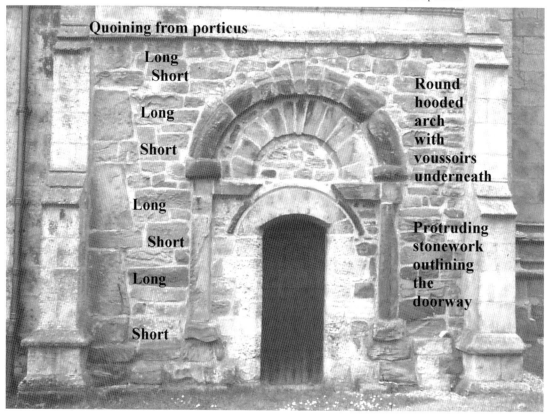

Quoining from porticus

Long
Short
Long
Short
Long
Short
Long
Short

Round hooded arch with voussoirs underneath

Protruding stonework outlining the doorway

LAUGHTON-EN-LE-MORTHEN
(2) Castle
SK 515882   Rating: ☆

23 Yds/21 M south of east end of the church of All Saints, turn off the main road which runs through the village (Rotherham Lane), and head in a southwest direction along the minor, no-through winding road "Church Corner" (there is a street sign with a no-through road indication).

Where Church Corner ends by a field fence (145 Yds/132 M from the street sign), cross over a stile and into the adjacent field. Proceed around the boundary edge of this field heading in a general northwest direction alongside the field fence behind which there are trees and vegetation. The site of the motte and bailey castle is on the east side of this field fence and is obscured from view by vegetation, trees, modern building and seemingly derelict land. The motte is about 170 Yds/155 M from the stile.

A view of the general area of the castle site can also be gained from the wall at the west end of the graveyard on the west side of All Saints Church and the adjacent graveyard extension. Here too the site is overgrown and derelict with features difficult to identify with certainty.

This castle stands on the site of a 7C hall of King Edwin of Northumbria. It was his Kentish wife who introduced Christianity to the area through the foundation of All Saints Church. However, Domesday Book (1086) records that site contained a hall of Edwin, Earl of Mercia. This Edwin was actively trying to resist the Normans and was treacherously murdered by his own followers in 1071.

MEXBOROUGH
St John's Church

SK 479997   Rating: ☆☆   Access is possible.

The church is located in the south, central, part of Mexborough, about 100 Yds/91 M north of the River Don. It is situated adjacent to the south side of "Church Street" (there are street signs) and about 880 Yds/804 M west of the eastern junction of Church Street with the A6023.

The present structure mainly dates from the 13C and the restoration in 1891.

Internally, there is a section of stonework from an 11C A-S cross-shaft. It stands on a plinth close to the north-east corner of the tower and behind (to the west) of the east door into the tower. The plinth measures 8 Ins/20 Cms H, by 23½ Ins/59 Cms W, by 12 Ins/30 Cms D. The section of stonework measures 57 Ins/144 Cms H, tapering 13½ Ins/34 Cms to 11¾ Ins/29 Cms W, tapering 8½ Ins/21 Cms to 7 Ins/17 Cms D. Due to weathering the only decoration that survives is two small circles within a panel on each of the two faces and the incised lines outlining the shape of the cross-shaft. There is no other decoration on the other two sides.

MORTHEN
A-S Cross-shaft

SE 476894   Rating: ☆☆

In the centre of Morthen, there is a section from an A-S cross-shaft standing on a plinth. It is situated on the east side of the road that runs in a southwest/northeast direction through the village. The cross-shaft is 132 Ins/335 Cms from the east side of the road. It is located 19 Yds/17 M north of the entrance to the disused chapel on the east side of the road, and 22 Yds/20 M south of the "Morthen Hall Lane" street sign on the north side of the road (there is a minor crossroads at this point and the road changes direction to resume its southwest/northeast direction).

The surviving section of stonework from the cross-shaft stands 32 Ins/81 Cms H by 11 Ins/27 Cms square. It stands on a solid, squat plinth, 19 Ins/48 Cms H by 25 Ins/63 Cms square. The cross-shaft leans slightly to the east and is very weathered with no trace of decoration surviving on any of its sides (the graffiti is not too intrusive). There is no identifying plaque or any other indication of what the cross-shaft commemorates.

Once recognised the cross-shaft can be definitively identified. The Ordnance Survey maps do not give the correct indication of the location of the cross-shaft; it is on the east side of the road and not on the south side of Morthen Hall Lane.

MORTHEN: An Anglo-Saxon Cross-Shaft. This cross-shaft commemorates King Athelstan's victory at the Battle of Brunanburh in 937.

Local sources indicate that the cross-shaft commemorates the battle of Brunanburh in 937 when King Athelstan defeated a combined Norse, Danish, Scottish and Welsh army and so became the first King of All England. The later stages of the battle took place in the vicinity of Morthen.

ROTHERHAM
(1) All Saints Church
SK 428928   Rating: ☆

In the centre of Rotherham and situated on a knoll, All Saints Church, with its distinctive tall spire, is easily located on the south-west side of "All Saints Square" and on the east side of "Church Street" (there are street signs).

A church was first founded on this site in 937. This church was replaced in the late 11C and was itself replaced by the present structure dating mainly from the 15C. The church was restored in 1873-75.

In the south-west part of the church there is an informative permanent exhibition on the history of the parish. The exhibition explains there is an A-S door jamb under the north-west pier of the tower and that the present chancel now covers the site of the A-S church.

Internally there are no A-S remains discernible in the chancel. However, the A-S door jamb referred to in the exhibition is separate from the present chancel. This door jamb is incorporated into the fabric of the north face of the north-west pier of the tower. It is situated at floor level, 16 Ins/40 Cms west of the north-east corner of the pier. The doorjamb measures 5 Ins/12 Cms H by 22 Ins/55 Cms W. The door jamb is an inverted trapezium in shape and it appears decorated with "herring-bone" type decoration. It certainly does look different from the surrounding stonework.

Internally, there is part of what is described as an A-S coffin lid. It has been incorporated into the west wall of the north aisle, in the northwest corner of the north aisle, and 36 Ins/91 Cms up from the floor. The coffin lid measures 8 Ins/20 Cms H by 28 Ins/71 Cms W. It is decorated with a sword. It is debatable whether this coffin lid is A-S; it appears to be later medieval.

ROTHERHAM
(2) Clifton Park Museum
SK 435927   Rating: ✰✰✰

The Museum is located about 300 Yds/274 M to the south-east of the central part of Rotherham. The building housing the Museum is situated within "Clifton Park". Clifton Park is situated adjacent to the east side of "Clifton Lane" (there are street signs).

In the flowerbeds on the north side of the entrance drive leading to the Museum, there is a free-standing notice "Clifton Park and Museum". The building housing the Museum is 30 Yds/27 M away from Clifton Lane and is easily identified. (By the Museum entrance, attached to the walling, there is a "Clifton Park Museum" etc notice.)

As with all museums, the displays and the exhibits they contain may be changed, re-sited, removed from display and/or put in store, or loaned to other museums or suitable repositories. Before visiting the museum it is worth checking in advance whether the displays listed in the text below are still in place in the same location(s) set out in the text. Individual exhibits may have been rearranged in terms of their display, the order in which they are displayed and their relationship to other exhibits, some exhibits may have been removed from display. The text in the entry reflects the descriptions and/or accompanying notices to the exhibits at the time of visiting. These too may have been revised, amended, added to or removed.

The Museum is housed in the home built for the Rotherham ironmaster Joshua Walker in 1783. The interior of the house retains much of its original decoration and has been little altered. Currently the Museum contains examples of Rockingham Porcelain and Swinton Pottery and other exhibits and displays relating to the social history of the area.

The Museum also has amongst its collections and now in reserve:

1.   An excellent example of a 10C Viking gold ring.

2.   A 9C Viking brooch.

3.   16 silver penny coins from the reign of Harold II (other Harold II coins are now in the British Museum in London).

4.   A sceat from the reign of Æthelred II of Northumbria (854-862).

5.   A silver penny from the reign of Edward the Confessor (1042-1066).

These pieces and some of the coins can now be viewed by contacting: The Museums, Heritage & Promotions Manager, Clifton Park Museum, Clifton Lane, Rotherham, South Yorkshire, S65 2AA.

ROYSTON
Kirk Cross
SE 363106   Rating: ☆

On the southern edge of Royston, there is an easy-to-identify section of stonework from an A-S cross-shaft standing on a plinth. It is situated on the west side of the B6132 standing on a sizeable grass verge. The section of stonework is 8 Yds/7 M west of the B6132, "Royston Lane" (there is a street sign affixed to the first floor of the nearby end house), and 5 Yds/4 M from the south side of "Kirk Cross Cres" (Crescent) (there is a street sign).

The section of stonework measures 22 Ins/55 Cms H by 11 Ins/27 Cms square. It stands on a tapered plinth 22 Ins/55 Cms H by 33 Ins/83 Cms square. The section of stonework is weathered and damaged and there is no decoration on any of its sides. There may be an A-S church in the vicinity but this could only be proved by excavation.

SHEFFIELD
(1) Millennium Galleries
SK 355870   Rating: ☆☆

The Millennium Galleries are easily located in the centre of Sheffield on the west side of the A621 (known as "Arundel Gate" – there are no street signs). Opposite Sheffield Hallam University, the Millennium Galleries are located in a modern building built mainly in glass and white concrete.

As with all museums, the displays and the exhibits they contain may be changed, re-sited, removed from display and/or put in store, or loaned to other museums or suitable repositories. Before visiting the museum it is worth checking in advance whether the displays listed in the text below are still in place in the same location(s) set out in the text. Individual exhibits may have been rearranged in terms of their display, the order in which they are displayed and their relationship to other exhibits, some exhibits may have been removed from display. The text in the entry reflects the descriptions and/or accompanying notices to the exhibits at the time of visiting. These too may have been revised, amended, added to or removed.

The Galleries concentrate on the visual arts, craft and design in Sheffield and includes a Special Exhibition Gallery. Included among the displays in the Metalwork Gallery, there is an A-S gold and garnet pendant from Womersley, West Yorkshire.

SHEFFIELD
(2) Weston Park Museum
SK 339873   Rating: ★☆☆☆☆

The Museum is located on the western side of the centre of Sheffield. It is set back from the north side of the A57 (known as "Western Bank" – there are no street signs) about 700 Yds/640 M west of the junction of the A57 and the A61 (there is a street sign "Brook Hill" at the junction). The Museum is located close to a large number of university and hospital buildings and is situated immediately to the west of a public park (Weston Park). The appropriate building housing the Museum has the words "City Museum" incised above the portal to its impressive entrance.

As with all museums, the displays and the exhibits they contain may be changed, re-sited, removed from display and/or put in store, or loaned to other museums or suitable repositories. Before visiting the museum it is worth checking in advance whether the displays listed in the text below are still in place in the same location(s) set out in the text. Individual exhibits may have been rearranged in terms of their display, the order in which they are displayed and their relationship to other exhibits, some exhibits may have been removed from display. The text in the entry reflects the descriptions and/or accompanying notices to the exhibits at the time of visiting. These too may have been revised, amended, added to or removed.

The Museum displays Sheffield metal ware, cutlery, natural history, geology, archaeology and ethnology. The items of A-S interest are located in the "Sheffield Life and Times" display. These are:

1.   The Benty Grange Helmet capped with its distinctive boar. The 7C Benty Grange helmet belonged to a princely warrior of the Pecsætan (the Peak-dwellers). The boar was a symbol of strength associated with the god Frey(a). It was found under an earth mound in a barrow only 24 Ins/60 Cms H at its highest point.

2.   A modern reconstruction of the Benty Grange helmet.

3.   Cup fittings from a cup made of wood or horn rather than leather from Benty Grange. These comprise silver bindings and ornaments decorated with four wheel-shaped pieces and two small crosses of silver affixed by pins.

4.   A modern reconstruction of the cup with silver fittings from Benty Grange.

5.   Fragments from a silver enamelled escutcheon from a hanging bowl from Benty Grange. They are decorated with a combination of spiral designs and stylised animal heads.

6.   A selection of glass beads from sites in the Peak District.

7.   One shield boss and handle grip from Hilton, Derbyshire.

8.   A knife, a spearhead, a silver strap end, a gold encased beaver toothed pendant (a similar pendant also found at the same site is now in the British Museum), a comb fragment with decoration, and a rock crystal ball used as a good luck charm retrieved, all from the excavations of a Bronze Age cairn at Wigber Low, near Kniveton, Ashbourne, Derbyshire. The cairn was reused in the 7C. These excavations revealed a total of seven burials involving nine individuals. The burials were made in a burial pit beneath the cairn and the finds included human skeletal remains, their weapons, tools and ornaments.

9.   A restored bronze hanging bowl found at Grindlow barrow in Derbyshire.

10.   An escutcheon from a hanging bowl found at Middleton Moor, Derbyshire.

11.   A 7C gold cross probably part of a pendant and a mid 7C gold disc from White Low, near Winster, Derbyshire.

12.   A late 7C gold and garnet necklace from Galley Low, Derbyshire.

13.   Linked pins, silver beads and a glass bowl from Cow Low, Derbyshire.

14.   A 9C sword found in the River Witham. The hilt and pommel are decorated with silver strips incised with animal designs.

15.   A circular escutcheon from a hanging bowl found at the excavations of medieval farm buildings at Roystone Grange. It is decorated with a combination of spiral designs and stylised animal heads.

16.   A replica of the section of stonework from cross-shaft known as the "Sheffield Cross". It stands 60¼ Ins/153 Cms H. On one face it is decorated with vine scroll design that includes an archer, holding a bow and arrow, dressed in ordinary clothing rather than the more usual traditional drapery. The other face is undecorated since the other face of the original was hollowed out so that it could be used as a trough. The two other sides are decorated with vine scroll design. (The original is in the British Museum in London and dates from the early 9C. It measures 60¼ Ins/153 Cms H, by 24 Ins/60 Cms W, by 12 Ins/30 Cms D.)

Other items of A-S/Viking interest are retained in store in the Museum. These include: cruciform and penannular brooches, necklaces, clasp and rings, pins, spearheads, swords, iron fittings from a wooden bed, a 10C/11C hog-back tombstone, a section of stonework from a 10C cross-shaft, a grave slab incised with runes "(orat) e pro Helg (a)" meaning "pray for Helga" and silver pennies of Alfred the Great (871-899), Sievert Siefred (877-894), Edward the Elder (899-924), Cnut (1016-1035).

SPROTBROUGH
St Mary's Church
SE 539020   Rating: ★★

The church is located in almost the centre of the southern part of Sprotbrough. It is situated adjacent to the south side of "Main Street" about 50 Yds/45 M east of its junction with "Boat Lane" (there are street signs).

The present structure dates mainly from 1170, the late 13C, 14C and 15C. It is possible that an A-S church existed on the site.

Externally, there is a section of stonework from an A-S cross-shaft incorporated into the fabric of the church. It is located on the east face of a buttress 27 Ins/68 Cms west of a blocked doorway into the south side of the chancel. It is 4½ Ins/11 Cms south of south wall of the chancel and 26 Ins/66 Cms up from the ground. The section of cross-shaft measures 4 Ins/10 Cms H by 11½ Ins/29 Cms W. It is decorated with scroll design and dates from the 11C.

THRYBERGH
(1) St Leonard's Church
SK 467955   Rating: ☆☆

In the northern part of Thryburgh, St Leonard's Church is located on the west side of the A630(T) where there is a partly concealed drive to the church about 70 Yds/64 M north of the junction on the east side of the A630(T), "Doncaster Road", and "School Lane" (there are street signs). On the west side of the entrance to the drive, attached to the top of the associated walling, there is a large "St Leonard's Church Thrybergh" directional sign, underneath which there is a notice about the times of the church services.

Proceed in a westerly direction along the drive towards the church, passing through a gate on the way – at this point the drive becomes more of a pathway. The church is about 100 Yds/91 M west of the A630(T).

The surviving fabric of the church dates mainly from 14C and 15C although there is also material from the 12C.

The churchyard contains a distinctive, decorated section of stonework from an A-S cross-shaft although it might be of later date but in the A-S style. It is situated 74 Yds/67 M west of the A630(T) and 26 Yds/23 M from the east end of the church. It is 5 Yds/4 M south of the pathway that leads up to the church, and 34½ Ins/87 Cms west of some nearby walling. It stands under a tree.

The section of stonework measures 52 Ins/132 Cms H, by 13 Ins/33 Cms W, by 9 Ins/22 Cms D. It stands on a plinth that measures 9½ Ins/24 Cms H, by 34 Ins/86 Cms W, by 30 Ins/76 Cms D.

The lower half of the west side of the section of stonework is decorated with the head and torso of a saint (in bas relief). On the top half of the west side there is clearly a four-legged animal above which there is the lower half of a human body with legs and feet – some imagination has to be used. The north and south sides are decorated with circular interlace design. The east side has some decoration but due to weathering the design cannot now be identified. Unfortunately the section of stonework is heavily weathered and needs protection from the elements.

THRYBERGH
(2) Anglo-Saxon Cross-shaft
SK 468954   Rating: ☆☆

In the northern part of Thryburgh, turn east side off the A630(T), "Doncaster Road", and proceed along "School Lane" (there are street signs). After 37 Yds/33 M turn off School Lane and head north along "Three Hills Close" (there is a street sign). The section of stonework from an A-S cross-shaft is easily identified standing on a paved area by the east side of Three Hills Close 46 Yds/42 M from its junction with School Lane.

The section of stonework itself stands within a distinctive surrounding framework of stonework that measures between 2¼ Ins/5 Cms to 4½ Ins/11 Cms H, by 47 Ins/119 Cms W, by 33 Ins/83 Cms D.

The section of stonework measures 44½ Ins/113 Cms H, tapering 14½ Ins/36 Cms to 7½ Ins/19 Cms W, tapering 10 Ins/25 Cms to 9½ Ins/24 Cms D. The top has a tenon so that the next section of cross-shaft can be joined on. The west face is decorated with vine scroll design. No other decoration can now be identified on any of the other sides due to weathering. However, on each of the four corners, the stonework has been alternately cut and left to provide consistently spaced and sized protruding pieces of stonework.

West Yorkshire

In West Yorkshire 47 sites of Anglo-Saxon/Viking interested have been entered in the text.

11 sites have been rated with one star ☆

This signifies that the material may be difficult to find or identify with confidence. These entries are:

Birstall – St Peter's Church
Bramham – All Saints Church
Darrington – St Luke and All Saints Church
Kirkheaton – St John the Baptist Church
Normanton – All Saints Church
Sandal Magna – St Helen's Church
South Kirkby – All Saints Church
Swillington – St Mary's Church
Thorp Arch – All Saints Church
Wakefield – Cathedral
Woodkirk – St Mary's Church

9 sites have been rated with two stars ☆☆

This signifies that the material can be found and identified but it is not particularly well looked after or a "good example". These entries are:

Aberford – St Ricarius Church
Adel – St John the Baptist's Church
Bradford – Cathedral
Calverley – St Wilfred's Church
Guiseley – St Oswald's Church
Keighley – Castle Cliffe Museum
Rastrick – St Matthew's Church
Shore – Crosshead and Cross-shaft
Wakefield – Museum

11 sites have been rated with three stars ☆☆☆

This signifies that the material can easily be found and identified. These entries are:

Barwick-In-Elmet – All Saints Church
Crofton – All Saints Church
Harewood – All Saints Church
Ilkley – Manor House Museum
Kippax – St Mary's Church
Kirkburton – All Hallows Church
Leeds – Royal Armouries Museum
Mirfield – St Mary's Church
Riddlesden – East Riddlesden Hall
Skelmanthorpe – St Aidan's Church
[See also the entry in private ownership after the star rating index.]

7 sites have been rated with four stars ☆☆☆☆

This signifies that material can easily be found and identified, and provides good examples. These entries are:

Addingham – St Peter's Church
Bingley – All Saints Church
Huddersfield – Tolson Museum
Otley – All Saints Church
Otley – Museum
Pontefract – Anglo-Saxon Church
Rothwell – Holy Trinity Church

9 sites have been rated with five stars ☆☆☆☆☆

This signifies that material can easily be found and identified, providing excellent examples that are full of interest. These entries are:

Bardsey – All Hallows Church
Collingham – St Oswald's Church
Dewsbury – The Minster Church of All Saints (includes a Heritage
    Centre area)
Hartshead – Walton Cross
Ilkley – All Saints Church
Ledsham – All Saints Church
Leeds – City Museum
Leeds – St Peter's Parish Church
Thornhill (Near Dewsbury) – St Michael and All Angels Church

ANGLO-SAXON STONEWORK IN PRIVATE OWNERSHIP (NO ACCESS)

Section of stonework from an A-S cross-shaft   Rating: ☆☆☆

The section of stonework from a 10C A-S cross-shaft measures 16 Ins/40 Cms H, by 13 Ins/33 Cms W, by 7½ Ins/19 Cms D. It is decorated on one of the faces with most of an animal, minus its neck. On the other face it is decorated with cable design. On one of the (narrower) sides is decorated with three panels each containing what appears to be a bird (the third, top, panel is mostly missing). The other (narrower) side is decorated with cable design.

ABERFORD
St Ricarius Church

SE 434372   Rating: ★★   Access is possible.

In the centre of Aberford, the church is easily located on the west side of the road that runs north/south through Aberford (there are no street signs in the vicinity of the church). There is a freestanding church notice board behind the churchyard wall.

On the site of an A-S church, the present structure dates mainly from 1861 although there is some 12C and 13C material.

Internally, on the window ledge at the west end of the south aisle, there are five sections of assorted stonework (the largest has been broken in two):

1.   A section of stonework from a 10C A-S cross-shaft broken in two but placed back together. It is the section closest to the south end of the window ledge and measures 10 Ins/25 Cms H (W), by 23 Ins/58 Cms W (H), by 8 Ins/20 Cms D. It is decorated with interlace design on all four sides despite weathering and damage.

2.   A section of stonework comprising the central section and lower vertical arm of a 10C A-S crosshead with a section of stonework from its cross-shaft attached. It is the section of stonework next to "1" above (to the north) occupying the middle and most of the northern part of the window ledge. They measure in total 10 Ins/25 Cms H (W), by 18 Ins/45 Cms W (H), by 6 Ins/15 Cms D. Both the east and west sides of the section of stonework from the crosshead are decorated with a central circle with parallel lines extending in the shape of a cross towards the end of each arm. These lines terminate in a cross-enclosed in a circle, as can be seen from the complete vertical arm that connects the crosshead to the cross-shaft. There is no decoration on the other sides of the section of stonework from the crosshead due to damage. The section of stonework from the cross-shaft is decorated with interlace design on all four sides.

3.   A section of stonework comprising most of an arm from a 10C A-S crosshead. It is the section of stonework next to "2" above (to the north) occupying the northern end of the window ledge. The section of stonework measures 12 Ins/30 Cms (maximum) H(W), by 8 Ins/20 Cms W(H), by 6 Ins/15 Cms D. It is decorated with interlace design on its north-west and south-east sides. It is too weathered and damaged for any decoration to survive on the end of the arm.

(There are also two later sections of stonework, not A-S, on the window ledge in front (to the east) of the A-S sections of stonework.)

The church guide refers to the Battle of Winwaed fought between King Penda of Mercia and King Oswiu of Bernica on 15 November 655. Penda was defeated and killed and many of his army were drowned in the River Cock. Whilst the Cock Beck does run through Aberford, and it may have well run red with blood after the battle, the site of the battle itself, although open to conjecture, is likely to have been fought to the west in the Stanks/Seacroft area of Leeds.

ADDINGHAM
St Peter's Church

SE 085497   Rating: ☆☆☆☆   Access is possible.

The church is located on the eastern edge of Addingham close to the west bank of the River Wharfe. Turn off the A65 (T) as indicated by the directional sign "Grassington 13, Burnsall 9, Addingham ½, Bolton Abbey 3" and proceed along a minor road (there is no street sign) to approach Addingham from a south-easterly direction. After about 1600 Yds/1463 M, there is in the grass verge on the south side of the road and by a road junction, there is a directional sign indicating "Bolton Abbey 3, Burnsall 9, Grassington 13". Beneath this sign there is a separate "Parish Church" directional sign. Turn off this minor road and proceed as indicated by these directional signs and head in a northerly direction along "Church St." (there is a street sign).

After about 300 Yds/274 M, turn off Church Street as indicated by another "Parish Church" directional sign and head in a north-easterly direction along a winding driveway. In front of the walling by the east side of the entrance to this driveway there is a freestanding church notice. The Church is about 150 Yds/137 M away from Church Street.

The present church mostly dates from 1757 but the surviving fabric includes 15C material. There probably was an earlier A-S church on or close to the site of the present church.

Internally, there is a section of stonework from a late 9C cross-shaft. It is located affixed to the north wall of the north aisle 60 Ins/152 Cms west of the easternmost window in the north aisle (this is the window behind, to the north of, the organ). The section of stonework is supported by a floor-standing iron frame that stands 17 Ins/43 Cms H. The section of stonework stands 40½ Ins/102 Cms H, tapering 15 Ins/38 Cms to 6 Ins/15 Cms W, by 4½ Ins/11 Cms D. It is decorated on its south face with two figures, a cross in a circular surround, and vine scroll pattern. The east and west sides are both decorated with vine scroll pattern. The north face cannot now be viewed but it is apparently decorated with vine scroll design according to the descriptive notice attached nearby to the north wall of the north aisle. This notice also says the decoration on the south face represents the apocalypse.

The church also has in its possession a small Viking Age case that is not currently displayed. This decorated case may have been intended to house a comb. The case is made from bone and is now in two pieces in total measuring about 3½ Ins/8 Cms L.

In the churchyard there is an A-S cross base with a large, distinctive slot for the base of the cross-shaft that it supports. It is located 31 Yds/28 M from the east of the east end of the church, 99 Ins/251 Cms south of the pathway that runs south of the church in the churchyard (15 Ins/38 Cms west of the table tomb to Sarah Hodgson died 1812 18 March). The cross base measures 12½ Ins/31 Cms H, by 27 Ins/68 Cms W, by 13½ Ins/34 Cms D. It is too weathered for any decoration to survive on any of the sides.

The site of an A-S cemetery is located outside the church, and to the west of the churchyard wall. The church hall and car park and the platform of land on which they stand cover the site. When excavated the cemetery revealed several burials and, following analysis, the bones discovered will be re-buried. The bones date from the 9C and it is hoped the research analysts will discover whether the people buried met a violent death since the Vikings were known to be in the area at the time. Due to the unrest Archbishop Wulfhere of York fled to Addingham in 867 for safety.

ADEL
St John the Baptist Church
SE 275403   Rating: ☆☆

The church is located on the northern edge of Adel on the east side of "Church Lane" (there are street signs). Enter the churchyard from the "west gate" entrance (there is a large free-standing church notice board behind the nearby walling).

In the churchyard there are a number of distinctive sections of stonework of various ages and uses. These are located just inside the churchyard from the west gate entrance, on the south side of the footpath, and placed on the grass.

There is a complete A-S coffin and coffin lid placed alongside each other 14 Yds/12 M from this entrance gate. This coffin is A-S rather than Norman because, unlike the two Norman coffins also displayed in the vicinity, it has no carved-out head section. The A-S coffin measures 74 Ins/188 Cms L, by 17 Ins/43 Cms H and its width tapers from 27 Ins/68 Cms to 22 Ins/55 Cms. The coffin lid has similar dimensions apart from its 5 inch/12 Cms H.

Also among these sections of stonework, there is a section of stonework on whose north face there is a carving resembling a Maltese/"St Cuthbert-style" cross. It is located 6 Ins/15 Cms north of the nearby churchyard wall, and 110 Ins/279 Cms south of the medieval coffin nearest to the A-S coffin. This section of stonework measures 12 Ins/30 Cms H, by 16 Ins/40 Cms W, by 7 Ins/17 Cms D. It is partially obscured by vegetation and there is a substantial part of a medieval grave cover lying flat on the ground in front (to the north) of it (at its nearest 4 Ins/10 Cms away). There are also various other sections of assorted stonework in close proximity.

The present church on this site mostly dates from 1150. The church is famous for its sculptured south porch and chancel arch both of which date from around 1160. A-S stonework has been incorporated into the foundations of the present church although it cannot now be identified.

BARDSEY
All Hallow's Church
SE 365431   Rating: ☆☆☆☆☆

The church is easily located in the centre of Bardsey. It is situated set back from the south side of "Church Lane" (there are street signs).

Despite 12C, 14C, 16C, 18C and 19C additions and alterations to the church, extensive 9C A-S material survives in the tower, and the south and west walls of the nave. Apart from the 14C battlements and the 9C lower stages, the remainder of the tower dates from the 11C.

Internally, and now enclosed at the west end of both the north and south aisles, A-S fabric and an A-S window 108 Ins/274 Cms above each of the later inserted doors, can be easily identified surviving in the north and south walls of the tower (formerly part of the 9C A-S porch).

Internally, the line of the A-S nave roof line can be identified in the east face of the east wall of the tower (the lower of the two lines visible) and also in the east face of the west wall of the chancel.

Internally, the fabric immediately above the later inserted arches in the north and south walls of the nave, above the later inserted arch in the tower, and above the later inserted chancel arch, is all A-S in origin.

Internally, and although not that easy to identify, the position of a blocked-up A-S window is indicated by the irregular stonework on the south face of the north wall of the nave, above the westernmost arch.

Internally, large side, alternate quoining from the A-S church survives at the north-west and south-west corners of the nave – this can be seen at the west end of both the north and south aisles. The quoining in the southeast corner of the nave, and viewed from inside the vestry, is not so well-defined, and the quoining in the north-east corner of the nave is even less well-defined.

Internally, on steps at the east end of the north aisle, there are a number of sections of stonework that appear to be of a later medieval date.

The lower stages of the tower originally formed part of a porch dating from the 9C, which, in the 10C, was incorporated into a new west tower. The tower now has A-S double belfry windows in the south face at the second and third stages and single windows on the east face (windows on the west and north faces do not appear to be A-S). Interestingly, it is clear from the external fabric of the tower that the quoining of the 9C porch was much larger than the quoining of the 11C – this can be seen on looking at the external former north-west and south-west corners of the tower.

Externally, the line of the roof of the 9C porch can be identified about 72 Ins/182 Cms above the top of the window inserted in the 15C into the west wall of the tower.

BARWICK-IN-ELMET
All Saints Church

SE 401374   Rating: ☆☆☆   Access is possible.

Near the eastern end of Barwick, the church is situated between the junction of "Potterton Lane" and "Aberford Road" (there are street signs). It is on the north side of Abberford Road and the south side of Potterton Lane.

The present church dates mostly from the 14C.

Internally, there are:

1.   A section of stonework from an A-S cross-shaft. It is located in the south aisle standing on small fragments of unrelated stonework that sit on the floor. The section of stonework is 154 Ins/391 Cms west of the east end of the south aisle and 12 Ins/30 Cms north of the south wall of the south aisle. The section of stonework from the cross-shaft measures 29½ Ins/74 Cms H, tapering 14½ Ins/36 Cms to 13½ Ins/34 Cms W, by 8 Ins/20 Cms D. Although weathered it is decorated with interlace, just possibly Ringerike design, on all four sides.

2.   A section of stonework from an A-S cross-shaft. It is located in the south aisle standing on small fragments of unrelated stonework that sit on the floor. The section of stonework is 169 Ins/429 Cms west of the east end of the south aisle and 9 Ins/22 Cms north of the south wall of the south aisle. The section of stonework from the cross-shaft measures 28 Ins/71 Cms H, by 22¾ Ins/57 Cms W, and between 10 Ins/25 Cms and 11 Ins/27 Cms D. Although weathered it is decorated on its north

side with the figure of Christ (without the head) giving a blessing to two complete figures below. (His hands are placed upon their heads). The figure of Christ is twice the height of the other two figures. The south side is decorated with vine scroll and "tree of life" design, the west side is decorated with vine scroll and interlace design. On the east side any decoration has been removed when it was rendered.

There is a large information notice entitled "Saxon History" attached to the south wall of the south aisle above these sections of stonework from cross-shafts. The notice records the details of these two sections of stonework from 11C A-S decorated cross-shafts. Both sections of stonework were recovered in 1900, one from outside the east end of the north aisle, and the other from inside the west end of the south aisle wall.

BINGLEY
All Saints Church

SE 105395   Rating: ☆☆☆☆

On the western edge of Bingley, the church is easily located set back from the west side of the A650. Behind the low churchyard wall there is a taller free-standing "All Saints, Bingley" church notice.

The present structure dates from the 13C although most of the surviving fabric dates from the 15C. There were further alterations in the 16C, 18C and 19C.

Internally, there is an 8C A-S font. It is located sitting on top of a 23 inch/58 Cms H octagonal plinth which itself stands on an 8 inch/20 Cms H plinth abutting the westernmost pillar on the north side of the nave. The font measures about 30 Ins/76 Cms square and is about 13 Ins/33 Cms H. It is weathered and uneven. However, on its eastern face there is a discernible runic inscription whose interpretation has not yet been definitively established. The present interpretation is considered "Eadbierht, King, hote (ordered) to hew this dipstone (font) for us, bid (pray) for his soul". Ring work decoration can be identified on the other three sides of the font, the west and south sides being the better preserved.

Internally, there is a section of stonework from an A-S cross-shaft. It is located resting on a bracket affixed to the westernmost pillar on the north side of the nave, some 14 Ins/35 Cms above the top of the A-S font. The section of stonework measures 16 Ins/40 Cms H, tapering 9 Ins/22 Cms to 1 inch/2 Cms D (W), by 4½ Ins/11 Cms W (D). The east side and the north face are clearly decorated with interlace design. Although much more damaged and weathered, there is some decoration, probably interlace design, on both the south face and west side.

BIRSTALL
St Peter's Chuch

SE 218262   Rating: ✩✩   Access is possible.

The church is located in the south-western part of Birstall. At the more northerly junction of the A652 and the A643, "Kirkgate" (there are street signs), turn off the A652 as directed by the "St Peter's Parish Church" sign. Proceed down the part of Kirkgate that runs in a south-westerly direction (on this side of the road there is one street sign) – it is no longer the A643. The church is easily located on the south side of Kirkgate about 130 Yds/118 M south-west of the A652.

Most of the present structure of the church dates from 1863-70 although some 12C material does survive.

Internally, there is a section of stonework from an 11C A-S cross-base. It is located lying flat on the floor, about 13 Ins/33 Cms from the east wall of the north aisle. The section of stonework measures 20 Ins/50 Cms L(H), by 19 Ins/48 Cms W, by 7 Ins/17 Cms H (D). It is decorated with circular motifs, in what is a key pattern design. This section of stonework is surrounded by other miscellaneous sections of stonework of varying antiquity, none of which are A-S.

BRADFORD
Cathedral

SE 166333   Rating: ✩✩✩

The Cathedral is situated in the centre of Bradford on the north side of the A658, "Church Bank" (there are street signs), 60 Yds/54 M east of "Forster Sq." (Square) (there are street signs). (At Forster Square there are also "Cathedral" directional signs pointing towards Church Bank.)

On the north side of Church Bank there is an open, gated entrance. Attached to the adjacent walling on the east side of this entrance there is a notice board: "The Cathedral Church of Saint Peter, Bradford". Pass through this entrance, up steps, and continue around the exterior of the Cathedral for about 110 Yds/100 M as directed to the "Main" entrance located on the north side of the building.

In 1327 Scottish raiders burned down an earlier church on this site. The church also figured in the defence of Bradford during the Civil War when the Royalists besieged the town in 1642 and 1643. The Cathedral contains fabric from the 14C, 15C, 18C and 19C. When the church became a cathedral in 1919 further extensions and alterations were made periodically up until 1987.

Internally, there is a section of stonework from a 10C A-S cross-shaft. It has been incorporated into the fabric of the north wall in what is known as the "north ambulatory" (behind the organ). There is a notice about this section of stonework attached to the adjacent walling. It is 60 Ins/152 Cms east of the nearby step up to the north ambulatory from the north aisle and 58 Ins/147 Cms up from the floor. The section of stonework measures 13 Ins/33 Cms by 10 Ins/25 Cms. It is decorated with knot work pattern.

Internally, there is another section of stonework from a 10C A-S cross-shaft near the entrance to St Aidan's Chapel. St Aidan's Chapel is some 10 Yds/9 M north of the altar in the chancel. The section of stonework is incorporated into walling 28 Ins/71 Cms west of the entrance to St Aidan's Chapel. This section of walling, which runs in a north/south direction, has three sections of obviously "old" stonework. These comprise: part of an A-S cross-shaft, a medieval piscina, and part of a medieval grave cover (female, with shears).

The section of stonework from an A-S cross-shaft is the most southerly of these three sections of stonework, i.e., the section of stonework under 20 Ins/50 Cms above the nearest step and next to the adjacent pillar. It has been set into a niche at an angle to display its width (9 Ins/22 Cms) and its depth (4 Ins/10 Cms). It is about 10 Ins/25 Cms H and is clearly decorated with knot work pattern.

BRAMHAM
All Saints Church

SE 427430 Rating: ☆☆ Access is possible.

The church, with its distinctive tower and short steeple, can easily be identified in the central, eastern part of Bramham. The church sits at the western end of an unusually-shaped oval churchyard. The nearest churchyard entrance is located at the junction of "Vicarage Lane", "Church Hill", "Low Way", "New Road" and "Back Lane" (there are street signs but those for Church Hill and New Road are not at the junction by the church).

The oval shape of the churchyard is explained by the recorded history that there was a mid 7C A-S monastery on this site following the Celtic monastic arrangements. It is believed that the site of this monastery was in the centre of the present churchyard, to the east of the church, possibly at the "highest" point in the footpath running roughly west/east through the churchyard where there is a small ridge. (There is no commemoration of the site. An A-D ivory bodkin discovered on the site is now in the possession of Leeds City Museum – see the entry for Leeds, West Yorkshire.)

The present church on the site mostly dates from the 12C, 13C, 14C and the restoration in 1853.

Internally, an A-S quoin has been incorporated into the newer fabric of the church – it may well be in its original position. It is located inside the stair turret attached to the tower, 30 Ins/76 Cms up from the second step up. The quoin is in an upright position and measures 24 Ins/61 Cms H by 7 Ins/17 Cms W. There may be other A-S quoins surviving but these are obscured by cement and restoration stonework.

Internally in the main body of the church, although the nave walls above the arcades are undoubtedly thin and suggestive of A-S origin, there is no discernible proof of surviving A-S fabric since the walls are plastered on both sides and so hide any confirming features.

Externally, the lower stages of the tower may incorporate A-S material. In particular the southern face up to the first three stages and the lowest, narrow window with its moulded top arch.

Externally, large A-S quoins have been reused in the north-east and south-east corners of the chancel (the south-east corner has the better examples).

CALVERLEY
St Wilfred's Church

SE 208372   Rating: ★★   Access is possible.

On the north-eastern edge of Calverley, St Wilfred's Church is easily identified set back from the east side of the A657. Behind the churchyard wall there are free-standing "Calverley Parish Church" notice boards that can be seen from the A657.

The present church dates from 1150 with additions and alterations in the 14C, 15C, 16C. It was restored in 1844 and 1869.

Internally, the nave walls apparently contain A-S material but this is difficult to identify with certainty because when the covering plasterwork was removed in the 1870s the stonework was left with a scouring design caused by chiselling.

However, internally, there is the top and west side of a blocked A-S window. It has been incorporated into the south wall of the nave, on the western side of the second arch west of the chancel. It can easily be identified.

Internally, there are seven large sections of stonework from grave slabs. These have been affixed to the east face of the west wall under the tower, and placed on a step. Of these sections of stonework:

1.   A section of A-S stonework. It is the southernmost section of stonework. It measures 65 Ins/165 Cms H, by 19 Ins/48 Cms W, by 3 Ins/7 Cms D and is incised with a cross with a long shaft design (this can still be seen despite weathering).

2.   A section of stonework that may be A-S. It is northernmost section of stonework, the one standing on top of another. This possible section of A-S stonework has been broken in two and put back together – there is a large hole near the top. It measures 36 Ins/91 Cms H, tapering 16 Ins/40 Cms to 9 Ins/22 Cms W, by 4 Ins/10 Cms D. It is incised with a circular design above a long shaft.

Externally, there are three slabs of ancient stonework. These have been incorporated into the fabric of the north wall of the north aisle, and immediately below the guttering. They are:

3.   A section of 14C stonework. It is located midway between the westernmost windows. This section of stonework is decorated with a foliated stem.

4.   A section of A-S stonework. It is located midway between the two windows, second and third farthest from the west end of the north aisle. The cross measures 12 Ins/30 Cms both in height and width. This section of stonework is clearly decorated with a cross within a circle: the eastern arm of the cross and the eastern arch of the accompanying circle have clearly been truncated to fit into the surrounding stonework.

5.   A section of A-S stonework. It is located midway between the two windows, third and fourth farthest from the west end of the north aisle, and immediately to the east of a vertical drainpipe. This section of stonework measures 12 Ins/30 Cms both in height and width. It is decorated with a cross with four little balls in the arms.

COLLINGHAM
St Oswald's Church

SE 389461   Rating: ✰✰✰✰✰   Access is possible.

The church is located on the northern edge of Collingham some 50 Yds/45 M north of the A58(T). To reach the church turn north of the A58(T) and proceed along "Church Lane" (there are street signs). The church can easily be identified on the east side of Church Lane.

Despite the extensive restorations in the 1840s and in 1870, discernible traces of 11C A-S fabric survive.

Internally, A-S stonework may survive in the western walling of the chancel, but this cannot be identified with certainty.

Internally, there are two decorated sections of stonework from A-S cross-shafts in the northeast corner of the nave/the southeast part of the north aisle. These are:

1.   A section of stonework from a cross-shaft known as the "Apostles Stone" which dates from around 800. The Apostles Stone is the more northerly of the two sections of stonework from cross-shafts. It comprises two sections from the same cross-shaft now put correctly back together. It is located 7 Ins/17 Cms west of the easternmost pillar on the north side of the nave.

The Apostles Stone stands on a floor-standing stone plinth that measures 11½ Ins/29 Cms H, by 27¾ Ins/70 Cms W, by 18 Ins/45 Cms D. The Apostles Stone measures 44 Ins/111 Cms H, tapering 13½ Ins/34 Cms to 10½ Ins/26 Cms W, tapering 10 Ins/25 to Cms 7½ Ins/19 Cms D. On all four sides it is decorated with figures. These include Christ (the west face) and the Apostles in whole or in part. Where the stonework survives, the heads of the figures are enclosed under an arch. The west and east sides have larger figures than those on the north and south sides.

2.   A section of stonework from a cross-shaft known as the "Ærswith Cross" (Aerswith Cross) which dates from around 875. The Ærswith Cross is the more southerly of the two sections of stonework from cross-shafts. It comprises two sections from the same cross-shaft now put correctly back together. It is located 10½ Ins/26 Cms west of the easternmost pillar on the north side of the nave.

The Ærswith Cross stands on a floor-standing stone plinth that measures 5¾ Ins/14 Cms H, by 26 Ins/66 Cms W, by 18 Ins/45 Cms D. The Ærswith Cross measures 55¼ Ins/140 Cms H, tapering 11½ Ins/29 Cms to 10 Ins/25 Cms W, tapering 8 Ins/20 Cms to 6½ Ins/16 Cms D. On the west face it is clearly decorated with dragons and knot work design. Also on the west face there is a runic inscription 5 Ins/12 Cms up from the base of the lower section. The runes that can now be identified spell the name "ÆRSWITH". The east side is weathered and the decoration appears to include the depiction of a dragon and cable and knot work design similar to that on the better-preserved west face. The north and south sides are clearly decorated with knot work and cable design.

Internally, on the ledge of the window at the west end of the nave, there are five assorted sections of stonework.

3.   A broken section of stonework from a 10C A-S crosshead (two pieces of stonework from the same crosshead have now been placed back together). It is probably from the same crosshead identified at "4" and "5" below. This section of stonework is located lying flat on the ledge between 1 inch/2 Cms and 3 Ins/7 Cms north of the southern end of the window ledge. In total it measures 2¼ Ins/5 Cms H (D), by 10 Ins/25 Cms W (H),

and between 6 Ins/15 Cms and 9½ Ins/14 Cms D (W). On its top side it is decorated with the same cable design as "4" below. All the other sides are too weathered or damaged for any decoration to survive.

4.   A section of stonework from the same 10C A-S crosshead identified in "3" above and "5" below. It is located 17 Ins/43 Cms north of the southern end of the window ledge. The section of stonework measures between 7½ Ins/19 Cms to 9¾ Ins/24 Cms H (W), between 9½ Ins/24 Cms and 11 Ins/27 Cms W (H), by 4 Ins/10 Cms D. It is decorated with cable design on its east and south sides. There is a suggestion of similar decoration on the north side. The west side has been rendered, so no decoration survives.

5.   A section of stonework comprising part of an arm from the same 10C A-S crosshead identified in "3" and "4" above. It is located in the middle of the ledge 35 Ins/88 Cms north of the southern end of the window ledge. The section of stonework measures 15 Ins/38 Cms H (W), tapering 10 Ins/25 Cms to 8¼ Ins/20 Cms W (H), tapering 5½ Ins/13 Cms to 4½ Ins/11 Cms D. It is decorated with ring work design on the east and west sides. On the north and south sides it is decorated with a grid iron design.

6.   The next section of stonework to the north of "5" above is of later medieval origin and not A-S.

7.   A section of stonework comprising part an arm of a 10C A-S crosshead. It is located 4 Ins/10 Cms south of the northern end of the window ledge. The section of stonework measures between 3¼ Ins/8 Cms and 8 Ins/20 Cms H, by 8 Ins/20 Cms W, by 5½ Ins/13 Cms D. It is decorated with ring work design on the west and east sides. Due to weathering and damage there is no decoration that can now be identified on the other sides.

Externally, surviving A-S stonework can be identified in the south wall of the nave.

Externally, A-S quoining survives in the southwest and southeast corners of the nave although buttresses added later have obscured the quoining. Similar quoining apparently survives at the northeast angle of the nave, in the wall of the east side of the nave above the roof of the vestry (it is not easy to identify).

CROFTON
All Saints Church

SE 377182   Rating: ☆☆☆   Access is possible.

In the north-western part of Crofton, opposite where the "High Street" becomes "Harrison Road" (there are street signs), take the minor, no-through road which heads uphill in a north-easterly direction (there are no street signs). The church is at the eastern end of this road, about 45 Yds/41 M from the High Street.

The church mostly dates from the rebuilding around 1430 and the restoration in 1875 but it does also contain some 12C and 13C material.

Internally, there is a section of early 10C A-S stonework comprising what appears to be part of the lower arm from a crosshead and a section from its attached cross-shaft. It is located by the north wall of the north transept and 21 Ins/53 Cms west of the east wall of the north transept. It stands on a plinth 24 Ins/61 Cms H. This section of stonework measures 12 Ins/30 Cms H, by 9 Ins/22 Cms W, by 9 Ins/22 Cms D. On the south face it is decorated with the figure of a bishop carrying a cross and wearing an A-S style mitre. On the north face it is decorated with a figure upside down, a head with horns, supposedly the devil. The two other sides are too weathered for any decoration to survive.

Internally, there is a section of stonework from a late 9C cross-shaft. It is located standing on a ledge by the north wall of the north transept 24 Ins/61 Cms east of the west wall of the north transept. This section of stonework measures 24 Ins/61 Cms H, by 13 Ins/33 Cms W, by 7 Ins/17 Cms D. It is decorated with a broad interlace design on three sides. On the south face it is decorated with two griffins with crossed necks.

DARRINGTON

St Luke and All Saints Church

SE 485202   Rating: ☆   Access is possible.

In the centre of Darrington turn off the minor road "Estcourt Road" (there are street signs) which runs west/east through the village and head in a northerly direction along "Church Lane cul de sac" (there is a street sign). After about 80 Yds/73 M Church Lane ends at the gates on the south side of the churchyard.

On the site of an A-S church, most of the current structure dates from the 12C to 15C. It was restored in 1880.

Although the lower parts of the tower may contain A-S material this cannot be verified since externally the tower has undergone several alterations over succeeding centuries, and internally the stonework is mostly covered by plasterwork.

However, internally, there is a section of stonework comprising A-S square strip work. It is visible from the south aisle, protruding from the south face of the south wall of the tower and above the arch. It is easy to identify. The strip work measures 140 Ins/355 Cms L.

Internally, the present archway on the east side of the tower is narrow and high and no doubt resembles its A-S predecessor. Similarly, the nave is tall and relatively narrow, and it too may be A-S in origin but this cannot be verified with certainty since the stonework is covered with plasterwork.

DEWSBURY

The Minster Church of All Saints (Includes a Heritage Centre Area)

SE 245215   Rating: ☆☆☆☆☆   Access is possible.

In the southern part of the centre of Dewsbury look for directional signs that include "Minster". The Minster Church of All Saints is easily identified adjacent to the south side of the A644, "Vicarage Road" at its junction with the B6409 "Wilton Street" (there are street signs).

(Note: At this junction there is a very short minor road known as "Savile Road" (there are no street signs) between the west end of the Minster and Wilton Street.)

On the site of an A-S church the present structure dates mainly from the 14C with material surviving from the late 12C and early 13C. There were alterations and additions in the 15C and 19C. The church was partially rebuilt in the 18C and in the 20C the internal arrangements were substantially altered.

Internally, A-S fabric survives in the walling above the later inserted arcades in both the north and south walls of the nave (it can also be seen from both the north and south aisles.)

Internally, incorporated into the present fabric of the church, there is a large A-S quoin that formed part of the northeast end of the nave wall of the A-S church. This can best be seen from the north aisle as it is the north face that can be viewed. This quoin is located abutting the western arm of the easternmost arch on the north side of the nave, twelve stones up from the supporting pillar for this arch. The quoin has had one corner cut off by this 13C arch and is evidently amongst other the A-S fabric on the north face of the north wall of the nave. The quoin measures about 24 Ins/60 Cms H by about 31 Ins/78 Cms W.

Internally and displayed on the floor at the west end of what was once the north aisle, there are a variety of medieval grave slabs including a replica of an A-S wheel head cross.

During restorations of the church in the 18C and 19C pieces of A-S sculpture were discovered. This included part of a mid 9C A-S crosshead with an inscription in Old English to the effect (Someone set this in memory of) "berht, a monument to his lord. Pray for his soul". This section of stonework is now in the British Museum in London.

Internally, in what would have formerly been described as the south transept, there is now a "Heritage Centre" whose displays include the ecclesiastical history of Dewsbury.

In the Heritage Centre there are 11 sections of A-S stonework displayed attached to a curved wooden display with accompanying descriptions in front of (to the north) the south wall of the south transept. The sections of stonework are minimally 63 Ins/160 Cms up from the floor and they are attached to the wooden display. (The sections of stonework below and sitting on the floor at the base of the display are later medieval, not A-S/A-D.) All the sections of A-S stonework date from the late 8C to mid 9C unless stated otherwise. From east to west these are:

1.   A section of stonework from a cross-shaft. It measures 22 Ins/55 Cms H, by 9½ Ins/24 Cms W, by 9½ Ins/24 Cms D. On its north face it is decorated with two scenes depicting the life of Christ. The upper panel shows the miracle of turning running water into wine. Christ, the central figure, is raising his right hand to bless the wine jars in front of him. To the right an onlooker presses a hand to his cheek in amazement. The lower panel depicts the miracle of the loaves and the fishes. Christ, identified by his halo, is the figure to the left of the panel. All the other sides are too weathered or damaged for any decoration to survive.

2.   A section of stonework from one of the arms of a large crosshead. It measures 15 Ins/38 Cms H, by 9½ Ins/24 Cms W, by 7 Ins/17 Cms D. On the north side it is decorated with the figure of a man kneeling at the feet of a winged angel. On the east side it is decorated with the figure of a man with his arms uplifted in prayer. The other two sides are too weathered or damaged for any decoration to survive.

3.   A wedge-shaped section of stonework. It measures 22 Ins/55 Cms H, by 15 Ins/38 Cms W, by 8 Ins/20 Cms D. On its north face the decoration would have originally depicted two rows of standing figures but now only the legs and feet of the upper figures, and the heads of the lower ones, survive. The figures may have been intended to represent some of the 12 apostles. All the other sides are too weathered or damaged for any decoration to survive.

4.   A section of stonework. It measures 23½ Ins/59 Cms H, by 9½ Ins/24 Cms W, by 7½ Ins/19 Cms D. On its north side it is decorated with two standing figures that may be intended to represent bishops as they appear to be wearing mitres of A-S design. One of the figures may be carrying a scroll in his hand. All the other sides are too weathered or damaged for any decoration to survive.

5.   A section of stonework from a cross-shaft. It measures 21½ Ins/54 Cms H, by 14 Ins/35 Cms W, by 11½ Ins/16 Cms D. On its east face it is decorated with a depiction of the Virgin and Child. It is said to be one of the earliest sculptural representations of the subject

in the country. The panel above the Virgin seems to have contained a seated figure, only the lower portion of which is now visible. The upper section of a third panel may also be distinguished on the lower part of the section of cross-shaft, but the carving is too worn to determine the subject. The north face of the section of stonework is decorated with vine scroll design above which there is a lower section of a panel that appears to have contained two standing figures. The two other sides are too weathered or damaged for any decoration to survive.

6.   A section of stonework comprising the centre of a crosshead (the arms are virtually non-existent due to damage). It measures 15 Ins/38 Cms H, by 11 Ins/27 Cms W, by 9 Ins /22 Cms D. The south side is decorated with a cross within an oval. The north side is decorated with a raised, round boss. Traces of flanking knot work design are also visible on both of the north and south sides. The two other sides are too damaged for any decoration to survive.

7.   A section of stonework from a crosshead comprising part of the central section and most of two arms. It measures 12 Ins/30 Cms H, by 13 Ins/33 Cms W, tapering 4½ Ins/11 Cms to 2½ Ins/6 Cms D. On both the north and south sides there are lines outlining the shape of the cross and it is decorated with cusped arms and cable moulding. There is no decoration on either of the other two sides. It probably dates from the mid 9C.

8.   A section of stonework from what appears to be the end of an arm from a crosshead. It measures 15 Ins/38 Cms H, by 7½ Ins/19 Cms W (D), by 14½ Ins/36 Cms D (W). On the north side it is decorated with vine scroll design along the edge. All the other sides are too weathered or damaged for any decoration to survive. It dates from the 9C.

9.   A section of stonework from a cross-shaft. It measures 13½ Ins/34 Cms H, by 5½ Ins/13 Cms W, by 6 Ins/15 Cms D. It is decorated on all four sides. On the southeast side there is what may be the lower part of a crucifixion scene. The upper part of the body and the extended arms would have filled the head of the cross. On the northwest side it is decorated with a grotesque figure with large legs and feet that may be a representation of death. The northeast and southwest sides are decorated with vine scroll and interlace design. It dates from the 10C.

There are two sections of stonework "10" and "11" displayed one under another. These are:

10.   The top section of stonework is part of a cross-shaft. It measures 8½ Ins/21 Cms H, by 9 Ins/22 Cms W, by 4½ Ins/11 Cms D. The northeast and southwest sides show a vine scroll and interlace design symmetrically arranged on either side of a central spine. There is some line decoration on the northwest side. The southeast side is too damaged for any decoration to survive. It dates from the 9C.

11.   The section of stonework below "10" is part of a cross-shaft. It measures 5 Ins/12 Cms H, by 4 Ins/10 Cms W, by 5 Ins/12 Cms D. This section of stonework was discovered during excavations within the Minster in 1994. The northwest side is decorated with vine scroll design The southeast side is decorated with what may be the draperies of a figure but the surviving section of decoration is too small to make this identification certain. The other sides are too damaged for any decoration to survive. It dates from the 9C.

Also in the Heritage Centre there is a section of stonework from a hogback grave cover. It is located near to the staircase on a free-standing wooden plinth 32 Ins/81 Cms H, by 31½ Ins/80 Cms W, by 27½ Ins/69 Cms D. The section of stonework measures 12 Ins/30 Cms H, by 15 Ins/38 Cms W, by 18 Ins/45 Cms L. This late 9C hogback has been made to resemble a small boat-shaped house and is in the "Anglian" rather than the "Danish" style. Roof tiles have been carved on the upper surfaces, but it should be noted that the pattern of the tiles is different on each side. It is decorated with interlace design along both the northwest and southeast sides. The southwest facing gable end of the hogback is carved with a cross. The northeast facing side is damaged and it has no decoration.

From the Heritage Centre proceed to the "Paulinus Pilgrimage Chapel". The Chapel is reached by going up the stairs in the Heritage Centre and passing through a door into a vestibule in the centre of the first floor of the church. Go into the Chapel through the doors on the west side of this vestibule. At the western end of the Chapel, on top of a framework above the altar, there is another section of 9C A-S stonework. It measures 23½ Ins/58 Cms H, by 8½ Ins/21 Cms W, by 5½ Ins/14 Cms D. The east side is decorated with the seated figure of Christ, who

DEWSBURY: The Minster Church of All Saints, The Heritage Centre. An Anglo-Saxon, rather than Anglo-Danish, grave cover. It takes the form of a small boat-shaped house. It is decorated with interlace design, the roof tiles have different patterns on each side, and there is a cross at the gable end. Photograph reproduced with the permission of the Team Rector and District Church Council of the Minster Church of All Saints Dewsbury.

is identified by a halo. All the other sides are too weathered or damaged for any decoration to survive.

The collection of stonework in the Heritage Centre and the section of stonework in the Paulinus Pilgrimage Chapel are thought to be the remains of the cross erected in the late 9C to commemorate the visit of St Paulinus to the area in 627 AD.

Inside the church there is a reredos screen dating from 1913 depicting Christ and the Twelve Apostles flanked by saints and monarchs associated with the area including Aidan, Hilda, Bede, Edwin, Ethelburga, Oswald and Paulinus. It is located on the ground floor, and has now been placed against the north wall in what was the north transept.

GUISELEY
St Oswald's Church
SE 194422   Rating: ☆☆

Towards the eastern side of Guiseley, turn off the A65, "Otley Road" (there are street signs), and head in a north-easterly direction along "The Green" (there are street signs). After about 370 Yds/338 M the church is easily identified adjacent to the east side of The Green.

On the site of an A-S church the present structure dates from 1150. It was extended in the 13C, 14C and 15C. The church was rebuilt in 1910.

Internally, it is just possible there may be some A-S fabric in the old nave walls above the later inserted arches and in the four corners of the old nave. The church guide refers to some masonry that may be A-S in the southeast corner of the old nave. This may be the darker masonry in the walling adjacent to the north side of the steps leading up from the east end of the old south aisle into the Lady Chapel on the south side of St Oswald's Chapel (the old chancel).

Internally, there are:

1.   A section of stonework comprising part of the base of an A-S pillar. It is located standing on the floor 10 Yds/9 M from the south door, by the south side of the westernmost pillar on the south side of the present nave (in the more northern of the two south aisles). The section of stonework measures 23 Ins/58 Cms square by 12 Ins/30 Cms H. Its northwest facing corner has been cut off. There is no decoration on any of the sides.

2.   A section of stonework from a 10C A-S cross-shaft. The part of the base identified at "1" above acts as a plinth for this section of stonework. The section of stonework stands 50 Ins/127 Cms H, tapering 12½ Ins/31 Cms to 10½ Ins/26 Cms W, tapering 8 Ins/20 Cms to 7 Ins/17 Cms D. Although weathered and damaged it is decorated with

knot work design on all four sides. Additionally, on the southeast facing side the decoration includes a grid-iron design.

3.   A section of stonework comprising an end of an arm from an A-S crosshead. It has been cemented onto the top of the section of stonework identified at "2" above. The section of stonework measures 8½ Ins/21 Cms H, between 6 Ins/15 Cms and 12 Ins/30 Cms W, by 7 Ins/17 Cms D. The northwest side is decorated with interlace design. The southeast side is decorated with what appears to be the head of an animal and possibly the top half of a human head. The end of the arm and the other sides are too weathered for any decoration to survive.

HAREWOOD
All Saints Church
SE 313451   Rating: ✩✩✩

Opposite the junction of the A659 and the A61, turn off the A61 and head in a westerly direction along the "main" drive towards Harewood House. After about 880 Yds/804 M, and past the "Entrance and Visitors' Reception" for Harewood House, there is an "All Saints Church" etc notice. This notice directs you off the main drive to the House and along another, narrower, drive. As directed by this sign proceed in a northerly direction along this narrower drive for about 170 Yds/155 M until reaching a gated track way. From the gate proceed along this track way as it sweeps in a northerly direction around to the north entrance into the church. The church is about 88 Yds/80 M from the gateway. The church is hidden among the trees and because of this it is not easy to identify the church in the near vicinity.

The A-S church on this site was replaced in 1410. The church was altered 1793 and restored in 1862-63.

Internally, there is a section of stonework from an A-D cross-shaft dating from the 10C. It can be viewed from the former south chapel at the eastern end of the south aisle. It is located attached to the south face of the walling on the south side of the chancel (the north wall of the chapel). The section of stonework is 12 Ins/30 Cms east of the north side of the arch separating the former south chapel from the rest of the south aisle and 45 Ins/114 Cms up from the floor. It measures 16 Ins/40 Cms H, by 4 Ins/10 Cms D, by 11 Ins/27 Cms W. It is protected by a Perspex cover and although not in the best of condition decoration can clearly be identified. This section of stonework is decorated with the scene of a wild boar hunt on its south face. On the north face and the two other sides it is decorated with interlace design. Underneath this section of stonework there is an information notice.

HARTSHEAD
Walton Cross

SE 175237   Rating: ☆☆☆☆☆

About 1900 Yds/1737 M north-west of the centre of Hartshead, locate a tall public footpath directional sign. This sign is on the west side of the B6119, "Windy Bank Lane", opposite its junction with "Second Avenue". There are Windy Bank Lane and Second Avenue street signs at the junction. [The footpath directional sign and the road junction is about 95 Yds/86 M north-west of "Walton Cross Farm". (There is a Walton Cross Farm sign affixed to the walling by the drive leading to the appropriate building).]

Take the footpath that heads in a south-westerly direction as indicated by the public footpath directional sign. About 25 Yds/22 M from the road Walton Cross is easily identified in a fenced enclosure on the north side of this footpath.

HARTSHEAD: Walton Cross. An Anglo-Saxon cross base. The hole for the insertion of the cross-shaft can clearly be identified on the top (sky) facing side. The cross-base is decorated with interlace designs, animals and birds, in a hybrid of Anglo-Saxon and Anglo-Danish styles.

Walton Cross is a substantial section of stonework comprising an A-S cross base. With a slightly tapered top, the cross base measures 58 Ins/147 Cms H, by 40 Ins/101 Cms W, by 27 Ins/68 Cms D. A hybrid of A-S and A-D styles, it is decorated with interlace design on all four sides. On both east and west sides it is also decorated with animals and birds. The hole for the insertion of the cross-shaft can easily be identified on the top (sky) facing side. It dates from the late 10C/early 11C.

HUDDERSFIELD
Tolson Museum

SE 162165   Rating: ✩✩✩✩

The Museum is located about a mile east of the centre of Huddersfield. The building housing the Museum is situated in the grounds of Ravensknowle public park on the south side of the A629.

Opposite the drive leading to the Museum there is a "Tolson Museum" directional sign. Behind the entrance to the drive that leads to the Museum there is a free-standing "Tolson Memorial Museum Ravensknowle Park" etc notice. Proceed along the drive and the building housing the Museum is reached after about 90 Yds/82 M. The appropriate building, which dates from 1859-62, has cut into the stonework over the entrance the words "The Tolson Memorial" and beneath these words there is a large "Museum" notice.

As with all museums, the displays and the exhibits they contain may be changed, re-sited, removed from display and/or put in store, or loaned to other museums or suitable repositories. Before visiting the museum it is worth checking in advance whether the displays listed in the text below are still in place in the same location(s) set out in the text. Individual exhibits may have been rearranged in terms of their display, the order in which they are displayed and their relationship to other exhibits, some exhibits may have been removed from display. The text in the entry reflects the descriptions and/or accompanying notices to the exhibits at the time of visiting. These too may have been revised, amended, added to or removed.

The Museum houses natural history, archaeology and history displays and collections relating to textiles, farming, social history and transport all connected with Huddersfield and its hinterland.

There are displays of Anglo-Saxon interest entitled: "The Anglo-Saxons", "Language", "Carved Stonework", "Place Names: The Viking Invasions". These displays are located on the first floor.

The display "Language" provides the opportunity to hear the spoken language. On pressing the appropriate button the Old Englisc rendition from the opening lines of the epic "Beowulf" can be heard. Another button provides a rendition in Old Norse of a quotation from "Thrimsk

Vitha", recounting the story of the famous hammer of Thor, described as "Chief God of the Vikings". A third button provides the "modern" rendition of the Holme Valley dialect.

Standing on a raised display 9½ Ins/24 Cms up from the floor entitled "Carved Stonework" there are:

1.　Two sections from a cast of a fragment of a grave cover. They are located lying flat on the base of the display under a plastic cover measuring just under 13 Ins/33 Cms W, by 11 Ins/27 Cms D, by 2 Ins/5 Cms H. The more easterly (left-hand side) section measures 6 Ins/15 Cms L (H), by 5 Ins/12 Cms W, by ½ an inch/1 Cms H (D). The more westerly (right-hand side) section measures 10 Ins/25 Cms L (H), by 6 Ins/15 Cms W, by ½ an inch/1 Cms H (D). The original dates from around 860 and is incised in Old English: "set this in memory of Osberht a monument over his grave. Pray for his soul." The original is in the St Michael's and All Angels Church Thornhill (see the entry for Thornhill, near Dewsbury, West Yorkshire).

2.　A section of stonework from a cross-shaft. It is located standing on a plinth, 18 Ins/45 Cms H, by 9 Ins/22 Cms W, by 7 Ins/17 Cms D. The section of stonework is affixed to the wall. It measures 9 Ins/22 Cms H, by 9 Ins/22 Cms W, by 6 Ins/15 Cms D. It is decorated on all four sides with knot work design. It dates from 875-900 and comes from St John's Church Kirkheaton (see the entry for Kirkheaton, West Yorkshire).

3.　A cast reconstruction of a complete cross-shaft and crosshead from All Hallows Church Kirkburton. It measures in total 96 Ins/243 Cms H, tapering from 20 Ins/50 Cms (crosshead) to 10 Ins/25 Cms (cross-shaft) W, by 6 Ins/15 Cms D. The decoration has been painted on the three sides on view. On its north side it depicts Christ Crucified and it is decorated with knot work design. The two other sides are decorated with a double edged rectangle enclosing a single painted colour. The original dates from 975-1025 and is located in All Hallows Church Kirkburton (see the entry for Kirkburton, West Yorkshire).

4.　An A-S window head. It is located on the floor of the display leaning against "3" above and "5" below. The window head measures 22 Ins/55 Cms W by 14 Ins/35 Cms H, by 5 Ins/12 Cms D. It comes from St John's Church Kirkheaton (see the entry for Kirkheaton, West Yorkshire).

5.　A section of stonework from a cross-shaft. It is located standing on a plinth measuring 12 Ins/30 Cms H, by 9½ Ins/24 Cms W, by 7 Ins/17 Cms D. The section of stonework is affixed to the wall. It measures 16½ Ins/41 Cms H, tapering 9 Ins/22 Cms to 8 Ins/20 Cms W, by 5 Ins/12 Cms D. Although weathered, on the north side the section of stonework it is decorated with the top half of a man with a halo holding palm branches (the halo denotes he was a saint and the palms were a symbol of martyrdom). Above the palm branches two animals, one above another, can also be identified on this side. The two other sides that can be viewed are decorated with interlace design. The fourth side has been affixed to the wall and so cannot be viewed. It dates from around 825-900 and comes from St John's Church Kirkheaton (see the entry for Kirkheaton, West Yorkshire).

6.   A cast copy reconstruction of the section of stonework from the cross-shaft at "5" above incorporated into a cast copy of its complete cross-shaft and crosshead. The cast copy of both cross-shaft and crosshead stand 50½ Ins/128 Cms H in total, tapering from 12 Ins/30 Cms (crosshead) to 10½ Ins/26 Cms (cross-shaft) W, by 5½ Ins/13 Cms D. The cast has been painted white. On the northeast side of the cross-shaft it depicts the saint, the palm branches, animals. There is knot work design on all four sides of both the cross-shaft and crosshead.

7.   A section of stonework from a cross-shaft. It measures 25½ Ins/64 Cms H, tapering 11 Ins/27 Cms to 9 Ins/22 Cms W, by 6½ Ins/16 Cms D. On the east side it is incised in A-S futhorc (runes) "Eoh worohtae" (Eoh made this). Despite weathering there are angular twist and spiral designs on the west, east and north sides. The south side is too weathered and damaged for any decoration to survive. It dates from 875-925. It comes from St John's Church Kirkheaton (see the entry for Kirkheaton, West Yorkshire).

8.   A section of stonework from a cross-shaft. It is located standing on a plinth 18 Ins/45 Cms H, by 9 Ins/22 Cms W, by 7 Ins/17 Cms D. The section of cross-shaft is affixed to the wall. The section of stonework measures 8 Ins/20 Cms H, by 9½ Ins/24 Cms W, by 5½ Ins/13 Cms D. It is decorated with interlace design on the east and south sides. The decoration on the other two sides is too damaged for any design to be identified. It dates from 875-900 and comes from St John's Church Kirkheaton (see the entry for Kirkheaton, West Yorkshire).

In a separate display there is a model of a Viking farmstead based on a farm excavated at Ribblehead. In another separate display there is a replica of a square, decorated, late A-S font, the original came from All Hallows Church High Hoyland but is now in St Aidan's Church Skelmanthorpe (see the entry for Skelmanthorpe, West Yorkshire).

ILKLEY
(1) All Saints Church
SE 116478   Rating: ★★★★☆

In the centre of Ilkley, the church is easily located adjacent to the north side of the A65(T) in the north-west quadrant of the cross-roads containing the A65(T), "Church Street", and "New Brook Street" (there are street signs).

When the first church was built in 627 material was utilised from the Roman fort that encompassed the site. The present church on this site contains 13C, 14C, and 15C fabric despite the rebuilding in 1861 and alterations in the 20C. It is just possible that the west wall of the nave incorporates A-S fabric.

Internally, there are three A-S cross-shafts one with an A-S crosshead. They are located in the centre of the floor under the tower each standing on a low plinth about 1 inch/2 Cms H. They comprise:

1.   A section of stonework from a cross-shaft. It is located 53 Ins/134 Cms north of the south wall of the tower and 126½ Ins/321 Cms east of the west wall of the tower. It measures 55 Ins/139 Cms H, tapering 12 Ins/30 to Cms 6½ Ins/16 Cms W, tapering 13 Ins/33 Cms to 8 Ins/20 Cms D. The top of the section of stonework has a tenon so that the next section of cross-shaft can be joined on. On its north side, in the lowest panel, it is decorated with the depiction of a man with a book (no halo so not a saint) and in the panel above there is an entwined animal. On the other three sides the panels that can still be identified contain decoration including entwined animals. (This is the most weathered of the three sections of stonework from cross-shafts in the church.) It dates from the mid 8C.

2.   A section of stonework comprising a virtually complete cross-shaft on top of which there is a section of stonework comprising most of a crosshead. They are known as "The Four Evangelists". They are located 67½ Ins/171 Cms north of the south wall of the tower and 82 Ins/208 Cms east of the west wall of the tower. Together they stand about 130 Ins/330 Cms H.

The section of stonework from the crosshead comprises the central section and two lateral arms, a section of modern stonework connects this central section to an original additional top vertical arm from a crosshead (but not the same crosshead), plus a modern lower vertical arm connecting the crosshead to the section of cross-shaft. The section of stonework measures 29 Ins/73 Cms H, by 23 Ins/58 Cms W, by 8 Ins/20 Cms D. Despite weathering it is possible to identify, on its west face, a bird and interlace design, and on its east face, a winged angel and birds pecking fruit. There is some indistinct decoration on the ends of the arms, but none on the south facing end. The top vertical arm is decorated on its east face with an angel and on its west face it is decorated with ring chain design.

The section of stonework comprising most of a cross-shaft measures 101 Ins/256 Cms H, tapering 16 Ins/40 Cms to 10 Ins/25 Cms W, tapering 14 Ins/35 Cms to 10 Ins/25 Cms D. On its west side each panel is decorated with one of the symbols denoting the saints. The top panel denotes the eagle for St John, the panel below denotes the bull for St Luke, the panel below denotes the lion for St Mark and the bottom panel denotes a man for St Matthew. The top panel of the east side is decorated with Christ enthroned in Majesty holding a palm branch in His left hand. His right hand is raised in a blessing. In the panel below there are two entwined animals, and in the lowest two panels each contains a single animal. The north and south sides are decorated with scroll, triple-knot and snake patterns. It dates from the early 9C.

3.   A section of stonework from a cross-shaft. It is located 39½ Ins/100 Cms south of the north wall of the tower and 109 Ins/276 Cms east of the west wall of the tower. It stands 65 Ins/165 Cms H, tapering 13 Ins/33 Cms to 8½ Ins/21 Cms W, tapering 11½ Ins/29 Cms to 3½ Ins/8 Cms D. On its east side, below the weathering and damage, the surviving panel nearest the top is decorated with Adam and Eve and a serpent. The panel below them contains a pair of animals confronting each other. Below this panel there is another pair of animals confronting each other. The bottom panel contains two birds confronting each other. Despite weathering and damage the lower panels of the west side are decorated with part of an animal in the higher surviving panel and a bird with its feet vertically rather than horizontally in the lower surviving panel. The north and south sides are decorated with vine scroll design. Some cable design edging also survives on all four corners of the edges of this section of stonework. It dates from the early 9C.

Internally there are three sections of Roman stonework taken from the nearby Roman Fort and used as church building material. These have been attached to the west wall of the tower and stand on separate shallow plinths. They comprise:

4.   A Roman altar. It is the section of stonework nearest the south wall of the tower. The altar measures 42 Ins/106 Cms H (W), by 14½ Ins/36 Cms W (D), by 20 Ins/50 Cms D (H). This altar has been re-shaped to serve as a window head for the A-S church. The inner curved surface has remains of fine white plaster still attached suggesting that the A-S church on this site may have been plastered inside.

5.   A Roman altar. It is the middle of the three sections of stonework attached to the west wall of the tower. The altar measures 39 Ins/99 Cms H (W), by 14 Ins/35 Cms W (D), by 17½ Ins/44 Cms D (H). This altar too has been re-shaped to serve as a window head for the A-S church. Like the Roman altar at "1" above the inner curved surface has remains of fine white plaster still attached similarly suggesting that the A-S church on this site may have been plastered inside.

6.   An incised section of Roman stonework. It is the section of stonework nearest to the north wall of the tower. The section of stonework

ILKLEY: All Saints Church. An Anglo-Saxon cross-shaft depicting a pair of animals confronting each other.

measures 53 Ins/134 Cms H, tapering 13 Ins/33 Cms to 8 Ins/20 Cms W, tapering 13½ Ins/34 Cms to 10 Ins/25 Cms D. This does not appear to have been re-used in the A-S church.

By, and close to, all the pieces of stonework there are descriptive notices and sketches.

ILKLEY
(2) "Manor House" Museum

SE 115478   Rating: ☆☆☆

40 Yds/36 M west of the south porch All Saints Church, on the north side of Church Street there is an arched entrance. A "Manor House Art Gallery Museum" sign at first floor level extends over the pavement by this arched entrance. On the internal west wall of this archway there is a "Manor House Museum" directional sign. Opposite this archway, on the south side of Church Street, there is a "Manor House Museum" directional sign. Pass through the archway and proceed in a northerly direction along a cobbled

roadway. This cobbled roadway reaches the building housing the Museum after about 52 Yds/47 M from Church Street. The appropriate building has a free-standing "Manor House Art Gallery and Museum" notice board attached to the walling adjacent to its entrance.

As with all museums, the displays and the exhibits they contain may be changed, re-sited, removed from display and/or put in store, or loaned to other museums or suitable repositories. Before visiting the museum it is worth checking in advance whether the displays listed in the text below are still in place in the same location(s) set out in the text. Individual exhibits may have been rearranged in terms of their display, the order in which they are displayed and their relationship to other exhibits, some exhibits may have been removed from display. The text in the entry reflects the descriptions and/or accompanying notices to the exhibits at the time of visiting. These too may have been revised, amended, added to or removed.

The Manor House occupies part of the site of the north-west quadrant of the Roman fort. The present building originates from the 13C but most of the fabric dates from the 16C and 17C.

The Museum exhibits are displayed on the ground floor and exhibitions and galleries are displayed on the first floor. On the ground floor the "house body" is furnished in the style of the 17C and 18C. The most easterly room downstairs, the "solar wing", contains archaeological and historical displays.

In a display showing a photograph of the A-S crosses and crosshead standing outside All Saints Church Ilkley, there is a section of stonework from a A-S cross-shaft. This section of stonework measures 15 Ins/38 Cms H, tapering 9 Ins/22 Cms to 6 Ins/15 Cms W, by 5½ Ins/13 Cms D. On the south side it is decorated with vine scroll design. On the east and west sides it is decorated with interlace design. The north side is too weathered and damaged for any decoration to survive.

Standing in the fireplace are four medieval sections of stonework, three A-S sections of stonework, and the large upper stone from a powder mill. Those of A-S interest are:

1.   A section of stonework comprising the central section and one arm from a crosshead. It is located in the back row of stonework leaning against the north wall of the fireplace. The section of stonework measures 26 Ins/66 Cms H (W), tapering 14 Ins/35 Cms to 8 Ins/20 Cms W (H), by 6 Ins/15 Cms D. Apart from some circular design on the central boss (on both the northeast and southwest sides) there is no decoration due to weathering and damage.

2.   A section of stonework from an arm of a crosshead. It is located lying flat in the front row of stonework in the fireplace, the second

section of stonework from the north wall of the fireplace. The section of stonework measures 5 Ins/12 Cms H (D), by 17 Ins/43 Cms W, by 9½ Ins/24 Cms D (H). There is some circular design with interweaving strands decoration on the top side and some interlace design on the side facing the front of the fireplace. The other sides are too weathered or damaged for any decoration to survive.

3.   A section of stonework from a cross-shaft. It is located leaning against the south wall of the fireplace. The section of stonework measures 31 Ins/78 Cms H, by 11½ Ins/29 Cms W, tapering 7 Ins/17 Cms to 6 Ins/15 Cms D. On the northwest side it is decorated with a fox eating grapes. On the northwest, southwest and northeast sides it is decorated with vine scroll design. The southeast facing side is too weathered and damaged for any decoration to survive. It dates from the early 10C.

KEIGHLEY

Castle Cliffe Museum

SE 057421   Rating: ☆☆

There are a number of "Castle Cliffe Museum" directional signs in Keighley. In the north-western part of Keighley, turn off the A629 and head in a north-westerly direction along "Spring Gardens Lane" (there are street signs). The entrance to the grounds containing the Museum, with its adjacent car park, is about 680 Yds/621 M from the A629 on the north side of Spring Gardens Lane.

Opposite the entrance to the grounds there is a "Cliffe Castle Car Park" directional sign. From the car park by the entrance to the grounds head in a south-easterly direction downhill along a roadway as indicated by the "Cliffe Castle Museum & Park" directional sign. The Victorian building housing the Museum is some 82 Yds/74 M away from the car park.

As with all museums, the displays and the exhibits they contain may be changed, re-sited, removed from display and/or put in store, or loaned to other museums or suitable repositories. Before visiting the museum it is worth checking in advance whether the displays listed in the text below are still in place in the same location(s) set out in the text. Individual exhibits may have been rearranged in terms of their display, the order in which they are displayed and their relationship to other exhibits, some exhibits may have been removed from display. The text in the entry reflects the descriptions and/or accompanying notices to the exhibits at the time of visiting. These too may have been revised, amended, added to or removed.

Inside the Museum the "Archaeology Room" is located on the ground floor towards the rear of the building behind the large gallery display entitled "Airedale. The formation and life of a valley". It is between the "Airedale Gallery" and the Activity/Lecture Room: and between the "Natural History Gallery" and the "Riches Underfoot" gallery.

The Archaeology Room houses the items of A-S interest in a display cabinet that contains descriptive notes and sketches of local A-S cross-shafts. Inside this cabinet there are:

1.   A section of stonework from what is described as a crosshead, part of one arm: however, it may just be from part of a cross-shaft. It is located towards the northern (right hand side) of the cabinet. The section of stonework measures about 20 Ins/50 Cms H, by 9 Ins/22 Cms W, by 4 Ins/10 Cms D. On its east side it is decorated with circular patterns (thought to represent a beast according to the descriptive notice). The three other sides are too weathered or damaged for any decoration to survive. It comes from All Saints Church Ilkley (see the entry for Ilkley, West Yorkshire).

2.   A section of stonework from a cross-shaft. It is located towards the southern (left hand side) of the cabinet. The section of stonework measures about 13 Ins/33 Cms H, by 11 Ins/27 Cms W, by 5 Ins/12 Cms D. On its northeast side it is decorated with what is described as a swastika design – but imagination has to be used. The southeast side is decorated with knot work design. The two other sides are too weathered and damaged for any decoration to survive. It comes from All Saints Church Ilkley (see the entry for Ilkley, West Yorkshire).

3.   The other A-S artefacts displayed in this cabinet are: a 6C glass bead found on Baildon Moor, a glass bead found on Ilkley Moor, and a small glass bead found on Hawkesworth Moor.

Also in the Archaeology Room, but in a separate display cabinet, there are 9 stone heads. A notice inside the cabinet states: "Stone Heads. Celtic and Later. These stone heads cover a wide range in style and date. Whilst none have been excavated from an archaeological site, which would have enabled them to be accurately dated, some have been dated on stylistic grounds from the Early Iron Age, some 2,000 years ago, and others from Medieval and later times." It is just possible that one of these heads may be A-S. It is the one displayed separately on a ledge at the back of the cabinet towards the north-eastern (right hand side) end of the cabinet.

KIPPAX
St Mary's Church

SE 416303   Rating: ☆☆☆   Access is possible.

In the southern part of Kippax, 40 Yds/36 M north of the roundabout that enables the B6137 to change direction from north/south to west/east, turn east off the B6137 and proceed along a minor no-through road (there are no street signs). The church is at the top of this minor road and is reached after about 130 Yds/118 M as the road winds its way uphill. There are no directional or street signs, but the church can be identified without too much difficulty.

The present structure includes A-S fabric although much of the material dates from the 12C and the later additions in the 13C, 14C and 15C. There were major restorations in 1884 and in 1982-4. The nave walls and the lower stages of the tower may all be A-S in origin.

Internally, it is not possible to detect any A-S fabric in the structure with confidence as the walls are covered with plasterwork. However, there are two separate sections of stonework from the same early 11C A-S cross-shaft attached to the east wall of the nave, 16½ Ins/41 Cms south of the chancel arch. These are:

1.   A section of stonework from an A-S cross-shaft. It is located 77 Ins/195 Cms up from the floor – it is above "2" below. The section of stonework measures 25½ Ins/64 Cms H, tapering 13 Ins/33 Cms to 11½ Ins/29 Cms W, by 6 Ins/15 Cms D. On its west face it is decorated with the figure of a man standing on two snakes below which there are the heads of two dragons. The other sides are damaged with no decoration identifiable.

2.   A section of stonework from an A-S cross-shaft. It is located 107 Ins/271 Cms up from the floor – it is below "1" above. The section of stonework measures 8½ Ins/21 Cms H, tapering 11 Ins/27 Cms to 9½ Ins/24 Cms W, by 4½ Ins/11 Cms D. On its western face it is decorated with circular motif design. The other sides are damaged with no decoration identifiable.

Externally, evidence of A-S material can be easily identified in the distinctive herring-bone masonry at various levels in the tower, on both sides of the nave, and in the south and east walls of the chancel. A-S material may survive in the lower courses of stonework and some of the quoining in the nave and chancel.

KIRKBURTON
All Hallows Church

SE 197125   Rating: ★★★   Access is possible.

The church is easily located at the southern end of Kirkburton and is situated adjacent to the west side of the B6116.

On the site of an A-S church the present structure mostly dates from around 1200 with some 19C additions.

Internally, there is what appears to be a complete 11C stone cross-shaft and its associated crosshead – there are modern additions to both the crosshead and cross-shaft. On their west faces the crosshead depicts the upper part of the body and the cross-shaft the lower part of the body in a Crucifixion scene.

There are four "original" sections of stonework:

1.   The crosshead apart from most of the lower vertical arm joining the crosshead to the cross-shaft and the part of the southern horizontal arm that depicts a hand on the west face.

2.   The lower "neck" of the crosshead, the part of the lower vertical arm that connects the crosshead to the cross-shaft.

3.   The upper half of the cross-shaft that depicts the legs and feet of the Crucifixion scene and the top part of the interlace design on the west face. This measures 20 Ins/50 Cms H.

4.   A section of stonework from the cross-shaft that is decorated with interlace design on the west face – below "3" above. This measures 3 Ins/7 Cms H.

Note: The modern sections of stonework can be clearly identified as such.

The crosshead and cross-shaft are located standing on a plinth on the floor in the southeast corner of the nave, with their east side affixed with two struts to the west wall of the chancel. In total the plinth, cross-shaft and crosshead stand 103½ /262 Cms H. The plinth measures 8 Ins/20 Cms H, between 13½ Ins/34 Cms and 15½ Ins/39 Cms W, tapering 9 Ins/22 Cms to 8 Ins/20 Cms D.

The crosshead with its modern additions measures 23½ Ins/59 Cms H, by 21½ Ins/54 Cms W, between 4 Ins/10 Cms and 6 Ins/15 Cms D. On the top of the crosshead there is a round tenon, presumably intended for joining on another section of stonework. It is decorated on its east face with concentric circles forming a central roundel with two parallel incised lines outlining the shape of the crosshead. On its west face it is decorated with the head, body, outstretched arms and hands of a Crucifixion scene with two parallel incised lines outlining the shape of the crosshead. Other than some indication of two parallel incised lines outlining the shape of the arms, there is no decoration on any of the ends of the arms.

The cross-shaft with its modern additions measures 72 Ins/182 Cms H, tapering 11½ Ins/29 Cms to 6½ Ins/16 Cms W, tapering 7 Ins/17 Cms to 4¾ Ins/12 Cms D. It is decorated on its east face with two parallel incised lines outlining the shape of the cross-shaft. On its west face it is decorated with the legs and feet of the body of the Crucifixion scene with interlace decoration separate and below the Crucifixion scene. The west face also has two parallel incised lines outlining the shape of the cross-shaft. The other two sides have no decoration apart from two parallel incised lines outlining the shape of the cross-shaft.

There is a cast replica of this crosshead and cross-shaft in the Tolson Memorial Museum in Huddersfield (see the entry for Huddersfield, West Yorkshire).

Not currently displayed, the church also has in its possession a section of stonework that may have come from a crosshead or cross-shaft. What might have been the curved end of an arm from a crosshead has been cut to a square shape and a hole made to accommodate a candle. This section of stonework measures between 6 Ins/15 Cms to 8 Ins/20 Cms H, by 9½ Ins/24 Cms W, by 3¾ Ins/9 Cms D. On both of its two faces there are incised parallel lines of the type often found on a crosshead or cross-shaft. It has no other decoration on any of its sides.

KIRKHEATON
St John the Baptist Church

SE 178172   Rating: ☆   Access is possible.

At the southern end of Kirkheaton (in the vicinity of "Hill Side" marked on Ordnance Survey maps), turn off the main road which runs north-east/south-west through Kirkheaton (as the street signs indicate this road has a number of names as it passes through Kirkheaton) and head in a general southerly direction along "Church Lane" (there are street signs). After about 100 Yds/91 M the church can be easily identified on the west side of Church Lane.

On the site of an A-S church the present church dates from 1887-8 and incorporates some 14C material.

When the church was rebuilt in the late 19C the following were found:

1.   A section of stonework from an A-S cross-shaft. It measures 9 Ins/22 Cms H, by 9 Ins/22 Cms W, by 6 Ins/15 Cms D. It is decorated on all four sides with knot work design. It dates from 875-900.

2.   An A-S window head. The window head measures 14 Ins/35 Cms H, by 22 Ins/55 Cms W, by 5 Ins/12 Cms D.

3.   A section of stonework from an A-S cross-shaft. It measures 16½ Ins/41Cms H, tapering 9 Ins/22 Cms to 8 Ins/20 Cms W, by 5 Ins/12 Cms D. Although weathered, on the north side (as displayed in the Tolson Museum in Huddersfield) the section of stonework is decorated with the top half of a man with a halo holding palm branches. The halo denotes he was a saint and the palms were a symbol of martyrdom. Above

the palm branches two animals, one above another, can also be identified on this side. The two other sides that can be viewed are decorated with interlace design. The fourth side has been affixed to the wall (as displayed in the Tolson Museum in Huddersfield) and so cannot be viewed. The section of stonework dates from around 825-900.

4.   A section of stonework from a cross-shaft. It measures 25½ Ins/64 Cms H, tapering 11 Ins/27 Cms to 9 Ins/22 Cms W, by 6½ Ins/16 Cms D. On the east side (as displayed in the Tolson Museum in Huddersfield) incised in A-S futhorc (runes) "Eoh worohtae" (Eoh made this). Despite weathering there are angular twist and spiral designs on the west, east and north sides (as displayed in the Tolson Museum in Huddersfield). The south side (as displayed in the Tolson Museum in Huddersfield) is too damaged and weathered for any decoration to survive. The section of stonework dates from 875-925.

5.   A section of stonework from a cross-shaft. The section of stonework measures 8 Ins/20 Cms H, by 9½ Ins/24 Cms W, by 5½ Ins/13 Cms D. It is decorated with interlace design on the east and south sides (as displayed in the Tolson Museum in Huddersfield). The decoration on the other two sides is too damaged for any design to be identified. The section of stonework dates from the 875-900.

All these five sections of stonework are now displayed in the Tolson Memorial Museum in Huddersfield (see the entry for Huddersfield, West Yorkshire).

There are no other items of A-S interest remaining in the church.

LEDSHAM
All Saints Church

SE 456298   Rating: ★☆☆☆☆

In the centre of Ledsham, the church is easily located on a small hill close to the north side of the road that runs west/east through the village. It is close to a sharp right-angled bend in the road.

The church retains much late 7C/early 8C material with 12C, 13C and 15C alterations and additions. It was heavily restored in 1871.

The lower part of the tower originally formed part of a late 7C/early 8C A-S porch. The tower now incorporates material from this A-S porch. On the south side of the tower, a doorway and two complete windows, one lighting the lower storey, the other the upper storey of the former porch, as well as the surrounding masonry, are all A-S. (Note: during the restoration in 1871 the ornamental carvings surrounding the doorway externally were embellished to take their present form. Also the doorway is round-headed externally and square-headed internally.) Both windows and doorway are still in use and can all be identified from the outside as well as the inside of the tower.

The present south porch contains a considerable amount of 7C A-S material evident in the west and east walling. The A-S material in the porch originally formed part of an A-S porticus comprising a chapel with an upper and lower chamber. Most of the A-S doorway into the upper chamber of the A-S porticus survives – it is now blocked. It is easily identified both internally and externally immediately above the south doorway into the church. This doorway is square-headed on its south (external) side, and round-headed on its north (internal) side.

Internally, A-S material survives in the west and south walls of the nave (almost intact), and above the later inserted arches on the north side of the nave.

Internally, an A-S window survives above the centre of the later inserted archway in the west wall of the nave.

By following the line of the tops of the later inserted windows and arches, two blocked A-S windows can be identified in the south wall of the nave. These can be identified:

1.   One window is to the west of the top of the eastern nave window. Its eastern arch now springs from the western arch of the later inserted window. It comprises most of the individual stones forming the window head and the stones forming the vertical supports on the western side.

2.   The other window is to the west of the top of the western nave window. Its eastern vertical support is now adjacent to the western arch of the later inserted window. It comprises the individual stones forming the window head and the stones forming the vertical supports on either side.

In the surviving walling in the north side of the nave there are the remains of four blocked A-S windows either side of the top of the westernmost and easternmost arches. The four blocked windows can only be viewed from inside the nave and not the north aisle. From west to east they comprise:

3.   The individual stones forming most of the western curve of the top of the window head and part of the eastern curve of the window head.

4.   The individual stones forming part of the western curve of the top of the window head, the individual stones forming the eastern curve of the arch of the window head and the individual stones forming part of the eastern vertical support.

5.   The individual stones forming the top of the window head and the individual stones forming the western vertical support.

6.   The individual stones forming most of the eastern curve of the top of the window head and part of the western curve of the window head.

Internally, the abacus on each side of the chancel arch have both been decorated with 7C carvings although they have been heavily "restored" during the 1871 renovations.

Internally, there are two sections of stonework from A-S cross-shafts. These are located opposite the south entrance to the church, and built into the north wall of the later inserted north aisle. These can be identified:

LEDSHAM: All Saints Church. Anglo-Saxon stonework, windows and side alternate quoining.

7.   One section of stonework is 10 Ins/25 Cms east of the western window and about 87 Ins/220 Cms up from the floor. It measures 8 Ins/20 Cms H by 24 Ins/61 Cms W. It is decorated with a design which loosely resembles ring chain design; in the middle of the central circle there is a cross.

8.   One section of stonework is 6 Ins/15 Cms west of the eastern window and about 95½ Ins/242 Cms up from the floor. It measures 8 Ins/20 Cms H by 25 Ins/63 Cms W. The eastern 15 Ins/38 Cms only of this section of stonework is decorated with a design which loosely resembles a mixture of ring chain design and vine scroll design.

Externally, 7C A-S material can be identified in the south wall of the nave, including three blocked 7C windows. From west to east these are located:

9.   A virtually intact A-S window, including its distinctive single stone window head, now blocked in. It is located about 12 Ins/30 Cms west of the top of the only window to the west of the south porch.

10.   Part of an A-S window comprising a section of stonework from the top of the eastern side of the single stone window head. It is located cut into by the east side of the top of the same window to the west of the south porch as "9" above.

11.   The distinctive upper part of an A-S window comprising a section of stonework forming its single stone window head (now seemingly broken in two but placed back together). It is situated 26 Ins/66 Cms west of the centre of the first window to the east of the south porch (its western side is behind a drainpipe).

Externally, the large corner stones used in the A-S side alternate quoining can be identified in all corners of the nave apart from the north-east angle. When the chancel was widened in the 13C some of the A-S quoins were repositioned to form part of the "join" between the south wall of the nave and the south wall of the realigned chancel.

LEEDS

(1) City Museum

Rating: ☆☆☆☆☆

Six sections of stonework from A-S cross-shafts dating from around 925 and found in St Peter's Parish Church (see the entry below) are now in the ownership of Leeds City Museum. These sections of stonework are currently being held in the "reserve" collection and can now be viewed by contacting: The Curator of Archaeology, Leeds Museum Resource Centre, 1 Moorfield Road, Yeadon, West Yorkshire, LS19 7BN. The location of these sections of stonework will be determined by the store in which they are being held.

1.   A section of stonework from a cross-shaft. It measures 14 Ins/35 Cms H, by 9 Ins/22 Cms W, by 5½ Ins/13 Cms D. The section of stonework is decorated on one face with part of a figure with a book with drapery below. This figure probably depicts one of the Evangelists. On one side it is decorated with an animal head with a long tongue. Due to weathering and damage no other decoration can be identified on the other face and side. Leeds City Museum Reference: D.1973.338.1.

2.   A section of stonework from a cross-shaft. It measures 9 Ins/22 Cms H, by 10 Ins/25 Cms W, by 9 Ins/22 Cms D. The section of stonework is decorated on one face with the left shoulder of a figure with drapery and the upper part of a book. This figure probably depicts one of the Evangelists. On one side it is decorated with vine scroll design. Due to weathering and damage no other decoration can be identified on the other face and side. Leeds City Museum Reference: D.1973.338.2.

3.   A section of stonework from a cross-shaft. It is from a different cross-shaft from all the other sections of stonework included in this entry. It measures 13 Ins/33 Cms H by 6 Ins/15 Cms square. The section of stonework is decorated on all four sides with both interlace and vine scroll design. Leeds City Museum Reference: D.1973.337.

4.   A section of stonework from a cross-shaft. It measures 14½ Ins/36 Cms H, by 9 Ins/22 Cms W, by 5 Ins/12 Cms D. The section of stonework is decorated on one face with the depiction of the flying machine of Weland (or Weyland or Wayland) the Smith. It is possible to identify the tail of the flying machine, the two straps encircling Weland's knees, bellows and pincers from his smithy. The other face is decorated with ring chain design. One of the sides is decorated with the depiction of a dragon head with a tail. The other side is too weathered and damaged for any decoration to survive. Leeds City Museum Reference: D.1973.339.3.

5.   A section of stonework from a cross-shaft. It measures 13½ Ins/34 Cms H, by 8 Ins/20 Cms W, by 7 Ins/17 Cms D. The section of stonework is decorated on one face with part of a figure whose right hand emerges from drapery and holds a book. This figure is thought to depict St John the Evangelist. The other face and two sides are decorated with ring plait design. Leeds City Museum Reference: D.1973.339.2.

6.   A section of stonework from a cross-shaft. It measures 12 Ins/30 Cms H, by 7½ Ins/19 Cms W, by 7 Ins/17 Cms D. The section of stonework is decorated on one face with the central part of a figure holding a book in two hands. This figure probably depicts one of the Evangelists. On the other face it is decorated ring plait design. One side

is decorated with interlace design and the other side is too weathered and damaged for any decoration to survive. Leeds City Museum Reference: D.1973.339.1.

[Numbers "1" and "2" above probably came from the same cross-shaft. Numbers "4", "5" and "6" above definitely come from the same cross-shaft.]

Separate from these sections of stonework the Museum Store also contains two further sections of stonework that may come from A-S cross-shafts. These are:

7.   A section of stonework measuring 15 Ins/38 Cms H, by 10 Ins/25 Cms W, by 7 Ins/17 Cms D. On one face it is decorated with a figure with an arm raised. The face of the figure is flat and there is drapery around the body. Arguably there is another, smaller figure underneath the raised arm. It could be a Crucifixion scene. The other face and two sides are too weathered and damaged for any decoration to survive.

8.   A section of stonework measuring 23 Ins/58 Cms H, by 15½ Ins/39 Cms W, by 9 Ins D. On one face it is decorated with a figure with its left hand raised, the right hand is missing. The other face and two sides are too weathered and damaged for any decoration to survive.

The Museum also has in its possession:

9.   A sheet bronze work-box and a small penannular brooch from Hawnby in North Yorkshire.

10.   A Scandinavian ivory bodkin from the churchyard of All Saints Church, Bramham (see the entry for Bramham, West Yorkshire).

11.   An iron shield boss, two iron spearheads and a silver gilt brooch with garnets, all from a burial at Guston, Dover in Kent.

LEEDS

(2) St Peter's Parish Church

SE 306333   Rating: ☆☆☆☆☆

In the centre of Leeds signposts refer to St Peter's as the "Parish Church". The church is situated in the south-eastern part of the city centre. The large church of St Peter is about 80 Yds/73 M west of the junction of "Kirkgate" and "Duke Street" (A61) and what is known as the "loop road": there are street signs. The church is easily identified situated on the south side of Kirkgate.

The first church on this site was burnt down in 633 and the church was subsequently rebuilt in stone. Further rebuilding and alterations took place in the 12C, 14C and 16C. The present church dates from the comprehensive rebuilding in 1838-41.

Internally, there is a reconstructed A-S cross-shaft (arguably not complete) with a complete wheel head cross. They are located standing on the floor on the south side of the chancel, underneath the second arch west of the altar. The cross-shaft stands about 156 Ins/396 Cms H, tapering 20 Ins/50 Cms to 14 Ins/35 Cms W, tapering 12 Ins/30 Cms to 8 Ins/20 Cms D. The wheel head cross has a diameter of about 24 Ins/60 Cms with a depth of about 8 Ins/20 Cms. Originally the cross-shaft and wheel head cross were not together; they each had a different cross-shaft and crosshead. There is an illustrated descriptive notice affixed to the pillar to the west of the cross-shaft and crosshead.

The sections of stonework now forming the reconstructed "Leeds Cross" were found during demolition of the old church on this site in 1838. Where there were "missing" sections new, conjectural ones were carved. It is possible that there are more sections of stonework missing from the centre of the cross-shaft than are presently indicated. The sections of stonework found in 1838 date from around 925 and come from more than one cross-shaft.

On the north and south faces of the wheel head cross there are central bosses and a single strand design following the shape of the arms of the cross entwined at the end of each arm There is no decoration on the surrounding edge of the wheel or the ends of the arms.

On the cross-shaft the decoration of elaborate carvings of human and animal figures, and knot work and vine scroll pattern, depict both Christian and pagan themes. Some replacement sections of stonework have been incorporated into the cross-shaft, whether these are accurate replicas of the stonework they replace, or whether they are positioned in the right place, is a matter still under discussion.

The north face of the cross-shaft is decorated with:

1.   In the lowest panel, clearly broken but put back together. There is the depiction of a figure of a man whose outstretched right hand holds a sword and above whose left shoulder there is a bird. There is some disagreement as to whether this figure represents Sigurd, Odin or Weland.

2.   The panel above the figure in "1" above. This panel too is clearly broken but put back together. The decoration on this panel comprises interlace decoration.

3.   The panel above the panel in "2" above. This panel too is clearly broken but put back together. There is the depiction of a figure with curly hair, with drapery ending in a wing and a tail, and hands or claws. With both animal and human characteristics this figure may represent an angel.

4.   The panel above the figure in "3" above. The decoration on this panel comprises knot work decoration.

The south face of the cross-shaft is decorated with:

5.   In the lowest panel, clearly broken but put back together. There is the depiction of a figure of Weland the Smith with his flying machine. It is possible to identify Weland's arms and his hands grasping the hair and the train of the dress of the figure of the woman above him (she is sometimes identified as Weland's wife or a valkyrie), the wings of the machine, the straps passing around his body, Weland's left leg and foot, and pincers, hammers, bellows and anvil-wedges from his smithy.

6.   In the panel above Weland in "5" above. This panel too is clearly broken but put back together. The decoration on this panel comprises a robed figure holding a book in his right hand.

7.   In the panel above "6" above. This panel too is clearly broken but put back together. The decoration on this panel comprises a figure whose body is separated by a missing section of stonework. This figure has a halo over its head and above the halo there seems to be the end of the claws and wings of a bird. With the halo denoting a saint and the claws and wings associated with an eagle this figure may represent Saint John the Evangelist.

The east side of the cross-shaft is decorated with vine scroll design. The west side of the cross-shaft is also decorated with vine scroll design on its upper part but on its middle and lower parts it is decorated with angular and circular varieties of interlace design.

LEEDS
(3) Royal Armouries Museum
SE 309329   Rating: ✩✩✩

The Museum is about a mile south-east of the centre of Leeds and is well signposted. Follow the "Royal Armouries" directional signs and turn east off the A61 along "Chadwick Street" (there is a street sign) and then, as directed, turn east along "Armouries Drive" (there are street signs). The building housing the Museum is easily located on the north side of Armouries Drive.

As with all museums, the displays and the exhibits they contain may be changed, re-sited, removed from display and/or put in store, or loaned to other museums or suitable repositories. Before visiting the museum it is worth checking in advance whether the displays listed in the text below are still in place in the same location(s) set out in the text. Individual exhibits may have been rearranged in terms of their display, the order in which they are displayed and their relationship to other exhibits, some exhibits may have been removed from display. The text in the entry reflects the descriptions and/or accompanying notices to the exhibits at the time of visiting. These too may have been revised, amended, added to or removed.

There are five main galleries depicting War, Tournament, the Orient, Self-Defence and Hunting. The galleries trace the development of arms and armour throughout the world through the use of displays, artefacts, paintings, photographs, films and computer technology. There are regular programmes of interpretation and demonstrations about a variety of related subjects.

In the "War Gallery" there are some exhibits of A-S interest including 10C and 11C spear heads, swords, Danish axes, spurs, stirrups.

The War Gallery displays exhibits from the 7C/8C Wollaston burial at the side of a Roman road in the Nene valley. The burial is of an A-S warrior prince some 25 years old at death. The exhibits from this burial include the "Pioneer" helmet with a boar crest like that of the Benty Grange helmet. There is also a reconstruction of this helmet. Other finds displayed are a hanging bowl, a sword, a small iron knife and 2 small iron buckles.

In the display area relating to early warfare there are constant audio renderings including, in modern English, part of the A-S poem "The Battle of Maldon" – the battle took place in 991.

MIRFIELD
St Mary's Church

SE 212204   Rating: ☆☆☆   Access is possible.

The church is located on the south-eastern edge of Mirfield. 700 Yds/640 M north of the junction of "Church Lane" (there are street signs) and the A644, St Mary's Church is easily identified adjacent to the east side of Church Lane.

Most of the present church on the site dates from 1871, although there is some material dating from the early 13C.

Internally, in the "Lady Chapel" at the east end of the south aisle, there is a section of stonework from an 11C A-S headstone (note, not a section of stonework from a cross-shaft). It is situated about 18 Ins/45 Cms east of the west end of the altar rail, and some 15 Ins/38 Cms south of the wooden screen on the south side of the chancel. Its base is enclosed in a box. It measures 30½ Ins/77 Cms H, by 11 Ins/27 Cms W, tapering 9½ Ins/24 Cms to 8 Ins/20 Cms D. The south side is decorated with a well-defined figure holding a cross, the west side is decorated with a beast, the north side is decorated with a grid iron pattern, and the east side is decorated with interlace and plait work design.

NORMANTON
All Saints Church

SE 387225   Rating: ☆   Access is possible.

In the centre of Normanton, the church is easily identified set back about 45 Yds/41 M from the west side of the B6133, "High Street" (there are street signs). It is about 260 Yds/237 M south of the junction of the B6133 and the A655.

Although the church contains some A-S material, most of the present structure dates from the 13C to the 16C and the 19C.

Internally, A-S fabric survives between the four arches on the south side of the nave. The fabric can be identified on the north face of the walling, between the top of the supporting pillars and the top of the arches.

Given later building work and the effects of chiselling when plasterwork was removed, it is difficult to identify whether any walling on the north side of the nave is A-S since none of it appears similar to the A-S fabric on the south wall of the nave.

OTLEY
(1) All Saints Church

SE 202453   Rating: ☆☆☆☆

The church is easily identified in the centre of Otley. It is 150 Yds/137 M south of the readily apparent "Market Place" (there are street signs) and on the west side of "Kirkgate" (there is a street sign).

The present church mostly dates from the 12C and the alterations and additions in the 14C. There probably was an earlier A-S church on or near to the site of the present church.

Internally, 6 Yds/5 M from the east end of the south aisle, and 32 Ins/81 Cms north of the south wall, there is a gravelled display area which measures 99 Ins/251 Cms W by 51 Ins/129 Cms D. On this display area there are:

1.   A section of stonework from the cross-shaft known as the "Dragon Cross". It is located at the western end of the southernmost line of stonework in the gravelled display area. It measures 38 Ins/96 Cms H, by 11 Ins/27 Cms W, by 8 Ins/20 Cms D. This section of stonework is decorated on both faces with a winged dragon with the portrait of

a haloed saint underneath. On its two other sides it is decorated with interlace design. It dates from the 9C.

2.   A section of stonework from a cross-shaft that is probably A-D. It is located in the same line of stonework as "1" above to the east, and next to, the Dragon Cross "1" above. It measures 12 Ins/30 Cms H, by 9 Ins/22 Cms W, by 5 Ins/12 Cms D. This section of stonework is decorated on the north and south faces with knot work design. On its two other sides it is decorated with vine scroll design.

3.   A section of stonework from the cross-shaft known as the "Evangelist Cross". It is located in the same line of stonework as "1" and "2" above, to the east, and next to, "2". It measures 16 Ins/40 Cms H, by 14 Ins/35 Cms W, by 9 Ins D. This section of stonework is decorated on the north face with part of an angel (the lower half of one wing, some drapery and lower part (cross-shaft) of a cross they are holding) and the head of a monk kneeling at the angel's feet. Unfortunately, because of the damage to this face, only part of the decoration is evident and a good deal of imagination has to be used. The south face is decorated with vine scroll design and the very top of the head of an angel. The other two sides are decorated with vine scroll design. It dates from the late 8C. [See also entry "5" below.]

4.   A section of stonework that dates from a later medieval time. It is located in the same line of stonework as "1", "2", "3" above to the east, and next to, "3". It measures 11 Ins/27 Cms H, by 19 Ins/48 Cms W, by 6 Ins/15 Cms D. There is a descriptive notice to the east, and next to, "4".

5.   A section of stonework from the cross-shaft known as the "Evangelist Cross". (The Evangelist Cross is sometimes also called the "Angel Cross".) It is the more easterly of the two sections of stonework forming the middle line of stonework in the gravelled display area. It measures 31 Ins/78 Cms H, by 11 Ins/27 Cms W, by 9 Ins/22 Cms D. This section of stonework is decorated on the north face with the three of the Evangelists, each beneath an arch and holding his Gospel. (Only the upper body, not the head, of the top Evangelist survives. Both the heads and upper bodies of the two Evangelists below survive.) The south face of this section of cross-shaft is decorated with part of two panels containing the head and body of an angel in the upper panel, and vine scroll design with part of the top of the head of another angel and part of a sword in the lower panel. The other two sides are decorated with vine scroll design enclosing birds and animals. It dates from the late 8C. [See also entry "3" above.] [Part of the crosshead to the Evangelist Cross is now in Otley Museum (see the entry for Otley Museum, West Yorkshire below).]

6.   A section of stonework from a cross-shaft that is probably A-D. It is the more westerly of the two sections forming the middle line of

OTLEY: All Saints Church. The "Dragon Cross".

stonework. It is to the west of "5" above. It measures 12 Ins/30 Cms H, by 8½ Ins/21 Cms W, by 5 Ins/12 Cms D. It is decorated with interlace and knot work design on all four sides.

7.   A section of stonework from an A-D grave cover. It is located at the western end of the northern line of stonework on the gravelled display area. It measures 4½ Ins/11 Cms H, by 22 Ins/55 Cms W, by 20 Ins/50 Cms D. On its top face it is decorated in Ringerike design. There is no decoration on any of the other sides. It dates from the 11C.

8.   A small fragment of stonework from a column of later medieval stonework. It is located in the same line of stonework as "7" above, to the east, and next to, "7".

9.   A section of stonework from an A-S grave marker. It is located in the same line of stonework as "7" and "8" above, to the east of "8" and to the east, and next to, the sketch showing the complete two faces and sides of the Evangelist Cross. The section of stonework measures 8 Ins/20 Cms H, by 10 Ins/25 Cms W, by 9 Ins/22 Cms D. On its northern face it is decorated with vine scroll design. The three other sides are too weathered and damaged for any decoration to survive.

10.   A tapering section of stonework from an A-D cross-shaft. It is located in the same line of stonework as "7", "8", and "9" above, to the east, and next to, "9". It measures 24 Ins/61 Cms H, by 11½ Ins/29 Cms W, by 7 Ins/17 Cms D. It is decorated on all four sides with knot work design.

[There are two other sections of stonework from later medieval grave covers, close to, but not on, the gravelled display area.]

OTLEY
(2) Museum
SE 204455   Rating: ☆☆☆☆

In the centre of Otley, the Museum is located about 380 Yds/347 M east of the readily apparent "Market Place" (there are street signs). It is on the north side of the A659, "Boroughgate" (there is a street sign but not at the junction) at its junction with the west side of "Garnett Street" (there is a street sign). (At this junction Boroughgate becomes "Cross Green and there is a street sign).

When the Museum is open an "Otley Museum Open" sign is propped up against the pillars by the entrance to the "Civic Centre". The appropriate building has on the glass to its entrance doors the Otley coat of arms and the words "Otley Civic Centre". As indicated by the signage inside the building, the Museum is housed in the ground floor of the Civic Centre. The exhibits are located in rooms at the rear of the building.

As with all museums, the displays and the exhibits they contain may be changed, re-sited, removed from display and/or put in store, or loaned to other museums or suitable repositories. Before visiting the museum it is worth checking in advance whether the displays listed in the text below are still in place in the same location(s) set out in the text. Individual exhibits may have been rearranged in terms of their display, the order in which they are displayed and their relationship to other exhibits, some exhibits may have been removed from display. The text in the entry reflects the descriptions and/or accompanying notices to the exhibits at the time of visiting. These too may have been revised, amended, added to or removed.

The Museum includes three display cabinets containing sections of stonework from eight A-S cross-shafts. Descriptive notices mostly accompany these sections of stonework. Working southwards along the display cabinets:

1.   A section of stonework comprising an arm from an A-S crosshead; it is part of the lower arm that connected the crosshead to the cross-shaft. It is located in the northernmost display cabinet, the section of stonework at the north end of the display cabinet next to, and to the north of "2" below. The section of stonework measures 10 Ins/25 Cms H, by 7 Ins/17 Cms W, by about 3 Ins/7 Cms D. Apparently the surface has been affected by fire, hence its reddened appearance.

On its west side it is clearly decorated with the depiction of an A-S/ Viking Warrior. The warrior has a helmet with a nosepiece, a chain-mail jerkin with padded shoulders, and a sword with a round pommel in his right hand. On his right a spear has been bent to fit the frame of the "picture". Alongside his left shoulder is a dagger and by his left knee an axe. In the upper right hand corner there are traces of a raven and in the upper left hand corner there are traces of a claw of a dragon.

On its north side it is decorated with circular vine scroll design and on the south side it is decorated with strap work design. The east side has been used as a paving stone and so the decoration has almost completely vanished and, although there is some slight trace of decoration, the design cannot now be identified. It dates from 950.

2.   A section of stonework comprising part of the central section and part of two arms of a wheel head cross. It is located in the northernmost display cabinet, next to and to the south of "1" above, and next to, and to the north of "3" below in the middle display cabinet. The section of stonework measures 8 Ins/20 Cms H, by 10 Ins/25 Cms W, by 4 Ins/10 Cms D. It was originally decorated with

plait-work design but due to weathering it is now difficult to identify any decoration on any of the sides apart from the central boss on the east side. It dates from 975.

3.   A section of stonework from what is described as an "Anglian" cross comprising the lower part of the centre of a crosshead. It is located in the middle display cabinet, the section of stonework at the north end of the display cabinet, next to and to the south of "2" above in the northernmost display cabinet, and next to, and to the north of "4" below in the middle display cabinet. This section of stonework measures 7 Ins/17 Cms H, by 8 Ins/20 Cms W, by 3 Ins/7 Cms D. On the east side it is decorated with vine scroll design. All the other sides and the ends of the arm of the crosshead are too weathered and damaged for any decoration to survive. It dates from around 900.

4.   A section of stonework from a cross-shaft and part of the connected arm from the crosshead. It is referred to as "The Saints Stone". It is located in the middle display cabinet, the section of stonework in the middle of the display cabinet, next to and to the south of "3" above, and next to, and to the north of "5" below. The section of stonework measures 9 Ins/22 Cms H, by 8 Ins/20 Cms W, by 3 Ins/7 Cms D. On the west side the upper part is decorated with the lower clothing, legs and feet of a human figure, below which there is part of a dragon lying on its back and eating itself. The east side is decorated with strap work design. The other sides are too weathered and damaged for any decoration to survive. It dates from the late 10C.

5.   A section of stonework comprising an arm from a crosshead. It is located in the middle display cabinet, the section of stonework at the south end of the display cabinet, next to and to the south of "4" above, and next to, and to the north of "6" below in the southernmost display cabinet. The section of stonework measures 9 Ins/22 Cms H, by 7 Ins/17 Cms W, by 3 Ins/7 Cms D. It is clearly decorated with vine scroll design on the east side and entwined strap work design on the west side. The "end" of the arm is too weathered and damaged to confidently identify any decoration. It dates from 850.

6.   A section of stonework comprising part of the central section and part of an arm from a crosshead. It is located in the southernmost display cabinet, the section of stonework at the north end of the display cabinet, next to and to the south of "5" above in the middle display cabinet, and next to and to the north of "7" below in the southernmost display cabinet. The section of stonework measures 7 Ins/17 Cms H, by 8 Ins/20 Cms W, by 4 Ins/10 Cms D. On the west side in the centre there is a flower-like design enclosed within two concentric circles with some lines above the circles that may represent the legs of a human. On the east side there are some traces of decoration but these are too weathered

for a design to be identified. The other sides and the end of the arm are too weathered and damaged for any decoration to survive. It dates from 900.

7.   A section of stonework from the arm of the crosshead of the "Angel/Memorial/Evangelist" cross. It is located in the southernmost display cabinet, the section of stonework in the middle of the display cabinet, next to and to the south of "6" above, and next to and to the north of "8" below. This section of stonework measures 9 Ins/22 Cms H, by 8 Ins/20 Cms W, by 6 Ins/15 Cms D. The west side and the end of the arm is decorated with vine scroll design. The east side is decorated with the depiction of a bull, the symbol of St Luke. There is no other decoration on any of the other sides. It dates from the late 8C. (See the entry for All Saints Church, Otley, West Yorkshire, above.)

8.   A section of stonework from a cross-shaft. It is located in the southernmost display cabinet, the section of stonework at the south end of the display cabinet, to the south of and next to "7" above. The section of stonework measures 7 Ins/17 Cms H, by 5 Ins/12 Cms W, by 2 Ins/5 Cms D. On the west side it is decorated with knot work design. The east side has been rendered. The other two sides are too weathered and damaged for any decoration to survive.

PONTEFRACT
Anglo-Saxon Church
SE 462224   Rating: ☆☆☆☆

In the north-eastern part of Pontefract, locate the distinctive parish church of All Saints on the north side of the A645. It is situated at the junction of the A645 and a minor road (there is no street sign). (All Saints Church was ruined in 1645 during the Civil War and although the western part is still ruined, the tower and transepts have been restored and a new, truncated, nave built. In the churchyard there is a large, free-standing church notice identifying "The Parish Church of All Saints".)

Turn off the A645 and proceed in a north-westerly direction along this minor road. (There are "Castle" word and symbol signs directing you along this minor road.) After about 75 Yds/68 M, on the south-western side of this minor road, turn off and proceed in a south-westerly direction uphill along a cobbled road "Booths" (there is a street sign) as directed by the "Castle" sign.

After about 16 Yds/14 M, there are the surviving foundations of an A-S church. These are located in a low, walled enclosure on the north side of the road,

The remains comprise the nave, 9 Yds/8 M by 7 Yds/6 M and part of the west end of the chancel, at its maximum 108 Ins/274 Cms by 180 Ins/457 Cms.

The accompanying notice displays a plan of the church indicating the location of a number of burials in the vicinity and an artist's impression of what the church looked like. The notice records: "The remains of this church are the only visible evidence of the earliest period of Pontefract's history. It seems to be the Saxon predecessor to the parish church of All Saints across the road. During the tenth century the Pontefract area lay within the royal estate of Tanshelf, where, in AD 947 King Eadred accepted the allegiance of the Northumbrians and Archbishop Wulfric of York. It may also have been a base for Eadred's campaign against the Viking, Erik Bloodaxe in AD 948. A priest is mentioned for Tanshelf in Domesday Book and this is probably his church. The church (kirk) may have given its name to the eleventh-century settlement of Kirkby. Two phases of burial pre-dated the stone building, and a timber structure may have been built here first. The earliest burials date to around AD 700. The chancel was the earliest part of the building, and stood alone on the site while more burials took place; many children were buried close to its west wall. Later the nave was added. Straight joints are visible in the stone wall, showing this to be an addition. The simple two-cell plan is typical of a church of the eighth to tenth centuries. The artists' impression (below) shows how it might have looked: very tall for its width, with a high pitched roof. The few windows would have been narrow and the walls, like the excavated foundations would include herringbone masonry. Standing churches of this date can be seen nearby at Ledsham and Burghwallis, Doncaster."

RASTRICK
St Matthew's Church

SE 137215   Rating: ☆☆   Access to the church is not essential.

The combined Anglican and Methodist Church of St Matthew is located in the centre of Rastrick, adjacent to the south side of the A643. (Note: the Ordnance Survey Map does not fully reflect the west/east direction of the A643 at this point.)

The present church on the site dates from 1796-98.

A section of stonework comprising a substantial 11C A-S cross base is situated in the north-western part of the churchyard, 11 Yds/10 M north-west of the northern churchyard entrance by the side of the A643.

The slightly tapered cross-base is 40 Ins/101 Cms south of the churchyard wall. It stands 42 Ins/106 Cms H, by 26 Ins/66 Cms W, by

26 Ins/66 Cms D. The cross base is heavily weathered. There is a recess in the top to house the accompanying cross-shaft. The north side is the least weathered and the decoration of plait work and circular design is the best preserved. On its south and east sides it is decorated with tree scroll design, although the weathering requires a good deal of imagination to be used. On the west side it appears that weathering has worn away all trace of decoration.

RIDDLESDEN
East Riddlesden Hall (NT)
SE 079421   Rating: ☆☆☆

At the south-east end of Riddlesden, turn off the B6265, "Bradford Rd." (there are street signs) and head in a southerly direction as indicated by the "East Riddlesden Hall" directional signs. In the grass verge on the south side of Bradford Road, and by the west side of the minor road which goes down to the entrance gateway and drive leading to the Hall, there is a large free-standing sign "The National Trust East Riddlesden Hall". The Hall is about 200 Yds/182 M south of Bradford Road.

The Hall is a manor house dating from the 1640s which had a west wing remodelled in 1692. Apart from the facade the west wing was demolished in 1905.

Inside the Hall, in the Great Hall, there is a section of stonework from an A-S cross-shaft. It is located in the south-west corner of the Great Hall, surrounded by a 31 Ins/78 Cms H wooden barrier (in the corner of the Hall farthest from the entrance). It is supported and enclosed by a purpose built tray – there are additional vertical supports to keep the section of stonework upright. This tray sits on a purpose built wooden plinth that stands on the floor. The purpose built tray measures 1¾ Ins/4 Cms H, by 13½ Ins/34 Cms W, by 8½ Ins/21 Cms D. The purpose built plinth measures 13 Ins/33 Cms H, by 19 Ins/48 Cms W, by 15½ Ins/39 Cms D.

This section of stonework from a cross-shaft comprises two sections of stonework correctly joined together. Together they measure 35½ Ins/90 Cms H, tapering 12 Ins/30 Cms to 10½ Ins/26 Cms W, tapering 6½ Ins/16 Cms to 4½ Ins/11 Cms D. The north-east (front) face is decorated on its upper section with a pelican tearing at her breast to feed her young, alternatively, a depiction of the symbol of St John, the eagle. The lower section of the north-east face is decorated with ring work design. The south-east side is decorated on its upper section with interlace design and on its lower section it is too weathered for any decoration to survive. The north-west side has no decoration surviving on either the upper or lower sections other than two incised parallel lines running down the centre. The south-west (rear) face is too weathered and damaged for any decoration to survive on either the upper or lower sections.

The guidebook ascribes a date of around 700 to this section of stonework – this seems about 200 years too early. It has been suggested the section of stonework was built as a doorpost, but this seems unlikely as they are typical sections of what one would expect from a cross-shaft. The two sections of stonework were found separately, the upper section in 1987 and the lower section in 1959. The lower section was found among graves in the cellar of the Hall and the upper section in grounds in the vicinity of the Hall.

Being in such a good defensive position and with the sections from an A-S cross-shaft found in the vicinity, it is likely that the site was occupied during the A-S period.

ROTHWELL
Holy Trinity Church
SE 343283   Rating: ☆☆☆☆   Access is possible.

In the southern part of Rothwell the church is easily located on the north side of "Church Street" (there are street signs). The churchyard is about 360 Yds/329 M north of the A654. It can be reached by taking "Butcher Lane" (there is a street sign) which runs north off the A654 to lead into Church Street.

The current church on the site dates from the 15C and the restoration in 1873.

ROTHWELL: Holy Trinity Church. Two sections of Anglo-Saxon stonework, possibly each from a lintel over a door. Both are clearly decorated with a series of arches under which there are a variety of designs including interlace, vine-scroll pattern and animals.

Internally, there are two sections of 8C/9C A-S stonework possibly each from a lintel over a door. At present these are located in the north-west corner of the nave. They are lying on a strip of polystyrene packing placed on top of a flat piece of wood lying on the floor, adjacent to the angled walling between the north side of the nave and the tower. The two sections of stonework have been placed one on top of the other and are separated from each other by another piece of polystyrene packing. (They are to be displayed at the west end of the north aisle along with a number of later medieval decorated pieces of stonework.)

The smaller "upper" section of stonework measures between 6½ Ins/16 Cms and 7½ Ins/16 Cms H, by 26 Ins/66 Cms W, tapering 10 Ins/25 Cms to 7 Ins/17 Cms D. It is clearly decorated on its south-east side with arches under which there are interlace and vine scroll pattern designs. The other three sides are too weathered and damaged for any decoration to survive.

The larger "lower" section of stonework measures between 7 Ins/17 Cms and 7 ¾ Ins/19 Cms H, by 34 Ins/86 Cms W, by 21 Ins/53 Cms to 9 Ins/22 Cms D. It too is clearly decorated on its south-east side with an elaborate design with arches under which animals can be identified. On the north-east side of this section of stonework that is 9 Ins/22 Cms D, it is decorated with the head, torso, arm and hand of what probably is an angel. The face on this head is very clear and the depth of the eye sockets indicate these may have been set with jewels. The two other sides are too weathered and damaged for any decoration to survive.

SANDAL MAGNA
St Helen's Church
SE 343182   Rating: ☆

In the centre of Sandal Magna, the church is easily identified set back from the east side of the A61. Behind the churchyard walling by the east side of the A61 there are large, free-standing "St Helen's" church notice boards.

The present structure on the site dates mostly from 1150 with alterations and additions in 1180, the 14C, 16C. It was restored in 1872.

That there was an A-S church on this site and this is confirmed internally by a distinctly A-S arrangement whereby the angles of the central square crossing project into the nave aisles.

Internally, it is likely that A-S material survives in the lower parts of the crossing and some of the fabric in the south transept walling. The surviving section of a plain, square section from an A-S string course that protrudes on the west face of the west wall of the south transept confirm this. This section is about 12 Ins/30 Cms above the top of the arch in the west wall of the south transept. This section measures about 108 Ins/274 Cms in length.

Internally, the four large supporting columns for the central crossing have "channelled bases" that may indicate A-S origin. This tooling can be identified in the stonework at the bases of these columns, above the plinths on which they stand, and below the circular moulded stonework. Although these features can be identified at the bases of all four columns, the south-west and south-east columns are the best preserved.

SHORE
Mount Cross

SD 915273   Rating: ☆☆

Mount Cross comprises an 11C A-S ring head cross and a cross-shaft. It is situated in an isolated location to the north the hamlet of Shore.

On the southern edge of Stansfield Moor there is a minor road that follows the contours of the hillside and links Hebden Bridge with Burnley and a number of isolated hamlets in between. North of Shore there is a road junction and on the south side of the road there is a directional sign "Shore ½, Todmorden 3¾". Turn off this minor road and head south along "Mount Lane" (there is a street sign) towards Shore as indicated by the directional sign. After about 300 Yds/274 M, there is a wooden "Public Bridleway" directional sign 72 Ins/182 Cms from the east side of Mount Lane. Beneath this public bridleway sign, and attached to it, there is a more distinctive "Lower Intake" sign. Proceed along the bridleway in a south-easterly direction for about 74 Yds/67 M. The cross, leaning southwards at a 45 degree angle, is easily identified in the field adjacent to the north side of this bridleway. It is located 12 Yds/10 M north of the field wall running along the north side of the bridleway.

The section of stonework comprising the ring head cross and cross-shaft stand in total 77 Ins/195 Cms H. The ring head cross measures 25 Ins/63 Cms H, by 22 Ins/55 Cms W, by 4 Ins/10 Cms D. There is no decoration on any of the sides of the ring head cross due to weathering and damage apart from the central boss on the south facing side and the damaged, incomplete, central boss on the north facing side. The section of stonework comprising the cross-shaft measures 52 Ins/132 Cms H, tapering 15 Ins/38 Cms to 12½ Ins/31 Cms W, by 6½ Ins/16 Cms D. There is no decoration on any of the sides of the cross-shaft due to weathering and damage.

SKELMANTHORPE
St Aidan's Church

SE 229104   Rating: ✩✩✩   Access is possible.

Towards the western end of Skelmanthorpe, turn off the B6116 and head in a south-westerly direction along "Cumberworth Road" (there are street signs) as directed by the arm "New Mill, Holmfirth" on the directional signpost at the junction.

After about 66 Yds/60 M turn off Cumberworth Road and head in an easterly direction along "Radcliffe Street" (there is a street sign). 15 Yds/13 M from Cumberworth Road, set back from the south side of Radcliffe Street, there is a free-standing "St Aidan's Church" notice board on the church green.

After about 43 Yds/39 M, on the south side of Radcliffe Street, there is an entrance to a drive that leads directly uphill to the church that can easily be identified. Pass through this entrance and proceed up along the drive to reach the church that is about 84 Yds/76 M away from Radcliffe Street.

The church dates from 1894-95.

Internally, the church contains an A-S font. It is situated in the centre of the west end of the nave, on a plinth. The font has been placed on a more recent 24 inch/60 Cms H pedestal. The font is 26 inch/66 Cms square by 24 Ins/60 Cms H. It is decorated with arch motifs, figures, circular and tree scroll design with large leaves. It is thought that A-S workman working in 1080 made this font. The font originally came from All Hallows Church, High Hoyland. There is a replica of this font in the Tolson Museum, Huddersfield (see the entry for Huddersfield, West Yorkshire).

SOUTH KIRKBY
All Saints Church

SE 453111   Rating: ✩   Access is possible.

In the centre of South Kirkby, the church is easily identified on the south side of the B6422, "Barnsley Road" (there is a street sign). There is a free-standing church notice board behind the walling on the south side of the B6422.

The present church on the site dates mainly from the 13C, 14C and 15C.

Internally, fabric in the walling in the four corners of the nave includes 11C A-S stonework. The stonework is not easy to identify due to later rebuilding and plasterwork. The stonework in the north-west and south-west corners of the nave is easier to identify.

SWILLINGTON
St Mary's Church

SE 385305   Rating: ☆   Access to the church is not essential.

Towards the northern end of Swillington, the church is easily located on the west side of the A642 at its junction with "Church Lane" (there is a street sign). The churchyard entrance is in Church Lane.

The present church on the site dates mainly from the 12C, the late 14C, the mid 15C, and the rebuilding in 1884.

Externally, there is an 11C "scratch" or "mass" dial incised on the face of one of the stones incorporated into the fabric of the south wall of the south aisle. This stone is 17 Ins/43 Cms west of the window nearest to the east side of the south porch and 85 Ins/215 Cms up from the ground. The circular incision on the stonework is much worn and the central gnomon is missing but its position is indicated. The diameter of the dial is 11 Ins/27 Cms.

THORNHILL (near Dewsbury)
St Michael and All Angels Church

SE 253188   Rating: ☆☆☆☆☆   Access is possible.

In the north-eastern part of Thornhill, the church is easily identified adjacent to the western side of the B6117.

On the site of a 9C A-S church the present structure dates mostly from the 15C and the rebuilding in 1875-76.

Internally, there are nine sections of A-S stonework displayed in the "Savile Chapel" located at the east end of the north aisle. These sections of stonework and the accompanying illustrated information notices have been placed on three purpose built floor-standing display stands.

The westernmost display stand is situated 50½ Ins/128 Cms south of the north wall of the Savile Chapel and 30 Ins/76 Cms east of the iron gates at the west end of the chapel. This display contains:

1.   A section of stonework from an arm from a crosshead. It is located sitting on a spike on the top display shelf of this stand and measures 7 Ins/17 Cms H (W), between 5 Ins/12 Cms and 7½ Ins/19 Cms W (H), by 5 Ins/12 Cms D. On the north and south sides, and the top "end", it is decorated with knot work design. There is no decoration on the other sides or the end of the arm. It is numbered "1A".

2.   A section of stonework from a cross-shaft. It is located sitting on a spike on the middle display shelf of this stand and measures between 2½ Ins/6 Cms and 4 Ins/10 Cms H, tapering 8 Ins/20 Cms to 7½ Ins/19 Cms W, by 5½ Ins/13 Cms D. On the south side it is decorated with knot work design. On all three of the other sides it is so weathered that no decoration survives apart from vertical lines providing a border for each edge of each side. It is numbered "1B".

3.   A section of stonework from a cross-shaft. It is located sitting on the bottom display shelf of this stand and measures between 14 Ins/35 Cms and 17½ Ins/44 Cms H, by 9 Ins/22 Cms W, by 5½ Ins/13 Cms D. On the south side it is decorated with a large "S" shaped curving design arguably above which there is a depiction of outward facing animals. However, below the "S" shaped curving design there are faint traces of a futhorc (runic) inscription on three lines: "Ethelberht settæfter Ethelwi(ni) O (ra)", meaning Ethelberht set up this cross in memory of Ethelwini. Pray for him. The north side is decorated with lines outlining an oblong with a smaller oblong inside. The east and west sides are each decorated with lines outlining a single oblong. It dates from the 9C. It is numbered "1C".

THORNHILL: St Michael and All Angels Church. A display of Anglo-Saxon stonework including parts of crossheads, cross-shafts (three with inscriptions) and a grave cover with an inscription.

The middle display stand is situated just under 40 Ins/101 Cms south of the north wall of the Savile Chapel and 73 Ins/185 Cms east of the iron gates at the west end of the chapel. This display contains:

4.   A section of stonework from a cross-shaft. It is located sitting on a spike on the top display shelf of this stand and measures between 10½ Ins/26 Cms and 11½ Ins/29 Cms H, tapering 8 Ins/20 Cms to 7½ Ins/19 Cms W, by 5 Ins/12 Cms D. On the south side it is decorated with knot work design. The west side is decorated with vertical lines. The two other sides are too weathered and damaged for any decoration to survive. It is numbered "2A".

5.   A section of stonework from a cross-shaft. It is located sitting on the middle display shelf of this stand and measures between 11½ Ins/29 Cms and 12 Ins/30 Cms H, tapering 12 Ins/30 Cms to 9½ Ins/24 Cms W, tapering 11 Ins/27 Cms to 8½ Ins/21 Cms D. Due to damage, it has clearly been shaped to fit in somewhere; only about 5 Ins/12 Cms of the width of the north side survives. The south side is decorated with vine scroll design. The north and west sides are decorated with vertical lines. The north side is also decorated with some plait work design. Any original decoration on the east side has been completely obliterated by later "shaping". It is numbered "2B".

6.   A section of stonework from a cross-shaft. It is located sitting on the bottom display shelf of this stand and measures between 19½ Ins/49 Cms and 20½ Ins/52 Cms H, tapering 8 Ins/20 Cms to 7½ Ins/19 Cms W, tapering 4½ Ins/11 Cms to 4 Ins/10 Cms D. On the south side it is decorated with knot work design including a pair of outward facing dragons below which there is a futhorc (runic) inscription on three lines: "Eadred sete æfta Eate eonne", meaning Eadred set this cross up to Eata. There is no decoration on the north and west sides apart from lines outlining an oblong. On the east side there is no decoration apart from vertical lines marking a border on each edge. It dates from the late 9C. It is numbered "2C".

The easternmost display stand is situated 30 Ins/76 Cms south of the north wall of the Savile Chapel and 117 Ins/297 Cms east of the iron gates at the west end of the chapel. This display contains:

7.   A section of stonework comprising part of an arm and possibly part of the central section from a crosshead. It is located sitting on a spike on the top display shelf of this stand and measures between 9½ Ins/24 Cms and 10½ Ins/26 Cms H, between 4½ Ins/11 Cms and 7 Ins/17 Cms W, by just over 4 Ins/10 Cms D. It is decorated on all four sides with vine scroll design. It is numbered "3A".

8.   A section of stonework from a 9C grave cover. It is located sitting on a spike on the middle display shelf of this stand. It has been

split vertically in two and placed back together. The section of stonework measures between 6 Ins/15 Cms and 10½ Ins/26 Cms H, between 6 Ins/15 Cms and 11½ Ins/29 Cms W, by 3¼ Ins/8 Cms D. On the south side there is a futhorc (runic) inscription on part of four lines: "æ æft (aer) Osber (ch) tæ bec(bnofe)r ber(gi (gebiddad dær saule)", meaning some person, whose name it is not now possible to identify, set this in memory of Osberht, a monument over his grave. Pray for his soul. The three other sides are too weathered and damaged for any decoration to survive. It dates from around 870. It has been suggested that it could have covered the coffin containing the body of King Osberht killed by the Danes near York on 21 March 867. It is numbered "3B". [A cast of this section of stonework from a grave cover is now in the Tolson Museum in Huddersfield (see the entry for Huddersfield, West Yorkshire).]

THORNHILL: St Michael and All Angels Church. An Anglo-Saxon cross-shaft. It is decorated with knot work design, below which there are three lines of futhorc/runic inscription.

9.   A section of stonework from a cross-shaft. It is located sitting on the bottom display shelf of this stand and measures between 19 Ins/48 Cms and 20½ Ins/52 Cms H, tapering 12½ Ins/31 Cms to 11 Ins/27 Cms W, by 7¼ Ins/18 Cms D. On the south side it is decorated with knot work design below which there are three lines from a runic inscription: there is a futhorc (runic) inscription on four lines: "(G)ilsuith arærde æft Berhtsuithe, becun (on) bergi. Gebiddath thær saule", meaning Gilsuith reared this cross to Berhtsuith, a monument on her grave. Pray for her soul. The three other sides are decorated with knot work design. It was carved in the late 9C. It is numbered "3C".

There is a modern reproduction of the complete cross-shaft that the section of cross-shaft at "9" above comes from. It is located leaning against the north wall of the Savile Chapel 13½ Ins/34 Cms east of the westernmost window on the north side of the Savile Chapel. It has been affixed to a wooden backing. The reproduction measures about 67 Ins/170 Cms H, 18 Ins/45 Cms W at its maximum, by 2¼ Ins/5 Cms D.

These sections of stonework represent at least six different crosses. It is possible that "1" above may come from the same cross as "3" above, although it is also possible that "1" above comes from the same crosshead as "7" above. It is possible that "2" above may come from the same cross-shaft as "3" above. It is possible that "4" above comes from the same cross-shaft as "6" above. It is possible that "7" above comes from the same cross as "9" above.

THORP ARCH
All Saints Church

SE 438461   Rating: ☆   Access is possible.

The church is located in an isolated position on the north-eastern side of Thorp Arch. The church is situated by the junction of "Church Causeway" and "Whins Lane" (there are street signs) on the east side of Church Causeway.

The church dates mostly from the restoration in 1871-2.

Internally, there is a section of stonework from an A-S cross-shaft. It has been incorporated into the fabric of the internal west wall of the south porch, underneath the northern end of the window ledge. It is located 13½ Ins/34 Cms south of the north wall of the porch and 28½ Ins/72 Cms up from the floor. The section of stonework measures 12 Ins/30 Cms H by 18 Ins/45 Cms W. Although weathered and damaged some knot work decoration can be identified.

(Note: The section of stonework underneath the southern end of the window ledge decorated with a chequer-board design is of later medieval date.)

WAKEFIELD
(1) Cathedral
SE 333208   Rating: ☆

In the centre of Wakefield, the Cathedral, with its tall spire (the highest in Yorkshire), is easy to identify. It is located on the north side of the paved area that forms a westerly continuation of "Kirkgate" (there is a street sign). The Cathedral is about 125 Yds/114 M west of where Kirkgate changes from running in a north-westerly to a westerly direction (there is another "Kirkgate" street sign at this point).

The Cathedral is built on the site of an A-S church of which nothing can now be seen. During excavations in 1974 A-S graves were found beneath the foundations of the Norman church surviving on this site. The present structure dates mainly from the 14C and the restoration in 1858-74.

Internally, by the east wall of the south transept, there is a replica of part of the cross-shaft known as the "Wakefield Cross". (The original, dating from around 940, is in Wakefield Museum – see the entry below). The replica is 63 inch/160 Cms tall and stands on a plinth. It is decorated on all four sides with interlace and plait work design. On the wall on the north side of the replica there is a pictorial reconstruction of the Wakefield Cross, and on the wall on the south side of the replica there is an information notice about the Wakefield Cross.

WAKEFIELD
(2) Museum
SE 331208   Rating: ☆☆

In the centre of Wakefield, the building housing the Museum is located on the south-west side of the A650, "Wood Street" (there are street signs). It is about 157 Yds/143 M north-west of the junction of Wood Street with the A642, "Marygate" and "Bull Ring" (there are street signs).

The appropriate building has: the words "Wakefield Museum" affixed to the exterior stonework at first floor level, the word "Museum" on the ironwork above the entrance doorway and a Wakefield Museum notice board by the steps adjacent to the entrance. The building was built 1820-21 as a music saloon and reading room.

As with all museums, the displays and the exhibits they contain may be changed, re-sited, removed from display and/or put in store, or loaned to other museums or suitable repositories. Before visiting the museum it is worth checking in advance whether the displays listed in the text below are still in place in the same location(s) set out in the text. Individual exhibits may have been rearranged in terms of their display, the order in which they are displayed and their relationship to other exhibits, some exhibits may have been removed from display. The text in the entry reflects the descriptions and/or accompanying notices to the exhibits at the time of visiting. These too may have been revised, amended, added to or removed.

On the first floor the Museum tells the history of Wakefield through informative displays (including "touch-screen") with illustrative artefacts. The displays of A-S interest are on the first floor.

There is a display on the "Dark Ages" and reference to the Kingdom of Elmet 400-617. This display contains a spearhead found at a burial dating from 600 at North Elmsall.

The display also contains the original of the section of stonework from a cross-shaft known as the "Wakefield Cross". It is on loan from York Museums. The section of stonework measures 60 Ins/152 Cms H, tapering 17 Ins/43 Cms to 13 Ins/33 Cms W, by 10 Ins/25 Cms D. The section of stonework is clearly decorated with plait work design on all four sides. It dates from 950. [A replica of the Wakefield Cross is displayed in Wakefield Cathedral (see the entry above).]

WOODKIRK
St Mary's Church

SE 272250   Rating: ☆

The church is located on the western side of Woodkirk. It is adjacent to the east side of the A653, about one mile south of the junction of the A653 with the A650 (T) (by Junction 28 of the M62). There is a church notice board behind the walling alongside the east side of the A653. There is also a free-standing "Public Footpath" directional sign in front of this walling, 4 Yds/3 M north of the church notice board. This public footpath passes through the churchyard and past the south porch of the church.

The church dates mostly from the rebuilding in 1831, but it does have a 13C tower.

Externally, there is a section of stonework from what may be an A-S cross base. It is located 24 Ins/61 Cms south of the western end of the south porch of the church. The section of stonework tapers from about 24 Ins/61 Cms square at its base to about 20 Ins/50 Cms square at its top. It stands about 23 Ins/58 Cms H. The cross base has a socket for a cross-shaft. It is weathered with no distinctive decoration on any of its sides.

York *(Including Fulford)*

In York, including Fulford, 19 sites of Anglo-Saxon/Viking interest have been entered in the text.

10 sites have been rated with one star ☆

This signifies that material may be difficult to find or identify with confidence. These entries are:

Fulford – St Oswald's Hall
Fulford – Battle
York – Archaeological Resources Centre
York – Friargate Wax Museum
York – Holy Trinity Church
York – Palace of Erik Bloodaxe
York – St Cuthbert's Church
York – St Mary Bishophill Senior Church
York – St Olave's Church

2 sites have been rated with two stars ☆☆

This signifies that material can be found and identified but it is not particularly well looked after or a "good example". These entries are:

York – All Saints Church
York – St Clements's Church

5 sites have been rated with three stars ☆☆☆

This signifies that material can easily be found and identified. These entries are:

York – Holy Redeemer Church
York – Minster Library
York – St Mary Bishophill Junior Church
York – Walls – The Anglian Tower
York – York Story Museum in the former church of St Mary (now no longer open)

1 Site Has Been Rated With Four Stars ☆☆☆☆

This Signifies That Material Can Easily Be Found And Identified And Provides Good Examples. This Entry Is:

York – Minster

2 sites have been rated with five stars ☆☆☆☆☆

This signifies that material can easily be found and identified, providing excellent examples that are full of interest. These entries are:

York – Jorvik
York – The Yorkshire Museum

ADDENDUM

THE HARROGATE HOARD

Location yet to be determined

Rating ☆☆☆☆☆

"The Harrogate Hoard" is a Viking hoard discovered in January 2007 in the Harrogate area.

It comprises a decorated silver guilt cup containing 617 coins dating from the late 9C to early 10C, 67 pieces of silver including arm-rings, silver ingots and "hack-silver" comprising silver that has literally been broken or chopped-up, a gold arm-ring and fragments of a lead sheet that it is thought formed part of a covering or box.

The latest coins date from the time of King Athelstan (924-939) and it is thought the hoard was deposited around 928.

The hope is that this hoard will be jointly acquired and exhibited by York Museums Trust, Harrogate Borough Council's Museums & Arts Service and the British Museum and displayed both in Yorkshire and elsewhere.

FULFORD
(1) St Oswald's Hall (Formerly St Oswald's Church)
SE 605496 Rating: ☆

In the northern part of Fulford, which is now a suburb of York, St Oswald's Hall is located on the north side of St Oswald's Road that leads off the A19 in a westerly direction. There are street signs either side of St Oswald's Road at its junction with the A19 identifying both St Oswald's Road and the fact that it is a no-through road and leads to Connaught Court and Atcherley Close.

The Hall is situated at the western end of St Oswald's Road, on the north-eastern corner of a very minor crossroads (including a south running rough drive cum track). St Oswald's Hall was formerly St Oswald's Church and the "grounds" to the Hall were the former churchyard.

There is a descriptive notice affixed to the wall adjacent to the eastern side of the gated entrance to the former churchyard. The notice is 48 Ins/121 Cms up from the ground. The notice records: "St Oswald's Hall. On this ancient site traces have been found of Roman, Pagan and Christian Saxon occupation including foundations of a late Saxon Church. The surviving 12C Norman Chapel belonged to St Mary's Abbey York throughout the Middle Ages. Victims of the Black Death were buried here in 1349. This chapel served the people of Fulford until the present parish church was built in 1866. Declared redundant in 1973 the building was restored as a private residence in 1981."

Enquiries should be made of the Tourist Information Centre in York to see if access is possible.

FULFORD
(2) Battle
SE 611487 Rating: ☆

The site of the battle is centered around the north and south bank of the small stream known as "Germany Beck", which is crossed by the A19, "Selby Road". On the west side of the A19, locate its junction with the no-through road "Landing Lane" (there is a street sign that also indicates no through road). Opposite the junction with Landing Lane, on the east side of the A19, there are two street signs "Main Street" (the more northerly) and "Selby Road" (the more southerly).

From these two street signs proceed in a northerly direction along the pavement for about 42 Yds/38 M. There is then a break in the adjacent fence (concrete pillars linked by low iron bars) separating the pavement from a recreation ground. [This break in the fence is located some 12 Yds/10 M south of the bridge carrying the A19 (Main Street) over Germany Beck.] 318 Ins/807 Cms east of this break in the fence, and incorporated into an identifiable west sloping earthen bank, there is a plaque commemorating the battle. The plaque lies in the ground some 46 Ins/116 Cms north-west of ten paving slabs that also lie in the ground. The surrounding grass is encroaching on both the plaque and paving slabs and consequently they are not easy to find.

The plaque measures 20 Ins/50 Cms by 18 Ins/45 Cms. Incised on it are the words: "This stone is to commemorate the battle of Fulford fought in this area between Hardrada and Morkere on September 20th 1066. Fulford Parish Council." Due to weathering and the surrounding vegetation the wording is not that clear.

The battle was fought on the 20 September 1066 and probably involved some 5,000 to 6,000 men on either side. Earl Morkere and Earl Edwin led the northern English army. The Norwegian army was led by King Harald Sigurdsson, "Harald Hardrada(i) or Harald the Ruthless", of Norway and Earl Tostig. The Norwegian army left their camp and ships at Ricall and marched towards York following the east bank of the River Ouse. The English army occupied the higher ground on the north side of a ford over the Germany Beck. The Norwegians formed a line of battle with their left (west) flank protected by the River Ouse and their right (east) flank protected by a ditch running parallel to the river. King Harald's position was in the Norwegian line closest to the River Ouse. After initial English success King Harald's personal intervention led to the English defeat. Casualties were heavy on both sides and many Englishmen were drowned in the River Ouse although some were able to return to York.

YORK

Street signs are readily visible and identifiable throughout the centre of York. "The centre of York" is defined as the area within Eastings 596 and 611 and within Northings 513 and 525.

YORK
(1) All Saints Church – Pavement
SE 604517   Rating: ★★

The church is located in the central part of the centre of York. It is situated on the north side of Coppergate, 18 Yds/16 M west of its junction with Piccadilly and on the corner of the junction of Coppergate and Parliament Street.

When St Cuthbert visited York in 685 to be consecrated Bishop of Lindisfarne an A-S church was established on this site. The present structure is particularly distinctive with its late 15C large octagonal Lantern Tower. The church was restored in 1835-37.

Internally, there is a section of stonework from an A-S coffin (probably a child's). It is located laying on top of a plinth that measures 11 Ins/27 Cms H, by 34 Ins/86 Cms W, by 12 Ins/30 Cms D. The plinth stands on the floor underneath the western arm of the second arch west of the altar on the north side of the nave. (It is 3 Ins/7 Cms east of the supporting pillar.) The section of stonework tapers 6½ Ins/16 Cms to 5½ Ins/13 Cms H, by 35½ Ins/90 Cms W, by 13 Ins/33 Cms D. The top face is clearly decorated with entwined beasts and interlace design. A stone ridge runs through the middle of this top face. There appears to be no decoration on the other sides.

YORK
(2) Archaeological Resources Centre (ARC)
SE 605519   Rating: ✫

The Centre is located in the northern part of the centre of York. It is easily located on the southeast side of St Saviourgate housed in the former church of St Saviour's. Attached to the walling by the side of the entrance doors there is an "ARC" notice.

The centre is intended to provide visitors with "hands on" experience of archaeology providing an opportunity to sort bones, tiles and pottery, make a "Roman" shoe and weave cloth on a "Viking" loom, and use computers to see how they help with excavations.

YORK
(3) Friargate Wax Museum
SE 604515   Rating: ✫

The Wax Museum is located in the southern part of the centre of York. It is situated on the north side of Lower Friargate, 46 Yds/42 M west from its junction with Clifford Street. The appropriate building has attached to the gates to the entrance to the building a large sign "Friargate Wax Museum and the Black Cave". There is also a large, vertical sign "Friargate Museum" attached to the front of the building.

The displays and the exhibits may be changed, re-sited or removed from display. Before visiting it is well worth checking beforehand that the displays referred to in the text below are still in place.

The waxworks contain a variety of displays relating to the various Dukes of York, Kings and Queens of England – including King Alfred, the Battle of Hastings, Francis Drake, the Great York Air Raid in 1942 and Gaming Machines.

YORK
(4) Holy Redeemer Church
SE 576526   Rating: ☆☆☆   Access is possible.

The church is located west of the central part of York. The churchyard is adjacent to the north side of the A59 in the part of the road known as "Boroughbridge Road" (there is a street sign). There is a freestanding church notice board facing the road.

The present structure was built in 1965. The church incorporates into its structure stones taken from the A-S church of St Mary Bishophill Senior, York. St Mary's Church was demolished in 1964(?).

Internally, fabric from St Mary's, possibly A-S and possibly dating from the 8C, is easy to identify in the south wall of the south aisle, in the pillars and arches in the south wall of the nave and in the stonework surrounding the south door into the church.

Internally, incorporated into the walling of the reading desk located on the north side of the chancel there are:

1.   A section of stonework from a cross-shaft. It has been incorporated into the west and south faces of the stonework in the reading desk, forming part of a corner, 17½ Ins/44 Cms up from the floor on the west face and 13½ Ins/34 Cms up from the floor on the south face. The section of stonework from the cross-shaft measures 20½ Ins/52 Cms H by 5½ Ins/13 Cms W on its west side, 20½ Ins/52 Cms H by 11½ Ins/29 Cms W on its south side and 19 Ins/48 Cms H and between 4½ Ins/11 Cms and 6½ Ins/16 Cms W on its east side. On both the west and south sides knot work design can be identified. On its east side the design includes a series of small squares reminiscent of tegulated roof design from a hogback grave cover.

2.   A section of stonework from a cross-shaft. It has been incorporated into the south face of the stonework forming the east arm of the reading desk, 14½ Ins/36 Cms west of the east end of the reading desk and 12½ Ins/31 Cms up from the floor. The section of stonework from a cross-shaft measures 8½ Ins/21 Cms H by 7 Ins/17 Cms W. It is decorated with two lines from a circle possibly enclosing a face.

Internally there is a section of stonework from an A-S cross-shaft incorporated into the west and south faces of the stonework in the pulpit on the south side of the chancel. It forms part of a corner of the pulpit, 31½ Ins/80 Cms up from the floor on the west face and 32½ Ins/82 Cms up from the floor on the south face. The section of stonework from a cross-shaft measures 16 Ins/40 Cms H by 8½ Ins/21 Cms W on its west side and 13 Ins/33 Cms H by 12 Ins/30 Cms W on its south side. Despite damage knot work design can be identified on both the west and south sides.

Internally, there is a damaged section of stonework from an A-S cross-shaft standing on the floor in front of the northwest angle of the pulpit on the south side of the chancel. The section of stonework measures up to 9½ Ins/24 Cms H, by 9½ Ins/24 Cms W, and up to 9½ Ins/24 Cms D. Both the north east and south west faces appear to be decorated with part of a figure (upside down when the more horizontal end of the section of stonework is placed on the floor). The other two sides are decorated with knot work design.

Internally, incorporated into the walling in the south wall of the south aisle there are:

3. A section of stonework from an A-S cross-shaft. It is located 102 Ins/259 Cms west of the east end of the south aisle and 44 Ins/111 Cms up from the floor. The section of stonework measures 10½ Ins/26 Cms H by 12½ Ins/31 Cms W. It is decorated with a diamond pattern design.

4. A section of stonework from an arm of an A-S crosshead. It is located 129 Ins/327 Cms west of the east end of the south aisle and 87½ Ins/222 Cms up from the floor. The section of stonework measures 8½ Ins/21 Cms H by 7 Ins/17 Cms W. It is decorated with knot work design.

5. A section of stonework that may be part of an A-D hogback grave cover. It is located between the second and third freestanding pillars (from the east end) on the south side of the nave and 90 Ins/228 Cms up from the floor. The section of stonework measures 12 Ins/30 Cms H by 22 Ins/55 Cms W. It is decorated with knot work design. (To the east of this section of stonework, and lower down the walling, there is a more distinctive later medieval gave cover.)

6. A section of stonework from an A-S cross-shaft. It is located 47 Ins/119 Cms east of the south door and 35 Ins/88 Cms up from the floor in a section of stonework that separates two niches. The section of stonework measures 22½ Ins/57 Cms H, tapering 13½ Ins/34 Cms to 10 Ins/25 Cms W, by 9 Ins/22 Cms D. It is decorated with knot work design on all three sides that can now be viewed.

Internally, at the east end of the church, and affixed to the wall behind the altar, there is a large iron cross. Attached to the centre of this iron cross, there is a section of stonework from an A-S cross-shaft. The section of stonework measures about 18 Ins/45 Cms H, tapering 8 Ins/20 Cms to 7 Ins/17 Cms W, tapering 8 Ins/20 Cms to 7 Ins/17 Cms D. On its west face it is clearly decorated with the head and torso of a saint (there is a halo) holding a book above which there are two human legs and feet. On its north and south sides it is decorated with ring chain design. It is not possible to view the east face at present but this too is likely to be well decorated given the given the quality of the decoration on the other sides.

Internally, additional to the A-S/Viking material identified, later medieval grave covers can also be identified incorporated into the fabric of the church utilising material taken from St Mary Bishophill Senior.

Externally, fabric from the St Mary Bishophill Senior Church has clearly been rebuilt into the present structure to form the wall of the south aisle, including a blocked doorway, and the south doorway into the church, now enclosed by a modern building. Some of the material used may be A-S in origin but it is difficult to confirm this with confidence.

See the entries for St Mary Bishophill Senior Church, York and St Clement's Church, York.

YORK: Holy Redeemer Church. Part of an Anglo-Saxon cross-shaft decorated with the figure of a saint – with halo – above which there are the legs and feet from another figure.

YORK
(5) Holy Trinity Church
SE 598516   Rating: ☆

The church is located in the south western part of the centre of York. It is set back from the southeast side of "Micklegate", less than 200 Yds/182 M northeast of Micklegate Bar.

A descriptive notice is attached to one of the entrance gates (the one on the west side) to the churchyard. This notice records that a religious house existed on this site before the Norman Conquest, a Benedictine Priory followed which then became ruined after the 1538 Dissolution.

The present structure is on the site of an A-S church ruined during the "Harrying of the North" in 1069-70. A Benedictine Priory built in

1089 replaced this ruined A-S church. The present, mostly 13C, structure occupies only part of the nave and the central crossing of the much larger Priory church. As well as 13C work, the fabric of the present structure includes material from the 12C, 15C, 16C and the rebuilding work undertaken in 1849, 1886 and 1903-5.

YORK
(6) Jorvik
SE 604516   Rating: ☆☆☆☆☆

"Jorvik" is located in the central part of the centre of York. On the south side of "Coppergate", opposite All Saints Church Pavement, turn off Coppergate and proceed in a southeast direction along "Coppergate Walk". After about 70 Yds/64 M the Jorvik is easily identified on the south side of Coppergate Walk. There is a distinctive "Jorvik" sign with logo extending over the pavement from the appropriate building. Jorvik houses a reconstructed Viking settlement and an exhibition on the Coppergate excavations.

Built on the site of the Coppergate excavations a time machine takes you back in time to 25 October 975. A "capsule" then takes you around a reconstructed Viking settlement that endeavours to show the development of the commercial part of the Viking city. The reconstruction shows the timber city of Jorvik comprising wooden houses, workshops and warehouses with thatched roofs. The reconstruction includes the sights, sounds and smells of the city with a wide variety of the people depicted undertaking everyday activities and using speech of the time. Part of the excavations have been reconstructed to show how and what the archaeologists discovered.

There are also displays showing various artefacts found during the excavations. These displays illuminate the particular object and the background scene depicted show the context in which the objects were used.

In Coppergate the buildings and artefacts were preserved by the damp soils in the vicinity. During the excavations that took place from 1976 to 1981 four rows of buildings were found along with a host of everyday utensils, tools and clothing, including the remains of boots and shoes, needles and pins, plants and insects.

[The Coppergate helmet is now displayed in the Yorkshire Museum in York, see the appropriate entry below. An incised slab incorporated into the floor of Jorvik marks the spot where the helmet was found in 1982. The incised slab is about 7 Yds/6 M from the end of the time car ride (landing platform) and about 13 Yds/11 M away from the exhibition. The commemorative slab records: "At this spot on the 12th May 1982 the

Coppergate helmet was found by Chris Wade and Andy Shaw during construction of the JORVIK Viking Centre."]

YORK
(7) Minster
SE 603522   Rating: ✰✰✰✰

The Minster is in the north western part of the centre of York. It dominates the locality. It is adjacent to the north side of "Minster Yard". The main western entrance is close to the junction of "Minster Yard", "High Petergate" and "Duncombe Place".

The present Minster and all its predecessors stand on part of the site of the Headquarters for the Roman fortress of York. A wooden church dedicated to St Peter was built on the site for the baptism on Easter Day in 627 of King Edwin of Northumbria (reigned 616-633). This church was then enclosed within a stone church completed by King (Saint) Oswald of Northumbria (reigned 634-641). When Wilfred became bishop of York in 629 he carried out repairs and improvements. The church was burnt in 741. The new building work undertaken by Archbishop Albert of York (767-80) and consecrated by him in 780, included a new altar in the church where Edwin was baptised. In 1069 the Normans burnt down the Church of St Peter and in 1075 the Danes broke into the church and departed with much booty.

The present structure, which dates from 1220, is the largest Gothic church in Northern Europe. It also includes "Early English", "Decorated" and "Perpendicular" styles of architecture.

The Eastern Crypt

In the eastern crypt beneath the present choir there are extensive remains probably dating from the church consecrated by Archbishop Albert in 780. The entrance to the eastern crypt is reached by proceeding down a flight of steps in the south-western part of the south transept and into the "Undercroft Museum". Proceed into Chamber II of the Undercroft Museum and take the steps up to the Treasury to the east. Proceed in an easterly direction through the Treasury, through the western crypt, and then into the eastern crypt.

The remains were discovered during the course of repairs following the fire in 1829. The information is based on the evidence discovered by John Browne during 1829-1847. The remains are now covered by modern paving or encased in later stonework. They are not accessible to the public.

The remains comprise foundations of concrete rubble and parts of the main sidewalls that by their layout indicate an apsidal church with aisles or porticus and with an eastern transept.

The foundations are apparently some 108 Ins/274 Cms below the floor of the south aisle of the present choir. Underneath the present structure, the foundations run eastwards from the base of the north-eastern pier of the central tower for about 43 Yds/39 M, and run westwards underneath the floor of the present central crossing and the nave for some 20 Yds/18 M. The foundations themselves are about 24 Ins/60 Cms in thickness.

The main sidewalls survive to about 16 Yds/14 M in length and stand up to 120 Ins/304 Cms H. The walls have a core 56 Ins/142 Cms thick faced on either side by herring-bone masonry. They enclose an area 9 Yds/8 M in width. The walls, including the herring-bone masonry are now encased on both sides by later masonry.

The foundations indicate a structure at least 66 Yds/60 M in length and 28 Yds/26 M in width. It is just possible that part of these foundations are displayed. These are located in the northern part of the eastern crypt where there is a small wooden fenced enclosure surrounding a small chamber below the present floor level. This chamber contains what the accompanying notice describes as a " Roman Column Base and late 11C Apse". The column base dates from the 4C and comes from a colonnade in the house of the commanding officer of the Roman legion. Part of the curved foundation of the eastern apse of the 8C A-S cathedral can also be seen in this small chamber although these foundations are usually attributed to the 11C Norman cathedral. The red studs in the floor of the eastern crypt mark the inner and outer edges of this apse wall. (Follow the outer, eastern lines of the red dots to identify the curved section of walling in the chamber.)

In a niche on the east face of the western wall of the eastern crypt there is a mid-15C font sitting in a well, now filled in, which sits on the traditional site of where King Edwin was baptised in 627. The font cover depicts the figures of Queen Ethelburga, King Edwin, Bishop Paulinus, St Hilda and James the Deacon. There is a descriptive notice.

The Undercroft Museum

In the Undercroft Museum, there is an exhibition displaying the foundations and the walling of the Roman basilica and part of the legionary fortress Headquarters building. The foundations of the Norman Cathedral are also displayed. The Museum also contains Roman and some of the A-S artefacts found in the vicinity. An extensive A-S cemetery was found under the present floor level in and around the vicinity of Chamber I. The cemetery was in use between 800 and 1080.

As with all museums, the displays and the exhibits they contain may be changed, re-sited within the museum, removed from display and/or put in store, or loaned to other museums or suitable repositories. Before visiting a museum it is well worth checking beforehand that the displays referred to in the text below are still in place and whereabouts they are in the museum. Even where the displays are in the same places as indicated in the text below, individual exhibits may have been rearranged in terms of their display, the order in which they are displayed and their relationship to other exhibits, some individual exhibits may have been removed from display.

The Undercroft Museum is entered down a flight of steps in the south-western part of the south transept. Precede into Chamber I where all the items of A-S/A-D interest are apart from the "Horn of Ulph" – see the paragraph below concerning "The Treasury". [Note: The current suggested, clockwise, tour of the Undercroft results in this Chamber being the last visited.]

On reaching the bottom of the steps in the southeast chamber (Chamber I) of the Undercroft Museum (the first chamber entered if the tour starts in an anti-clockwise direction) there are:

1.   A grave cover of a 6-year-old A-S child. It is located on a specifically built floor standing stand 3 Yds/2 M from the bottom of the steps. It is in its own display on the left (west) side of the steps and 4 Yds/3 M south of the freestanding display indicating the Roman, Saxon, Norman and Medieval levels of stonework underpinning the present Minster. The grave cover measures 28½ Ins/72 Cms L, by 14 Ins/35 Cms W, by 8½ Ins/21 Cms D. It is decorated with a cross and interlace design on its top side: there is no other decoration on any of the other sides.

2.   A section of stonework from an A-S cross-shaft. It is located on a specifically built floor standing stand 4 Yds/3 M from the bottom of the steps. It is in its own display on the right (east) side of the steps and in the opposite location to "1" above. The section of stonework measures between 31 Ins/78 Cms and 38 Ins/96 Cms H, tapering 14 Ins/35 Cms to 11 Ins/27 Cms W, by 8½ Ins/21 Cms D. Despite damage and weathering the section of stonework is clearly decorated. On the northeast side it is decorated with three figures, possibly representing Christ blessing two saints. The three other sides are decorated with interlace design and entwined animals. It dates from the 10C.

3.   The site of the grave cover of a 6-year-old A-S child referred to in "1" above. It is located 7 Yds/6 M from the bottom of the steps and is situated among the freestanding display indicating the Roman, Saxon, Norman and Medieval levels of stonework underpinning the present Minster. The site is indicated by a flat stone marked with a cross and two upright stones. (There is an information notice about the grave attached to the stonework.). See ☆☆ below – a display cabinet in the centre of the floor in Chamber I.

4.   A display containing a number of items of A-S/Viking interest. This separate self-contained display is part the freestanding display

indicating the Roman, Saxon, Norman and Medieval levels of stonework underpinning the present Minster (also referred to in "1" and "3" above). This display is situated on the north facing part of this Minster levels of stonework display. The A-S/Viking display contains the numbered items:

On the upper shelf numbers 1 and 2:

1. A section of stonework from an Anglian grave cover. It measures 6 Ins/15 Cms H, by 9 Ins/22 Cms W, by 5 Ins/12 Cms D. It is decorated on its north side with a cross and an inscription: "+ HIC. CES. ITEM. RA. VVLFHER (ERE) QUIESC (UN)T" denoting the grave of Wulfhere. Despite damage there may be some decoration on the other sides but these cannot be viewed at present.

2. The section of stonework comprising part of the central section and part of an arm from a small 8C crosshead. It measures 17 Ins/43 Cms H, by 8½ Ins/21 Cms W, by 9½ Ins/24 Cms D. On the north side it is decorated with an Evangelist holding a Gospel. On the south side it is decorated with vine scroll design – mostly on the part of the arm of the crosshead. Due to weathering and damage there is no other decoration on any of the other sides of this section of stonework.

On the lower shelf numbers 3 to 8:

3. A chalice and paten made for burial, pewter with high lead content, with no date attributed. They mark the grave of a priest.

4. A 13C Wolfshead in stone. Its purpose is unknown.

5. A bone stylus for writing on wax tablets, probably A-S.

6. An Anglo-Scandinavian bone comb.

7. An Anglo-Scandinavian bone cloak pin.

8. An Anglo-Scandinavian Bone Skate made from horse bone.

Some of the finds from the A-S cemetery found under the Minster are exhibited in a display cabinet in the centre of the floor in Chamber I. This display cabinet is located 11 Yds/10 M from the bottom of the steps into Chamber I, and 3 Yds/2 M east of the display of the levels of stonework containing the site of the burial of the 6 year old referred to in ☆☆ above – the freestanding display indicating the Roman, Saxon, Norman and Medieval levels of stonework underpinning the present Minster. In this display cabinet there are the numbered items:

1. A section of stonework from an A-S cross-shaft. It measures 11 Ins/27 Cms H, by 14 Ins/35 Cms W, by 6 Ins/15 Cms D. On

the south side there is an unfinished decoration depicting birds and foliage in an "inhabited" vine scroll design. The north side is decorated with basket ware design. The two other sides have been rendered so no decoration survives. It dates from the 9C. It is numbered "1".

2. A section of stonework from an A-S grave marker. It measures 16 Ins/40 Cms H, by 10 Ins/25 Cms W, by 4 Ins/10 Cms D. It is decorated on both north and south sides with a cross on a stepped base (a rare example). Due to weathering no decoration survives on the other two sides. It is numbered "2".

3. An Anglian "stele". It measures 6 Ins/15 Cms H, by 8½ Ins/21 Cms W, by 3½ Ins/8 Cms D. It is decorated on its south side with "+LEOB" and "DEH". There is no decoration on any of the other sides. It dates from the late 7C/early 8C. It is numbered "3".

4. One damaged arm from an A-S crosshead. It stands 6 Ins/15 Cms H, by 4 Ins/10 Cms W, by 3 Ins/7 Cms D. It is decorated with vine scroll design on both north and south sides, but due to damage no decoration survives on the other two sides. It is numbered "4".

Sections of A-S stonework are also displayed in an open area in front of walling in the south-eastern part of Chamber I, 12 Yds/10 M from the bottom of the steps leading into the Chamber. These sections of stonework are all numbered in a descriptive notice attached to the front of one of two wooden bench-like stands describing them as "Re-Used Roman Stones, Anglian (8th Century), Anglo-Scandinavian Gravestones with crosses and interlace". The front wooden stand stands 27¾ Ins/70 Cms H. It has numbers "4", "5", and "6" (see below) placed upon it. The rear wooden stand stands 39½ Ins/100 Cms H. It has numbers "2", "3", and "9" (see below) placed upon it. Number "1" (see below) is displayed separately, to the left (north) of the front wooden stand and in front (west) of the rear wooden stand.

These sections of numbered stonework are:

1.　What the notice describes as a "Large flat complete gravestone with interlace." A large A-S/Viking grave slab. It is located to the left (north) of the front wooden display stand. It is supported by two purpose-built 18¾ Ins/47 Cms high supports. A 24-Ins/60 Cms high "wall" of stonework encloses both the slab and the supports on which it sits. The almost complete (there is part of a corner missing) grave slab measures 4 Ins/10 Cms H(D), by 53 Ins/134 Cms L, by 19 Ins/48 Cms D (W). The top face is decorated with knot work design. There is no decoration on the other three sides.

2.　What the notice describes as an "Incised grave slab with cross and interlace (rope border)." A section of stonework from an A-S grave slab. It is the section of stonework nearest to the left (north) end of the rear wooden stand. The section of stonework measures 12 Ins/30 Cms H(W), by 27½ Ins/69 Cms W(L), by 6½ Ins/16 Cms D. On both the west and east sides it is decorated with a large cross that intersects in the centre of the grave cover and divides the sides into quarters containing interlace design. The other two sides are too weathered for any decoration to survive.

3.   What the notice describes as a "Fragment of grave slab with stepped base." A section of stonework from an A-S grave slab. It is the second section of stonework from the left (north) end of the rear wooden stand, between the sections of stonework numbered "2" and "9". The section of stonework measures 21½ Ins/54 Cms H(L), by 21½ Ins/54 Cms W, by 6 Ins/15 Cms D. On its west (top) side it is decorated with interlace design. There is no decoration on the other three sides.

4.   What the notice describes as a "Weathered grave slab with scroll work." A section of stonework from a Viking grave slab. It is located towards the right (south) end of the front wooden stand. The section of stonework measures 5½ Ins/13 Cms H (D), by 12½ Ins/31 Cms W, by 15 Ins/38 Cms D (L). It is decorated with cross and interlace design in the Jellinge style on all four sides (it has two broken edges).

5.   What the notice describes as a "Hogback gravestone." A section of stonework from a hogback grave cover. It is the section of stonework near the left (north) end of the front wooden stand. The section of stonework measures 17 Ins/43 Cms L, by 15½ Ins/39 Cms W, by 7 Ins/17 Cms H. Although weathered the section of hogback does retains some vestiges of tegulated roof decoration. The sides are too weathered for any decoration to be confidently identified.

6.   What the notice describes as a "Fragment of grave slab with bird decoration." A section of stonework from an A-S cross-shaft. It is the section of stonework towards the centre of the front wooden stand between the sections of stonework numbered "4" and "5" above. The section of stonework measures 21 Ins/53 Cms H, by 16¾ Ins/42 Cms W, by 4¼ Ins/10 Cms D. It is decorated with vine scroll design including four birds on its west side. It is decorated with basket ware design on its three other sides.

7.   What the notice describes as a "Re-used Roman stone – originally a memorial with a Latin inscription "To the spirits of the departed and of Antonius Gargilianus, of equestrian status, formerly prefect in the Sixth Legion. He lived 56 years 6 months, Claudius Florentinus, Decurion, his son-in-law (set this up)." This section of stonework also bears an Anglo-Scandinavian inscription, prefaced by a cross, "Pray for the soul of Costaun." It is the section of stonework sitting on a concrete ledge 25 Ins/63 Cms south of the front wooden display stand. The section of stonework has been broken and divided into three sections but all three sections have now

been placed back together. Overall this section of stonework measures 74¼ Ins/188 Cms L, by 19 Ins/48 Cms H(W), and between 4 Ins/10 Cms and 4½ Ins/11 Cms D. All three sections of stonework have the same dimensions in height (width) and depth. The most easterly (left-hand) section of stonework measures between 28¾ Ins/75 Cms and 29¼ Ins/74 Cms L, the middle section of stonework measures between 22½ Ins/57 Cms and 23¾ Ins/60 Cms L, the most westerly (right-hand) section of stonework measures between 19 Ins/48 Cms and 21¼ Ins/53 Cms L. Apart from the inscriptions referred to in the notice on the north side of this section of stonework, no other decoration can be identified on any of the other sides.

8.   What the notice describes as a "Re-used Roman column incised with a cross". It is the section of stonework sitting on the same concrete ledge as "7" above and 11½ Ins/29 Cms southwest of "7" above and 56 Ins/142 Cms south-west of the barrier in front of the front wooden display stand. The column has been broken in two with the two sections placed together. It measures 52 Ins/132 Cms L overall. The more easterly (left-hand) section of stonework measures 27¼ Ins/69 Cms L, between 13½ Ins/34 Cms and 15 Ins/38 Cms H(W), by 7½ Ins/19 Cms D. The more westerly (right-hand) section of stonework measures 24¾ Ins/62 Cms L, between 15 Ins/38 Cms and 15½ Ins/39 Cms H(W), by 7½ Ins/19 Cms D. Although weathered the column is decorated on its top face with vine scroll design, including, apparently, four birds, but these are difficult to identify because of weathering. It is not possible to view all sides but some basket ware design can be identified on the sides that can be viewed.

9.   What the notice describes as "Part of an Anglian gravestone or stele shape with simple markings on the edge." Number "9" labels three sections of stonework. They are located near the right (south) end of the rear wooden stand.

a.   The section of stonework towards the rear of the rear wooden stand, behind the left-hand (northern) section of stonework of the three sections of stonework numbered "9" (this entry). This section of stonework measures 11 Ins/27 Cms H, by 7¾ Ins/19 Cms W, by 6½ Ins/16 Cms D. It is damaged with little trace of any decoration surviving on any of its sides.

b.   The section of stonework in front of "a." above and on the left-hand (northern) side of the three sections of stonework numbered "9" (this entry) on the rear wooden stand. This section of stonework measures 4 Ins/10 Cms H, by 5¼ Ins/13 Cms W, by 5¾ Ins/14 Cms D. On the west side it is incised with the letters "PRO ANI". It is damaged with little trace of any decoration surviving on any of the other sides.

c.   The section of stonework on the right-hand (southern) side of the three sections of stonework numbered "9" (this entry) on the rear wooden stand. This section of stonework measures between 5½ Ins/13 Cms and 6 Ins/15 Cms H, by 5½ Ins/13 Cms W, by 3½ Ins/8 Cms D. It is damaged with little trace of any decoration surviving on any of its sides.

The Treasury

The A-S "Horn of Ulf" is displayed in "The Treasury" (on the site of the Roman HQ building). The Treasury is entered up steps leading from Chamber II in the Undercroft Museum. The Horn of Ulf is exhibited placed on supports on the bottom shelf in the second display cabinet on the left from the entrance to the Treasury (about 6 Yds/5 M from the top of the steps). The "Horn" is a drinking horn made from an elephant's tusk. It measures 27 Ins/68 Cms L. The Horn was carved and decorated at Salerno in Italy in the first half of the 11C. The nobleman "Ulf" gave it to the Minster before 1066. It now has 17C silver mountings. The Horn is numbered "12" on the information notice attached to the adjacent wall.

[There are helpful descriptive notices identifying the items of interest in the various chambers in the Undercroft Museum and The Treasury.]

YORK
(8) Minster Library
SE 603523   Rating: ☆☆☆

The Library is in the north western part of the centre of York. The building housing the Library is about 100 Yds/91 M north of the north transept of the Minster. The building is on a north-west/south-east alignment. The entrance to the Library and its grounds is through a gated enclosure. The relevant entrance doorway has a "York Minster Library" sign affixed to the adjacent wall.

The Library was once the chapel of the Archbishop of York's Palace.

The Library contains the "York Gospel Book" which was made by monks at Canterbury around 1000 AD. Wulfstan, Archbishop of York 1003-23, brought it to York.

YORK
(9) Palace of Erik Bloodaxe
SE 605519   Rating: ☆

The site of the palace is in the centre of the northern part of the centre of York. The site of the palace is situated on the north side of Saint Andrewgate, at the junction of "Colliergate", "King's Square" and "St. Andrewgate". The modern building housing "Newitts" sports shop now occupies the site. Extending over the pavement from the first floor of the building is a sign "Newitts of York Established 1902". Erik Bloodaxe was King of York between 947 and 948 and between 952 and 954.

YORK
(10) St Clement's Church
SE 600509   Rating: ☆☆   Access is possible.

The church is located south of the southern part of the centre of York. It is situated on the north side of Scarcroft Road, at the junction of "Scarcroft Road" and "Nunthorpe Road" (there are street signs for Scarcroft Road but not Nunthorpe Road). It is about 100 Yds/91 M from the eastern end of Scarcroft Road.

The church was built in 1874.

Internally, the there is what appears to be a complete A-S grave cover. It is located affixed to the western wall of the nave behind the font. It is also affixed to the plinth on which the font sits. The grave cover measures 48 Ins/121 Cms H, tapering 16½ Ins/41 Cms to 15½ Ins/39 Cms W, by 6 Ins/15 Cms D. On its east face it is decorated with a large cross dividing the face into four segments that each contain knot work design. On the north and south sides there are some traces of knot work design despite the weathering.

Internally, there is what is described as an A-S child's coffin. It is located lying on the floor in the centre of the north aisle. The coffin measures 7 Ins/17 Cms H, by 36 Ins/91 Cms L, tapering 16½ Ins/41 Cms to 12 Ins/30 Cms W. It is not decorated.

The grave cover and coffin came from St Mary Bishophill Senior Church in York (now demolished). See the entries for St Mary Bishophill Senior Church, York and Holy Redeemer Church, York.

YORK
(11) St Cuthbert's Church
SE 607521   Rating: ☆

The church is located in the centre of the northern part of the centre of York. It is situated adjacent to the northwest side of Peasholme Green, under 80 Yds/73 M south west from the junction of Peasholme Green and "Jewbury".

A church was founded on this site possibly around 687. There is a legend that St Cuthbert blessed the city of York in the vicinity of where the church now stands. The present structure incorporates some A-S material but it was largely rebuilt around 1430.

Externally, on the east face of the chancel wall, the gable end of the 10C A-S church can be identified high up in the wall. The age and irregularity of some of the stones incorporated into the fabric of this wall indicate the use of both A-S and Roman material.

YORK
(12) St Mary Bishophill Junior Church
SE 599515   Rating: ☆☆☆   Access is possible.

The church is located in the south western part of the centre of York. It is adjacent to the north side of the road "Bishophill Junior" opposite its junction with Smales Street.

The tower is A-S in origin and dates from the 11C; the internal tower arch separating the tower from the nave is A-S. The walls of the nave may be A-S in origin. Most of the present body of the church dates from the 12C, 13C and 14C. The church was restored in 1860.

Internally, there is a section of stonework from an A-S cross-shaft. It is located standing on the floor at the west end of the nave, 1½ Ins/3 Cms east of the stonework supporting the south side of the eastern arch of the tower. The section of stonework measures 34½ Ins/87 Cms H, tapering 14½ Ins/36 Cms to 10 Ins/25 Cms W, by 7 Ins/17 Cms D. On all four sides the decoration indicates a transitional design merging vine scroll, strap work, and basket plait design. It dates from the mid 10C.

A section of stonework from an A-S cross-shaft, a section of stonework from part of an A-S crosshead and a section of stonework from probably another A-S cross-shaft found in St Mary Bishophill Junior are now displayed in the Yorkshire Museum (see the entry for the Yorkshire Museum, York).

Externally, the tower contains examples of A-S features including:

1.   Side alternate quoining on the four corners of the tower. Some of the examples nearer to ground level are quite large.

2.   Double belfry windows each framed by pilasters. These are located in the fourth (top) stage of the tower on all four sides of the tower.

3.   Single windows in both the second and third stages of the tower. These are located on the north and south sides of the tower.

4.   A mixture of re-used Roman material and herring-bone masonry. This is evident on all four sides and all stages of the tower.

YORK
(13) St Mary Bishophill Senior Church
SE 602514   Rating: ☆

The site of this church is located in the south western part of the centre of York. The site is situated in a walled and gated enclosure, now distinguishable only as a former graveyard and a flat grass-covered area with some trees. It is located on the east side of the road "Bishophill Senior" at its junction with the passage "Carr's Lane".

The church has been demolished and whilst the outlines of some of the foundations are clearly visible in the grass there is no descriptive plaque. Apparently, incorporated into the fabric of the nave was A-S material possibly dating from the 8C. The name "Senior" indicates that this church was older than St Mary Bishophill Junior that survives.

Some A-S material from St Mary Bishophill Senior has now been taken to the Holy Redeemer Church in Boroughbridge Road, York, and an A-S grave slab from St Mary Bishophill Senior is now in St Clements's Church, Scarcroft Road, York – see the entries for Holy Redeemer Church, York and St Clement's Church, York.

YORK
(14) St Olave's Church
SE 598522   Rating: ☆

The church is located on the west side of the centre of York. It is situated adjacent to the northeast side of "Marygate", under 25 Yds/22 M north of the gatehouse and western entrance to the gardens containing St Mary's Abbey and the Yorkshire Museum.

On the site of an A-S church, the present 15C structure was damaged during the siege of York in 1642 and was rebuilt in 1721-22. It also has 19C additions.

This church was dedicated to St Olave (the patron saint of Norway) in 1050. Although no fabric from this early church survives, the founder of the church, Earl Siward of Northumbria, who died in 1055, lies buried under the original site of the high altar of the church (now near the present chancel steps). There is no commemorative plaque.

YORK
(15) Walls – the Anglian Tower
SE 599522   Rating: ☆☆☆

The Anglian Tower is located on the western side of the centre of York.

The city walls run for some 2¾ miles and whilst most of the surviving fabric dates from the 13C and from the 19C and 20C restorations, there are identifiable stretches of the wall incorporating Roman and A-S fabric.

In the extreme north eastern section of the Yorkshire Museum Gardens separate from, but adjacent to the York Central Library building, are the substantial 13C remains of St Leonard's Hospital SE 599521 (formerly St Peter's, an A-S foundation). Close to St Leonard's the medieval walls are clearly standing on a Roman base. Less than 100 Yds/91 M west of St Leonard's Hospital (in the Yorkshire Museum Gardens) there are the distinctive remains of the Roman Multangular Tower SE 599521. Although repaired with both modern and medieval masonry, distinctive Roman workmanship can be identified particularly on the inside of the tower. (There are also Roman coffins placed on the ground on the inside of the tower.)

Less than 50 Yds/45 M north of the Multangular Tower there are the simple remains of the Anglian Tower, which comprises a square tower with two narrow arched side doorways. The lower storey is tunnel-vaulted. This tower filled a breach in the Roman Wall, which, as can be seen, is separate from the medieval wall.

Almost immediately to the north of the Anglian Tower there is a grassed bank on which there are a number of plaques attached to stonework denoting the various building stages of the walls in the vicinity.

YORK
(16) The Yorkshire Museum
SE 599522   Rating: ☆☆☆☆☆

The Yorkshire Museum is located on the western side of the centre of York. The gardens containing the Museum can be entered through the imposing gated drive and pedestrian entrance on the west side of "Museum Street". Attached to the adjacent south pillar to the pedestrian entrance on the south side, there is a small plaque denoting "Yorkshire Philosophical Society". Inside the gardens, in front of railings, there are freestanding notice boards and signs identifying the "Yorkshire Museum". Free-standing Museum signs in the gardens themselves provide directions to the Museum that can be reached by more than one footpath.

The Museum is situated in the northern section of the Yorkshire Museum Gardens, east of the St Mary's Abbey ruins. It is located in a distinctive "Doric" style building dating from the early 19C.

As with all museums, the displays and the exhibits they contain may be changed, re-sited, removed from display and/or put in store, or loaned to other museums or suitable repositories. Before visiting the museum it is worth checking in advance whether the displays listed in the text below are still in place in the same location(s) set out in the text. Individual exhibits may have been rearranged in terms of their display, the order in which they are displayed and their relationship to other exhibits, some exhibits may have been removed from display. The text in the entry reflects the descriptions and/or accompanying notices to the exhibits at the time of visiting. These too may have been revised, amended, added to or removed.

This Museum contains exhibits covering archaeology, natural history, geology and pottery. The extensive displays and reconstructions cover Roman, A-S, Viking and Medieval periods of York's history. It also has many artefacts from St Mary's Abbey including walling and stonework with a reconstruction of the entrance to the Chapter House.

Items of A-S and Viking are to be found in the "Anglo-Saxon and Viking Galleries" located at the rear of the building on the ground floor and basement floor (with a connecting staircase).

NOTE: The numbers indicated below are the same numbers identifying artefacts in their respective displays. Likewise most of the descriptions detailed below are those descriptions that accompany the displays themselves.

Displayed in Galleries on The Ground Floor

These galleries contain a number of illustrated notices: "British Kingdoms and Anglo-Saxon Settlement"; "West Heslerton, 6th Century Settlement"; "Northumbria and Christianity, The Conversion of Edwin"; "The Irish Mission, Conflict with the Church of Rome"; "Uncleby, 7th Century Cemetery"; "Monasteries, Lastingham"; "Monasteries, Crayke"; "Wilfred, Bishop of York"; "Monasteries, Whitby & Jarrow"; "Alcuin, York's Greatest Scholar"; "The Golden Age of York"; "Alcuin and Charlemagne"; "Daily Life, Freemen and Peasants"; "King and Council"; "History through Coinage, Northumbrian Rulers"; "Troubled Northumbria, Internal Strife"; "Troubled Northumbria, Viking Raiders"; "Viking Settlement, The Danelaw"; "Viking York"; and "The York Master".

(A)   A DISPLAY CONTAINING THE FOLLOWING ITEMS AND ARTEFACTS:

"The Heworth Cemeteries":

1. Biconical urn with a footing decorated with stamps and oval bosses outlined with carved grooves and slashes.
2. Shouldered urn with multiple bosses.
3. Plain shouldered urn with grass tempering visible on the surface.
4. Biconical bowl with linear and chevron design.

5.   Biconical urn decorated with long bosses and line and dot decoration.

6.   Two urns, probably made by the same potter. They have the same grid and rosette stamps which occur in horizontal and linear panels.

7.   Stamped biconical urn with bosses and arched "Stenhende Bogen" decoration. This type of urn is known in the Saxon homeland of north-west Germany.

"5C/6C house at Catterick":

1.   Cooking pot from house

2.   Sherd with stamped decoration.

The display includes an illustrated reconstruction of a sunken floor house, a "grubenhaus", found at the site that measured 3 M (118 Ins) by 4.5 M (177 Ins).

"Finds from 5th - 6th Century Inhumation Cemeteries on the Wolds":

Hornsea Cemetery:

1.   Two cruciform brooches with animal head terminals, together with two small long brooches.

Cheesecake Hill Cemetery:

2.   Two annular brooches, amber necklace and cruciform brooch arranged, as they would have been worn.

3.   Pair of cruciform brooches with exaggerated animal headed terminals.

4.   Gilt and silvered cruciform mount.

5.   Two pairs of wrist clasps.

6.   Bronze tweezers engraved with geometric ornament.

7.   Two crystal beads.

8.   Necklace made of polychrome glass beads.

9.   Three small long brooches.

10.   Two iron knife blades.

11.   Socketed iron spearhead.

12.   Large spearhead.

Londesbrough Cemetery:

13.   Square headed brooch with head decorated with debased animal ornament.

14.   Square headed brooch with silver disc shaped extensions.

15.   Pair of wrist clasps decorated with debased animal heads.

16.   Buckle loop decorated with debased animal ornament.

17.   Necklace with mixed polychrome glass, plain glass and amber beads.

Kilham Cemetery:

18.   Cruiciform brooch.
19.   Necklace with polychrome and monochrome glass beads.
20.   Square-headed brooch with openwork foot.
21.   Copper alloy buckle.
22.   Radiate-headed brooch with chip-carved decoration inlaid with garnets.
23.   Two pairs of annular brooches.
24.   Amber necklace with pendant.
25.   Three pairs of wrist clasps.
26.   Three socketed spearheads.

"West Heslerton Grave Number 46":

1.   Objects from a woman's grave. Clothes have disintegrated leaving only small traces of textiles on the backs of some of the jewellery. The annular brooches on the shoulders pinned together the over garment. The cruciform brooch at the neck probably fastened a cloak and the wrist clasps secured the sleeves. The necklace is made of glass and amber beads (on loan from Malton Museum). The display contains an illustration of the grave with the artefacts attached.

2.   Over 90 graves were discovered containing grave goods. The women were buried with necklaces, with brooches at the shoulders and carried keys, small knives and other domestic articles at the waist. The men were buried with weapons including swords and spears. Both framed and sunken houses were found. Domestic remains found included animal bones, loom weights, pottery, combs and quern fragments.

(B)   A DISPLAY ENTITLED: "FINDS FROM THE UNCLEBY CEMETARIES".

It contains:

1.   Iron annular brooch.
2.   Iron buckle.
3.   Two iron knives.
4.   Two single edge short swords (scramasaxes).
5.   Large, tapered whetstone found standing upright near grave 11 which contained a scramasax, a smaller whetstone and other objects. The large whetstone has clearly never been used for sharpening objects and its size and fine finish suggest it was used for ceremonial purposes, like the whetstone of similar size from the royal burial at Sutton Hoo Suffolk. The Uncleby whetstone

may have been used to mark the burial place of an important person.

6. Grave 38. Necklace of amethyst and coloured glass beads.

7. Grave 29. Cylindrical bronze workbox with an iron chain attached containing a mass of threads.

Grave 62:

8. A bone, double-sided comb.

9. A bone spindle whorl.

10. Bronze pyramidal stud decorated with ring and dot design.

11. Bronze annular brooch decorated with two pairs of confronted animal heads.

12. Two silver wire earrings.

13. Necklace of blue and green glass beads with a bossed silver pendant at the centre.

14. Circular gold pendant decorated in filigree with a star pattern. When found, the setting contained a white substance which held a garnet.

15. Small piece of gold jewellery decorated with garnets. The use of carefully cut garnets placed in small cells edged with gold demonstrates craftsmanship of a very high order.

16. Two copper alloy buckles.

17. A bronze brooch.

Grave 31:

18. A silver pin.

19. A necklace of coloured beads with a gold pendant. The pendant is made from sheet gold and decorated with spiral ornament in filigree. In the centre is a setting for a garnet or other gemstone.

20. An annular silver brooch with a conventionalised animal head on either side of the attachment for the pin.

21. A bronze buckle decorated with openwork and ring and dot design.

22. A bronze bowl with drop handles and a foot ring.

(C) A DISPLAY ENTITLED: "WILFRED BISHOP OF YORK".

It contains:

Three funerary monuments and a stele from under York Minster:

1. Fragments from the top of a stele which dates to about 700 and has an incised cross with splayed ends and the letters of a personal name "LEOB DEIH". It measures 13

Ins/33 Cms H, tapering 5½ Ins/13 Cms to 3½ Ins/8 Cms W, by 4 Ins/10 Cms D. (NOTE: This is not currently displayed.)

2.   Corner fragment of a stele with incomplete text reading "PRO ANI (MA)" or "For the soul". (NOTE: This is not currently displayed and has not been displayed for some time – hence it has not been possible to check the dimensions.)

3.   Base of a stele with the form of the cross in the Celtic tradition. The marigold motif with the cross base shows Gaulish influence and is highlighted with red paint. It measures 22½ Ins/57 Cms H, tapering 10½ Ins/26 Cms to 9 Ins/22 Cms W, tapering 8½ Ins/21 Cms to 7 Ins/17 Cms D.

Cross fragment found near Ripon:

4.   Grave marker, probably early 8C, with the Latin text inscription reading "Adhuse the priest". It measures 13 Ins/33 Cms H, by 5½ Ins/13 Cms W, by 4 Ins/10 Cms D.

7C finds:

5.   Copies of gold thrymsas found in York. They bear a cross and a "church" motif and have a legend in runic and miniscule letters.

6.   Pear-shaped pendant of olive green glass with enamelled design in yellow.

7.   Bezel of a bronze finger ring with a device showing a horse above a prostrate figure transfixed by a spear.

Attached to the north-west facing (left-hand) side of the display entitled "Wilfred Bishop of York" there is a wooden replica of the front of the Easby Cross. There is an adjacent notice: "The Easby Cross. Monumental stone cross from Easby, of late 8th or early 9th century date. Depicted on the cross-head is Christ in Majesty, giving a Roman blessing. The top of the shaft shows Christ in Judgement with attendant angels and the panels below are of the apostles. The figures are finely carved with classical style of drapery and overlapping heads to create depth, reminiscent of the Carolingian tradition." (See the appropriate entry for Easby, North Yorkshire.)

(D)   A FREESTANDING DISPLAY IN THE CENTRE OF THE FLOOR ENTITLED: "BRONZE HANGING BOWL FROM YORK".

It contains:

A bronze hanging bowl from York. The 8th century bowl has three bird-shaped escutcheons, with wings of the birds silvered. The base of the bowl is decorated on the interior and exterior with applied silver foil decorated with interlace. Bowls such as this were possibly containers for holy water.

(E) A FREESTANDING DISPLAY IN THE CENTRE OF THE FLOOR ENTITLED: "THE ORMSIDE BOWL".

It contains:

Late 8th century bowl composed of a plain gilt-bronze inner shell and a silver-gilt outer shell ornamented with repousse decoration. Metal bosses surrounded by filigree conceal the rivets holding the two shells together. The ornament on the outer bowl is divided into quadrants, each decorated with fantastic birds and beasts in a vine scroll. The inhabited vine motif is derived from Eastern Christian traditions, but the fantastic beasts and miniature style suggest a southern Northumbrian origin.

The base of the outer bowl is decorated in repousse with an equal-armed cross and metal bosses mounted in false filigree. On the interior, a corresponding medallion is edged with twisted wire and has knot work patterns originally separated by four blue glass studs, only one of which survives.

This bowl is one of the finest pieces of Anglo-Saxon metalwork to survive in Britain. It would have been treasured by its original owner and was buried in the churchyard at Ormside probably to save it from plundering Vikings.

(F) A DISPLAY ENTITLED: "UPPER POPPLETON STRAP ENDS AND BROOCH FRAGMENTS".

It contains:

1. Six rare silver strap ends found near York made in around 850 AD, which are decorated with depictions of animals and inlaid with niello. They are designed to accommodate either leather straps or textiles.

2. Four small pieces from brooch fragments.

(G) A DISPLAY ENTITLED: "ANGLO-SAXON MONASTERY AT WHITBY".

It contains:

1. Broken cross in red sandstone found at Whitby. It measures 13 Ins/33 Cms H, by 16 Ins/40 Cms W, by 4 Ins/10 Cms D. On the front (west) side it is incised with the word "Abbae". The quality of the lettering is such as

would have been used in manuscripts. The script, known as majuscule, came to Northumbria through Iona and the Celtic missionaries.

2.   Three bronze styli used in the scriptorium at Whitby.

3.   Reed and quill pens (replicas).

(H)   A DISPLAY ENTITLED: "8TH – EARLY 9TH CENTURY YORK FINDS".

It contains:

1.   Double-sided comb and two combs with handles.

2.   Bone pins with decorated triangular heads.

3.   Caterpillar brooch from the Low Countries.

4.   Garment hook decorated with an equal-armed cross.

5.   Copper alloy cross brooch of a type common in Germany.

6.   Cross brooch, with traces of red and yellow enamelling.

7.   Viking lead weight inset with a piece of 8th century enamel, decorated with a winged animal.

8.   Bronze pins with flat expanded heads decorated with ring and dot.

9.   Gold ring with bezel in the form of a human head flanked by confronted animals, viewed from above. This is probably a southern English product.

10.   Gilded copper alloy pin-head decorated with a pair of animals biting each other's wings.

11.   Copper gilt garment hook decorated with interlace triquetra.

12.   Copper gilt fragment decorated with a pair of out-turned animal heads.

13.   Bronze loop with a terminal in the shape of an animal head.

(I)   A DISPLAY ENTITLED: "THE CAROLINGIAN TRADITION".

It contains:

1.   Fragment of a grave marker of the 1st half of the 9th century from the monastery at Whitby. The carving shows strong Carolingian influence in the use of pelleting on the borders and the naturalistic rendering of the animal.

2.   Single leaf from a Latin text of the four Gospels written in southwest Germany in the 9th century. The text which is of St Mark's Gospel, is carefully written in the Carolingian miniscule style, a script devised at the Court of Charlemagne.

(J)   A DISPLAY ENTITLED: "ANGLO-SAXON ARMS AND ARMOUR".

It contains:

1.   Sword from Gilling West of 9th century date. The grip, guards and pommel are enriched with applied silver strips and plates decorated with conventionalised foliage, originally inlaid with niello. The sword has a two-edged fullered blade with pattern welding. This was one of the commonest types of 9th century sword, much prized by both Anglo-Saxons and Vikings.

2.   Iron pommel, found in York, dating to the 9th century, and from which decorated silver plates have been stripped.

3.   Part of the grip, upper guard, and pommel of a sword decorated in the 9th century Trewhiddle style, found in Acomb, York. The grip was encircled by silver bands decorated with foliage, of which one survives. The upper guard and pommel have applied silver plates decorated with foliage or animal heads.

4.   THE YORK HELMET, formerly known as the "Coppergate Helmet". An Anglo-Saxon helmet of 8th century date. The iron cap is made in sections and edged with brass. On the crest is an inscription in Latin, which translated reads "In the name of our Lord Christ, the Holy Spirit (and) God; and to all we say Amen Oshere".

The helmet was discovered during the excavations in "Coppergate", York in May 1982. The helmet was made between 750 and 775 for a royal or noble family. It was possibly made for, or by, or commissioned by, a man named Oshere. The helmet has had a lot of use and the dent and a cut identified suggested it had been used in battle. In "Jorvik" in York there is an incised slab marking the place where the helmet was found during the excavations. (See the entry for "Jorvik", York.)

The helmet comprises the cap, two hinged cheek pieces and a curtain of mail to protect the neck. It is made of iron with brass fittings and would have originally had a padded lining of either a textile or leather. There is animal and interlace decoration on the nose guard, the join of the "eyebrows", and at the back of the helmet. The Christian Latin inscription identifying Oshere is incised on the brass strip running from the top to the back of the helmet cap. The brass strips running from the top to the ears of the helmet cap are also incised with Christian Latin text.

5.   Two single-edged swords or scramasaxes, of late 7th or early 8th century date, found in graves at Uncleby.

The longer sword was from the burial which had the ceremonial whetstone as its marker. Scramasaxes first appear in Anglo-Saxon England in the 7th century.

6.   Iron shield boss and spearhead of 6th century date from a tumulus at Sowerby. The boss is all that survives of the shield which was about two feet in diameter and made of wood, possibly covered by leather.

7.   Iron socketed spearhead with a pointed leaf-shaped blade, found near Kelfield. The socket is vertically grooved and has projecting wings. Winged spearheads are thought to have been imported from the Carolingian Empire in the 9th century.

8.   Three socketed spearheads with leaf-shaped blades dating to the late 5th or early 6th century from Sweden.

(K)   A DISPLAY ENTITLED: "NORTHUMBRIAN COINAGE".

It contains:

Sceattas of southern type:

1.   Kentish bird on cross type – Whitby.
2.   East Anglian "porcupine" type – Whitby.

Northumbrian Sceattas:

3.   Aldfrith 685-704.
4.   Eadberht.
5.   Eadberht.
6.   Archbishop Ecgberht.
7.   Aelfwald.

Northumbrian Stycas Phase I (796 – c835):

The silver content is relatively Hat first, but becomes noticeably debased by about 830. The name of the king or archbishop is given before the moneyer's.

8. – 9.   Aethelred I – moneyer Ceobald.
10. – 12.   Archbishop Eanbald II: Eadvvlf, Cunvvulf, Edilveard.
13. – 15.   Eanred: Hvaetred, Vilheah, Eadvini.
16. – 19.   Eanred: Daegberct, Eadvini, Heardvvulf, Herred.

Northumbrian Stycas Phase II (837 – 855):

After 837 the system was reorganised to allow new teams of moneyer's for King and Archbishop to produce a more prolific coinage which lasted until early in the reign of Osberht. Differences in spelling and style on the dies seem to indicate that several separate workshops were in operation, not necessarily all at York.

Workshop 1:

20. – 24. Eanred: Brodr, Fordred, Monne, Wihtred.
25. – 33. Aethelred II: Leofdegn, Brother, Wihtred.
34. – 35. Archbishop Vigmund: Coenred.
36. – 38. Redvvlf: Hvaetnod, Coenred.
39. – 40. Osberht: Vvlfsixt.

Workshop 2:

41. Eanred: Aldates.
42. – 45. Aethelred II: Alghere, Eanred.
46. – 47. Redvvlf: Alghere.

Workshop 3a:

48. – 51. Eanred: Fulcnod, Odilo, Monne.
52. – 58. Aethelred II: Leofdegn, Eanred, Monne, Vvlfred, Eardvvlf.
59. – 62. Archbishop Vigmund: Edilveard, Hunlaf.
63. – 65. Redvvlf: Cudberht, Monne.
66. – 67. Osberht: Viniberht.
68. – 69. Archbishop Vvlfhere: Vvlfred.

Workshop 3b:

70. – 71. Eanred: Fordred.
72. – 74. Aethelred II: Brother, Vendelberht.
75. – 76. Archbishop Vigmund: Edelhelm.
77. – 78. Redvvlf: Vendelberht.
79. – 80. Osberht: Edelhelm.

Workshop 3c:

81. – 83. Eanred: Monne, Fulcnod.
84. – 86. Aethelred: Fordred, Vvlfsic.
87. – 89. Redvvlf: Brother, Fordred.
90. – 92. Osberht: Eanvvlf, Monne.

(L)   A DISPLAY ENTITLED: "9TH CENTURY FINDS FROM YORK".

It contains:

In the 9th century, Anglo-Saxon metalwork was ornamented with small, lively animals and stylised leaves, usually in silver against nielloed backgrounds. This style of decoration, known as "Trewhiddle" style, was used all over England, indicating the close cultural links between the kingdoms at the time. Later in the century, England was split in two by the Vikings and thereafter the north and south had different art styles.

1.   Pewter disc brooch with rosette pattern.
2.   Bronze pins with polyhedral heads, decorated with punched dots or ring and dots.
3.   Polyhedral bronze weight.

4. Two bone trial pieces with Trewhiddle style animals. They may have been used as sketch pads to work out designs for transfer onto metal objects.

5. Strap ends with animal head terminals and Trewhiddle beasts and leaf patterns.

6. Silver ring with circular bezel, decorated with an animal.

7. Silver strap end with animal head terminal inlaid with niello.

8. Strap end inlaid in silver with a human half-length figure.

9. Pendant made from a Y-shaped antler tine. The animal heads on the sides closely resemble those on the Trewhiddle style strap ends.

10. Bronze strap end with animal head terminal decorated with a series of horizontal zones of geometrical ornament alternating with plain bands. Piece enriched with metal rivets.

11. Two narrow strap ends with animal head terminals.

(M) A DISPLAY ENTITLED: "TROUBLED NORTHUMBRIA".

It contains:

Whitby finds:

1. A stone mould (replica) for casting ingots. Anglo-Saxon metalwork was probably melted down by the Vikings and cast into moulds such as this.

2. Decorated mounts cut for re-use.

3. Gilt-bronze openwork mount, decorated with interlace, and with a pattern of two equal-armed crosses. The mount has been deliberately cut and would originally have come from a book cover.

4. A bird escutcheon from a hanging bowl.

5. Thistle brooch.

6. Bossed penannular brooch.

7. Two pieces of cut silver.

York finds:

8. Blue glass stud in a silver mount of false filigree. The stud has been removed from a larger object of 8th century date, possibly a bowl.

9. Pictish brooch of 8th century date which has been cut.

Bolton Percy coin hoard:

10. A small Badorf ware pot, found containing 1,775 stycas. The coins were probably concealed at the time the Vikings captured York in 866, or soon afterwards.

(N) **A SECOND DISPLAY ENTITLED: "TROUBLED NORTHUMBRIA".**

It contains:

Viking weapons and riding equipment from York:

1. Iron battle-axe with convex cutting edge.
2. Lobed whalebone sword pommel and plain bone sword guard, not from the same sword.
3. Iron arrow-head with leaf shaped blade.
4. Two iron swords with double-edged fullered blades, straight guards and semi-circular pommels.
5. Part of a wooden saddle-bow decorated with a series of interlocking triangular fields filled with interlace. The fields are outlined by beaded mouldings and separated by strips of horn and tinned nail head ornament. The technique of decoration parallels that found on wooden objects in the Norwegian royal ship-burial at Oseberg.
6. Iron snaffle bit with inverted Y- shaped cheek pieces.
7. Tinned iron prick spur with the loop decorated on each side with three equally spaced mouldings. One of the attachments for the leather strap survives.
8. Iron stirrup made from a rod of circular section hammered flat to provide the foot rest. The loop at the top of the stirrup is leather.
9. Iron horse shoe.

(O) **A DISPLAY ENTITLED: "VIKING SETTLEMENT".**

It contains:

1. Oval tortoise brooch from a woman's grave at Bedale.
2. Incomplete antler comb from York with teeth broken off.
3. Bronze chape from York with Jellinge style animal ornament. 10C.
4. Pewter disc brooch decorated with Jellinge style animal – probably made in York.
5. Twisted gold ring from York.
6. Fragment of open work in Jellinge style found in York.
7. Strap end decorated in "Borre" style ring chain from York.
8. Silver armlet from Flaxton with punched decoration.
9. Cylindrical bone object from Sawdon decorated with pelleted interlace.10C.

(P) **A DISPLAY ENTITLED: "FINDS FROM THE FARMSTEAD AT RIBBLEHEAD".**

It contains:

1. Iron socketed spearhead with long, narrow blade.
2. Part of an iron bridle bit.

3.   Iron knives with scramasax-shaped blades.
4.   Bell with loop for suspension.
5.   Stone spindle whorl.
6.   Three stycas: Archbishop Vvlfhere: Moneyer Vvlfred
        – 853/4/5.
        Aethelred II: Moneyer unknown – 841/2-9.
        Aethelred II: Moneyer Odilo.
7.   Rotary quern of millstone grit.
8.   Honestones.

(Q)   A DISPLAY ENTITLED: "DRESS IN ANGLO-SCANDINAVIAN YORK".

It contains:

1.   Two iron knives, one with bone handle with ring and dot.
2.   Copper alloy buckle with plant ornament on loop.
3.   Bronze buckle with ring and dot ornament.
4.   Two bone buckles, one dyed green.
5.   Copper-alloy strap end decorated with Borre-style ring chain.
6.   Grave group from St Mary Bishophill Junior including an iron knife, copper alloy buckle plate, and pendant whetstone.
7.   Jet snake pendant.
8.   Bronze stud with beast.
9.   Rectangular lead alloy brooch decorated with a pair of saltires.
10.   Lead alloy brooch with equal-armed cross.
11.   Copper alloy disc brooch with bosses and beaded mouldings.
12.   Copper alloy suspension loop decorated with animal ornament.
13.   Garment hook decorated with ring and dot.
14.   Bronze ear scoop and tweezers.
15.   Silk cap. Originally the cap had linen ribbons on either side to tie it under the chin.
16.   Beads and a circular lead alloy pendant, with a boss and crescent motifs. They have been positioned to resemble a necklace.
17.   Amber pendant, beads and ring.
18.   Two pins, one with a spiral head.
19.   Silver ring of twisted wire.
20.   Armlet, decorated with punched dots and attached ring.
21.   Tinned, twisted armlet.

(R)   A DISPLAY ENTITLED: "YORK WOODWORKING".

It contains:

Coppergate finds:

1.   Unfinished bowl and turning cores.
2.   Wooden cup, small dish, bowl, platter and lid.

Other York sites:

3.   Iron axe – main woodworking tool.
4.   T-shaped axe, both ends of blade are broken away.
5.   Adze for shaping curved structures such as ship timbers.
6.   Iron spool-bit.
7.   Two decorated wooden spoons.

Traders and York (In the same display cabinet as "York Woodworking"):

1.   Two copper alloy balance beams, one of which is folding. Portable balances were common, possibly used to weigh silver.
2.   Shallow, circular scale-pan.
3.   Three metal weights.
4.   Lead pendant in the form of a ship. The tall mast is lightly incised with a pattern, possibly the rigging, and lines of the ship's sides may indicate the planks of the hull. Ships were essential to the livelihood of the traders and were often depicted on jewellery.
5.   Hones made from Norwegian schist.
6.   Part of a soapstone bowl from Norway or Shetland.
7.   Selvedge of silk tabby which has come from Byzantine or Islamic weaving centre.
8.   Two banded slate whetstones, one with a suspension loop.
9.   Three ringed pins, a type which originated in Ireland.

Fishing (In the same display cabinet as "York Woodworking"):

1.   Net-sinker decorated with interlace pattern where the rope passes through the stone.
2.   Iron fish-hook with a barbed tip.
3.   Iron double-pronged implement which may have been an eel spear.

SEPARATE DISPLAYS OF INDIVIDUAL SECTIONS OF STONEWORK

(AA) STONEWORK ENTITLED: "CHAIR-END FRAGMENTS LASTINGHAM".

North Yorkshire 8th – early 9th century. A chair side and finial. The finial is in the form of a finely-carved animal head, and the side or support is decorated with interlace. This is a rare survival from the furnishings of an important Anglo-Saxon monastery; it may even be the chair of the abbot. Lastingham was founded by St. Chad in the 7th century, and was probably important in Alcuin's day.

The upper and lower decorated sections of stonework ends from an 8C abbot's chair: there is a modern intermediate section separating the two original sections. In total these three sections of stonework measure 33½ Ins/85 Cms H. They are displayed standing on a purpose built supporting stand that measures 31½ Ins/80 Cms H, by 14 Ins/35 Cms W, by 6 Ins/15 Cms D.

The top section of stonework measures 7½ Ins/19 Cms H, by 9 Ins/22 Cms W, by 3¼ Ins/8 Cms D. It is sculptured in the shape of a dragon's head. This section of stonework is on loan from St Mary's Church at Lastingham (see the appropriate entry Lastingham, North Yorkshire).

The lower section of stonework measures 10½ Ins/26 Cms H, by 11 Ins/27 Cms W, by 3¼ Ins/8 Cms D. It is decorated on all four sides: there are triangular shapes on the two narrow sides and irregular shapes on the two wider sides. This section of stonework is on loan from Ryedale Folk Museum (see the appropriate entry Hutton-le-Hole, North Yorkshire).

(BB) STONEWORK WITHOUT A TITLE BUT ATTACHED TO THE ILLUSTRATED NOTICE "MONASTERIES CRAKE".

Two small sections of stonework from a late 8C crosshead. These are attached to a purpose built supporting stand on which is drawn the outline of a crosshead. These two sections of stonework have been placed to form part of the left lateral arm of the crosshead. One section measures, 5½ Ins/13 Cms H, by 7 Ins/17 Cms W, by 3 Ins/7 Cms D. The second section measures 5½ Ins/13 Cms H, by 3 Ins/7 Cms W, by 3 Ins/7 Cms D. On the front faces of both the sections of stonework they are decorated with vine scroll design. In the centre of the larger section of stonework the figure of Christ can apparently be identified – but it is not clear. Due to weathering and damage there is no other decoration on any of the sides that can now be viewed of either these sections of stonework or the end of the arm. Both these sections of stonework were found at Crayke. A monastery was founded at Crayke in the 7C on a site covered by the present St Cuthbert's Church and churchyard (see the appropriate entry Crayke, North Yorkshire).

(CC) STONEWORK ENTITLED: "CROSS-SHAFT FROM ST MARY BISHOPHILL JUNIOR YORK".

Cross-shaft from St Mary Bishophill Junior, York. Cross-shaft fragment of the mid 9th century showing two Anglo-Saxon secular figures dressed in shin length tunics with belts and a cloak. A sword and horn are worn at the waists. The secular figures on the stone may represent the patrons who commissioned the monument. It is displayed standing on a purpose built supporting stand that measures 35 Ins/88 Cms H, by 19¾ Ins/50 Cms W, by 19¾ Ins/50 Cms D.

The section of stonework measures 22 Ins/55 Cms H, tapering 13 Ins/33 Cms to 11 Ins/27 Cms W, by 10½ Ins/26 Cms D. It is decorated on one face with two secular figures each dressed in shin-length tunics with a belt and a cloak. One of these figures has a hunting horn attached to his belt and the other figure has a sword attached to his belt. Two of the other sides are decorated with vine scroll and interlace design. The other face is too damaged for any decoration to survive. This section of stonework comes from St Mary Bishophill Junior, York – see the entry for St Mary Bishophill, York. (Note: it is displayed separately from the St Mary Church Tower display in the basement to the Yorkshire Museum.)

(DD) STONEWORK ENTITLED: "CROSS-FRAGMENT FROM WESTON CHURCH".

Part of an arm from an A-S crosshead that has been re-cut in Viking times. It is displayed sitting on top of a purpose built supporting stand that measures 47¼ Ins/120 Cms H, by 9¾ Ins/24 Cms W, by 9¾ Ins/24 Cms D.

The section of stonework from a crosshead measures 15½ Ins/38 Cms H, by 7 Ins/17 Cms W, by 4½ Ins/11 Cms D. On one face it is decorated with a helmeted Viking warrior holding a battle axe and a sword – the panel below is too damaged for any decoration to survive. The opposite face has a man holding a sword, thrusting back a female figure with his right hand, and in the panel below, there is knot work decoration. There is no decoration on the other two sides due to weathering and damage. From Weston Church, North Yorkshire (Note: there are now no items of A-S/Viking interest now in Weston and so it does not have an entry in North Yorkshire.)

(EE) STONEWORK ENTITLED: "HOGBACK FROM INGLEBY ARNCLIFFE".

It is located sitting on top of a purpose built supporting stand that measures 31½ Ins/80 Cms H, by 39½ Ins/100 Cms W, by 13¾ Ins/34 Cms D.

The section of stonework from a hogback grave cover measures 10 Ins/25 Cms H, by 29 Ins/73 Cms W, tapering 9½ Ins/24 Cms to 6 Ins/15 Cms D. There is a slight suggestion of a tegulated roof decoration and there is a distinctive ridge running around the edge of the top face. It is very weathered and no decoration can be identified with certainty on any of the other sides.

(Note: there are now no items of A-S/Viking interest in Ingleby Arncliffe and so it does not have an entry in North Yorkshire.)

(FF)   STONEWORK ENTITLED: "GRAVE SLAB FROM UNDER YORK MINSTER".

A 10C grave slab. It lies on top of a purpose built stand that measures 19¼ Ins/48 Cms H, by 78¾ Ins/200 Cms W, by 19¼ Ins/48 Cms D.

The grave slab measures 11 Ins/27 Cms H(D), by 51 Ins/129 Cms long, by 19 Ins/48 Cms D (W). On its top side it is decorated with Sigurd killing Fafnir the dragon (the slab is badly worn obscuring much of the illustration). Around three of the edges there is decoration including the figure of a dragon and vine scroll design. The fourth edge is broken off and damaged and no decoration survives. This grave slab was found in the A-S cemetery under York Minster (see the appropriate entry for York Minster, York and in particular the section relating to the Undercroft Museum).

(GG)   SECTION OF STONEWORK NOT CURRENTLY DISPLAYED.

Part of an early 9C grave marker with a decorated border and a depiction of an animal. The grave marker measures 8 Ins/20 Cms H, by 12 Ins/30 Cms W, by 4 Ins/10 Cms D. It was found on the site of the monastery at Whitby (see the entry for Whitby, North Yorkshire).

A SEPARATE DISPLAY OF STONEWORK ADJACENT TO THE NOTICE "THE YORK MASTER"

a.   A section of stonework from a grave slab. It is attached to the left hand side of the display stand, to the left of, and above, "b" below. It measures between 16 Ins/40 Cms and 16½ Ins/41 Cms H, between 22 Ins/55 Cms and 23½ Ins/59 Cms W, by 7 Ins/17 Cms D. The Jellinge style of decorative design has been divided into two panels. In the upper panel there is a distinctive dragon like animal and in the lower panel there is an abstract design. The "frame" enclosing these panels is decorated with interlace design. There is no other decoration on any of the other sides. It was found in Clifford Street, York.

b.   A section of stonework from a 10C grave slab. It was attached to the left hand side of the display stand, to the right of, and below, "a" above. It is decorated with interlace on all four sides. It was found underneath York Minster. (NOTE: This is not currently displayed and has not been displayed for some time – hence it has not been possible to check the dimensions.)

c.   The corner of an unfinished grave slab. It is attached to the right hand side of the display stand, to the left of, and above "d" below. This section of stonework measures 8¾ Ins/22 Cms H, by 9 Ins/22 Cms

W, by 4½ Ins/11 Cms D. One face is decorated with a stylised hound like animal and some other design that it is difficult to identify. The other sides are too weathered and damaged for any decoration to be identified. It is no later in date than 920. It was found in Coppergate, York.

d. A section of stonework from an early 10C cross-shaft. It is attached to the right hand side of the display stand, to the right of, and below "c" above. It measures 25 Ins/63 Cms H, by 12½ Ins/31 Cms W, by 13½ Ins/34 Cms D. On one side it is decorated with a portrait of Christ with a dished halo in the A-S tradition (this can easily be identified despite the damage). Although damaged the three other sides are decorated in the Jellinge style, including a chained beast and a fettered bird. From Newgate Street, York.

A SEPARATE DISPLAY RELATING TO A VIKING SHIP

This display comprises a cross-section of a Viking cargo ship based on a late 10C coastal trading vessel found in Roskilde Fjord, Denmark.

DISPLAYED IN GALLERIES ON THE BASEMENT FLOOR

These galleries contain the following illustrated notices: "York: Growth of the Town" and "Norman Devastation".

(S)   A DISPLAY CONTAINING A RECONSTRUCTION OF PART OF A VIKING HOUSE.

On reaching the bottom of the steps linking the Ground Floor and Basement Floor displays of A-S and Viking interest, there is a reconstruction of part of a Viking house discovered in the Coppergate excavation. The building's floor is sunk 1.5 M below ground level. The walls, made of oak, have squared uprights with horizontal planks. The lower part of the wall is a copy of the timbers as found in the excavation.

(T)   A DISPLAY ENTITLED: "YORK METALWORKING".

It contains:

Coppergate Finds:

1.   Piece of galena, lead ore.
2.   Clay crucible for melting silver.
3.   Lead from spillages.
4.   Two stone ingot moulds.
5.   Cut length of a bronze ingot.

Finds from other York sites:

6.   Matrix made of lead probably used for producing moulds from which pendants could be cast. It is decorated in the Borre style.
7.   Clay mould for a trefoil brooch.
8.   Replica of a trefoil brooch such as would have been made in the mould.
9.   Two disc brooches with identical Jellinge style animals, probably made in the same workshop. Unfinished example comes from Coppergate.

(U)   A DISPLAY ENTITLED: "YORK TEXTILES".

It contains:

Pavement finds:

1.   A plain woven wool cloth, with a piece of worsted lozenge twill stitched to the upper corner.
2.   Fragment of fine worsted lozenge twill, which would have required three shafts on the loom.
3.   Short length of yarn.
4.   Spindle and spindle whorls.
5.   Clay loom weights.

Finds from other York sites:

6.   Bone thread maker.
7.   Bone pin-beater for picking out threads and beating up the weft.
8.   Wooden bobbin for carrying weft.
9.   Rectangular weaving tablet for making narrow, flat braids.
10.   Bone lucet for making tabular braids.
11.   Iron shears.
12.   Glass linen smoothers probably used for smoothing or pleating linen.
13.   Wool comb for preparing wool for spinning worsted yarn.

(V)   A DISPLAY CONTAINING A RECONSTRUCTION OF AN UPRIGHT LOOM

Most of the display comprises a reconstruction of an upright warp-weighted loom. The loom weights are of baked clay. These looms were used in the home to make woollen and linen cloth. Coarse fabrics were often undyed. Finer fabrics were dyed, using madder for red, woad for blues, lichens for purple and assorted plants for yellows.

Also, sitting on this display there is a replica wooden trough for kneading bread, and a wooden ladle, both based on Scandinavian originals.

(W)   A DISPLAY ENTITLED: "YORK LEATHERWORKING".

It contains:

Pavement finds:

1.   Leather offcuts.
2.   Iron awl.
3.   Shoe last.

Tools and leather objects found at other York sites:

4.   Iron scraper for preparing hides for tanning.
5.   Leather boot.
6.   Leather boot with toggle.
7.   Child's ankle boot.
8.   Child's shoe.
9.   Leather scabbard with decoration reflecting the shape of the knife originally inside. The blade and handle are represented by two panels of interlace and the guard by a coiled animal.
10.   Leather scabbard decorated with panels of interlace and a fret pattern.

(W)   A DISPLAY ENTITLED: "POTTERY PRODUCTION".

It contains:

1.   Torksey ware storage pot with thumb applied strips.
2.   York ware cooking pot and lamp.
3.   Stamford ware glazed jugs, one with tubular sprout.
4.   Stamford ware unglazed cooking pots.
5.   Shelly cooking pot with rouletted decoration and lamp.
6.   Badorf ware amphora with applied strip decoration.
7.   Pingsdorf ware amphora with painted decoration.
8.   Tating ware jug.

(X)   A DISPLAY ENTITLED: "YORK ANTLER AND BONE WORKING".

It contains:

Clifford Street finds:

1.   Rough-outs for comb-backs, made of antler.
2.   Antler blanks for the tooth-plates of combs.
3.   Unused comb-backs.
4.   Finished combs.
5.   Red deer antler sawn into lengths ready for use.
6.   Bone skates.
7.   Knife with bone handle with incised decoration.
8.   Bone pin in imitation of bronze ringed pin.

9.   Bone pins with animal heads.
10.   Bone pin carved with winged beast at the end.
11.   Bone pins with spatulate heads.
12.   Bone pins with facetted heads.

Objects from other sites:

13.   Two long antler combs with incised decoration, one in the form of interlace.
14.   Bone comb case decorated with ring and dot.
15.   Bone comb case scored with runic letters.
16.   Matching comb and comb case.
17.   Antler die with the numbers indicated by ring and dot.
18.   Bone plaque with the rough-out for an openwork rectangular design.
19.   Bone strap end decorated with conventionalised plant ornament.
20.   Bone face-plaque.
21.   Two bone plaques, one decorated with interlace.

(Y)   A DISPLAY ENTITLED: "GRAVE-SLAB WITH ENDS FROM YORK MINSTER" and showing a drawing of the tower of St Mary Bishophill Junior Church, York.

It contains:

A broken, but placed back together, section of stonework from an A-S crosshead comprising the central section and one arm. It is located attached to the rear of the display 8½ Ins/21 Cms from (to the right of) the representation of St Mary's Church tower. The section of stonework measures between 7¾ Ins/19 Cms and 13 Ins/33 Cms H, by 16½ Ins/41 Cms W, by 6¼ Ins/16 Cms D. One side is decorated with the body of Christ with an arm outstretched (the head and part of one arm are missing). There is knot work decoration on the edge of the crosshead arm. The other sides are too damaged for any decoration to survive. This is from St Mary Bishophill Junior, York – see the entry for St Mary Bishophill Junior, York.

In the centre of the display, on a floor standing raised wooden display plinth, there are four sections of stonework from A-S gravestones found under York Minster (see the entry for the Undercroft Museum, York Minster). Two sections of stonework have been placed in a horizontal position and two sections of stonework have been placed at opposite ends of the display in an upright position. These are:

1. A section of stonework from a grave slab. It is located standing in an upright position at the left end of the display, next to, and to the left of, "2" below. The section of stonework measures 26 Ins/66 Cms H(L), tapering 6½ Ins/16 Cms to 4½ Ins/11 Cms W(D), by 15¾ Ins/40 Cms D (W). Although weathered some interlace decoration

survives on two faces of the slab. No decoration survives on the other two sides due to rendering or damage.

2. A section of stonework from a grave slab. It is located lying in a horizontal position next to, to the right of "1" above, and next to, and to the left of "3" below on the display. The section of stonework measures 26½ Ins/67 Cms L, by 15½ Ins/38 Cms D (W), by 6½ Ins/16 Cms H(D). On the top side there is interlace decoration and although weathered some similar decoration can also be identified on two of the other sides currently on view.

3. A section of stonework from a grave slab. It is located lying in a horizontal position next to, to the right of "2" above, and next to, and to the left of "4" below on the display. The section of stonework measures 26½ Ins/67 Cms L, by 17½ Ins/44 Cms D (W), by 6½ Ins/16 Cms H(D). On the top side there is interlace decoration and although weathered some similar decoration can also be identified on two of the other sides currently on view.

4. A section of stonework from a grave slab. It is located standing in an upright position at the right end of the display, next to, and to the right of "3" above. The section of stonework measures 26 Ins/66 Cms H(L), tapering 7½ Ins/19 Cms to 5½ Ins/13 Cms W(D), by 15¾ Ins/40 Cms D (W). Although weathered some interlace decoration survives on the two faces of the slab. No decoration survives on the two sides due to weathering and damage, rendering.

[There is a descriptive notice: "The grave-slab is ornamented with interlaced animals in low relief, framed by a central "cross" and a border with incised cabling. The end stones are carved on both faces. The grave-slab and end stones both date to the 10th century and were repositioned as shown in the 11th century cemetery under York Minster."]

A section of stonework probably part of a cross-shaft. It is located attached to the walling on the right hand side of the display. The section of stonework measures 7 Ins/17 Cms H, tapering 9½ Ins/24 Cms to 8¾ Ins/22 Cms W, by 6½ Ins/16 Cms D. Despite damage Jellinge style decoration can be identified on all four sides. An animal can be identified on the front side and there is knot work design on the edges. From St Mary Bishophill Junior, York – see the entry for St Mary Bishophill Junior, York.

YORK
(18) York Story Museum (In the Former St Mary's Church)
SE 604516   Rating: ✰✰✰

The former church of St Mary used to house the York Story Museum but the Museum has now closed. The church is easily identified adjacent to the east side of "Castlegate".

The church includes A-S material but the present structure mostly dates from the early 13C. It was subsequently altered in the 14C and 15C.

The Museum included models, reconstructed scenes and an audio-visual display of York's history.

Internally, A-S material is clearly evident in the northeast and southeast corner walling of the nave, from the ground upwards to the base of the chancel arch.

The original dedication stone for the church remains within the church. It is located attached to the northeast wall of the nave, near the base of the eastern arch in the north aisle. When the church was used as the York Story Museum the dedication stone could be viewed from a landing by "The J.B. Morrell Theatre". This dedication stone records the founding of the church by Efrard, Aesc and Grim in 1020.